The Software Interface between Copyright and Competition Law

Information Law Series

VOLUME 20

General Editor

Prof. P. Bernt Hugenholtz
Institute for Information Law
University of Amsterdam

The titles published in this series are listed at the back of this volume.

KLUWER LAW INTERNATIONAL

The Software Interface between Copyright and Competition Law

A Legal Analysis of Interoperability in Computer Programs

Ashwin van Rooijen

AUSTIN BOSTON CHICAGO NEW YORK THE NETHERLANDS

Published by:
Kluwer Law International
PO Box 316
2400 AH Alphen aan den Rijn
The Netherlands
Website: www.kluwerlaw.com

Sold and distributed in North, Central and South America by:
Aspen Publishers, Inc.
7201 McKinney Circle
Frederick, MD 21704
United States of America
Email: customer.service@aspenpublishers.com

Sold and distributed in all other countries by:
Turpin Distribution Services Ltd.
Stratton Business Park
Pegasus Drive, Biggleswade
Bedfordshire SG18 8TQ
United Kingdom
Email: kluwerlaw@turpin-distribution.com

Printed on acid-free paper.

ISBN 978-90-411-3193-5

Printed in Great Britain.

Table of Contents

Acknowledgments

First and foremost, I would like to thank my advisor, Bernt Hugenholtz, and my daily advisor, Lucie Guibault, for their truly superb guidance and feedback. The discussions with Bernt and Lucie were among the most rewarding and challenging moments of my research. I am very grateful for their critical input, and I recognize that their dedication to PhD supervision is not a given. In general, I have found the Institute for Information Law (IViR) to be a very inspiring and fun research environment, and I have benefited enormously from the interdisciplinary expertise of IViR's staff – notably Egbert Dommering, Nico van Eijk, Natali Helberger, Joris van Hoboken, Wolfgang Sakulin and Stef van Gompel. I would also like to thank Stef for being a great roommate and for many other useful exchanges of views on such topics as coffee, *droit d'auteur*, Amsterdam's Noord-Zuid metro line, formalities, the local sandwich shop and orphan works.

During my time at Berkeley, I was fortunate enough to be assigned Pamela Samuelson as my thesis supervisor. Her supervision was superb, and I have greatly relied on her enormous expertise on software protection and interoperability in this research. On visits to other universities and places, I received immensely valuable input from Pierre Larouche, Giuseppe Dari-Mattiacci, Howard Shelanski, François Lévêque, Thomas Vinje, Josef Drexl, Frank van Iersel and Samuel Miller. Thank you very much.

I am very grateful to my parents, Nico and Alice, and my sister, Asha, for their support throughout this project. This study is no exception to the rule that PhD projects have their more and less interesting moments, and my family has shown great and necessary support during the latter moments.

Finally, I would like to thank my girlfriend Anna for her fantastic support and patience, which I have abused at times – in particular, by giving Anna entire chapters to read and enjoy. If parts of this thesis prove understandable to non-lawyers or non-geeks, chances are this is because of Anna's feedback.

Brussels, December 2009

List of Abbreviations

A-G	Advocate-General
AMI	*Auteurs-, Media- en Informatierecht* (journal)
API	Application Programming Interface
BC	Berne Convention
BGH	Bundesgerichtshof
BIE	*Bijblad bij de Industriële Eigendom* (journal)
BIOS	Basic Input/Output System
C	Programming language
C++	Programming language
CFI	European Court of First Instance
COM	European Commission document number
CONTU	Commission on New Technological Uses
CR	*Computerrecht* (journal)
DG	Directorate-General of the European Commission
DOJ	Department of Justice (United States)
ECIS	European Committee for Interoperable Systems
ECJ	European Court of Justice
ECLR	European Competition Law Review
ECR	European Court Reports
EIPR	European Intellectual Property Review
EPC	European Patent Convention
EPO	European Patent Office
EU	European Union
F.2d	Federal Reporter, second series
F.3d	Federal Reporter, third series
F.Supp	Federal Reporter, supplement
FCC	Federal Communications Commission

FTC	Federal Trade Commission
GC	General Court of the European Union
GUI	Graphical User Interface
GRUR (Int.)	*Gewerblicher Rechtsschutz und Urheberrecht* (International) (journal)
HHI	Herfindahl-Hirschman Index
HTML	HyperText Markup Language
IER	*Intellectuele Eigendom en Reclamerecht* (journal)
IIC	International Review of Intellectual Property and Competition Law
InfoSoc	Directive 2001/29/EC on the harmonization of certain aspects of copyright and related rights in the information society
IP	Intellectual Property
IPR	Intellectual Property Right
IT	Information Technology
NJ	*Nederlandse Jurisprudentie* (Dutch case reporter)
NRA	National Regulatory Authority
NRF	New Regulatory Framework
OJ	Official Journal
ONP	Open Network Provisions
PC	Personal Computer
QWERTY	Keyboard layout
RAM	Random Access Memory
RAND	Reasonable and Non-Discriminatory (licensing terms)
ROM	Read Only Memory
SAGE	Software Action Group for Europe
S.Ct.	Supreme Court Reports
SMP	Significant Market Power
SSNIP	Small but Significant, Non-transitory Increase in Price
SSO	Standard Setting Organization Structure, Sequence and Organization (of a computer program)
TFEU	Treaty on the Functioning of the European Union
TPM	Technical Protection Measure
TRIPS	Agreement on Trade-Related Aspects of Intellectual Property
USC	United States Code
VCR	Video Cassette Recorder
W.Comp.	World Competition
WCT	WIPO Copyright Treaty
WIPO	World Intellectual Property Organization
WPPT	WIPO Performances and Phonogram Producers Treaty

Chapter 1
Introduction

When IBM approached William H. Gates III to supply the operating system for IBM's Personal Computer (PC) in the early 1980s, Mr. Gates recognized the opportunity of a lifetime. Although he had no operating system completed at the time, Gates managed to purchase one from a local developer for $50,000. He then licensed it to IBM for $80,000. The license has been described as the deal of the millennium, albeit not for the modest profit. The opportunities Gates envisioned stretched far beyond IBM's PC and the $30,000 gain. Gates anticipated attempts to reverse engineer the PC's copyrighted core, the BIOS chip, resulting in PC 'clones'. In order for the clones to run the same software as IBM's PC, the clones would also require a license for Gates' operating system MS-DOS. Before long, there would be a PC on every single desk, all running Microsoft's operating system. And so it happened: within months, the first cloners presented a fully IBM compatible PC and obtained a license for MS-DOS. This newcomer named itself after its achievement: *Compaq* is short for compatibility and quality.

More than twenty years later, this interoperability between PC manufacturers has proven more advantageous for Gates than for IBM. Increased competition in fully compatible PC hardware has forced IBM to abandon the PC business; however, it has enabled Gates to roll out successive versions of his proprietary operating systems. Microsoft now serves the vast majority of consumers and businesses with its *Windows* series of operating systems. However, Gates' own failure to provide interoperability with other software firms also turned against him. Competitors, supported by IBM, have attempted to create software that interoperates with the dominant Windows system but have failed due to Microsoft's refusal to disclose its interfaces. Microsoft defended its refusal relying on intellectual property rights. Its conduct, nonetheless, led the European Commission to find an abuse of a dominant position under competition law. The software giant was ordered to pay a record EUR 1.7 billion fine and to supply all specifications required to create interoperable software. The European Union's second-highest court, the General Court (GC), upheld the Commission's decision, and Microsoft chose not to appeal.

1.1. BACKGROUND AND OBJECTIVE

These brief excerpts from the history of the PC[1] illustrate that the success of computer programs often depends on their ability to *interoperate* – or communicate – with other systems. This is due to *network effects* – the demand for a particular program often increases with its number of users. Network effects cause consumers to select the product with the largest number of other users, which can ultimately lead to all consumers using the same vendor's product. Absent interoperability with that product, competitors often will be unable to attract any consumers to their rival products. However, the substantial market power associated with exploiting network effects can also stimulate significant innovation efforts. Network effects and interoperability thus significantly affect innovation and competition in many software industries.

This raises the question of whether the effects of interoperability on innovation and competition are recognized in the law. Innovation and competition are primarily affected by two legal disciplines: intellectual property rights – primarily copyright law – and competition law. In order to create interoperable software, a developer must use and have access to the target program's interoperability information, or interface specifications. For example, all programs designed for the Windows operating system rely on Windows' interfaces. This information, however, can be protected by intellectual property rights, enabling the rightsholder to control the development of competing, interoperable software. However, a refusal to supply this information to competitors could fall under scrutiny of competition law.

Although the exclusivity awarded by intellectual property rights might appear to conflict with free competition, there is an increasing awareness in the legal and economic community that intellectual property rights and competition actually serve complementary purposes: both regimes stimulate and balance innovation, or dynamic efficiency, and price competition, or static efficiency. Intellectual property rights accomplish this by structurally establishing in advance (*ex-ante*) what is protected and under what conditions. Competition laws accomplish this by after-the-fact (*ex-post*), case-by-case review of a firm's behavior. The objective of this study is to contribute to

1. Cringeley 1996. IBM had first sought to contract Gary Kildall, the creator of the highly regarded CP/M operating system. However, Kildall refused upon advise of his lawyers, who were concerned about IBM's insistence on signing non-disclosure agreements. Clearly, law and business are separate arts. The operating system purchased by Gates was, ironically, a reverse engineered version of Kildall's CP/M.

the debate about the complementary relationship between intellectual property rights and competition laws by introducing the network effects prominent in the software industry as a complicating factor.

1.2. PROBLEM DEFINITION

As part of their complementary relationship, intellectual property and competition laws are increasingly called on to anticipate matters traditionally addressed primarily by the other. Thus, intellectual property rights must be curtailed to allow for sufficient static competition despite the existence of the exclusive intellectual property right, whereas competition laws, in addition to the more traditional goal of stimulating static competition, must also safeguard innovation, or dynamic competition. Against this background, the following questions arise: *(i) how interoperability affects the balance between innovation and free competition in software; (ii) which of two regimes – copyright law or competition law – primarily should be concerned with striking this balance as affected by interoperability; and (iii) which particular instruments are suitable to approach this problem within these respective regimes.*

1.3. OUTLINE AND METHODOLOGY

In order to answer its three-layered research question (*supra*), this study first evaluates, based on a normative framework (Chapter 2), the current law addressing interoperability in software (Chapters 3 and 4), followed by a comparison with related legal disciplines (Chapter 5), and, finally, conclusions and recommendations (Chapter 6).

Thus, Chapter 2 of this study first provides a normative framework, determining the effects of interoperability (openness) versus non-interoperability (control) based on economic theory. It will demonstrate, first, that the strong need for interoperability in computer programs causes a degree of interdependency between firms, which affects both innovation and competition. Thus, in software development, competing firms are more dependent on each other than in many other industries, in which firms can innovate and compete more independently. Subsequently, Chapter 2 will demonstrate that both interoperability and absence of interoperability can yield positive effects and that a balance must be struck between these two extremes. An analysis of empirical data falls outside the scope of this study. Instead, the focus lies on the legal framework in which the relevant determinations can be made by the appropriate institutions. Chapter 2 will also introduce the two main legal approaches to interoperability – namely, more rigid but certain *ex-ante* intellectual property rights and more flexible *ex-post* competition laws – and demonstrate that there is a trade-off involved in selecting either one of these approaches to addressing interoperability.

Drawing on the normative framework, Chapters 2–4 aim to provide an analysis of the current respective *ex-ante* copyright and *ex-post* competition approaches to interoperability. The legal analyzes in Chapters 3 and 4 are limited to the laws of the European Union and its implementation in the Member States. Chapter 3 will demonstrate how copyright protection of computer programs can enable rightsholders to control interoperability with their programs and which instruments have been implemented to limit such control. It will also demonstrate that, notwithstanding these limiting instruments, copyright law still leaves the rightsholder with substantial control over interoperability. Conversely, competitors may have insufficient means to establish interoperability with a copyright-protected computer program. This outcome does not correspond with the normative balance established in Chapter 2. Since the problems related to the interaction between copyright law and interoperability have been harmonized at a European level, this analysis will primarily focus on this harmonization instrument – the European Software Directive – and will study the Member States' national copyright laws insofar as they implement or interpret this directive. Whether copyright law provides for legal certainty will be analyzed in the abstract – that is, by identifying any open norms, and subsequently examining whether a coherent interpretation of these norms exists in the literature and by the judiciary.

Chapter 4 discusses the *ex-post* application of competition law to interoperability. It first focuses on the trade-off between the *ex-ante* copyright approach and the *ex-post* application of competition laws, and demonstrates that there are several arguments to address interoperability within copyright law rather than through application of competition laws. The second part of the chapter demonstrates that, should competition law nonetheless be applied, it does not necessarily lead to a more adequate balancing of interests involved in interoperability. The rigid application of the established case law on anticompetitive conduct neither comfortably nor adequately accommodates the specific concerns of a refusal to provide interoperability information. This rigidity also undermines the flexibility that application of competition law is designed to offer. The analyzes in Chapters 3 and 4 demonstrate that both copyright and competition law essentially promote a model of completely independent competition, rather than the type of partial interdependency present in the software industry. In sum, the evaluative analyzes in Chapters 3 and 4 reveal that neither current copyright nor competition laws provide entirely adequate frameworks to balance the interests of interoperability and non-interoperability.

In Chapter 5, the copyright approach to software interoperability will be compared to two legal disciplines in which an *ex-ante* approach to interconnection is rooted more solidly: European design protection law and telecommunications law. Design protection laws are of interest because they explicitly exclude from intellectual property protection those elements of a design that are necessary for interconnections. A similar approach could eliminate much of the uncertainty surrounding the use of interface specifications under copyright law. Telecommunications law is not an intellectual property right, but it offers an interesting comparison because it is a body of law in which courts and regulators have accumulated substantial experience with interdependent competition and network effects through *ex-ante* interconnection regulation. Moreover, some of its instruments, in particular regulatory oversight of interconnection negotiations, appear suitable to facilitate access to interface specifications within copyright law.

Chapter 6 will summarize and combine the findings of previous chapters in order to draw conclusions and to discuss several recommendations, which are aimed at aligning the treatment of software interoperability in copyright and competition laws more closely with the normative framework established in Chapter 2. Some of its recommendations are inspired by U.S. copyright law because there is a substantial body of U.S. case law and accompanying literature on the interaction between interoperability and copyright law.

1.4. SCOPE

A number of issues are related to but beyond the scope of this study. This study will focus on two main legal disciplines: copyright law and competition law. The focus on copyright law, rather than other intellectual property regimes, follows from the historical tendency to protect computer programs primarily through copyright rather than other intellectual property regimes. Whether copyright law is indeed the most suitable regime to protect computer programs has been subject to some debate previously. Although this debate will not be revisited, the peculiar role of copyright law in protecting computer programs will be examined in depth in section 3.1 in the context of its implications for interoperability.

Software interoperability is a form of standardization: where two or more manufacturers' products interoperate, there is a (limited) standard. Standards can emerge *de-jure* – by law, formal agreement or consent – or *de-facto*, that is, without a formal act. Each standard raises different issues. *De-jure* standardization primarily raises issues of anticompetitive cooperation between multiple firms (collusion), whereas the principal risk of *de-facto* standards is a possibly anticompetitive refusal to allow others to use the standard. The focus of this study is on single-firm (*unilateral*) conduct and *de-facto* standardization, rather than *de-jure* standardization and concerted practices between multiple firms.

The problem of software interoperability manifests itself primarily in so-called *proprietary* software markets, where software is distributed without the original 'blue print' (or *source code*) of the program. By contrast, the *open source* model allows the source code of the program to be distributed and modified, which enables other developers to improve the software. The release of a computer program's source code under an open source license generally obviates the need to regulate access to interface information, while the underlying economics are fundamentally different. The focus of this study will be on interoperability in proprietary software rather than under open source models.

Chapter 2

Interfaces and Interoperability in Context

The present chapter aims to establish a background and normative framework on software interoperability, against which subsequent chapters will analyze the relevant law. First, it provides a business and technology context of interoperability in the software industry. Second, it provides an analysis of the effects of interoperability, which will serve as the normative basis to analyze the relevant laws in subsequent chapters. Third, it introduces the two principal legal approaches to addressing interoperability.

Section 2.1 will first demonstrate the critical role of interoperability in the software industry. Computer programs generally interoperate with and rely on other software and hardware for their proper functioning, and enable users to exchange their data. This interoperability introduces a degree of interdependency in the software industry that is not found in most other industries. Section 2.1 also offers a technical background to interoperability. In particular, it demonstrates that software interoperability hinges on (lawful) use of and access to a computer program's interface specifications, and that these interface specifications can be obtained, *inter alia*, through the time-consuming process of reverse engineering.

Section 2.2 provides an analysis of the effects of interoperability. It demonstrates that interoperability generally benefits end-users due to a greater realization of network effects, while it facilitates competition as entry barriers are lowered. However, absence of interoperability can also prove welfare enhancing. The ability to exploit a closed network or system can provide significant incentives to innovate, while a need to adhere to existing interoperability standards can limit innovation. Section 2.2, therefore, concludes that, in the laws affecting software interoperability, a balance must be struck between interoperability and a lack of interoperability.

Section 2.3 introduces the two principal legal approaches to addressing interoperability, namely, an intellectual property and a competition approach. These approaches will be further examined in Chapters 3 and 4, respectively.

Section 2.4 concludes this chapter by establishing a normative and an instrumental benchmark for the analysis of the relevant law.

2.1. SOFTWARE, INTERFACES AND INTEROPERABILITY

This section aims to provide an industry (section 2.1.1) and technology (section 2.1.2) context of interfaces and interoperability in computer programs. These sections provide background to the subsequent economic and legal analyzes.

2.1.1. Interoperability and Interdependency

This study is concerned with the legal treatment of interoperability between computer programs. *Interoperability* may be defined as 'the ability to exchange information and mutually to use the information which has been exchanged'.[2]

Interoperability in the computer industry is a big deal, and lack of interoperability even more so. Whereas most people unconsciously rely on interoperability between computer programs every day, many others will recall instances of unreadable e-mail attachments, presentations that failed to display on the projector or word-processing documents that were delivered by the printer in an unreadable form. In such instances, it might have crossed the mind of the frustrated computer user that the lack of interoperability was perhaps deliberate and that whoever caused it probably sought to persuade the user to switch to a different vendor or to upgrade to a new version – both of which typically come at a price. Part of this study is devoted to demonstrating that this could quite possibly be true.

A fully functional computer system, comprising the computer hardware, an operating system and application programs, such as a word processor, is a function of tens of thousands of interoperating hardware and software components. All components must be designed to interoperate seamlessly with one another, or the system could malfunction, or functionality offered by one component could be left unused as other components fail to respond to it.

In addition to this type of vertical interoperability– or interoperability between components of a single computer system, in which each component serves a distinct purpose – horizontal interoperability denotes interoperability between components on different computer systems.[3] This enables users to

2. Software Directive, §10; McKean 2005.
3. Lea & Hall 2004, p. 73.

communicate and exchange documents – for instance, by e-mail or instant messaging – and to connect computers in a local or a worldwide network, such as the internet. As more people use a particular product, such as a word processor from a particular vendor, the value of that component or product increases for other users as well. This is known as a *network effect* and will be further explored in section 2.2.

This vertical and horizontal interdependency of components in the computer industry is remarkable because many of the components of the user's computer system are manufactured by different firms. This implies a substantial degree of coordination among vendors, as they must design their products according to a set of detailed, common rules, or *interfaces*, in order to provide for interoperability. This need for coordination among firms has led to extensive use of interface *standards*, some of which can barely go unnoticed even to novice computer users.[4] Section 2.1.2 will demonstrate how interoperability is technically achieved.

Although such interdependency is not unique to the computer industry, the *degree* of interdependency – particularly in horizontal relationships – probably is. In most other industries, firms innovate and compete largely independently of each other. These firms, therefore, are not (or not to the same extent) dependent on (the specifications of) each other's particular products. For example, film studios create their own movies and are not generally technically dependent on films created by competing studios. By contrast, computer programs structurally need to offer horizontal interoperability: one vendor's word processor ideally should be able to exchange documents with another vendor's word-processing program. This type of horizontal interdependency is not typical in many industries, where, instead, independency is the general rule. Of course, in many industries, vertical relationships among suppliers similarly require substantial interdependency. For instance, a manufacturer of a jet turbine engine for Airbus is restrained by quite a complex set of design and manufacturing requirements. However, in many such vertical relationships, one vendor – in this case, Airbus – is responsible for the end product. Airbus thus supervises the coordination of parts and absorbs the coordination costs. A computer system, by contrast, often has no central brand name 'responsible' to the end-user but, instead, is the product of components from multiple vendors combined by the user.

The substantial interdependency in the software industry can significantly affect innovation and competition. First, software developers cannot innovate completely independently because their products must interoperate with those of others. Thus, innovation, to some extent, is limited by requirements determined

4. Robinson & Cargill 1996. Well-known computer standards include: 801.1X, AC3, ASCII, ASP, AVI, BAS, BIOS, BMP, BSD, C++, CSV, DHCP, DIVX, DNS, DLL, DOC, EGA, FAT32, FTP, GIF, HTML, HTTP, HTTPS, IMAP, IP, JAVA, JPEG, K56, LAN, LDAP, MD5, MIDI, MP3, MPEG, NTFS, ODBC, ODF, OLE, PCI, PCL, PDF, PNG, POP3, PPP, QWERTY, RAR, RSS, RTF, SCSI, SMB, SMTP, SQL, SSH, TCP/IP, TIFF, TLS, TWAIN, TXT, USB, UTF-8, UTP, VCARD, VPN, W3C, WAV, WEP, WMA, WPA, X86, XGA, XLS, XML, ZIP and ZSH.

by competitors or by industry associations. In particular, interfaces of competitors must be copied in order to enable interoperability with their products.[5] Second, firms cannot compete entirely independently because the need for interoperability among their products causes a need for coordination and sharing of information. Moreover, if a firm cannot offer interoperability with existing and widely used components, its product might have no chance of success, and the firm could, therefore, abandon competition and new-product development (innovation) altogether. In sum, the interdependency and standardization in the software industry alters both innovation and competition.

The contrasting model of *in*dependency is not only the general rule elsewhere in business but, accordingly, also in the relevant laws addressing innovation and competition. These laws concern primarily intellectual property rights and competition rules. Because the computer industry is regulated by the same laws on intellectual property and competition as other industries, the application of these laws could jeopardize the need for standardization and interoperability in the software industry. This will be examined in Chapters 3 and 4, respectively. Indeed, in accordance with the generally prevailing model of independency, intellectual property and competition laws prescribe that competing software manufacturers largely refrain from copying (parts of) each other's products, including, as it turns out, their interfaces necessary for interoperability. Sharing among competitors is not warmly embraced by these laws. Again, this is a problem for an industry that is so firmly based on a need to coordinate, standardize and interoperate. As this study will demonstrate, application of these laws to the software industry can significantly (and negatively) affect innovation and competition.

At the same time, the law arguably should recognize that interoperability and network effects, caused by the increased value of a particular product due to a larger number of users, alter the opportunities and threats for firms in the software industry, and that these opportunities and threats affect competition and innovation. Interoperability with other products can contribute significantly to the success of a computer program. Conversely, once a computer program has become successful due to network effects, preventing interoperability with other programs can exclude such competition and, therefore, serve to establish a lucrative, *de-facto* situation of exclusivity over a network or platform. The significant opportunities and threats in the software industry were demonstrated, for example, by the story about Bill Gates and IBM in the introduction of this study. The software and computer industries are increasingly characterized by similar *standard wars*, in which competing firms attempt to establish their technology as the *de-facto* industry standard, which can contribute to significant market power and associated profits.[6]

---

5. See also section 2.1.2b.
6. Lea & Hall 2004, p. 74. Recent such examples include the rivalry between Microsoft's OpenXML standard and the ODF format for word-processing documents, as well as Sony's BlueRay technology versus HD-DVD.

In such instances, firms compete for the entire market, rather than a share within the market. As will be demonstrated in section 2.2.2d of this chapter, this has its own effects on innovation and competition.

Whereas intellectual property and competition laws thus generally stimulate a model of independent innovation and competition, there are exceptions elsewhere in the law. Telecommunications law, for example, recognizes the structural interdependency in the telecommunications industry. It does not require competing networks to operate completely independently but, instead, prescribes competing networks to interconnect. By the same token, design protection laws recognize that, particularly in the automotive industry, there similarly is a substantial degree of vertical interdependency in (spare) parts, which has resulted in special provisions related to interconnections between product and spare parts protected by design protection laws. Both areas – telecommunications law and design protection laws – will, therefore, be studied for comparison in Chapter 5.

2.1.2. Technology and Terminology

In order to enable an understanding of how the law affects interoperability, it is important to provide some insights on how interoperability between computer programs is technically achieved. To that end, this section summarizes how computer programs are developed (section 2.1.2a), and how interoperability between computer programs is technically implemented as part of that process (section 2.1.2b).

a. Software

Software is the set of instructions aimed at having computer hardware perform a specific task,[7] thereby turning versatile but idle machines into useful tools. Software is used to control general-purpose computers, such as desktop, laptop and handheld PCs, and devices with specific purposes, such as televisions, washing machines, cameras and aircraft. Software also controls more complex systems, such as the internet, defense systems and air traffic control. In this study, the terms *software* and *computer programs* are used interchangeably.

The common distinction in two main types of computer programs is still relevant (albeit far from exhaustive): *application programs*, such as word processors, image editors and spreadsheets, are designed to enable the user to perform specific tasks, whereas *operating systems* function as intermediaries between these application programs and the computer hardware.[8]

7. Band & Katoh 1995, p. 3; European Commission 1988, §5.1.1; National Commission on New Technological Uses of Copyrighted Works 1978, p. 9.
8. Band & Katoh 1995, p. 3.

Many application programs can only be run in conjunction with a specific operating system and hardware architecture and must, therefore, be interoperable with those systems.[9] For present purposes, an important third category is middleware. This type of program is functionally situated between operating systems and application programs, thereby enabling the same application to be run on different operating systems. As this categorization already indicates, computer systems generally comprise different layers of abstraction. Technologies and concepts in computer systems can often only be properly understood in the context of the applicable layer of abstraction. This also applies to reverse engineering and interoperability (see *infra*).

Computers can only run programs distributed in object code. This is a binary and hardware-specific format, consisting only of ones and zeros. Object code is effectively incomprehensible to humans, which would make software development in object code a nearly impossible task.[10] This has stimulated the development of high-level *programming languages*.[11] A programming language is a collection of instructions and 'grammar' rules that enable the programmer to enter commands that more closely resemble (simple) English.[12] The expression of a program in a programming language is known as the source code of the program, which is the form used for its development. A compiler reads the source code and generates machine-readable and machine-specific object code.[13] This is the form in which computer programs are generally distributed to end-users. Distribution in object code enables end-users to run the software directly for its intended purpose, rather than having to compile it first, while the incomprehensible object code prevents exposure of the valuable know-how originally contained in the source code.[14] This model is referred to as the *closed code* practice.[15] Source code is often compared to a recipe: like a computer program distributed in object code form, one may enjoy a dish prepared according to a recipe that cannot easily be extracted from the meal.

---

9. The difference between application programs and operating systems is not always clear: see, for example *Microsoft Decision* (European Commission 2004), §800–§813 (on the question of whether a media player is part of the operating system, or a separate piece of software).
10. Carr 2008, p. 53; Johnson-Laird 1994, p. 888.
11. Ramamoorthy & Tsai 1996.
12. See also Sammet 1972; Webber 2003. Apart from improving the comprehensibility of the program's code, programming languages also make the code *portable*: because the instructions written in a programming language are less machine-specific, they can more easily be adapted for a different type of machine. Ramamoorthy & Tsai 1996.
13. In reality, the path from finished source code to executing a program typically comprises a more complex, four-stage process: compiling, assembling, linking and loading. Furthermore, a compiler does more than mere translation of source code into assembly language: she or he also optimizes the code, which makes the program run faster, require less memory or both. Webber 2003, p. 47.
14. Band & Katoh 1995, p. 14; Holmes & Torok 2006.
15. Gibson 2005, p. 175.

Unlike the recipe behind the dish, however, the source code behind a computer program distributed in object code can be extracted using a *decompiler*. A decompiler attempts to reverse the conversion of object code into source code, thus reconstructing human-readable source code from a program's distributed object code.[16] Decompilation is discussed in more detail in section 2.1.2b as it can be a necessary tool for establishing interoperability between computer programs.[17]

In contrast to the previously described closed code model, the *open source* model denotes free availability of the software's source code, enabling other developers to improve and modify the software.[18] Although it has long been commercially neglected, open source has matured into a viable alternative for proprietary (closed code) software.[19] Reliable open source software, such as the *Linux* operating system, the *OpenOffice* suite, the *MySQL* database and the *Apache* web server, contributes to the success of open source. In the open source model, where the underlying source code is essentially freely available,[20] the interface specifications are necessarily disclosed, such that, at least in theory, establishing interoperability with computer programs licensed as open source should not raise substantial (legal) complications.[21] Open source models, therefore, are not discussed at length in this study.

b. Interoperability

Previously in section 2.1.1, we observed that software substantially relies on other software by *interoperating* with such other software. For example, application programs need to interoperate with the computer's operating system; different application programs need to read and write each other's file formats, program modules call on each other's functionality, and programs on different computers must communicate with each other using common network protocols. The terms *interconnection* and *compatibility* are sometimes used to indicate connections between systems at a lower, mechanical level (rather than a higher, logical level), such as in telecommunications.[22]

Technically, interoperability is achieved through special parts of the computer program called *interfaces*.[23] Achieving interoperability with another component requires logical access to that component's interfaces. This is

16. Breuer & Bowen 1994.
17. For other motives, see Staffelbach 2003, p. 50.
18. Guibault & Van Daalen 2006.
19. Goth 2005.
20. Weber 2005.
21. However, a recent report by the Open Source Alliance suggests that open source developers neglect the critical role of interoperability in the success of open source software. Open Source Alliance 2007. On open source licensing, see Guibault & Van Daalen 2006.
22. See also Staffelbach 2003, p. 69.
23. Software Directive, §10.

necessary both for the development of the component and during runtime, at the end-user's computer.[24]

The *Posix Open Systems Reference Model* distinguishes four types of interfaces in software.[25] Each program or component may have many interfaces of all four types to respond to corresponding functions. In this study, the most important type of interface is the *Application Programming Interface*, or *API*, which is an interface for interoperating with other programs. The term has been defined as 'any well-defined interface that defines the service that one component, module or application provides to other software elements'.[26] APIs are a crucial part of operating systems and many applications. For instance, Microsoft Windows' APIs are crucial to any developer of application programs for this operating system. Similarly, the APIs of the popular image-editing program *Adobe Photoshop* enable third parties to create image effect filters that can be used within Photoshop, and the open source web browser *Mozilla Firefox* enables others to create plug-ins through its API.

Other interfaces include the *user interface*, which allows a user to interact with a system. Because user interfaces, by definition, do not involve software-to-software interaction, they are largely ignored in this study.[27] *Data interfaces* are responsible for storing and retrieving data in a specific format. Common formats are JPEG for images, HTML for web pages, PDF for online and print documents and MP3 for music. These formats can be read and written by computer programs from many different developers. Many application programs contain data interfaces for both common or open formats and for one or more proprietary or native formats. The former allows the program to read and write formats used by other applications, ensuring compatibility. The latter usually takes better advantage of the program's specific functionality. For instance, Adobe Photoshop's native PSD format can store an image in separate layers and in a high resolution. The more common and popular JPG format does not allow images to be stored in separate layers, nor in high resolution, but, due to its smaller size, is more suitable for transfer over relatively slow internet connections. Finally, *communications interfaces* or communication *protocols* enable computer programs to communicate over telecommunications equipment. The communications interface defines the protocols or rules used in communicating data. Among the more familiar communications interfaces are HTTP for transferring web content and SMTP, IMAP and POP3 for sending and receiving e-mail.

Interfaces are present at different levels of abstraction. They are used at lower, physical levels (such as an Ethernet connector plug) and at higher,

24. McKean 2005.
25. Severance 1999.
26. Souza et al. 2004, p. 64.
27. Nonetheless, for purposes of copyright law, so-called command-line user interfaces are very similar to application programming interfaces and are, therefore, examined in some detail in Chapter 3.

logical levels (such as data interfaces between word processors). Arguably, an operating system taken as a whole provides an interface between the computer hardware and other (application) programs.[28] Each individual function or subroutine of a computer program could be considered an interface as well.

As noted, software-to-software interfaces or APIs are central to this study. APIs are comprised of two parts: the interface *specification* and its *implementation*. The interface specification is the part of the interface that may be disclosed to other computer program(mer)s.[29] It instructs the program(mer) about the name, purpose and calling convention of the interface; that is, what it does, what information to provide it with and what information to expect from the interface in return. In effect, the specification of the interface defines the rule of how (in which format) to interoperate through the interface.[30] For two computer programs to be interoperable, they must thus adhere to the *exact* same interface specifications. API interface specifications are often concretely expressed in the source and object code of the computer program. These interface specifications, therefore, are not to be confused with the use of the word *specifications* in the typical, more abstract meaning of 'characteristic'. In the latter sense, the specifications (characteristics) of the Airbus A330-200 airliner include its maximum operating Mach number, which is 0.86.[31] By contrast, the interface specifications (interface rules) of Microsoft's Windows operating system are expressly contained in each copy of the program, albeit in unreadable object code form.

The interface implementation, then, is the functional part of the interface, or the body of the interface. An interface implementation constitutes instructions similar to any other part of the program but with the specific purpose of interoperating with other programs in the format defined by the interface specification. The following example lists the source code of a simple interface that finds a keyword in a text and returns a value of true or false to indicate whether the keyword was found. The first (marked) line of the

28. Samuelson 2008a, p. 28.
29. The practice of separating interface specification and implementation is a form of information hiding: software engineers only disclose the interface specifications on a need-to-know basis. Other developers must understand what an interface does and what parameters it requires to complete its task (the specification) without necessarily having any knowledge of the internal functioning of the interface (its implementation). The programmer may thus change the implementation of the interface (e.g., to improve its performance or compatibility with internal components) without changing its specification. Well-defined APIs, thus, also serve to facilitate the coordination of interoperability development among developers and are considered as a contract between different groups of developers (Ghezzi et al. 1991, p. 81; Parnas 1972; Souza et al. 2004).
30. Band & Katoh 1995, p. 7.
31. Airbus, *Specifications Airbus A330-200*, available at <http://www.airbus.com/en/aircraftfamilies/a330a340/a330-200/specifications/> (last visited December 31, 2009).

interface is its specification; the subsequent lines together constitute the implementation.

```
BOOL SearchInText( CString strText, CString strKeyword )
{
 if( strText.Find( strKeyword ) )
 return TRUE;
 return FALSE;
}
```

Note that interoperability is a matter of degree: in particular for more complex interoperating systems, interoperability may be stronger or weaker depending on the mutual use of and access to the relevant interface specifications.[32] If only some interfaces can be used, interoperability may not be complete.[33] However, not all potential interfaces in a computer program are indeed intended to function as interfaces to other programs or systems. An interoperable developer may seek to access interfaces in a program that the original developer had not anticipated. Thus, the term *interface* is not reserved for points of entry set by the original developer. What constitutes a (useful) interface is sometimes determined by third parties.[34]

Interface specifications can be a species of standards.[35] The interfaces themselves may become a recognized manner of calling on a computer program's interfaces (e.g., the VESA-bus standard), or the underlying product may become so popular that its interfaces necessarily become a standard in the industry (e.g., Microsoft Windows' interfaces). What precisely constitutes a standard, however, is difficult to define, even in the abstract. Lea & Hall observe, 'both surprisingly and ironically, there is no commonly agreed definition [of a technical standard]'.[36] A technical standard often pertains to some form of communication between different vendors' products. Hovenkamp offers a definition of a technical standard that can also encompass interface specifications: 'a set of technical specifications that provides a common design for some product or process'.[37] As already observed, these standards are a crucial ingredient of an industry so strongly characterized by coordination and interdependency, such as the computer industry.[38] Evidently, most interface specifications never become standards. However, the controversies surrounding interface specifications – and the observations regarding interface specifications in this study – primarily concern those that

32. Band & Katoh 1995, p. 8; Samuelson 2008a, p. 7.
33. See, for example, *Microsoft Decision* (European Commission 2004), §750; *Microsoft* (GC 2007), §210; Shapiro & Varian 1999, p. 148.
34. Band & Katoh 1995, p. 10.
35. Samuelson 2008a, p. 5.
36. Lea & Hall 2004, p. 69. See also McKean 2005 ('an idea or thing used as a measure, norm, or model in comparative evaluations'). For other definitions, see Lea & Hall 2004, p. 71.
37. Hovenkamp 2007, p. 87.
38. See section 2.1.1.

have become standards. It is also true that not all (technical) standards concern interface specifications, and the function and effects of control over such other standards may be very different from control over interface specifications. Thus, this study's observations regarding interface specifications may also apply to some standards that do not concern interface specifications, but this is not necessarily true.

Standards, including standards for interfaces, can principally emerge in two different ways: *de-jure* or *de-facto*.[39] A de-jure standard is created by formal agreement or consent. It may also be defined by a governmental body or industry organization. Many standards used in telecommunications and broadcasting are *de-jure* standards, such as ISDN, PAL and NTSC. Private industry groups known as Standard Setting Organizations (SSOs) play an increasingly important role in *de-jure* standard setting – particularly in interface standards.[40] By contrast, a de-facto standard emerges without any formal act; it simply arises as a widely recognized way of doing or creating something in the market. Many computer-related standards originate as *de-facto* standards: the Windows operating system and its interfaces, the QWERTY keyboard and the HTTP protocol are all examples.

Standards, including standards for interfaces, can be proprietary or open. A proprietary standard is controlled by one or more private parties. Control can be based on intellectual property rights, such as patents or copyrights, on secrecy, or on both. By contrast, an open standard is made publicly available. It may not be protected by intellectual property rights at all, the rights may not be enforced, or they may be licensed under Reasonable and Non-Discriminatory (RAND) terms.[41]

Recall that achieving interoperability with another computer program requires adherence to that program's interface specifications. Hence, in order to achieve interoperability, the competing developer must obtain the target program's interface specifications. These specifications may be obtained either with or without assistance from the target program's developer.

The most obvious means of obtaining interface specifications is by simply requesting them from the target program's developer. Software developers regularly document their interface specifications for use by other programmers.[42] The main disadvantage of relying on the developer's documentation is the potential lack of accuracy and comprehensiveness.[43] First, the documentation process is notoriously neglected in software development,

39. Lea & Hall 2004, p. 69.
40. Lemley 2002, p. 1891.
41. Tiemann 2006.
42. See, for example, Microsoft, MSDN, available at <http://msdn.microsoft.com/> (last visited December 22, 2008); Sun Microsystems, OpenOffice.org 2.0 Developer's Guide, available at <http://api.openoffice.org/docs/DevelopersGuide/DevelopersGuide.xhtml> (last visited July 26, 2006).
43. Johnson-Laird 1994, p. 846.

leaving friend and foe uninformed about the functioning of the software.[44] Second, the developer may limit disclosure and documentation to those interfaces he or she deems necessary or desirable for interoperability with third-party software. There may be many reasons for a developer to hide interfaces. For example, it may be inefficient or even harmful for another program to call upon a certain interface. Making variables and interfaces subject to unanticipated calls is also considered contrary to industry practice.[45] Developers may thus have legitimate reasons for withholding many of their interfaces. However, there may be less sincere concerns involved as well: a developer can gain a significant competitive advantage by withholding certain interfaces of a popular computer program. The effects and legal implications of such control over interfaces are central to this study and will be discussed in the following chapters.

If not voluntarily disclosed, the interoperable developer can attempt to extract the interface specifications from a copy of the computer program.[46] The specifications are embedded in the object code of that copy, which is, however, not a human-readable form (see section 2.1.2a). Undisclosed interface specifications are thus not normally readily accessible. Reverse engineering techniques, however, may be employed to extract the interface specifications from the copy of the program.[47]

Reverse engineering is 'the reproduction of another manufacturer's product following detailed examination of its construction or composition'.[48] Reverse engineering has its origins in *hardware* analysis, in which its first and foremost purpose was to create a clone of a competing product, regardless of a need to interoperate with that product.[49] In software, reverse engineering has been described as 'the process of analyzing a subject system to create representations of the system at a higher level of abstraction'.[50] This definition encompasses different reverse engineering methods, including black-box testing and decompilation (see *infra*).[51] The former achieves a higher level of abstraction by deducing specifications from observing a program's operations, whereas the latter deducts high-level source code from low-level object code.

Thus, the black-box analyst closely observes the computer program in operation and, by observing exactly *what* it does, attempts to reconstruct *how* it does it. Without actual knowledge of the program's source code (it is treated as a 'black box'), the engineer attempts to reconstruct how the program works and, particularly, which interface specifications it uses to interoperate with

44. Ghezzi et al. 1991, p. 227; Souza et al. 2005.
45. Fowler 2002. See also Ghezzi et al. 1991, p. 9; Webber 2003, p. 312.
46. Band & Katoh 1995, p. 12.
47. See, for example, Weiser 2003, p. 552 (reporting several real-world examples of reverse engineering for purposes of interoperability).
48. McKean 2005.
49. Samuelson & Scotchmer 2002, p. 1582.
50. Chikofsky & Cross II 1990, p. 15. See also Gowers 2006, §2.20.
51. Schricker 1999, p. 1119.

other programs.[52] Black-box testing is a commonly used method of obtaining interface specifications and has proven a successful method in the past. Compaq successfully employed this technique to reverse engineer IBM's BIOS-chip, a critical part of the first IBM PC. The Samba team also relied on black-box analysis to achieve interoperability with Microsoft's networking protocols.[53] Nonetheless, although it is potentially useful, black-box testing requires a substantial investment in time and resources. It can be extremely difficult and time consuming to establish all interface specifications a program uses, as it requires simulating an environment in which all possible circumstances are duplicated.[54]

Decompilation, then, is a partly automated method of reconstructing the human-readable source code from a program's object code.[55] Reconstructing the source code enables a programmer to study and modify a program in a way that object code does not allow her or him to do. In some respects, decompilation, therefore, is opposite to black-box testing. Decompilation is aimed directly at the inner workings of a program: it attempts to extract the source code rather than reconstructing such code from observing the product's functioning. Decompilation is, therefore, also known as white-box testing.[56] In theory, decompilation could be helpful to an engineer in search of a target program's interface specifications. Moreover, it should provide the interoperable developer with *all* the existing interfaces, not merely the ones disclosed by the original developer, or those discovered by black-box testing.[57] Indeed, successful decompilation could potentially reveal considerably more: because the source code is reconstructed, decompilation also exposes the *implementation* of the interfaces and all other parts of the program, including any valuable know-how other than interfaces.[58] Software engineers typically use black-box testing and decompilation complementarily.[59]

Even if decompilation is successful, however, some valuable information in the original source code, such as the original names for interfaces and variables as well as comments, can never be reconstructed.[60] Because these names and comments are useless to the computer and, therefore, would take up unnecessary space, they are often stripped from the program during compilation.[61] Without these original names and comments, however, it is more

---

52. Band & Katoh 1995, p. 14.
53. Tridgell, *How Samba Was Written*, available at <http://samba.org/ftp/tridge/misc/french_cafe.txt> (last visited April 11, 2006).
54. Madou et al. 2005.
55. Band & Katoh 1995, p. 15; Cifuentes 1999.
56. Cifuentes & Fitzgerald 1998, p. 271.
57. Staffelbach 2003, pp. 50, 120.
58. Cifuentes et al. 1998.
59. Johnson-Laird 1994.
60. Cifuentes et al. 1998, p. 236; Souza et al. 2005.
61. Johnson-Laird 1994.

difficult to comprehend the source code.[62] Consider the following example: a simple interface written in C++ that confirms the presence of a keyword in a text.[63] As parameters, the interface expects the text to search in (`strText`) and the keyword to search for (`strKeyword`). The original source code, including the developer's comments (written between `/*` and `*/` marks) as well as the original names of the function and parameters, immediately reveals the code's functionality to any programmer:

```
/* this function looks for a keyword in a text and returns true if found */
BOOL SearchInText ( CString strText, CString strKeyword )
{
 if( strText.Find( strKeyword ) )
 return TRUE; /* yes, keyword found */
 return FALSE; /* no, keyword not found */
}
```

Unlike this original source code (*supra*), the source code generated by the decompiler is difficult to understand in isolation:

```
int function057 ( class094 var822, class094 var823 )
{
 if( method012( var822, var823 ) ) return 1;
 return 0;
}
```

Without further knowledge of what each variable and data type actually represents in the context of the entire computer program, it is difficult to understand the function of this decompiled source code, even for a skilled software engineer.[64]

In the current state of the art, decompilation, like black-box analysis, is still very difficult.[65] This difficulty can give the target program's developer a significant lead-time, while fruitful reverse engineering efforts could further be frustrated by periodical changes in interface specifications.[66] Decompilation may also become more difficult as a result of the increasing complexity of software.[67] Nonetheless, reverse engineering techniques are used commonly in the software industry.[68] Moreover, studies suggest advances in decompilation

62. Teasley 1994. See, for example, *Creative v. Aztech* (Singapore Court of Appeal 1996), 499.
63. For more examples, see also Walter et al. 2001, p. 232.
64. See also Band & Katoh 1995, p. 15.
65. *Microsoft Decision* (European Commission 2004), §685. See, for example, Boomerang, available at <http://boomerang.sourceforge.net/> (last visited January 12, 2009); ExeToC, *ExeToC*, available at <http://sourceforge.net/projects/exetoc> (last visited January 12, 2009).
66. See, for example, *Microsoft Decision* (European Commission 2004), 184.
67. Spoor 1994.
68. Samuelson & Scotchmer 2002, p. 1578.

technology, based in part on improved artificial intelligence.[69] Furthermore, there are specialized decompilation firms.[70]

In addition to voluntary disclosure and reverse engineering, forced access can be a third means of obtaining interface specifications. As demonstrated in Chapter 3, the European copyright regime addressing interoperability relies on a combination of voluntary access and reverse engineering for access to interface specifications of a copyright-protected computer program, while forced access could, under exceptional circumstances, be obtained by applying competition law (Chapter 4).

2.2. EFFECTS OF INTEROPERABILITY

The previous section demonstrated the relevance of interfaces for software interoperability. The purpose of the present section is to examine some of the effects of software interoperability on consumers, as well as on innovation and competition. Section 2.2.1 first underscores the difference between the value of interface technology as such and its value for interoperability. Section 2.2.2 examines some effects of interoperability in horizontal relationships, in which network effects play a key role. Section 2.2.3 examines some effects of interoperability in vertical relationships. Finally, section 2.2.4 examines the implications of these horizontal and vertical effects for the central normative concern of this study: the extent of control over interface specifications. This normative framework will be used to evaluate the substantive effects of the relevant intellectual property rights (Chapter 3) and competition laws (Chapter 4) on the control over interfaces and, thereby, on interoperability, innovation and competition.

2.2.1. INTERFACES AND INTEROPERABILITY

Recall that interfaces, and particularly their specifications, are the key to interoperability. Interface specifications, therefore, should not only be regarded as technology as such but also and primarily as the technological key that competitors need to achieve interoperability. Crucially, control over interfaces (e.g., through intellectual property rights) can thus yield two types of effects: direct effects (control over interface technology as such) and, more importantly, indirect effects (control over interoperability).

The direct effects of control over interfaces follow from the value of exclusivity over the interface itself. This could also be called the interface's *ex-ante* value, or its value before the underlying product has attracted demand in the market. In particular for the specification of the interface, this value is

69. Gowers 2006, §2.20; Sparta 2005.
70. Staffelbach 2003, p. 55; Walter et al. 2001, p. 213.

modest; it is little more than a format through which the interface operates with other systems. This format is relatively arbitrary, as different formats will initially produce identical results.[71] Even if some interface specifications, such as those of operating systems, can be quite complex,[72] their complexity relative to the program they form part of is still modest. The *ex-ante* value of an interface specification may thus be relatively low.

Indeed, the value of interfaces primarily lies in their *in*direct function: by controlling interfaces, firms obtain *de-facto* control over interoperability with their product. By controlling interfaces, firms can thus control access to their product's network of users (horizontally), or to their product's functionality (vertically). As demonstrated in the following two sections, the value of interoperability can be significant for horizontal and vertical competitors. This relates to their *ex-post* value, or the value of interoperability with the underlying product. The interface specification is a *sine-qua-non* to achieving interoperability, and, depending on the value of such interoperability, the *ex-post* value of the interface specification, therefore, can be quite substantial.[73]

2.2.2. Horizontal Effects of Interoperability

This section examines the effects of interoperability on innovation and competition among horizontal competitors. Interoperability increases network effects (section 2.2.2a). Section 2.2.2b examines various types of network effects. Section 2.2.2c examines the effects of interoperability as a trade-off between standardization and variety. Section 2.2.2d demonstrates that interoperability and network effects are determinative for the type of competition and innovation that firms are likely to engage in.

a. Interoperability and Network Effects

Computer software is generally subject to relatively strong network effects.[74] Network effects denote an increase in value as more people consume the good; the value of a network good is, in other words, a function of its number of users.[75]

For a network good, there are different demand curves for different numbers of users. The demand for a network good is not only determined by its price but also by the number of other people using it.[76] Thus, prices and

71. See also section 3.1.1a. See also Farrell 1989, p. 47; Hovenkamp et al. 2002–2007, §12.3a.
72. Band & Katoh 1995, p. 7; Farrell & Katz 1998, p. 649; Lemley & McGowan 1998, p. 533; Pilny 1992, p. 197; Samuelson 2007b, p. 218; Staffelbach 2003, p. 70.
73. See, for example, *Microsoft* (GC 2007), §694.
74. Lemley et al. 2000, p. 31.
75. Farrell & Klemperer 2004, p. 2007; Katz & Shapiro 1998, p. 3; Shapiro & Varian 1999, p. 174.
76. Menell 1998, p. 655; Scotchmer 2004, p. 293.

qualities of two products being equal, consumers would prefer the product with the larger network benefits. The presence of network effects in software can have a profound impact on its innovation and dissemination and on consumer welfare.[77]

Consumer welfare could, simplistically, be viewed as the product of two primary efficiencies: dynamic and static efficiency. Static efficiency relates to the optimal dissemination of existing goods, or maximizing people's access to goods. Dynamic efficiency relates to innovation, or the optimal replacement of older technologies by newer ones. The competitive process should normally promote an optimal mix of static and dynamic efficiency. However, law and policy influence firms' behavior. For example, firms' pursuit of dynamic efficiency is influenced by intellectual property rights, of which the scope and term are defined by the legislator. From a policy perspective, then, there is an inherent tension between these two efficiencies; dynamic efficiency (innovation) requires firms to be able to set a higher price in order to recoup investments in innovation, whereas static efficiency (dissemination) requires a low price. Intellectual property and competition laws both aim to balance these two efficiencies, each in their own manner.[78]

If network effects are important, consumer welfare is not only stimulated by a lower price (static efficiency) and innovation (dynamic efficiency) but also by connection to the largest number of other users. If two non-interoperable network products A and B cost the same, but product A is used by 1,000 other users and product B by only 10, consumer welfare is better served if network product A were further disseminated. In other words, in addition to stimulating a lower price and innovation, network effects must also be maximized.[79] Like the conflicting interests of promoting innovation and dissemination thereof (*supra*), network effects have their own effect on dynamic efficiency, as the standardization involved in having consumers benefit from the same network inherently limits the possibilities for change, and, thereby, for further innovation. Chapters 3 and 4 will demonstrate that, unlike the former tension between exclusivity for innovation and openness for dissemination, the latter tension between standardization and variety is not yet substantially recognized in intellectual property (copyright) and competition laws.

Network effects are generally strongest where the relevant good allows for communication with other users of the good, such as a telephone.[80] In order to allow for communication, the goods must interoperate with each other. As noted, whether software systems are interoperable depends on the openness of their respective interface specifications; open interface specifications enable

---

77. See also Katz & Shapiro 1994, p. 106.
78. See section 4.1.2a.
79. Menell 1998, p. 664. Menell 1998, p. 664. Because different business strategies may be employed to market products subject to network effects, price only partly reflects costs and demand. See, for example, Farrell 1989, p. 42. See also section 2.2.2d.
80. Menell 1998, p. 656.

interoperability; closed specifications obstruct interoperability.[81] Users of interoperating goods are part of the same network; users of non-interoperating goods are not part of the same network. Because intellectual property right can be used to control use of and access to interfaces, they can have a profound impact on interoperability, and, thereby, on network effects. Section 2.2.4 will explore this relationship in some detail.

Network effects can thus be generated within a network of goods from a single vendor – for example, all Microsoft Word documents – or across networks of goods from different vendors – for example, web pages in HTML format. In the latter case, the different vendors' goods are interoperable; in the former, they are not. When two vendors' products are interoperable through open interfaces, the network encompasses users of both products. Thus, interoperability between vendors can increase the size of the network and, therefore, the network benefits of each individual good.[82] In the software industry, users can often select from a variety of products that are interoperable through common standards. For example, regardless of one's choice of word processor, most word processors can handle documents in TXT, RTF or HTML formats. The network effects of each of these products should thus be comparable.[83] The former type of network effects is also referred to as proprietary network effects. In this model, network effects can still be maximized if all users select a single vendor.

Because the demand for a network good increases with the number of people using it, demand is greatest for the network with the largest number of users.[84] Conversely, networks that are already small tend to lose customers.[85] This process reinforces itself. Network industries, therefore, are subject to *tipping*: eventually, one network good among a number of competing, non-interoperable network goods could win the race for the vast majority of consumers as consumers seek to join the network with the largest number of other users.[86] Tipping thus excludes competition from non-interoperable vendors. Nevertheless, some consumers may have a sufficiently strong demand for variety, which may prompt them to accept the lesser network benefits of a rival, smaller network (such as Apple's MacOS).[87]

Because reverse engineering can help to achieve interoperability,[88] it may serve as a means of 'self help' for one firm to develop products interoperable

81. See section 2.1.2b.
82. Farrell & Katz 1998, p. 611; Lemley & McGowan 1998, p. 491; Page & Lopatka 2007, p. 92.
83. Due to imperfect interoperability, network effects may, in reality, not be equal.
84. Shapiro 2000, p. 10.
85. Shapiro & Varian 1999, p. 176.
86. Farrell & Klemperer 2004, p. 2034; Farrell & Saloner 1985, p. 71; Katz & Shapiro 1994, p. 106; Samuelson & Scotchmer 2002, p. 1624; Scotchmer 2004, p. 295; Shapiro 2000, p. 7; Shapiro & Varian 1999, p. 176.
87. Shapiro & Varian 1999, p. 188.
88. See section 2.1.2b.

with those of another firm, which is particularly relevant after tipping has occurred.[89] For instance, RealNetworks reverse engineered Microsoft's Windows Media Player format for streaming media, whereas Apple reverse engineered Adobe's PDF standard for use within its operating system MacOS X. The role of reverse engineering for interoperability will be examined in Chapter 3.

b. Types of Network Effects

Katz & Shapiro categorize goods along a continuous scale of actual networks, virtual networks and positive feedback effects. The principal criterion for this categorization is to what extent the good provides any value separately from its network effects.[90] Most computer programs fall in one of these three categories.

It follows that the strongest type of network effects, namely actual networks, comprise goods that have no inherent value apart from their ability to connect to others in the network: '[t]he benefit to a purchaser [. . .] is access to other purchasers.'[91] The telephone and fax machine are classic examples.[92] However, many computer programs can also be categorized under this label: e-mail clients and instant messengers, for instance, have virtually no inherent value apart from their ability to connect to other users in the network.[93] The same applies to some social networking applications, such as Facebook and LinkedIn.

Virtual networks consist of goods that, unlike goods in actual networks, possess some inherent value separate from their network value, yet have increased value with more people consuming the good. Most computer programs fall in this category: they enable an individual user to perform useful tasks, yet they become more valuable as the user can connect to other users. For instance, an individual user benefits from a word processor by the ability to create, edit and print documents. However, as more people use the same word processor, they can also exchange their documents and edit and review each other's work.[94] Such *horizontal* or *direct* effects are particularly present in application programs, due to the ability to exchange data[95] (e.g., a Microsoft Excel spreadsheet) or communications (e.g., AIM instant messenger) between users of the same program.[96] Even if a particular computer program provides limited functionality to exchange data with other users, network effects may

89. Menell 1998, pp. 680, 691; Samuelson & Scotchmer 2002, p. 1621; Weiser 2003, p. 551.
90. Katz & Shapiro 1985, p. 424. See also Lemley & McGowan 1998.
91. Lemley & McGowan 1998, p. 488.
92. See also Benjamin et al. 2006, pp. 698, 705; Farrell & Klemperer 2004, p. 2009; Larouche 2000, p. 365; Lemley et al. 2000, p. 31; Page & Lopatka 2007, p. 91.
93. Farrell & Klemperer 2004, p. 2007; Goldberg 2005, p. 134; Shelanski & Sidak 2001, p. 8.
94. Lemley & McGowan 1998, p. 491; Lemley et al. 2000, p. 32.
95. Samuelson et al. 1994, p. 2376.
96. Lea & Hall 2004, p. 73; Page & Lopatka 2007, p. 97.

still be generated as a result of shared learning costs. With more people using the same program, there are better opportunities to exchange knowledge about the program, and network effects may increase.[97]

Software may additionally be subject to *vertical* or *indirect* network effects, or network effects caused by complementary products.[98] Thus, a developer of a word-processing application will typically prefer to develop the application for the operating system with the greatest market share. As more application developers choose to develop for a particular operating system or platform, the success of the operating system is reinforced.[99] In *Microsoft v. European Commission*, a case discussed in more detail in Chapter 4 the General Court similarly considered that, as more content would become available exclusively in Microsoft's Windows Media format because it was bundled with the popular Windows operating system, the demand for Windows Media Player would be reinforced.[100] Thus, vertical or indirect network effects are particularly relevant for operating system or platform developers.[101]

Lastly, there are positive feedback effects. Goods in this category are not actually part of a network, but derive their value principally from inherent qualities. Nonetheless, although these goods do not interoperate or communicate, their value may still increase with others consuming the same goods. This is due mostly to supply-side economies of scale: it becomes more attractive for suppliers to supply complementary goods for a larger customer base because the fixed costs of production can be divided over a larger number of sales. The large number of complementary goods, in turn, reinforces the popularity of the primary product. These effects, therefore, are to be contrasted with true network effects, which are demand-side economies of scale.[102] Earlier computer games – which often lacked networking functionality – may fall under this category. Although the games only provided value to each individual consumer, popular games frequently induced spin-off products such as *cheat sheets*.[103]

---

97. *Apple v. Microsoft* (US Court of Appeals, Ninth Circuit 1994); Barton 1997, p. 444; *Microsoft Decision* (European Commission 2004), §338; Farrell 1989, p. 37; *Lotus v. Borland* (US Court of Appeals, First Circuit 1995), 821; Menell 1989, p. 1066; Menell 1998, p. 662; Samuelson 2001, p. 17; Samuelson et al. 1994, p. 2375; Shapiro & Varian 1999, p. 121; Sheremata 1997, p. 967.
98. See also Farrell & Klemperer 2004, p. 2013; Lea & Hall 2004, p. 74; Scotchmer 2004, p. 298.
99. Lemley & McGowan 1998, p. 491. See also *Microsoft Decision* (European Commission 2004), §340.
100. *Microsoft* (GC 2007), §983, §984.
101. See also Larouche 2000, p. 365.
102. Lemley & McGowan 1998, p. 495; Shapiro 1999a, p. 5; Shapiro & Varian 1999, p. 179.
103. A 'cheat sheet' lists hints on how to circumvent some of the video game's (artificial) limitations.

c. Standardization and Variety

This section demonstrates the consequences of network effects and interoperability for consumers. The most obvious and direct benefit of interoperability between different vendors' products is a greater realization of network effects. When multiple vendors' computer programs are interoperable, users benefit not only from an increase in the number of users of their particular vendor's program but also from increased use of other vendors' programs. Network effects are not fragmented but instead encompass users of all interoperable vendors and products.[104]

Interoperability also safeguards individual consumers against lock-in effects, which is sometimes referred to as stranding or path dependency.[105] Absent interoperability, a consumer will incur switching costs when migrating from one vendor's product to another vendor's product.[106] First, users switching to a new system from a system with a large installed base incur opportunity costs caused by the relatively low network benefits of the new system in comparison to the old system,[107] while switching by each individual user also reduces the network benefits for the remaining installed base. Second, switching costs are caused by sunk costs or investments in the use of the current network good. Switching between non-interoperable computer programs, for example, may entail not only discarding investments in a computer program but also a need to convert data into the new format and having to learn a new user interface.[108] As a consequence of switching costs, users can be locked into a particular vendor's products. By contrast, if multiple vendors' programs are interoperable, a user is not restricted to the same vendor's products in subsequent software purchases.[109]

Lock-in and coordination costs can have a profound impact on the innovation and dissemination of goods subject to these effects. The adoption of the QWERTY keyboard is a classic example.[110] Reportedly designed to actually reduce the speed of typing rather than facilitating it, consumers had nonetheless grown accustomed to this design. Despite the development of improved keyboard designs, QWERTY had already become the *de-facto* standard by the beginning of the nineteenth century.[111] As the QWERTY keyboard demonstrates, the switching costs incurred by consumers willing to migrate

---

104. Farrell & Klemperer 2004, p. 1976; Katz & Shapiro 1985, p. 424; Shapiro 2000, p. 8; Shapiro & Varian 1999, p. 229.
105. Farrell 1989, p. 38; Farrell & Klemperer 2004, p. 2015; Shapiro & Varian 1999, p. 230; Shelanski & Sidak 2001, p. 8.
106. Farrell & Klemperer 2004, p. 1977; Katz & Shapiro 1998, p. 5.
107. Lemley & McGowan 1998, p. 722. See, generally, Farrell & Klemperer 2004.
108. Klemperer 1987, p. 375; Menell 1998, p. 659.
109. Katz & Shapiro 1998, p. 5; Page & Lopatka 2007, p. 94; Scotchmer 2004, p. 298; Shapiro 2000, p. 8.
110. Lemley et al. 2000, p. 34. But see Liebowitz & Margolis 1990.
111. David 1985, p. 334. See also Farrell & Klemperer 2004, p. 2011.

to a new technology may be prohibitively high.[112] Consequently, innovative new products, such as the DVORAK keyboard, may not be optimally disseminated.[113] A new entrant will generally be unable to introduce an incrementally better product because compatibility requires adherence to the 'older' standard.[114] Conversely, as the same example demonstrates, dissemination of older yet successful network goods, such as the QWERTY keyboard, may be excessive.[115] Accordingly, rewards for network products may be equally excessive.[116] In other words, by exploiting network effects, a developer can potentially earn more than the social value of the innovation would justify (see also section 2.2.2d).

With competition between incompatible products, consumer expectations are critical.[117] Because consumers benefit from operating on a single network as this maximizes the benefit of being part of the network, they may anticipate which network will acquire the largest installed base.[118] In deciding which product is likely to bring the most network benefits (and will emerge as the *de-facto* standard), consumers must make some predictions as to the behavior of other consumers. They are likely to make these predictions based on factors such as quality, price and reputation of the suppliers. Among the principal proxies relevant to that determination is the quality or innovation of the software product.[119] Consequently, vendors have a strong incentive to win consumer confidence by being innovative, and dynamic efficiency may be strongly stimulated (see also section 2.2.2d).[120]

Nonetheless, there is a risk of selecting an inferior standard. Naturally, anticipating which standard will prevail *ex-ante* is more difficult than choosing which standard has proven to be superior *ex-post*. This may cause a welfare loss because new and innovative technology might not be optimally disseminated.[121]

Even after recognizing the adoption of an inferior technology, the same principle of anticipation that led to the adoption of the inferior standard may prevent consumers from switching to a new, superior standard: generally, consumers may assume that others will refrain from switching due to the associated costs.[122] Some would argue, for instance, that the widespread use of the

112. Lemley & McGowan 1998, p. 497; McGowan 1996, p. 843.
113. Farrell 1989, p. 46.
114. Katz & Shapiro 1998, p. 38.
115. Farrell 1989, p. 46. See also Scotchmer 2004, p. 295.
116. Farrell 1995, p. 47; Farrell & Katz 1998, p. 46.
117. Lemley & McGowan 1998, p. 722; Page & Lopatka 2007, p. 91; Shapiro & Varian 1999, p. 211; Sheremata 1997, p. 953.
118. Katz & Shapiro 1985, p. 425; Katz & Shapiro 1998, p. 4.
119. Katz & Shapiro 1998, p. 5. See also Farrell & Klemperer 2004, pp. 2028, 2041.
120. Farrell 1995, p. 47; Farrell & Klemperer 2004, pp. 2029, 2041; Katz & Shapiro 1994, p. 106; Katz & Shapiro 1998, p. 38; Scotchmer 2004, p. 296.
121. Katz & Shapiro 1994, p. 106.
122. Farrell & Saloner 1986, p. 940; Lemley & McGowan 1998, p. 497.

Microsoft Windows operating system is comparable to that of the QWERTY keyboard – that is, there are superior alternatives, but strong network effects prevent consumers from switching. Interoperability between programs obviates such coordination problems.

Interoperability between systems reduces the possible negative effects caused by a need for consumers to select a standard among multiple, competing and non-interoperable standards. This reduces coordination costs between consumers, including costs of selecting an inferior standard.[123]

Absent interoperability between vendors, adoption of a new technology can be delayed altogether if there are several rival standards for similar technology. Each competing standard risks individually failing to gain sufficient momentum. This effect is referred to as splintering, and it impedes the maximization of network effects.[124] Recent examples include different standards for recordable DVD disks and high definition television, as well as the variety of UNIX implementations.[125]

Although interoperability thus has many positive effects for consumers, there can also be negative effects. Interoperability limits variety: if computer programs must interoperate, they are, to a certain extent, limited in their design.[126] If the new product must interoperate with other vendors' products,[127] or with previous versions of the rightsholder,[128] it must meet certain interoperability requirements.[129] These requirements may imply severe design restrictions and, therefore, a loss in variety.[130] Interoperability not only limits variety between firms horizontally[131] but also for successive product versions of the same firm.[132] For example, some observers, including Microsoft itself, believe that the Windows operating system has become inefficient due in part to backwards-compatibility with older ('legacy') versions, which have limited Microsoft's ability to redesign Windows in its entirety.[133] Farrell & Saloner present the question of whether to mandate interoperability as a trade-off between standardization and variety, or a choice between increased network effects and less variety or lower network benefits with more variety.[134]

---

123. Farrell 1989, p. 37; Farrell & Klemperer 2004, pp. 2021, 2029; Katz & Shapiro 1998, p. 6.
124. Farrell & Klemperer 2004, p. 2023.
125. *Id.*, p. 2024; Shapiro & Varian 1999, p. 229; Stuurman 1995, p. 123. See also Zittrain 2008, p. 7 (noting that none of the proprietary networks in the 1990s, such as America Online, CompuServe and Prodigy, tipped the market).
126. Farrell & Saloner 1992, p. 10.
127. Katz & Shapiro 1998, p. 38.
128. See section 2.2.3.
129. Band & Katoh 1995, p. 8.
130. Farrell 1989, p. 36; Farrell & Klemperer 2004, p. 2033.
131. See section 2.2.2c.
132. Menell 1998, p. 678; Merges 2007, p. 1642; Samuelson 2008a, p. 49.
133. See also Merges 2007, p. 1642.
134. Farrell & Saloner 1985, p. 71. See also Shapiro & Varian 1999, p. 188.

The limitations imposed by a requirement of interoperability depend on the extent to which the product offers any inherent functionality beyond that of its network functions, or, in other words, on the strength of the network effects. For some products, such as server operating systems, interoperability with other components in the network is the central task. The design of such programs is significantly determined by network protocols, such that there may be little room for innovation beyond the scope of these protocols. Breakthrough innovation would require a redesign of the network protocols and cannot be achieved only at the level of the individual components.[135] Conversely, the network protocols, to a large extent, impose design limits on the server operating system. One solution is to support different interfaces (native and non-native interfaces; see section 2.1.2b).

The process of achieving interoperability between competitors may introduce coordination costs:[136] the stronger the network effects, the more significant the need for interoperability with other products that determine the overall design of the product, and the more closely different vendors must coordinate their product development. For example, fully interoperable word processors, ideally, should coordinate the distribution and layout of documents in considerable detail, such that each word and element appears in the exact same position in the document, regardless of which of the interoperable word processors is used to open and save the document. This, in turn, implies coordination of hyphenation; word, sentence and paragraph spacing; document margins and more. This coordination process is aided by standard setting, which, however, introduces costs in and of itself. *De-jure* standardization can involve significant delays,[137] whereas *de-facto* standardization may induce duplicate research efforts and reverse engineering costs.[138]

Interoperability between components not only allows for exchange of data between consumers but also introduces security risks: viruses and other malicious content spread more quickly between interoperable systems.[139] For instance, while Apple's MacOS operating system was long believed to be less vulnerable to viruses than Microsoft's considerably more widespread Windows, Apple's more recent launch of the popular iPhone, which is interoperable with Apple's MacOS operating system, could increase security problems on the entire MacOS platform.[140]

Finally, mandated interoperability could have a negative effect on innovation to the extent that the interface technology necessary for interoperability

135. Note that a single firm might not be able to carry out the type of breakthrough innovation required to displace the incumbent, such that imposing interoperability might not pose too large a limitation.
136. See also section 5.2.1b.
137. Farrell & Saloner 1992, p. 10; Pilny 1992, p. 204.
138. David & Bunn 1988, p. 172; Farrell & Saloner 1992, p. 10. See section 3.2.2a.
139. Samuelson 2008a, p. 1.
140. Raikow, *iPhone Hacker Slams Apple Security*, available at <http://www.crn.com/security/201202993> (last visited February 19, 2009). See also Zittrain 2008, p. 40.

is innovative and must be shared with competitors to enable interoperability.[141] If a firm is forced to share its intellectual property, the incentives to innovate could diminish. Section 4.1.2 elaborates further on this issue.

d. Competition, Innovation and Market Power

Previously, it was demonstrated how interoperability and network effects affect consumers. As software firms seek to satisfy consumers' demand for a maximization of network effects, these network effects also affect the type of innovation and competition in the industry, as well as the market power of individual firms.[142] Besen & Farrell distinguish three principal strategies that firms may embrace to meet consumers' demand for a maximization of network effects:[143] first, they could attempt to establish a *de-facto* standard unilaterally and obtain a dominant position; second, they could adopt an existing standard; or, third, they could establish a new standard in cooperation with other firms. The focus in this study lies on the first two strategies.[144] Firms can implement their strategy of how to compete by maintaining either open or closed (controlled) interfaces.

When firms use closed interfaces, they compete with non-interoperable products, and each firm's product generates its own network effects (the first strategy, or 'standard war'). Users of firm A's product do not have access to users of firm B's product, as the products use different interfaces and are non-interoperable. Consequently, if network effects are important, users will tend to select the firm with the largest network or installed base. Thus, if firm A's product already has 1,000 users and firm B's product only has 10 users, subsequent buyers will likely prefer product A. As already noted, this process reinforces itself, and the market may eventually tip to firm A (see section 2.2.2a). Firm B may eventually be excluded from the market because of lack of interest. Firm A, meanwhile, obtains a position of significant market power. Firm A's substantial market power is an attractive proposition, and firms, therefore, may be inclined to compete vigorously *ex-ante* to tip the market to their product.[145] In other words, firms compete for the entire market, rather than within it.[146]

141. Hovenkamp et al. 2002–2007, §12.3d1.
142. Menell 1998, p. 663.
143. Besen & Farrell 1994. See also Larouche 2000, p. 383; Menell 1998, p. 665.
144. The cooperation between firms necessary to establish a standard raises different issues under competition law, which are beyond the scope of this study. See, for example, Hovenkamp 2007, p. 91; Lemley 2002, p. 1939; Shapiro 2000.
145. Dam 1995, p. 350; Hovenkamp 2007, p. 88; Katz & Shapiro 1998, p. 42; Koelman 2006, p. 839; Merges 2007, p. 1657; Samuelson & Scotchmer 2002, p. 1617; Scotchmer 2004, p. 305; Weiser 2003, p. 536. See also Bartmann 2005, p. 124.
146. Shapiro 2000, p. 89. See also Lea & Hall 2004, p. 70; Merges 2007, p. 1634. One can also distinguish between competition *ex-ante* (for the market) and *ex-post* (in the market). See Katz & Shapiro 1985, p. 424; Lemley & McGowan 1998, p. 525; Shapiro 2000, p. 9.

By contrast, with open interfaces and interoperable products, firms cannot compete in network size because the network effects of all interoperable products are equal (second strategy). It is difficult for any particular firm to obtain a significantly larger installed base than other firms and to use that larger installed base to capture the entire market. A user of one competitor's product benefits from the network effects caused by all competitors' products combined. For instance, standardized formats for word-processing documents allow users of different word processors to exchange documents. Interoperable products of different firms are, to some extent, substitutes for each other because they offer the same network benefits. This stimulates the more traditional competition in the market, in which firms do not compete for the largest installed base or network size, but rather at the product or service level.[147] There may, however, be less of an incentive to offer the type of breakthrough innovation stimulated by competition for the market.[148] Instead, firms may be over-stimulated to develop interoperable products, or marginal improvements over existing products, rather than engaging in an entirely new standard that could be beneficial to society.[149] There may be increased competition and innovation in individual components, which should result in lower prices and more variety in these components, but possibly less breakthrough innovation.[150]

The distinction between the effects of interoperability and non-interoperability is certainly not as black-and-white as presented earlier, however. Interoperability may also stimulate significant innovation.[151] For new market entrants, keeping interfaces open and safeguarding interoperability may be an important 'driver' for their new platform: if other firms develop complementary products for a platform due to its open interfaces, the popularity of the platform may increase more rapidly (vertical interoperability).[152] Conversely, follow-on innovation may be stimulated by open interfaces, as a follow-on innovator can expect a large audience for the new product.[153] Indeed, the economic purpose of a standard is to 'freeze' development in one stage (i.e., the standard) in order to enable or accelerate (follow-on) innovation in a second stage. Thus, standardization removes the uncertainty about the outcome of the innovative process, thereby facilitating follow-on innovation. The internet, in particular, is a sublime example of an

147. Farrell 1989, p. 42; Farrell & Klemperer 2004, p. 1971; Lea & Hall 2004, p. 70; Shapiro 2000, p. 89.
148. Katz & Shapiro 1985, p. 439.
149. Farrell 1989, p. 48.
150. *Id.*, p. 36; Shapiro 2000, p. 8.
151. Scotchmer 2004, p. 304.
152. Katz & Shapiro 1985, p. 425; Katz & Shapiro 1994, p. 111; Samuelson & Scotchmer 2002, p. 1616; Shapiro & Varian 1999, p. 199.
153. Large firms can also benefit from open interfaces. For instance, IBM's use of open interfaces accelerated support for its new PC platform. Farrell 1989, p. 42; Hovenkamp 2007, p. 100; Katz & Shapiro 1994, p. 103.

innovation-driver based on open standards.[154] Interoperability with the incumbent will also aid the new entrant in persuading consumers to switch to its new product (horizontal interoperability).

Because interoperability can substantially affect the form of competition (in or for the market), it can also significantly affect market power. Due to strong network effects in software, consumers seek to maximize their network benefits. If the different manufacturer's products are not interoperable (controlled interfaces), consumers, therefore, will tend to choose the brand with the largest number of other users. The market may eventually tip to that product. Such tipping reduces competition from other firms, causing substantial market power. Competitors anticipate this and, therefore, may compete for that tipped position. By contrast, with interoperable products, firms compete in the market, and the market power of any one firm may be less substantial. These two different forms of competition – for and in the market – are depicted in the diagram below

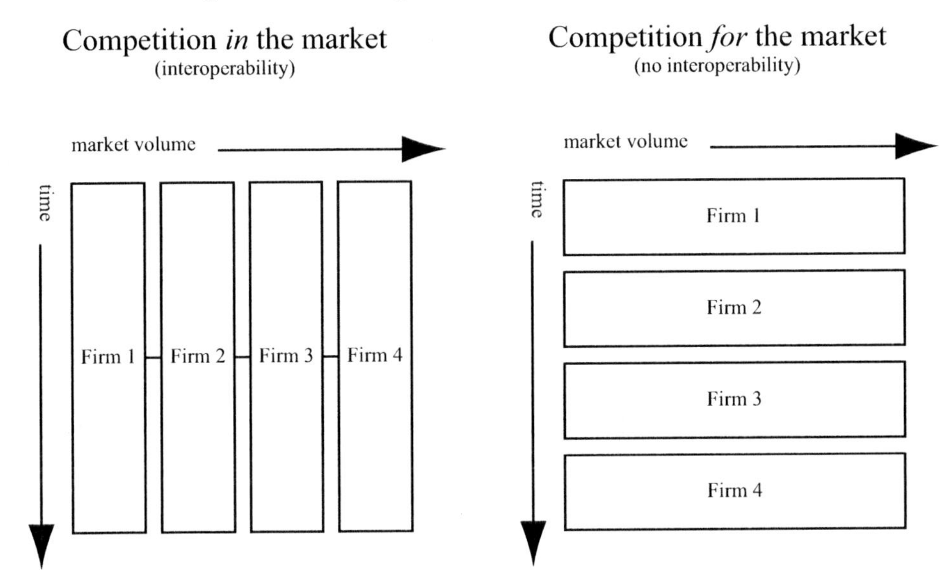

The notion of innovation by subsequent dominant firms can be traced back to Austrian economist Schumpeter's theory of *creative destruction*:[155] a process of continuous innovation rather than (mere) price and output competition, in which rivals compete for the entire market rather than a share in the market. In Schumpeter's view, these subsequent periods of dominance and resulting monopoly rents are the primary drivers for innovation. Large firms could

154. See, generally, Carr 2008, p. 107. See also Frischmann & Weber-Waller 2008; Weiser 2003.
155. Schumpeter 1942, p. 83. See also Katz & Shelanski 2005.

have better opportunities to innovate than smaller firms because of more resources and better abilities to deploy new innovations.[156] According to the Schumpeterian school, monopoly power in such markets should not be a primary concern. Monopoly power will only exist until a competitor has introduced another innovation, thereby replacing the incumbent.[157] The significant market power is thus not necessarily sustainable. Conversely, the threat of entry by other firms should stimulate the incumbent to maintain a high rate of innovation. Furthermore, although prices may be high as a result of the monopolist market structure, these higher prices could merely be a recoupment of investments made earlier (*ex-ante*), namely, during the competition for becoming the *de-facto* standard.[158] The difference with competition in the market is that competitive pressure primarily comes from subsequent, rather than concurrent, competitors. The substantial market power associated with winning competition for the market may incline firms to take more radical steps in innovation and competition than in models of competition in the market.[159]

Thus, in order to *obtain* a monopoly position, firms must offer significantly more attractive products than their rivals, in particular when another firm already has a large installed base.[160] A more attractive product is a more innovative product offered at a lower price. According to some, a product must be 'ten times better' in order to persuade users to switch from an established (tipped) network product.[161] This process is demonstrated, for example, by Adobe's reliance on network effects in the development of its PDF standard for electronic document storage[162] and by Nintendo's replacement of Atari as the standard game console in the 1970s, which itself was followed by Sega.[163] Earlier, Bell's initial patents in the telephone enabled it to exploit network effects so as to expand significantly – although initially only among urban, business users.[164]

Conversely, in order to *maintain* the monopoly position, the incumbent must itself innovate significantly in order to prevent entry by other firms. This was demonstrated, for example, by Bell's development of amplifying technology in order to improve the quality of its telephone lines when confronted with competition from independent carriers[165] and by Microsoft's

156. Lea & Hall 2004, p. 75.
157. See also Korah 2006, p. 2; Turney 2005, p. 181.
158. Katz & Shelanski 2005, p. 7.
159. See also Larouche 2008, p. 8 ('a fairly granular form of competition').
160. Weiser 2003, p. 586.
161. See also Farrell & Klemperer 2004, p. 2029; Shapiro & Varian 1999, p. 196.
162. Shapiro & Varian 1999, p. 189.
163. Shapiro 1999b, p. 676; Weiser 2003, p. 588.
164. Mueller 1993, p. 357. In the few years prior to the invention of the switchboard, the telephone only enabled two-way communications. Benjamin et al. 2006, p. 695; Lloyd & Mellor 2003, p. 7.
165. Benjamin et al. 2006, p. 700. See also Nihoul & Rodford 2004, p. 271. But see Zittrain 2008, p. 80.

development of Windows as a response to Apple's graphical user interface (GUI). Thus, Schumpeterian competition for the market may stimulate considerable innovation efforts, both from new entrants and from incumbents. However, the same principle may also induce duplicate research and innovation efforts because only one of the innovators will win the race for the entire network.[166] Incompatibility and competition for the market, therefore, can cause welfare losses similarly to a patent race.[167]

However, the effects of competition for the market are not limited to innovation; they may also affect prices. For example, penetration pricing may be necessary to win consumers from the incumbent and to establish an installed base for a new standard.[168] Profits could be made at a later stage, for instance, by selling complementary products (see section 2.2.3). Thus, for instance, after Bell's initial patents in the telephone had expired, competition arose from independent carriers. As Bell and the independents did not interconnect each other's networks, this resulted in competition for the market, which, in turn, resulted in substantial telephony coverage at affordable prices in the United States.[169]

Schumpeter's theory of innovation by subsequent dominant firms is not uncontroversial.[170] As Katz & Shelanski point out, the notion that innovation is driven by large firms (less concentration) has not been corroborated by substantial empirical evidence.[171] Studies suggest an inverse U-shaped relationship between innovation and concentration: neither cutthroat competition in highly concentrated markets nor monopoly power (unconcentrated markets) are greatly beneficial to innovation. Innovation may benefit most from a concentration level between these two extremes.[172] Nevertheless, the software industry may well be an example of an innovation-based industry with Schumpeterian characteristics.[173] Indeed, software firms with a larger installed base may also be in a better position to disseminate innovation among their installed bases – for instance, through automatic product updates. In any event, Schumpeter's theories have prompted a more prominent role for

166. Farrell & Saloner 1992, p. 10; Samuelson & Scotchmer 2002, p. 1625.
167. Farrell 1995, p. 48.
168. See, generally, Farrell & Klemperer 2004, p. 2036. See also Shapiro & Varian 1999, pp. 196, 273; Weiser 2003, p. 586.
169. Benjamin et al. 2006, p. 697; Mueller 1993, pp. 358, 362, 363.
170. See also Dommering et al. 2001b, p. 28; Drexl 2004, p. 796; Federal Trade Commission 2003, §2.II.A.3.
171. Katz & Shelanski 2005, p. 18. Such a determination is typically made using the *Herfindahl-Hirschman Index* (HHI). See also Katz & Shapiro 1998, p. 15; Merges 2007, p. 1634. See also Dommering et al. 2001b, p. 28; Katz & Shelanski 2007, p. 17; Zittrain 2008, p. 80.
172. Federal Trade Commission 2003, p. 83 (Box 2-1). See also Merges 2007, p. 1636.
173. Evans & Schmalensee 1996, p. 36; Merges 2007, p. 1636; Page & Lopatka 2007, p. 103; Shapiro 1999a, p. 3; Shapiro & Varian 1999, p. 173.

scrutiny of the effects of competition on innovation, where this analysis had traditionally focused on price and output levels.[174]

An analysis of entry barriers and the pattern of innovation is an important element of competition scrutiny in Schumpeterian markets.[175] Because innovation in such markets is undertaken primarily by subsequent dominant firms, it is paramount that, at any given time, the incumbent be subject to sufficient pressure from subsequent firms. Competitive pressure translates into low entry barriers or a quick rate of innovation. Low entry barriers thus ensure that the current firm maintains incentives to invest its monopoly rents in further innovation, thereby staying ahead of competitors, while they enable other firms to acquire the incumbent's position by innovating even further. Although significant temporary market power need, therefore, not be harmful, sustainable market power due to high entry barriers should be avoided, as this reduces the competitive pressure on the currently dominant firm.[176] In the software industry, control over interfaces and standards can constitute a significant entry barrier. Conversely, interoperability or open interfaces lower entry barriers for competitors.[177] It is easier to compete with the incumbent in a network market if the interfaces are open because the new entrant does not have to persuade customers to abandon the network benefits of their current network good; instead, the new entrant's product increases the total network effects.

Competition in and for the market could thus represent two alternative means of maximizing network effects. Competition in the market is enabled through open interfaces and interoperability. In this model, network effects are maximized by a variety of interoperable products from different vendors. Competition for the market is stimulated through control over interfaces and incompatibility. Rather than multiple firms, network effects in this model are maximized by a single firm serving the entire market. In comparison to competition in the market, incentives to innovate may be more significant due to the prospect of substantial market power. There are also lower coordination costs because firms do not need to coordinate their product offerings. This, indeed, was one argument Bell raised when it sought to establish itself as the monopoly provider of telephony in the United States (which it called 'universal service'): interconnection with the other carriers, or competition in the market, would entail significant coordination costs.[178] However, the innovation rate after tipping may be suboptimal.[179] Moreover, competition for the market could reduce innovation and variety at the component level, while prices could be higher. Some of these negative effects of competition for the market (higher prices and less innovation at the component level) may be mitigated if the incumbent is under sufficient competitive pressure from possible new entrants.

---

174. Katz & Shelanski 2005, p. 19. See also Shelanski & Sidak 2001, p. 11. See also section 4.1.2a.
175. Katz & Shelanski 2005, p. 11. See also Drexl 2004, p. 796; Merges 2007, p. 1636.
176. Drexl 2008, p. 9.
177. Farrell & Klemperer 2004, p. 1998; Farrell & Saloner 1986, p. 942; Katz & Shapiro 1998, p. 5.
178. Benjamin et al. 2006, p. 700; Mueller 1993, p. 363.
179. Farrell & Klemperer 2004, p. 2046; Shapiro 1999b, p. 675.

If it is accepted that both competition in and for the market could serve to maximize network effects, but that Schumpeterian competition for the market leads to more radical innovation and market power, while competition in the market leads to more incremental innovation and less market power, the question remains as to which one of these two models is to be preferred. This trade-off appears to be a matter of policy, but the choice may depend on such factors as the strength of network effects, coordination costs, the rate of innovation and the investments required to enter the market. However, as Weiser observes, one need not chose between either a fully proprietary model (stimulating competition for the market) and a fully open model (stimulating competition in the market). Even if a single standard, in which multiple firms compete, is eventually likely to dominate the market, it still appears preferable to have multiple firms or standards compete for that position in order to ensure that the best standard prevails.[180] In order to stimulate innovation and investments in the development of strong standards, which can then serve to maximize network benefits, permitting competition for the market temporarily (until a *de-facto* standard has emerged) might, therefore, be the best option.[181]

In sum, interoperability can have both positive and negative effects on innovation and competition. Conversely, mandating interoperability, although welfare enhancing in some instances, may be detrimental in other instances.[182] Due primarily to its *in*direct role of controlling access to the underlying network and network effects, the ability to control interfaces and interoperability can contribute more quickly to a position of significant market power. However, it may be precisely this significant market power that drives innovation and competition. This form of competition for the market need not necessarily be detrimental as long as sustainable market power is prevented, in particular through sufficiently low entry barriers. Section 2.2.4 will demonstrate that this has implications for the (intellectual property) control over interfaces.

2.2.3. Vertical Effects of Interoperability

The previous section examined the role of interoperability and control over interfaces among horizontal competitors. In that relationship, network effects play a key role. The present section examines the role of interoperability and control over interfaces in relationships among vertical competitors.

a. Systems or Components Innovation

As already noted, computer programs do not only interoperate horizontally but also vertically. That is, a system comprises many components, each

180. Weiser 2003, p. 585.
181. See also Koelman 2006.
182. Farrell & Klemperer 2004, p. 2054; Weiser 2003, p. 583.

responsible for a distinct task, which must interoperate closely with each other. For example, an application program must interoperate with the operating system, which, in turn, must interoperate with the computer's random access memory, its disks, display and other resources. Thus, control over interfaces by one component's manufacturer can limit other component manufacturers' abilities to market their products.

In vertical relationships, interoperability tends to stimulate component innovation. This is also known as mix-and-match compatibility. As interfaces are open, vendors have more incentives to develop new and useful components rather than entire systems.[183] Users can combine components from different vendors to create a system – for example, a printer from firm 1 and ink cartridges from firm 2. By contrast, incompatibility induces systems innovation because the innovator cannot rely on components from other vendors. Furthermore, the innovator can recoup development costs across different components and does not run the risk of facing competition in one or more components that make up the system.[184] Thus, firm 1 creates both printers and ink cartridges; firm 2 does the same.[185] The difference between components and systems innovation, also distinguished as intrabrand versus interbrand competition, is depicted in the diagram below.

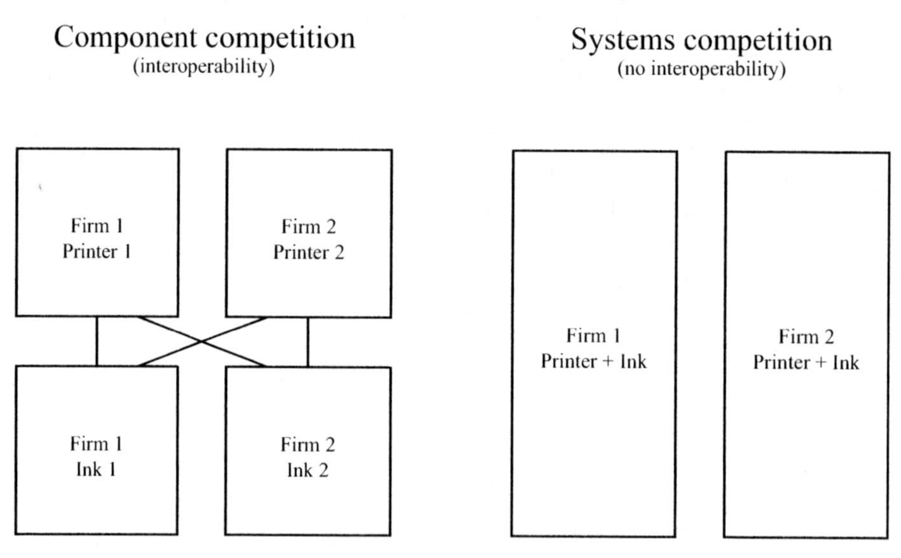

Interoperability between vertical components also allows for specialization within the system. For example, it is very common for the operating system and application programs to be developed by different manufacturers, even if

183. Katz & Shapiro 1994, p. 110. See also Farrell 1989, p. 36; Shapiro & Varian 1999, p. 232.
184. Samuelson & Scotchmer 2002, p. 1623; Shapiro & Varian 1999, p. 232.
185. See also Samuelson & Scotchmer 2002, pp. 1617–1622.

the application program substantially relies on functionality provided for by the operating system. For instance, a word processor that enables the end-user to print a document actually relies on printing functionality built into the operating system. Similarly, the means by which the word processor offers the user a selection of different fonts, or allows the user to browse through his or her documents, are often provided for by the operating system.[186] Interoperability is, therefore, not only important to enable horizontal data exchange, as examined section 2.2.1, but also to vertically call or rely on functionality of another program.

b. Controlling Secondary Markets

Control over interface specifications and interoperability may be used to foreclose competition in an adjacent market. For instance, a refusal by an operating systems manufacturer to disclose its interface information to application program developers limits the latters' abilities to develop applications for that particular operating system.[187] Such control may have positive or negative welfare effects.

Controlling a secondary market is not always possible. There must be separate primary and secondary markets. For instance, the markets for operating systems and office suites generally appear to be separate,[188] but there is a single market for office suites, rather than separate ones for word processors, spreadsheets and presentation software. Moreover, there must be some type of lock-in effect or sunk costs in the primary market: if consumers can easily switch to competitors, control of the secondary market will yield no results. These effects may be caused by lack of interoperability, contracts or intellectual property rights.[189] Finally, consumers are presumed to purchase the primary and secondary products at different stages.[190]

The effects of such control have been analyzed by two partly opposing schools: the Chicago school, which tends to emphasize the positive effects of such vertical integration, and the post-Chicago school, which tends to focus on negative effects.

---

186. Evans et al. 2002, p. 509; Samuelson 2008a, p. 5.
187. See section 2.1.1. Note that a refusal to supply interface information to vertical competitors is only one strategy to gain a foothold in such adjacent markets. A firm may also change its existing interfaces, such that existing products in that adjacent market become incompatible with the firm's changed interfaces (Borenstein et al. 1995, p. 455; Hovenkamp et al. 2002–2007, §12.3d2). Alternatively, a firm may tie or bundle products without offering the tied product separately, or it may offer a second product following a predatory pricing strategy. The result of all of these practices could be foreclosure of competition on the secondary market. See also Evans et al. 2002, p. 509; Page & Lopatka 2007, p. 47.
188. However, commentators caution that market definitions in software are relatively short-lived due to the rapid innovation in the software industry. Katz & Shapiro 1998, p. 13.
189. Bechtold 2007, p. 79; Whinston 1990, p. 839.
190. Shapiro 1995, p. 486.

According to the Single Monopoly Theorem, which is typically associated with the Chicago school of economics,[191] there are generally no anti-competitive rationales for a monopolist to attempt to monopolize a secondary, complementary market because the monopoly rent can only be extracted once.[192] For instance, a monopolist in the market for printers would generally be unable to profitably raise prices for ink cartridges because consumers are only willing to pay one monopoly price for both products combined. Thus, a price increase in ink cartridges would require compensation by a price decrease for printers. According to commentators of the Chicago school, attempts to control a secondary market must, therefore, necessarily have a procompetitive (and welfare-enhancing) effect.[193] Note that this conclusion has been nuanced by insights offered by the post-Chicago school (see *infra*).

One such procompetitive rationale may be the ability to engage in Ramsey pricing.[194] The theory of Ramsey pricing holds that, if there is a need to recoup sunk costs for a series of related (complementary) products or services, these costs are most efficiently recouped by pricing that does not alter the relative usage of the individual products. This implies that the component of the total product or service that demonstrates less price elasticity of demand be increased in price, while the component that is more price elastic be reduced in price. As demand for the former is less sensitive to price, the price increase will not cause substantial reductions in its demand. Thus, the total sunk costs for both products can be recouped while maintaining the relative consumption level of both products. Ramsey pricing enables a firm to recoup sunk costs more efficiently, namely, over a longer period of time.[195] Rather than being forced to recoup all sunk costs from the sale of the primary product, causing higher prices for the primary product and, therefore, ignoring those customers willing to pay a lower price, the manufacturer may be able to recoup part of the development costs for the primary product in the secondary market.[196] Such price discrimination may also help to serve those customers anticipating less frequent use of the product. These customers will be willing to pay a lower price for the primary product and a higher price for the secondary product, of which they expect to consume less.[197] Significantly, because computer programs are often subject to strong network effects (see section 2.2.1), it may be important for a new entrant to establish an installed base first by pricing low (e.g., video consoles) and to earn profits later (e.g., by selling video games).[198]

191. Evans et al. 2002, p. 511.
192. Bork 1978; Hovenkamp et al. 2002–2007. See also *Microsoft Decision* (European Commission 2004), §765; Helberger 2005, p. 47.
193. See also Kuhn & Van Reenen 2007, p. 18.
194. Benjamin et al. 2006, p. 765; Ramsey 1927, p. 47; Schotter 2003, p. 394; Shapiro 1995, p. 498.
195. Bechtold 2007, p. 29.
196. See also Herndon 2002, p. 326; Kuhn & Van Reenen 2007, p. 21.
197. Bechtold 2007, p. 31.
198. O'Donoghue & Padilla 2006, p. 105.

Another such rationale may involve concerns over a producer's reputation in the primary product market.[199] A manufacturer of goods in the primary market may fear that inferior complementary products in the secondary market could undermine its reputation. This may cause a welfare loss. To combat this loss, the manufacturer may attempt to control which products are offered on the secondary market, or, alternatively, the manufacturer may choose to control this market itself.[200] Thus, a developer of operating systems might fear that the reputation of its operating system was vulnerable due to virus attacks, with current developers of antivirus software unable to combat viruses adequately. Consequently, by withholding interoperability information, the operating systems vendor could enter the market for antivirus software itself, thereby possibly improving its reputation through better antivirus software.[201] Alternatively, the developer might require a license to access the interface information, which could then be used to enforce quality standards.

Vertical product integration through foreclosure of vertical competitors could also diminish coordination costs: as achieving interoperability with horizontal and vertical competitors involves coordination costs, having these products developed by a single firm may reduce these costs. Transaction costs may also be saved due to economies of scale in marketing, distribution and licensing.[202] Similarly, vertical integration can bring product improvements. For example, vertical integration of a computer and hard drive can significantly benefit consumers.[203]

Whereas economists of the aforementioned Chicago school have questioned the ability of a monopolist to profitably raise prices in a secondary market by monopolizing that market, economists of the post-Chicago school have advanced arguments rebutting some of these findings. Post-Chicago school economists point at circumstances in which it may be possible for a monopolist to raise prices in an adjacent market through foreclosure – thus, circumstances in which the Single Monopoly Theorem does not hold.[204] Essentially, the Single Monopoly Theorem assumes that two products are fully complementary.[205] In other words, an increase in demand for product A should lead to an increase in demand for product B. This is not always

199. Hovenkamp et al. 2002–2007, §12.3c1; Shapiro 1995, p. 491.
200. For instance, Philips Electronics, which had developed a popular coffee machine that used coffee pads, attempted to maintain a foothold in the market for coffee pads by arguing that competitors' inferior coffee pads could damage its coffee machine and were, therefore, a threat to its reputation. The court rejected this reasoning; see *Philips v. Vomar* (Voorzieningenrechter Rechtbank Haarlem 2002). See, generally, Zittrain 2008.
201. See also Katz & Shapiro 1998, p. 43.
202. European Commission 2009, §62; Katz & Shapiro 1998, p. 42; Page & Lopatka 2007, p. 55.
203. Evans et al. 2002, p. 510; Hovenkamp et al. 2002–2007, §12.3d3.
204. Lévêque 2005, p. 81; Whinston 1990.
205. Hovenkamp et al. 2002–2007, §12.3c2.

the case. Where leveraging or foreclosure is applied to two goods that are not fully complementary, a monopolist could raise prices by tying the goods or foreclosing competition for product B.[206]

Furthermore, the Single Monopoly Theory presumes that the monopolist enjoys an unchallenged position in the primary market. If, however, this position were to be threatened in the future – which can often happen in markets with a quick rate of innovation – leveraging the monopoly power into a secondary market could be profitable.[207] A related, anticompetitive rationale for leveraging monopoly power involves raising barriers to entry.[208] If a manufacturer of video game consoles leverages its monopoly power into the market for video games, there would be no more competition in the market for that console's video games. A developer of video games will be forced to manufacture its own consoles as well, which constitutes a significant barrier to entry.[209]

The Single Monopoly Theory associated with the Chicago school presumes that consumers are aware of, or at least are able to calculate, the costs of both the primary product and any secondary products purchased during the product's lifecycle, such that the market for the primary and secondary products can be treated as a single one.[210] Several theories contradict this assumption. Consumers might not be able to calculate the lifecycle costs of the primary and secondary products combined (the costly information theory),[211] or locked-in consumers might be surprised by a sudden price increase (the surprise theory).[212] Alternatively, a systems vendor might increase prices only in the secondary market and compensate this increase by a lower price in the primary market. According to the lack of commitment theory, such a price change would help to extract profits from locked-in, existing costumers – which, after all, are 'surprised' by the price increase in the secondary market – while new customers are compensated by the lower price in the primary market. The result is a higher income on average.[213]

---

206. *Microsoft Decision* (European Commission 2004), §768; Lévêque 2005, p. 81.
207. *Microsoft Decision* (European Commission 2004), §770; Hovenkamp et al. 2002–2007, §12.3c2; Kuhn & Van Reenen 2007, p. 18.
208. See also *Microsoft Decision* (European Commission 2004), §769.
209. Hovenkamp et al. 2002–2007.
210. Herndon 2002, p. 333.
211. Bechtold 2007, p. 22; Shapiro 1995, p. 492. For instance, the lifecycle costs may depend to a large extent on the costs of the secondary product. If the buyer cannot accurately anticipate the quantity of the secondary product she or he will consume, as, for example, in the case of spare car parts, calculating the lifecycle costs may accordingly be difficult (Drexl et al. 2005, p. 450). See also Bechtold 2007, p. 22; Shapiro & Teece 1994, §IV.C. for more causes of 'costly information'. See also section 5.1.1b.
212. Shapiro 1995, p. 488; Shapiro & Teece 1994, p. 149. But see Bechtold 2007, p. 23; McGowan 1996, p. 795; Shapiro 1995, p. 493; Shapiro & Teece 1994, §IV.C. See also Drexl 2004, p. 797; Herndon 2002, p. 316; *Kodak* (US Supreme Court 1992); McGowan 1996, p. 794; Shapiro 1995, p. 493; Shapiro & Varian 1999, p. 146.
213. Bechtold 2007, p. 25; Borenstein et al. 1995, p. 460. But see Shapiro & Teece 1994, §IV.D.2.

Buyers might only partly be able to anticipate such price increases through contracts.[214]

A final argument against control of complementary products through controlled interfaces is that it impedes user innovation. This concept has been studied by scholars such as Von Hippel, Zittrain & Benkler.[215] An open platform enables end-users to create complementary computer programs or services that can offer substantial added value for all users of the platform.

In sum, the control of complementary products and markets through control over interface specifications can induce systems competition and enable foreclosure of vertical competitors. This, in turn, can have positive effects, emphasized by the Chicago school, and negative effects, highlighted by the post-Chicago school.

2.2.4. Openness Versus Control of Interfaces

Thus far, section 2.2.1 has demonstrated that control over interfaces is not primarily relevant to *directly* control access to interface technology as such, but rather *indirectly* to control interoperability with the firm's product. Sections 2.2.2 and 2.2.3 have demonstrated that interoperability can have both positive and negative effects on innovation and competition. This is true in both horizontal and vertical relationships. The present section demonstrates that these effects have implications for the control over interfaces, which is the central normative issue in this study.

The law typically provides for some control over intellectual creations in order to stimulate innovation by introducing the ability to exclude others from using the protected subject matter. In general, this right of control or exclusivity, typically granted through intellectual property rights, enables the rightsholder to raise the price above the negligible marginal costs of production, thereby recouping the more substantial fixed costs of innovation and thus enabling such innovation in the first place. However, such control is generally limited in scope and term to allow for sufficient openness. Openness, then, allows competitors to duplicate the rightsholder's innovation, including for follow-on innovation. Intellectual property rights and competition laws thereby aim to stimulate and balance, on the one hand, dynamic efficiency or innovation through control and, on the other hand, static efficiency or dissemination as well as follow-on innovation through openness.[216]

When control is exercised over interfaces, this balance may need to be recalibrated. This is a result of the larger indirect effects that control over interfaces can have on interoperability, network effects and systems competition,

214. Borenstein et al. 1995, p. 473. See, however, Shapiro 1995, p. 496.
215. See, generally, Zittrain 2008, p. 86 (with accompanying notes).
216. Lévêque & Méniere 2004, p. 4; Menell 1998, p. 669; Valkonen & White 2007, p. 372.

and, thereby, on innovation and competition.[217] These effects of control over interfaces can generate considerably more market power than control over regular subject matter. Network effects may increase the market power among horizontal competitors (section 2.2.2), whereas the control over interoperability with complementary components can increase the market power *vis-à-vis* vertical competitors (section 2.2.3). If this increased market power also becomes sustainable, it can undermine a balanced promotion of dynamic and static efficiency. This is depicted in the table below.

	Direct function	Horizontal effect	Vertical effect
Control over interfaces	Stimulate *dynamic* efficiency (interface innovation)	No interoperability: competition *for* the market	No interoperability: *systems* competition
Openness of interfaces	Stimulate *static* efficiency (dissemination of interface technology)	Interoperability: competition *in* the market	Interoperability: *component* competition

Thus, because control over interface specifications not only has a direct function of excluding competitors' use of the interface technology as such (which is similar to control over any other subject matter) but also and primarily an indirect function of controlling access to interoperability with the rightsholder's network or platform, the control over interface specifications may result in significantly more market power than control over other subject matter. In order to correct for this 'amplifying effect', the control over interface specifications may need to be more limited than control over other, 'regular' subject matter.[218] Most importantly, this balance should be struck with express consideration of the indirect effects of control over interface specifications on interoperability, innovation and competition. An approach that treats interface specifications on par with other subject matter may thus result in too much control and too little openness.

Lowering the level of protection for interface specifications could be accomplished through a reduced term or scope of protection.[219] Still, reducing the *scope* of protection would likely yield little effect because interface

217. Farrell 1989, p. 47; Menell 1998, p. 673.
218. See also Farrell 1995.
219. Valkonen & White 2007, p. 374. The distinction between limiting the scope and term of protection is not black-and-white. Notably, a rule permitting reverse engineering takes the form of a limitation on the scope of protection, yet it can also effectively limit the term of protection. See also Chapter 3.

specifications must be duplicated verbatim; there is no room for variation. Consequently, regardless of the (reduced) scope of protection, as long as the intellectual property right 'reads on' the interface specification, it cannot be copied verbatim in order to achieve interoperability. A reduced *term* of protection, then, might be more fruitful. A rightsholder's control over its interface specifications could extend only to a relatively short period of time, after which openness of these interface specifications could enable competitors to develop interoperable products. There are two advantages to such temporally limited control over interface specifications. First, limiting the term of control over interface specifications enables a balance to be struck between competition for and in the market, which, as noted, can both be efficient. Thus, the limited control over their interface specifications enables rightsholders to compete for the market during a limited time, allowing them to compete for the monopoly position by establishing a *de-facto* standard. Such competition can help ensure that the best standard prevails and that a valuable platform is created for further innovation.[220] However, after control over the interface specifications has ended, competition in the market and interoperable program development is reinstated. Second, limiting control over interface specifications intensifies competition for the market, as it ensures that the competitive pressure caused by possible entry from successive competitors during any single period of dominance remains high.[221] As further explored in section 2.3, there are two principal legal approaches to limiting the duration of control over interfaces: by intellectual property rights and by competition rules.

One might argue that development of new interface specifications could be impeded if the control of these interfaces were weakened, thus provoking firms to develop more 'closed' systems.[222] Consequently, network effects might not be fully realized.[223] It was already noted, however, that the *ex-ante* value particularly of an interface specification is very low, and any development costs in such specifications can normally be recouped from the sale of the primary product (the computer program).[224] Moreover, interfaces must be developed in any event, if only to allow one's own programs to interoperate. In other words, a software firm typically does not require a separate incentive to develop interface specifications.[225]

---

220. Weiser 2003, p. 585.
221. Turney 2005.
222. Lemley & McGowan 1998, p. 533. See also Koelman 2006; Pilny 1992, p. 205; Samuelson et al. 1994, p. 2404.
223. Koelman 2006, p. 839.
224. Lemley & McGowan 1998, p. 533; Samuelson & Scotchmer 2002, p. 1620. See also Drexl et al. 2005, p. 455. See also section 5.1.1a.
225. However, if interface specifications are not protected by any intellectual property right, it may be difficult for a rightsholder to license the information because the information could be freely distributed to third parties upon release and because it would be more difficult for the rightsholder to impose conditions on use of the specifications. Conversely, some means to control the specifications after their disclosure could provide greater incentives to disclose them and foster interoperability.

In sum, the intellectual property protection of interface specifications may have a profound indirect effect on interoperability, and thereby, on innovation and competition. This indirect effect of control over interfaces can cause an amplifying effect on the market power caused by the control over the interfaces. This may warrant a lower level of protection for interface specifications than for other subject matter, in particular through a shorter term of protection. In any event, the balance of openness versus control of interface specifications should be struck based on the indirect effects of such control on interoperability, innovation and competition.

2.3. FLEXIBILITY VERSUS CERTAINTY

Section 2.2 demonstrated that both interoperability and lack of interoperability can be beneficial to society, while section 2.1 demonstrated that interoperability with a particular computer program primarily hinges on whether that program's interface specifications are controlled by the rightsholder, or open. It follows that, ideally, a balance should be struck between openness and control of such interface specifications (section 2.2.4). This section introduces two principal legal approaches to striking this balance, which, in subsequent chapters, will be studied in more detail: first, an *ex-ante* approach, based on intellectual property rights, and, second, an *ex-post* approach, based on competition law.

In an *ex-ante* intellectual property rights approach, the balance between openness and control of interoperability information is structurally fixed in advance. Rather than a consideration of individual cases, this approach would prescribe that all firms can maintain control over their interface specifications under certain conditions and for a particular duration. This approach enables firms and their competitors to coordinate their actions with the law but cannot consider the particularities of individual cases. Rather, it requires an analysis of the ideal balance between control and openness of interface specifications that produces an outcome which nears the optimal outcome in the largest number of foreseeable cases.

Section 2.2.4 suggested that control over interface specifications might need to be more limited than control over regular subject matter based on the indirect effects of such control on interoperability. In particular, a shorter term of protection may be warranted. As already observed, one means to limit the term of control over the specifications is to permit competitors to reverse engineer them (see Chapter 3).

The second approach to balancing control and openness of interface specifications is through application of competition law. Competition law could be used to force a dominant firm to supply its interface specifications to competitors *ex-post* (see Chapter 4). In this approach, the balance between openness and control is reviewed after-the-fact and adjusted based on the particularities of the individual case. The *ex-post* analysis enables a careful consideration of the welfare effects of either openness or control of interface information in this particular case. This is because the relevant authority reviewing the individual case after-the-fact, can conduct the analysis relying on considerably more information than the *ex-ante* legislator. The authority may consider factors mentioned in this chapter, as well as other factors, in its determination as to whether the subject firm should be allowed to continue to control its interfaces. The flexibility of an *ex-post* approach is, therefore, potentially more accurate than the *ex-ante* approach in striking the optimal balance between openness and control of interface information. However, this flexibility necessarily impedes the certainty enabled by an *ex-ante* approach.

These respective approaches will be studied in more detail in Chapter 3 and section 4.2, whereas the trade-off between both approaches is further examined in section 4.1. For present purposes, it suffices to observe that there are two principal legal approaches to striking the balance between openness and control of interface information: an *ex-ante* intellectual property approach, which provides for more certainty but also more rigidity, and an *ex-post* competition law approach, which offers more flexibility and less certainty. There is thus an inherent tension between these approaches because certainty and flexibility are, to some extent, mutually exclusive.

2.4. CONCLUSION

This chapter has analyzed the technical and economic context of software interfaces and interoperability in order to establish a normative framework for the analysis of laws dealing with innovation and competition.

Section 2.1 demonstrated that computer programs typically rely on both horizontal and vertical interoperability with other hardware and software. Vertical interoperability with other computer programs enables each program to fulfill a particular task within a system. Horizontal interoperability enables users of different computer programs to exchange data. Although firms in most industries compete and innovate largely independently of each other, the stronger need for horizontal and vertical interoperability in software has introduced a more substantial degree of interdependency in this industry.

Section 2.1 also demonstrated how interoperability with another vendor's computer program is achieved at a technical level. Interoperability requires access to the target program's interface specifications, which are embedded in the code of that program. If not properly documented or if deliberately maintained as secret, these specifications could be obtained by reverse engineering technologies, notably black-box testing and decompilation. Both reverse engineering technologies require a considerable investment in time and resources, and their success depends significantly on the state of the art in reverse engineering technology.

Section 2.2 examined the effects of interoperability between horizontal competitors, in which network effects play a key role, and interoperability between vertical competitors, which relates to systems and components.

Software is subject to relatively strong network effects: typically, the value of a computer program increases when more people use the same program. Because users, therefore, will choose the program with the most number of users, markets for computer programs and other network goods are subject to tipping: eventually, one network of goods could win the race for all or most users and emerge as the *de-facto* standard. Network effects need not be limited to a particular vendor's product, however. If two vendors' programs are interoperable, users of both products benefit from the combined installed base and increased network effects.

Interoperability and network effects may have both positive and negative effects for society. Generally, users benefit from interoperability between vendors as the network effects increase due to a larger number of network participants. Interoperability also protects consumers against lock-in effects. However, mandating interoperability may impede incentives to innovate in software and interface development because it removes the opportunity for any single firm to capture the entire market by establishing a new, *de-facto* standard.

Similar to these effects of horizontal interoperability, vertical interoperability can also have pro- and anticompetitive effects. Generally, interoperability stimulates component innovation, whereas absence of interoperability would stimulate systems competition. Interoperability facilitates vertical competition with different vendors, whereas a lack of interoperability can be used to control a secondary market. Section 2.2.3b introduced several theories of the Chicago and post-Chicago schools of economics, which tend to emphasize, respectively, the positive and negative effects of such control over adjacent markets.

From the mixed horizontal and vertical effects of interoperability, it can be concluded that, ideally, a balance must be struck between interoperability and lack of interoperability. Because interoperability primarily hinges on availability of interface specifications, this balance can be struck by regulating control over these interface specifications. It follows that a balance must be struck between control and openness of interface specifications. Based on the significant indirect effects of control over interface specifications on interoperability, and, thereby, on innovation and competition, this balance may be different from the balance struck for most 'regular' subject matter.

As demonstrated in section 2.3, this balance can instrumentally be struck in two principal ways: with or without consideration of the particular circumstances of the case. In the former case, the balance between openness and control of interface specifications can be different in each situation, thus allowing for a balance that potentially more accurately represents the optimal balance between open and controlled interfaces. In the latter case, the balance is fixed *ex-ante* so as to represent an optimal mix of control and openness of interface specifications in all (foreseeable) cases. The former approach requires flexibility and is principally implemented through application of competition law, which permits a review of a firm's control over interface specifications after-the-fact on a case-by-case basis (*ex-post*). The latter approach requires more certainty and is implemented through *ex-ante* intellectual property rights.

Hence, the following two benchmarks are formulated:

(1) *Openness versus control*: a balance between openness and control of interface specifications based on indirect effects of such control on interoperability, innovation and competition (section 2.2);
(2) *Flexibility versus certainty*: a trade-off between a more rigid and certain *ex-ante* approach to interoperability, and a more flexible *ex-post* approach (section 2.3).

Chapter 3
Copyright Law

Chapter 2 established benchmarks for the analysis of laws affecting innovation and competition in software that is subject to network effects. It suggested that a balance should be struck between a rightsholder's ability to control its computer program's interface information and competitors' abilities to access and use that information in order to develop interoperable software. Chapter 2 also identified two legal approaches to this balance: an *ex-ante* approach based on intellectual property rights, which offers more certainty to facilitate investment decisions in innovation, and an *ex-post* approach based on competition law, which offers more flexibility to assess the effects caused by either control or openness of interface information in individual cases. The present chapter focuses on the former, *ex-ante* copyright approach, whereas the next chapter will focus on the *ex-post* competition approach, as well as the trade-off between both approaches.

The purpose of this chapter is twofold. First, against the normative scale of openness versus control, identified in Chapter 2, the present chapter aims to demonstrate that the current copyright regime affecting interoperability in computer programs provides rightsholders with too much control over interoperability information and thus offers too little openness of this information to competitors, notwithstanding several instruments specifically designed to allow competitors to access this information. Second, against the instrumental trade-off between an *ex-ante* approach, offering more certainty, and an *ex-post* approach, offering more flexibility, this chapter will demonstrate that copyright law, as an *ex-ante* instrument, is unsuccessful in providing competitors with sufficient certainty as to their ability to use and access interface information. This uncertainty effectively reinforces the rightsholder's control over his or her program's interface information.

Copyright's effect on the normative balance between control and openness of interface information can be examined in two stages. In the first stage, copyright protection of computer programs may directly and indirectly confer control over interoperability information (section 3.1). In the second stage, specific limitations may be used to reduce this control for more openness (section 3.2). The interaction between these two stages determines the balance between control and openness.

Section 3.1 focuses on the first stage. It establishes how, in the absence of specific provisions to limit such control, copyright protection of computer programs may directly protect interface specifications as copyrighted, original expression, which allows for control of their *use* by competitors. Moreover, copyright law can indirectly prevent *access* to interface information. An appreciation of how copyright may confer control over use of and access to interoperability information is paramount to an understanding of the second stage, or the necessity and effect of the specific instruments designed to limit such control (section 0). Section 3.2 focuses on the second stage. It evaluates, first, to what extent the control of interface information (section 3.1) is limited by the provisions affecting use of and access to interoperability information in the European Software Directive, and whether this regime is successful in striking a balance between control and openness of interface information. Second, it evaluates whether these provisions offer sufficient certainty as *ex-ante* instruments. It will be demonstrated that these provisions are largely insufficient to provide for openness of a computer program's interface specifications. They could well enable rightsholders to maintain substantial and sustainable control over access to their programs' interoperability information, while, moreover, they confront competitors with a significant degree of uncertainty surrounding the lawful use of interface information. Section 3.3, therefore, concludes that copyright law fails to balance control of interface specifications with sufficient openness.

3.1. COPYRIGHT AND CONTROL OF INTERFACE INFORMATION

This section demonstrates how the choice of copyright protection for computer programs may have introduced the ability for rightsholders to directly control the *use* of (section 3.1.1) and indirectly control *access* to (section 3.1.2) their program's interface information. Because both use of and access to interface specifications are prerequisites to interoperable program development, both forms of control independently enable a rightsholder to prevent such development. In the second part of this chapter (section 3.2), it will be demonstrated how the European Software Directive aims to limit both forms of control over interface specifications.

3.1.1. Use

The free use of interface specifications for interoperability is impeded by a combination of two partly overlapping aspects of copyright protection of computer programs: first, the protection of functional expression in computer programs (section 3.1.1a), and, second, the failure to balance the promotion of originality in such expression with interests of standardization (section 3.1.1b). The accompanying diagram illustrates these two causes.

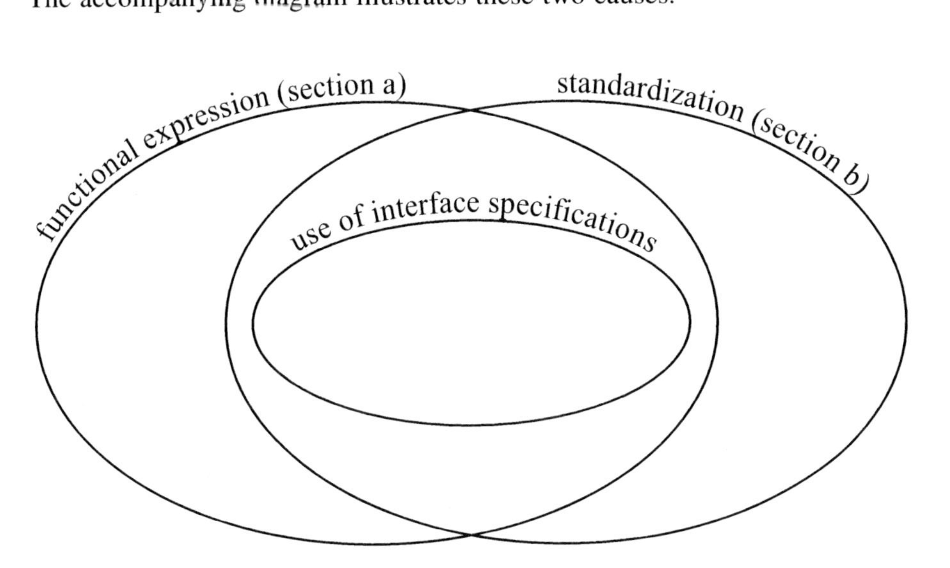

a. Copyright Protection of Functional Expression

This section will demonstrate that the protection of computer programs as Literary Works under copyright means that computer programs are primarily protected at the level of their written program code, rather than on their functionality or behavior.[226] Interface specifications are part of this code and, therefore, could be copyrightable. Two important copyright subject matter doctrines – the idea/expression dichotomy and the originality requirement – may, in the context of computer programs, not be sufficient to exclude interface specifications from protection.

The need for legal protection of computer programs emerged with the recognition of the vital importance of software for society and with its high development costs and the relatively low costs of copying.[227] Legal protection

226. Samuelson et al. 1994, p. 2360. The behavior or functionality of the program may be eligible for patent protection. See Bakels & Hugenholtz 2002.
227. See, for example, European Commission 1988, §5.2; National Commission on New Technological Uses of Copyrighted Works 1978.

of computer programs was thus primarily aimed at providing for strong protection in order to stimulate software development. The effects of such protection on interoperability and a maximization of network effects was only recognized as a problem at a later stage, and, indeed, the present section will demonstrate that the regime chosen to provide for protection – copyright protection as Literary Works – appears difficult to reconcile with the need to facilitate interoperability between computer programs.

In providing for legal protection of computer programs, there was a preference for applying an existing intellectual property regime over the introduction of a new, tailor-made (*sui generis*) regime of legal protection.[228] Although the latter type of protection would allow for consideration of the highly functional nature of software and the corresponding need for protection,[229] applying an existing intellectual property regime was considerably less cumbersome to implement; it would provide a more immediate answer to the needs of the software industry. Of these existing instruments – mostly copyright, patent, trade secret and unfair competition law – the former was regarded as the most appropriate.[230] A narrowly construed definition of patentable subject matter, according to which only inventions that brought about some physical change of matter were patentable, excluded most computer programs from patent protection. Furthermore, the incremental nature of software development was difficult to reconcile with patent law's requirements of novelty and inventive step.[231] Copyright law, then, would allow for immediate and effortless protection because its legal framework was already established and because it did not require authors to comply with any formalities.[232] Moreover, copyright law was considered to provide a solution to the industry's need for strong international protection, as copyright law was extensively harmonized in international treaties – most notably the Berne Convention.[233]

In order to enable full, international copyright protection of computer programs within the framework of the Berne Convention, it was considered necessary to treat computer programs as *literary works* within the meaning of

228. European Commission 1988, p. 175; Menell 1998, p. 681; National Commission on New Technological Uses of Copyrighted Works 1978; Plana 2007, p. 92; Spoor et al. 2005, p. 589. See also section 2.1.
229. See, for example, Guibault 1997; Lewinski 2008, p. 234; Menell 1987; Samuelson 1985; Samuelson et al. 1994; Stern 1986; Vandenberghe 1984; World Intellectual Property Organization 1978.
230. Bently & Sherman 2004, p. 63; Cornish 1993, p. 185; Czarnota & Hart 1991, p. 30; European Commission 1985, §149; European Commission 1988, §5.3; Haberstumpf 1993, p. 74; Software Directive, Proposal (1989), §3.6; Spoor et al. 2005, p. 589.
231. Samuelson et al. 1994, p. 2343. See also Software Directive, Proposal (1989), §3.2.
232. Cornish 1993, p. 187; Ricketson 1987, p. 897. See also section 3.1.2c.
233. Cornish 1993, p. 185; Dreier 1991a, p. 578; Dreier 1993, p. 35; Spoor 1994, p. 1082. The European Software Directive, TRIPS agreement and the WIPO Copyright Treaty (WCT) all rely on the Berne Convention for protection of computer programs. See Articles 1(1), 10(1) and 4, respectively.

the convention, rather than as utilitarian works, works of applied art or a new category of works.[234] The comparison to literary works was based on the source code: a program is essentially a series of instructions in textual form, which might be compared to the text of a novel or poem.[235] Although that code – particularly the object code – was admittedly intended for interpretation by a computer rather than a human being, this was not considered to constitute a substantial obstacle to copyright protection.[236]

There was a concern of protecting software – an essentially functional product – without applying the substantially higher thresholds for protection of technical inventions, which are safeguarded by patent law.[237] Proponents of a copyright approach counterargued, first, that copyright protection did not extend to the functionality of the software itself, which thus remained unprotected, but only to the particular expression thereof in the code. Second, the fact that that expression was of a highly functional nature did not preclude copyright protection because copyright had long protected other functional works, including maps and user manuals.[238] It will be demonstrated how these two arguments relate to the use of interface specifications.

The first argument – that of the unprotectability of the functionality itself – is primarily based on the idea/expression dichotomy. This copyright doctrine safeguards authors' freedom to build on ideas developed by others. These ideas can be copied, provided that each author uses his or her own expression.[239] Traditionally, the idea/expression dichotomy has been viewed

---

234. Cornish 1993, p. 190; Walter et al. 2001, p. 120. See also Ricketson & Ginsburg 2006, p. 517. It was also considered necessary to introduce no or only few exceptions to the general rules applying to these Literary Works. For instance, whereas Berne's term of protection of fifty years after the death of the author was clearly excessive for software, this term was maintained for purposes of compatibility with the convention. Berne Convention, Article 7(1). See also Cornish 1993, p. 186; Dreier 1991a, p. 583; Hugenholtz & Spoor 1987, p. 32; Lehmann 1993, p. 26; Ricketson & Ginsburg 2006, p. 562; Vandenberghe 1984, p. 104.
235. Gibson 2005, p. 176; Gordon 1998, p. 10; Haberstumpf 1993, p. 86; Lewinski 2008, p. 232; Software Directive, Proposal (1989), 9; Walter et al. 2001, p. 126. See also section 2.1.2a.
236. Lewinski 2008, p. 233. According to some commentators, it was inherent in copyright's requirements of originality that, regardless of the degree or originality, humans be able to perceive the originality of the work's expression. See National Commission on New Technological Uses of Copyrighted Works 1978, p. 36; Vandenberghe 1984, p. 98. See also Cornish 1993, p. 190; Derclaye 2000, p. 11; Goldstein 1986, p. 1127; Gordon 1998, p. 10; Ricketson 1987, p. 897. But see Hugenholtz 1989, p. 18; Hugenholtz & Spoor 1987, p. 31. See also Quaedvlieg 1987, p. 112.
237. Band & Katoh 1995, p. 100; Samuelson 2007c. See also section 3.2.1a.
238. See, for example, Goldstein 1986, p. 1120; Goldstein 1993, p. 205; Quaedvlieg 1987, p. 116; Samuelson et al. 1994, p. 2349; Spoor et al. 2005, p. 589; Vandenberghe 1984, p. 92. See also Dam 1995, p. 323; Ginsburg 1994, p. 2567; Goldstein 1986, p. 1121; Hugenholtz & Spoor 1987, p. 31; Software Directive, Proposal (1989).
239. Cornish 1993, p. 191; Haberstumpf 1993, p. 100; Haeck 1998, p. 85; Samuelson 2007c, p. 1927.

as a continuum of more abstract ideas, which are not protected, to more concrete expression, which is eligible for copyright protection.[240]

Applying this distinction between idea and expression to software was less than straightforward.[241] However, both in the literature[242] and in the case law,[243] a general consensus has emerged that software functionality is typically to be considered as a pattern of unprotected ideas, whereas the programmer's expression thereof in the source code is eligible for copyright protection.[244] Copyright law thus does not grant an exclusive right in the (more valuable) ideas or functionality of a computer program,[245] but rather in the developer's efforts in implementing those ideas in (source) code.[246] Importantly, because there are various possible expressions to implement each more abstract idea or functional element, these ideas and functional elements are not themselves 'locked up'.[247] The idea/expression dichotomy thus serves as a crucial limitation on the scope of protection for computer programs. This proved a central argument in favor of copyright protection for software.[248]

However, although the parameter of concreteness under the idea/expression dichotomy thereby nicely separates protectable code from unprotectable functionality, it does not necessarily exclude interface specifications from the scope of protection. Unlike the functionality of the program, interface specifications are very concrete pieces of information. They are reduced to a written form as part of the program code.[249] Indeed, the very purpose of an interface specification lies in its concreteness: the concreteness of the

---

240. *Nichols v. Universal Pictures Corporation* (US Court of Appeals, Second Circuit 1930), 121; Nimmer & Nimmer looseleaf, §13.03[A][1][a].
241. Newman 1999; Quaedvlieg 1987, p. 104. See also Drexl 1994.
242. Czarnota & Hart 1991, p. 36; Walter et al. 2001, p. 129. See also Cornish 1993, p. 191; Dreier & Schulze 2004, p. 854; Hugenholtz 1989, p. 39; Lehmann 1989, p. 1058; Quaedvlieg 1987, p. 104; Ricketson & Ginsburg 2006, p. 517.
243. See, for example, *Computer Associates v. Altai* (US Court of Appeals, Second Circuit 1992); *Navitaire v. EasyJet* (UK High Court of Justice, Chancery Division 2004), §94; *Softimage* (Supreme Court 2005).
244. The Software Directive also extends protection beyond the literal code to the structure, sequence and organization (SSO) of a program. See Czarnota & Hart 1991, p. 36.
245. Investments in software development as well as the value for users lie primarily in this unprotected functionality (or behavior) of the program rather than the particular expression thereof in the code. Quaedvlieg 2006, p. 159; Samuelson et al. 1994. See also section 3.1.2a.
246. Hugenholtz & Spoor 1987, p. 32; Software Directive, Proposal (1989), §3.6; Quaedvlieg 2006, p. 159.
247. Bakels & Hugenholtz 2002, p. 7; Newman 1999, p. 693.
248. Software Directive, Proposal (1989), §3.7. ('But the main advantage of this type of intellectual property protection relate to the fact that the protection covers only the individual expression of the work and gives thus sufficient flexibility to permit other authors to create similar or even identical programs provided that they abstain from copying.')
249. See also section 2.1.2b. See also Pilny 1990, p. 434.

specification enables the computer to verify whether a valid reference to the underlying interface is made. Because of their concreteness, interface specifications, therefore, could be regarded as protectable expression, rather than unprotected ideas.

The second argument of the proponents of a copyright approach to computer programs – that of the protectability of functional expression in program code notwithstanding its largely functional nature – related mostly to copyright's requirement of originality. Copyright law generally only protects *original* expression.[250] Originality typically comprises two aspects: first, the work must be original in the sense of originating from the author's independent creation, rather than from copying, and, second, it must bear the author's personal 'mark' or 'imprint'. The latter originality 'threshold' varies per jurisdiction.[251] In most jurisdictions, however, only a modicum of personal originality is required.[252]

Although courts and legislators have, in theory, sought to apply the same two-limbed originality test to computer programs, the application of the originality test to computer programs has, in practice, mostly been limited to the first limb – that is, whether the program is the result of the author's independent creation. The second limb – the presence of a modicum of personal input – has had little practical meaning in the context of computer programs. There are various reasons for this reduced originality approach. For instance, the program's source code allegedly containing the original expression is, as noted, often kept secret,[253] prompting courts to infer the originality of the code from indirect factors such as the program's size or externally visible complexity.[254] It is, furthermore, extremely difficult for a lay person (including a Judge) to recognize any originality attributable to the author in a program's source code – even if different programmers do have different styles of coding.[255] It is, moreover, utterly pointless to require more from the software author than that the code has not been copied: the public does not have access to the source code in which the originality should be expressed, such that any originality will generally go unnoticed. Moreover, originality in code expression is not necessarily functionally superior and is, therefore, not directly beneficial.[256]

---

250. On the relationship between the requirement of originality and the idea/expression dichotomy, see Drexl 1994, p. 74; Hugenholtz 1989, p. 78.
251. Haeck 1998, p. 55; Hugenholtz & Spoor 1987, p. 35.
252. Goldstein 2001, p. 161.
253. See section 2.1.2a.
254. See also van Rooijen 2007a.
255. Weber 2005, p. 136. See also Hugenholtz & Spoor 1987, p. 31.
256. Goldstein 1986, p. 1122; Hugenholtz 1989, p. 38; Weinreb 1998, p. 1179. However, the promotion of originality in expression of computer programs forces competing firms to use different, non-infringing expression when duplicating another computer program's functionality, which effectively creates some lead-time for the first programmer. It thereby serves to establish a temporary, *de-facto* term of exclusivity. Hugenholtz 1989, p. 38; Johnson-Laird 1994, p. 843; Menell 1998, p. 680; Quaedvlieg 1987, p. 92. Note, however, that the problem of duplicating functionality using non-infringing

These and other factors have contributed to a starkly objectified originality test for computer programs in which 'originality' has essentially been reduced to an inquiry into the author's freedom of choice: the work (the code) is original and is assumed to bear the author's 'mark' or 'imprint' if the author has selected the expression from a sufficient variety of possibilities.[257]

The originality in a computer program is thus considered to subsist in the countless number of choices generally made by the programmer in writing the program code: no two programmers would typically implement certain functionality using identical expression.[258] As noted, these are often relatively arbitrary choices:[259] ultimately, both the author and the end-user will evaluate the computer program by the functionality it performs,[260] rather than the particular expression chosen to implement such functionality. However, because originality in software is an objective criterion, the functional nature of these choices does not in itself preclude originality. There is ample room for variations in code expression, and this room for variation constitutes the basis for originality.

Under this starkly objectified originality test, it is difficult to maintain that interface specifications cannot demonstrate originality. Interface specifications, as part of the computer program's code, can similarly be conceived in various formats, and, depending on the actual originality threshold, could thus be considered original.[261] As the interface's specification follows largely from the function the interface must perform, and due to industry standardization, the freedom to choose a format for an interface specification is more limited than the freedom to express the entire program's functionality.[262] Particularly for simple interfaces, it is conceivable that two independent authors would use the exact same interface specification for an interface performing a given function. Nonetheless, there is still room for choices.

---

expression is somewhat academic because competitors often do not have access to each other's source code in the first place. See also section 3.1.2a.

257. Gervais 2003, p. 134; Hugenholtz 1991, p. 61; Hugenholtz 1989, pp. 33, 36; Hugenholtz & Spoor 1987, p. 31. See, for example, *Computer Associates Int'l* (Tribunal de Commerce de Bobigny 1995), 336; *Lotus v. Borland* (District Court Massachussetts 1992), 217.
258. Hugenholtz & Spoor 1987, p. 34; Software Directive, Proposal (1989), §2.7; Quaedvlieg 1987, p. 94; Spoor et al. 2005, p. 592.
259. See, generally, Farrell 1989.
260. Schmidtchen & Koboldt 1993, p. 423. See also *Whelan v. Jaslow* (US Court of Appeals, Third Circuit 1986), 1231 (observing that much of the investments in software development go into the design of the functionality and the structure, sequence and organization (SSO) of the program, such that protection of only the literal code would result in suboptimal incentives). See also *Inkassoprogramm* (Bundesgerichtshof 1985), §72.
261. Farrell 1989; Gordon 1998, p. 11.
262. See also *Computer Associates Int'l* (Tribunal de Commerce de Bobigny 1995), 337; Dreier 1991a, p. 583; Lehmann 1992, p. 364; Stuurman 1995, p. 457.

When a programmer designs a new API specification,[263] for example, she or he can generally choose from a variety of options that will produce identical technical effects. For instance, a specification for a simple interface that searches for a keyword in a text and then returns a value of '`true`' if found could be conceived as, *inter alia*, one of the following formats:

(1) `bool Search(CString strKeyword, CString strText);`
(2) `bool FindInText(CString strText, CString strKeyword);`
(3) `bool FINDKEYWORD(CString thetext, CString theword);`
(4) `bool Find(CString findwhat, CString text);`
(5) `bool myInterface(CString variable1, CString variable2);`
(6) `bool LookForText(CString lookforwhat, CString text).`

All six specifications are functionally identical, as they all contain the same number and type of parameters (two parameters of type `CString`, which is a type of variable used to store alphanumeric data), as well as the same return type (`bool`, for a 'true' or 'false' value). Given the functionality to be performed by the interface, the programmer has some freedom to choose a preferred format for the interface specification: he or she can specify the name for the interface (**`Search`** or **`FindInText`**, for instance) and for the parameters (`strKeyword` or `variable1`, for instance), as well as a particular arrangement of the parameters (`strKeyword`, then `strText` – or `strText`, followed by `strKeyword`). This freedom to choose among functionally identical formats constitutes the basis for any originality in the expression.[264]

On closer examination, however, the room for originality is (even) more limited than it may appear. For example, the number and type of the parameters (in this case: two, of type `CString`) are dictated by the function the interface is designed to perform and thus leave no room for any originality.[265] Furthermore, although the naming of an interface and its variables might appear to leave room for ample originality,[266] industry practice prescribes that these names be purely descriptive. Thus, the name of an interface and its parameters is typically not original but rather informs developers of (and is, therefore, determined by) its function.[267] In the previous example, the fifth alternative (**`myInterface`**) would likely not be selected because it does not properly describe the interface's purpose.

For these API specifications, the remaining freedom of choice primarily lies in the *arrangement* of the parameters. The developer can typically determine the order of the parameters arbitrarily: their initial arrangement has no

263. See also section 2.1.
264. It is not suggested that these choices amount to sufficient originality. See section 3.2.1b.
265. Lehmann 1989, p. 1059. See also section 3.2.1a.
266. This was argued in Clapes et al. 1987, p. 1534.
267. Simonyi, *Hungarian Notation*, available at <http://msdn.microsoft.com/library/default.asp?url=/library/en-us/dnvs600/html/hunganotat.asp> (last visited July 25, 2006). See also section 2.1.

effect on the functioning of the interface.[268] In the previous simple examples, this freedom is negligible, yet there may be more freedom for more complex interface specifications.[269] The precise freedom depends on the type of interface being specified as well as the programming language. Whether this freedom of choice amounts to sufficient originality depends on the applicable originality threshold. The effect of the European Software Directive's originality threshold on the protection of interface specifications will be explored in section 3.2.1b.

The eligibility of interface specifications for copyright protection could perhaps be questioned under a different approach to copyrightable subject matter.[270] For example, one might seek to apply an 'elevated' originality threshold, in which certain freedom of choice, such as the freedom to format an interface's specification, does not amount to originality because it is highly arbitrary or highly functional. Dutch commentator Quaedvlieg, for example, distinguishes between subjective and objective expression by considering the author's *evaluation* of his or her work, rather than the *creation* of the work. Thus, a painter evaluates her or his work using a subjective standard (the painter's personal taste), whereas a computer programmer evaluates her or his choices using an objective standard (of functionality and performance). The difference in the methods of evaluation, Quaedvlieg argues, supports an exclusion of the latter type of works (the functional works) from copyright protection.[271] However, Quaedvlieg's distinction between a subjective and objective evaluation of a work has not been reflected in Dutch case law.[272] Under an alternative (subject matter) approach, certain subject matter is entirely excluded from copyright protection, thereby obviating the application of the idea/expression dichotomy and originality requirement. The subject matter approach will be studied in further detail in Chapter 6.

In conclusion, based in part on the protection of computer programs as literary works within the meaning of the Berne Convention, which was considered necessary to provide for strong, international legal protection of software, copyright law protects computer programs at the level of their concrete code rather than their more abstract functionality. Because interface specifications required for interoperability are part of this code, they could potentially be considered protectable expression. The highly functional nature of interface specifications does not preclude a finding of originality (and, thus, copyrightability) because originality in computer programs has primarily been interpreted as a purely objective standard (freedom of choice) rather than a subjective standard. The creation of interface specifications may

268. See also Meyer & Colombe 1990b, p. 81; *TIPS v. Daman* (UK High Court of Justice, Chancery Division 1991), 172.
269. See also Staffelbach 2003, p. 70.
270. Haeck 1998, p. 109. See also European Commission 1988, §5.5.12.
271. Quaedvlieg 1987, p. 111.
272. See, for example, Quaedvlieg 2006; *Technip* (Hoge Raad 2006).

allow for limited freedom of choice, and, therefore, originality. Thus, neither copyright's idea/expression nor its originality requirement, as applied to computer programs, appear necessarily capable of separating interface specifications from the rest of the code of a computer program, which is eligible for protection. The possibility for a rightsholder to prevent interoperability through copyright protection of his or her program's interface specifications thus remains open.

b. Copyright and Standardization

Previously, it was examined how copyright law protects computer programs at the level of their written program code rather than their functionality, thus potentially protecting the interface specifications, which are part of that code. Such protection of functional expression is not normally problematic because different (original) expression can generally be used to accomplish the same functional result. As noted, this rhetoric of the possibility of variation in code expression was an important argument in favor of using copyright law to protect computer programs.

However, there are instances in which only use of the rightsholder's particular expression suffices for the purpose, such that variation in expression is *not* possible. Thus, as illustrated in the earlier Venn diagram, there is a subset of functional expressions that must be duplicated verbatim, and this is the separate problem of standardization of expression. Importantly, those instances include the need to copy a computer program's interface specifications verbatim in order to achieve interoperability. Thus, the protection of functional expression (see section 3.1.1a) is not the only cause for the tension between copyright protection of computer programs and the interests in interoperability. There is a second, partly overlapping cause: copyright's failure to accommodate the interests of standardization, of which interoperability is a species.

Interoperability is a form of standardization. At the end-user's level, this is apparent from the communication and data exchange between different vendors' computer programs and components. At a technical level, interoperability is accomplished by having firms adhere to the exact same interface specifications in their computer programs. Interoperability thus requires some standardization of expression: firms must use identical expression in interface specifications in order to establish interoperability.[273]

However, copyright law stimulates precisely the opposite of standardization: through its originality requirement, copyright law promotes diversity in expression. For most literary works, such as novels, paintings and plays, society generally benefits from a variety of original, rather than identical expressions.[274]

273. Clapes et al. 1987, p. 1562; Dreier 1991a, p. 583; Farrell 1989, p. 47; Goldstein 1986, p. 1127. See also Sucker 1993, p. 13. See also section 2.1.2b.

274. Goldstein 1986, p. 1122; Concurring opinion judge Boudin in *Lotus v. Borland* (US Court of Appeals, First Circuit 1995), 820.

However, diversity (originality) in expression and standardization in expression are mutually exclusive. The need to use identical expression in the interests of interoperability and standardization is thus directly at odds with copyright's focus on originality. It follows that, to the extent society benefits from software interoperability, it is necessarily hampered by the originality promoted by copyright law. If certain subject matter, such as interface specifications, generally benefits more from standardized expression than from original expression (diversity), one might question whether the copyright regime should be applied to it in the first place.

Moreover, copyright law does not offer a framework to assess whether such original expression is actually beneficial in the particular instance, or whether identical expression is more beneficial instead – for example, in the interest of interoperability. Within copyright's system of exclusive rights, on the one hand, and limitations to those rights, on the other, there appears to be little room to consider whether original expression (diversity) or identical expression (standardization) is more beneficial in the particular case. Using identical expression is only possible if the expression is not protected by copyright law (which precludes the author's exclusive control over such expression) or if the use made of protected expression is expressly permitted under any applicable limitations. Although copyright law contains various such limitations, these limitations are primarily designed to increase the dissemination of original expression among the general public or particular interest groups, rather than to balance originality (diversity in expression) with standardization.[275] Accordingly, courts, when confronted with a compelling need to use standardized or identical expression under copyright law, have sought to solve these cases by denying copyrightability altogether, or by interpreting statutory limitations more broadly (see *infra*). As the standardization problem is thus not recognized in copyright law as such, and as courts must, therefore, find other ways to accommodate the interests of standardization in copyright law, it may not always be readily apparent from a court's opinion that a standardization problem or a need to use identical expression actually underlies the case.

A few copyright doctrines may allow for some use of identical expression (and, thus, allow for standardized expression) within the realm of more traditional literary works.[276] For example, copyright law generally recognizes the right to quote from a copyrighted work without authorization.[277] This enables an author on copyright law, for example, to quote Judge Learned Hand's seminal explanation of the idea/expression dichotomy in *Nichols v.*

275. See also Guibault 2002, p. 27; Hugenholtz & Okediji 2008, p. 43. There appears to be more room for such considerations under the fair use defense in U.S. copyright law. See also section 6.3.1b.
276. For an analysis under U.S. law, see Samuelson 2007b, p. 193.
277. Dreier 2001, p. 307; Guibault 2002, p. 30; Hugenholtz & Okediji 2008, p. 15.

Universal Pictures.[278] As Learned Hand's discussion of the idea/expression dichotomy has arguably become a *de-facto* standard, there is a significant interest in enabling others to duplicate his particular words rather than having to paraphrase the more general concept he describes. Copyright limitations permitting quotations provide for this necessity. The European Information Society Directive also provides for an optional limitation that permits protected expression to be copied for certain incidental use.[279] Copyright law furthermore and to a limited extent recognizes the right to create a parody of a copyright-protected work, which also requires substantial duplication of existing expression. However, although these limitations might suffice for traditional, literary works, or the relation between authors and the public, in which there is only a limited need to use expression of others, they may not suffice in an industrial context, or the relationship between competitors, in which there is a more substantial need for use of identical expression in the interest of standardization.[280]

There is some overlap between the problem of protection of functional expression (see section 3.1.1a) and copyright's failure to accommodate standardization or use of identical expression because many standardization cases happen to involve functional expression. These two causes were clearly articulated, for example, in the U.S. case of *Lotus v. Borland.* In this case, Borland had copied the menu interface of Lotus' then-popular 1-2-3 spreadsheet program for use in its rival spreadsheet, Quattro Pro. Lotus' menu (its structure and labels) had benefited from substantial network effects based on a very large installed base, such that Borland would likely have difficulty attracting any users to Quattro Pro if they had to learn a new menu interface. Because of network effects, standardized expression (identical menus) appeared more beneficial to competition and innovation than original expression (different menus).[281] Lotus sued Borland for copyright infringement. The U.S. Court of Appeals for the First Circuit, in its majority opinion, held that Lotus' menu was an uncopyrightable (functional) 'method of operation' under Section 102(b) of the U.S. Copyright Act. This meant that Borland could copy Lotus' menu.[282] Although Lotus' menu might indeed be called a method of operation, similar to the buttons on a VCR, this by itself was arguably not a compelling reason to allow Borland to copy it because the same 'method' could

---

278. *Nichols v. Universal Pictures Corporation* (US Court of Appeals, Second Circuit 1930). Judge Learned Hand's expression may also be used without authorization because it is part of a government-created – and, therefore, unprotected – work. 17 U.S.C. §105.
279. InfoSoc Directive, Article5(2)(i). Note, however, that the extensive list of (mostly optional) limitations in Article 5 of this directive does not apply to software. InfoSoc Directive, Recital 50.
280. See also Newman 1999, p. 692; Samuelson 2007c, p. 1976. But see Spoor 1994, p. 1075 (arguing that use of interface specifications could be made without authorization under the Berne Convention's limitation permitting quotations).
281. Menell 1998, p. 680.
282. See also section 6.3.1a.

still be implemented with different, non-infringing expression (different menu labels). By contrast, Judge Boudin's insightful concurring opinion directly related the need to duplicate Lotus' menu to the fact that it had become a *de-facto* standard.[283] As recognized by Judge Boudin, the compelling reason for denying protection to Lotus' menu interface was primarily that Lotus' particular expression in its menu had become a standard, such that using different expression by Borland would forgo the benefits associated with that standard. Unlike Judge Boudin's concurring opinion, *Lotus*' majority 'method of operation' approach thus arguably conceals the more fundamental problem: whether copyright's promotion of originality should yield to the conflicting interests in standardization.[284]

However, the problem of the need to use identical expression does not entirely coincide with that of protection of functional expression. In some instances, non-functional or aesthetic expression might also need to be duplicated verbatim.[285] In such instances, copyright doctrines that limit the scope of protection for functional works do not apply and cannot, as they did in *Lotus v. Borland*'s majority opinion, obviate the separate problem of a need to use identical expression. Examination of such cases, therefore, may be useful to expose the problem of using identical expression under copyright law and to isolate it from that of protection of functional expression (see the accompanying diagram. In the Dutch case of *Dior v. Evora*, for instance, perfume maker Dior relied on copyrights in its packaging to prevent low-cost retailer Evora from displaying that packaging in its advertisements. Dior thereby indirectly sought to prevent Evora from reselling and discounting its perfumes. Unlike Lotus' menu structure (*supra*), Dior's packaging design was not a functional work but clearly constituted copyrightable, aesthetic expression. As in *Lotus v. Borland*, however, there was a need for Evora to use identical expression rather than to create original expression. The question was whether Evora could use expression identical to Dior's protected expression in order to advertise Dior's products, for which only use of Dior's particular, exact expression sufficed.[286] This need to use identical expression proved difficult to accommodate under Dutch copyright law because Dior's expression was clearly copyrightable and because there were no directly applicable limitations permitting Evora's use of the expression. The Appeals

283. Concurring opinion Judge Boudin in *Lotus v. Borland* (US Court of Appeals, First Circuit 1995), 821. See also Weiser 2003, p. 606.
284. See, for example, Menell 1998; Samuelson 2007b, p. 193; Samuelson 2008b.
285. See also Menell 1998, p. 680.
286. In a related U.S. case, a manufacturer of vacuum cleaners advertised its product using, verbatim, favorable evaluations made by a Consumers' Union Report. The Second Circuit held that the manufacturer's use of the remarks constituted fair use, observing, '[w]here an evaluation or description is being made, copying the exact words may be the only valid way precisely to report the evaluation.' *Consumers Union v. General Signal Corp.* (US Court of Appeals, Second Circuit 1983), 1049.

Court found a solution, holding that Evora's use was permissible by analogy to the limitations permitting quotations and reproduction of works in catalogs, and the Supreme Court affirmed.[287] Although the *outcome* of *Dior v. Evora* might again be considered satisfactory, the *reasoning* for that outcome was, again, less solid. Like in *Lotus v. Borland*, the Dutch courts were essentially forced to find an escape route to allow Evora to copy Dior's expression because the central trade-off underlying the case – whether original expression by Evora or whether identical expression was more beneficial – could not be addressed directly under Dutch copyright law. Indeed, the validity of the *Dior* approach has been questioned, in particular since the subsequent European Information Society Directive underscored the closed system of harmonized European copyright limitations, including the limitation for quotations.[288] In sum, *Dior v. Evora* demonstrates the failure of copyright law to balance the benefits of original and identical expression, and the difficulty of resolving this issue under existing copyright doctrines. The case also demonstrates that not all need for identical expression emerges from standardization in functional works: these problems may also occur in relation to more aesthetic expression. The accompanying diagram compares *Lotus v. Borland* and *Dior v. Evora*: both cases involve a need for identical expression, yet *Lotus* could also be approached as a problem of functional expression, whereas *Dior* could not.

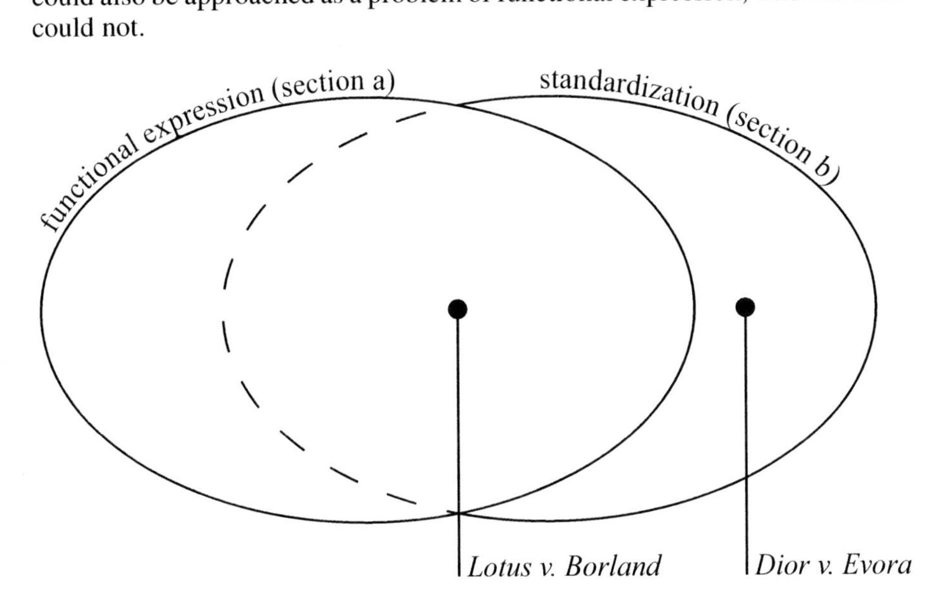

287. *Dior v. Evora* (Hoge Raad 1995), §3.6.2.
288. Guibault 2002, p. 17. An alternative solution might have been to apply a more general misuse doctrine. See van Rooijen 2006. See also Dreier 2001, p. 302; Goldstein 1986, p. 1127.

In sum, copyright's basic premise of promoting original expression conflicts with a need to use identical expression, and, thereby, with standardization of expression, such as using expression in interface specifications for interoperability.

Tensions between copyright's promotion of originality and standardization are also caused by the difficulty of anticipating standards *ex-ante*. Whether certain subject matter becomes a standard, or whether certain use of protected subject matter should be permitted in the interests of standardization, is often not discernable until well *after* the creation of the work. Thus, the need to copy subject matter in the interest of standardization can generally not be anticipated *ex-ante* but must be established *ex-post.*[289] However, copyright laws, like many other intellectual property rights, are primarily *ex-ante* regimes.[290] Accordingly, courts will typically determine whether a work constituted original expression at the time of its creation. Subsequent (*ex-post*) use made of the work does not normally affect originality.[291] Copyright law thereby provides certainty to rightsholders and competitors as to what is protected and to what extent. This *ex-ante* certainty is difficult to reconcile with the *ex-post* emergence of standards.[292]

Notwithstanding the difficulty of anticipating standards *ex-ante* in general, it may be possible to anticipate *specific* forms of standardization *ex-ante* if it can be established in advance which (type of) subject matter is likely to become a standard, or which uses may be necessary in the interest of standardization. For example, European design protection laws contain a subject matter exclusion to permit for reuse of interconnections and a limitation to allow for reuse of parts necessary for repairs. Design protection laws are further examined in Chapter 5. Interface specifications could similarly be anticipated as standards *ex-ante* through specific exclusions or limitations in copyright law (see section 6.3.1c).

A related reason for copyright's failure to allow for free use of standards in the interests of standardization, such as the use of interface specifications for interoperability, is that such a general *ex-ante* standardization exception can undermine the economic incentive function of copyright law for other subject matter. Although, as demonstrated in Chapter 2, there are stronger arguments for more limited control over standards than for other subject matter, the difficulty of distinguishing and isolating standards *ex-ante* (see *supra*) in order to reduce their control may mean that control is also reduced for other, non-standard subject matter, thus risking to reduce incentives to innovate in general.

---

289. See also Menell 1998, pp. 689, 700.
290. See section 4.1.2.
291. See, for example, *Bigott v. Doucal* (Hoge Raad 1999) (with case comment by Hugenholtz). See also section 6.3.1b.
292. See also section 6.3.1c.

In sum, the free use of standardized features in works, such as a program's interface specifications for interoperability, is hindered by copyright's failure to balance the benefits of original expression (different interface specifications) with those of identical expression, which may be needed to allow for standardization (duplicating another program's interface specifications).[293] Furthermore, copyright determines the eligibility for protection *ex-ante* and, therefore, cannot adequately deal with standardization issues, which generally emerge *ex-post*. This is not to suggest that copyright law *should* generally balance the interests in originality and standardization; it is merely observed here that this is one of two principal impediments to the free use of interface specifications (the other one being the protection of functional expression; see section 3.1.1a).

3.1.2. ACCESS

This section examines how copyright law indirectly provides for control over *access* to interoperability information. This is caused, first, by the distribution of computer programs and their specifications in unreadable object code form and the protection of the program in this form (section 3.1.2a). Second, a broad definition of the reproduction right limits possibilities to reverse engineer the original source code (section 3.1.2b). Third, copyright is merely a right to prohibit copying; it does not normally entail any positive obligations for rightsholders to provide access to their works (section 3.1.2c).

a. Object Code and Source Code

Most copyrighted works cannot be appreciated – and, therefore, not exploited – without access to the work's copyrighted expression. Because the user's appreciation lies in the original expression protected by copyright law (e.g., the text), *use* of a copyrighted work (e.g., a novel) generally coincides with *access* to the work. Consequently, the rightsholder typically enriches the public by disclosing the expression protected by her or his copyrights.[294] Access to the copyrighted expression is, therefore, not normally an issue in copyright law: copyright typically protects the subject matter in the same form in which it is exposed to the human audience.[295]

---

293. Unlike copyright law, trademark law does contain instruments that allow for (*ex-post*) considerations of standardization, in particular through its 'genericide' doctrine. Koelman 2006, p. 832; Merges 1999, p. 33.

294. Even if the rightsholder only provides conditional access to the work, the user generally still obtains access to the protected expression on meeting the rightsholder's conditions. For instance, one may typically only enjoy a movie at the cinema after paying an entrance fee. On payment, however, the user can appreciate the protected expression (the moving picture).

295. Cornish 1993, p. 197.

It was already observed that this is different for software.[296] Unlike the more traditional literary works, users of a computer program do not appreciate (or even see) the original expression in the source code, but rather the functionality it provides when executed by the computer in object code form. Distribution of the protected expression in source code form is, therefore, not required for appreciation by end-users, and, due to technology, not necessary. Indeed, it is industry practice to distribute the executable yet incomprehensible object code of a computer program to end-users, while the comprehensible source code is safely stored in-house.[297] This closed code practice allows users to run the computer program and benefit from the functionality it offers, yet without understanding how it works.

However, because the interface specifications required for interoperability are embedded in the distributed object code of the program, these specifications are hidden along with the know-how in that code. This practice severely restricts competitors' ability to develop interoperable software. Since the distributed object code is not readable by a human, while the source code is not distributed, both the know-how and the interoperability information are effectively kept secret.[298]

b. Reverse Engineering and Reproduction

Reverse engineering could theoretically enable a skilled software engineer to reconstruct the human-readable source code from the distributed object code, thus providing access to the know-how and interoperability information.[299] This process, however – like virtually every use made of a computer program – requires multiple intermediate and temporary copies of the object code to be made:[300] a computer generally cannot run or process software without first loading it into the system's random access memory (RAM).[301] Thus, for black-box testing, the interoperable developer must cause reproductions to be made in order to run and observe the program in operation. For decompilation, temporary reproductions are necessary to analyze the object code of the target program – possibly by loading the program into an automated decompiler – and to translate the object code into source code.[302]

---

296. See section 3.1.1a.
297. Gibson 2005, pp. 173–175; Holmes & Torok 2006; Samuelson & Scotchmer 2002, p. 1608. See also Visser 1997, p. 61. See also section 2.1.2a.
298. Bartmann 2005, p. 122; Menell 1998, p. 691.
299. See section 2.1.2b.
300. Band & Katoh 1995, p. 17; Gibson 2005, p. 214; Haberstumpf 1993, p. 160; Lemley & McGowan 1998, p. 525.
301. Guibault & Van Daalen 2006, p. 100; Schneider 1990, p. 506. However, on loading the program into RAM memory, the act of running the program is not considered a separate reproduction. See Haberstumpf 1993, p. 136; Schelven & Struik 1995, p. 57; Schneider 1990, p. 506. See also Spoor et al. 2005, p. 595.
302. Staffelbach 2003, p. 88.

These temporary reproductions, then, have been accommodated under a rather broad reproduction right,[303] which is part of the bundle of exclusive rights conferred by copyright law. Save any express limitations to that end (see *infra*), the rightsholder, therefore, normally would have the right to prevent the temporary acts required for reverse engineering the computer program.[304] This, in turn, prevents access to the source code, including the interoperability information.[305]

The reproduction right has effectively been expanded: copyright owners have not traditionally been able to prevent analysis and private use of their works.[306] Of course, most of those traditional works did not require reproduction in order to be analyzed or used[307] – although some did.[308] It follows that a technical or 'political' interpretation of the reproduction right, rather than a teleological one,[309] has enabled rightsholders of computer programs to control the use of their works in fine detail.

In part, however, the broad reproduction right serves to compensate for copyright's failure to protect the computer program's more valuable aspects – the functionality or know-how embedded in the (object) code.[310] The valuable know-how can only be obtained by studying the source code of the program.[311] This process may require reverse engineering. By preventing direct access to this know-how through a broad reproduction right, which limits competitors' abilities to reverse engineer this know-how, copyright effectively provides for some protection of these more valuable features.[312] In effect, by preventing reverse engineering, copyright law thus protects the software's shell or tissue, thereby limiting access to its more valuable inner ideas and principles, or know-how.[313] Herein lies the essence of copyright protection for computer programs:

---

303. Software Directive, Article 4; Guibault & Van Daalen 2006, P. 100; Samuelson 2007a, p. 563; Spoor et al. 2005, p. 594; Sucker 1993, p. 15. The broad reproduction right is also apparent from the absence of a right to make copies for private use. Lehmann 1989, p. 1062. See also Haberstumpf 1993, p. 133; *MAI v. Peak* (US Court of Appeals, Ninth Circuit 1993); Samuelson et al. 1994, p. 2391; Staffelbach 2003, p. 89.
304. See, for example, Vinje 1993, p. 49 (discussing the lack of a reverse engineering exception in the Commission's original Proposal for the Software Directive).
305. See also Dreier 1991a, p. 581; Schulte 1992, p. 653.
306. Dommering 1994; Guibault 2002, pp. 3, 48; Hugenholtz 1998, p. 5; Legal Advisory Board 1995; Lehmann 1993, p. 11.
307. Dommering 1992, p. 88; Dreier 1991a, p. 581; Guibault & Van Daalen 2006, p. 100; Haberstumpf 1993, p. 160; Schelven & Struik 1995, p. 57; Visser 1997, p. 70.
308. Visser 1997, p. 77. Playing music from a digital medium, such as a CD or MP3 file, similarly requires temporary copies to be made for digital processing. See also Verstrynge 1993, p. 6.
309. Dreier 1991a, p. 579; Lehmann 1989, p. 1062. See also Schneider 1990.
310. See section 3.1.1.
311. See also Samuelson & Scotchmer 2002, p. 1590.
312. Bartmann 2005, p. 123; Samuelson et al. 1994, p. 2392; Spoor 1994, p. 1082.
313. Spoor 1994, p. 1083. Note, however, that much of the value in the functionality of a program is revealed by simply running the program. This 'behavior' does not require reverse engineering in order to be exposed. Johnson-Laird 1994, p. 852.

notwithstanding its formal adherence to copyright principles, it is essentially a *sui generis* regime that restricts *access* to (rather than use of) know-how in computer programs – similarly to strong trade-secret protection.[314]

Even if the rightsholder's broad reproduction right covers the temporary reproductions necessary for reverse engineering, a right to reverse engineer can still be created, but it must be based on an explicit copyright limitation. This, in turn, enables legislators or courts to regulate reverse engineering by imposing conditions on the reverse engineer. Conditional reverse engineering would not have been possible if these temporary reproductions were not covered by the rightsholder's reproduction right.

Of course, preventing reverse engineering by providing the rightsholder with a broad reproduction right not only impedes access to such know-how but also to the program's interface specifications, which are embedded in the know-how or source code.[315] Conversely, *permitting* reverse engineering for purposes of interoperability is in some tension with strong protection for software, as it additionally enables the reverse engineer to obtain access to a computer program's know-how.[316]

However, even in the absence of legal conditions, reverse engineering does not present an immediate threat of exposure of the know-how embedded in the program's source code because reverse engineering requires considerable time.[317] Until a competitor has managed to successfully reverse engineer the program, the rightsholder, therefore, still effectively enjoys exclusivity.[318] This lead-time could be sufficient to recoup investments in this know-how and, therefore, mitigates the tension between effective protection of know-how and access to interoperability information. Much depends, however, on the evolving state of the art in reverse engineering technology.[319]

These concerns were at the heart of debates about the legality of reverse engineering for purposes of interoperability.[320] Notwithstanding copyright's protection against the making of temporary copies and its relevance for preventing direct access to know-how, it was recognized that interoperable developers still required access to the rightsholder's interoperability information.[321] In Europe, this has resulted in a statutory limitation allowing some reverse engineering for the purpose of establishing interoperability, which will be explored in section 3.2.2. In the United States, courts have accepted reverse engineering for purposes of interoperability under the fair use defense.[322]

314. Samuelson 1994, p. 279; Samuelson 2008a, p. 20; Schulte 1992, p. 658.
315. Schmidtchen & Koboldt 1993, p. 425.
316. See also Vinje 1991, p. 5; Vinje 1993, p. 73.
317. Samuelson et al. 1994, p. 2392. See also section 2.1.2b.
318. Reichman 1994, p. 2441; Samuelson & Scotchmer 2002, p. 1589.
319. See section 2.1.2b.
320. Bartmann 2005, p. 123; Samuelson 1994, p. 291; Sucker 1993, p. 17.
321. Lehmann 1992, p. 366; Vinje 1993.
322. De Cock Buning 2007, p. 126; Goldstein 2001, p. 299; Samuelson 1994, p. 285. See, for example, *Atari v. Nintendo* (US Court of Appeals, Federal Circuit 1992); *Sega v. Accolade* (US Court of Appeals, Ninth Circuit 1992), 1526.

c. Copyright as an Exclusive Right

The two preceding sections have demonstrated why copyright protection of a computer program limits the end-user's ability to obtain access to the program's interface specifications: these specifications are distributed in unreadable object code form (section 3.1.2a), while the possibility to reverse engineer the specifications from this object code is limited by copyright's broad right of reproduction (section 3.1.2b). Whereas copyright thus limits an *end-user*'s possibility to obtain a computer program's interoperability information, the *rightsholder* is also an unlikely source for the information, due to the very nature of copyright. The copyright in the computer program merely entails a right to *exclude* others from copying (using) the protected subject matter.[323] Copyright is not concerned with guarantees for *access* to (elements of) the work, even if the rightsholder has no (copy)right to prevent its use.[324] Although copyright law does contain several statutory limitations in favor of certain use of copyrighted works, these limitations similarly do not guarantee factual *access* to the protected work; rather, they limit the rightsholder's right to prohibit certain *use*.[325]

As noted, *supra*, this is not normally a concern because the rightsholder must typically make the work's protected expression available to the end-user in order to exploit the work. If, however, the end-user's appreciation of the work lies in something other than its expression – as in the case of software's functionality – the rightsholder can sometimes exploit the work without providing access to the protected expression, and access *can* become a concern.[326]

The nature of copyright as a mere right to prohibit is underscored by several rights within copyright law. For instance, the moral right droit de divulgation emphasizes the rightsholder's power to decide on first publication, and even to refrain from publication altogether.[327] Furthermore, the explicit prohibition on formalities, as codified in Article 5(2) of the Berne Convention, protects the rightsholder against the need to comply with any formal requirement as a condition for the enjoyment and exercise of his or

323. Spoor et al. 2005, p. 2.
324. Spoor 1994, p. 1080.
325. Guibault 2002, p. 109. For instance, a limitation in favor of making a backup copy of a computer program merely limits the rightsholder's abilities to prohibit copying for this purpose; it offers no guarantee that the work can actually be backed up. If the rightsholder has installed copy prevention technologies, for example, the statutory limitation may not be of any practical use. Spoor et al. 2005, p. 599. Similarly, a limitation permitting reverse engineering in order to extract interface information does not guarantee access to such information; it merely limits the rightsholder's possibilities to prohibit reverse engineering.
326. Lehmann 1989, p. 1060; Spoor 1994, p. 1081; Vandenberghe 1989, p. 409. See also *Sega v. Accolade* (US Court of Appeals, Ninth Circuit 1992), 1525.
327. Goldstein 2001, p. 289; Guibault & Van Daalen 2006, p. 124.

her rights. Consequently, the rightsholder cannot be required to disclose information about the work or the work itself in order to secure copyright protection. This is to be contrasted with, for instance, trademark and patent law, which generally do impose detailed disclosure obligations on rightsholders to ensure that the protected subject matter be adequately disseminated on expiration of the exclusive right.[328]

In sum, copyright is only a right to prohibit copying. It offers no instruments to obtain access to an undisclosed work, such as a program's interface specifications.

3.1.3. Conclusion

The protection of computer programs as literary works under copyright law has far-reaching implications for interoperability because it may bring control over the computer program's interface specifications within the effective scope of the rightsholder's exclusive rights. Copyright could enable the rightsholder to control both the use of and the access to the program's interface specifications. It may directly affect the *use* of interface information as it protects computer programs as 'literary works' at the level of their program code, of which the interface specifications form a part. Under the starkly objectified originality test applied to computer programs, the highly functional nature of interface specifications does not necessarily preclude protection. Copyright's general promotion of originality in expression also appears difficult to reconcile with the type of standardization in expression that is required for interoperability. In some respects, copyright protection for computer programs as literary works was, in software terms, a *quick and dirty* solution: it provided the fast and effective protection that was considered necessary to stimulate software development, but it was arguably far from elegant. As with most *quick and dirty* solutions, the lack of elegance inevitably showed: by treating computer programs as text, the interface specifications necessary for interoperability risked becoming part of the protected aspects of the program.

Moreover, the rightsholder may also indirectly exercise control over *access* to these specifications because copyright effectively protects the 'shell' around them. A broad interpretation of copyright's reproduction right brings the temporary reproductions required for reverse engineering within the scope of the rightsholder's exclusive rights. Were it not for the broad reproduction right, reverse engineering could enable competitors to reconstruct the source code, which, in turn, contains the interface specifications necessary for interoperability. The protection of the shell around the computer program's know-how leads to a second conclusion: notwithstanding

---

328. Samuelson & Scotchmer 2002, p. 1584. See also section 6.5. See also Kroes 2008, p. 3.

the accommodation of computer programs under copyright law, protection of computer programs as literary works is essentially a *sui generis* form of protection. Copyright's primary role in protecting computer programs is not to directly protect the know-how in the program: this information is typically hidden and, hence, not readily copyable, while it may not generally constitute original expression. Rather, copyright's role is to maintain the secrecy of this know-how by protecting computer programs in unreadable object code form and by preventing access to the source code.

In sum, copyright law can impede interoperability between computer programs through (in)direct control over use of and access to interface specifications.

3.2. INTEROPERABILITY UNDER THE SOFTWARE DIRECTIVE

Section 3.1 demonstrated how the protection of computer programs as literary works under copyright law could affect rightsholders' abilities to control the use of and access to their interface specifications. This section examines to what extent such control over use of and access to interface specifications has been limited by specific instruments – in particular under the Software Directive, which harmonizes the protection of computer programs by copyright law in Europe.[329] The following sections will analyze, first, to what extent these provisions actually limit control over use of (section 3.2.1) and access to (section 3.2.2) a computer program's interfaces, and whether these limitations, in conjunction with rightsholders' control of interoperability information (section 3.1), are successful in striking a meaningful balance between control and openness of interface information. Second, these sections will examine whether the Software Directive's provisions provide for sufficient certainty to rightsholders and competitors as *ex-ante* instruments. The analysis of these provisions reveals that the current regime is unsuccessful on both accounts. First, the provisions enabling access to interface information prove insufficient, thus enabling rightsholders to maintain factual control over access to their program's interface information. Moreover, the provisions related to use of such information leave open the possibility of direct copyright protection for interface specifications. The control over interface specifications (section 3.1), therefore, is not

329. The legislative history of the Software Directive began with a 1985 White Paper and a subsequent Green Paper. European Commission 1985; European Commission 1988. Upon a public consultation, the Commission issued a Proposal, and, after intense lobbying efforts on issues of interoperability, an Amended Proposal. Software Directive, Amended Proposal (1990); Software Directive, Proposal (1989). Where necessary, these documents will be referenced in this section for interpretation. The Software Directive was issued in 1991, and a consolidated version, incorporating changes brought by various other copyright directives, followed in 2009. For a comprehensive overview of the Software Directive's legislative history, see Vinje 1993.

substantially limited in favor of more openness. Second, due to the uncertainty as to the copyrightability of interface specifications, in addition to a complex system of conditions for reverse engineering, the directive largely fails to provide competitors with certainty as to the openness of interface information.

3.2.1. Use

Whether a balance between openness and control of interface information exists depends, in part, on the extent to which a rightsholder can directly control the use of such information and the extent to which this control has been limited by specific instruments. This section, therefore, examines whether copyright law, particularly as harmonized under the Software Directive, contains any limiting principles that could mitigate control over use of interface specifications (see section 3.1.1) in favor of more openness. Section 3.2.1a examines the idea/expression dichotomy; section 3.2.1b examines the originality requirement.

a. Idea/Expression

Copyright law generally protects the concrete expression of an idea, whereas the more abstract idea itself remains unprotected. Section 3.1.1 thus noted that interface specifications could possibly be considered copyrightable due to their highly concrete nature. Article 1(2) of the Software Directive refers to the idea/expression dichotomy and applies it to computer programs and their interfaces alike:

> Protection in accordance with this Directive shall apply to the expression in any form of a computer program. Ideas and principles which underlie any element of a computer program, *including those which underlie its interfaces*, are not protected by copyright under this Directive. [emphasis added][330]

The Software Directive thus fails to address the protection of interface specifications explicitly.[331] Instead, it leaves the protection of interfaces to be analyzed under the idea/expression dichotomy. Section 3.1.1 already observed that mere application of the idea/expression dichotomy might leave open the question as to the protectability of interface specifications. Indeed, the directive's protection of interfaces according to the idea/expression dichotomy is primarily the result of a compromise between two opposing industry groups: European Committee for Interoperable Systems (ECIS), which sought to explicitly exclude interface specifications from protection,[332]

330. Software Directive, Article 1(2).
331. See also Bainbridge 2006, p. 245.
332. Cornish 1989, p. 391; Meyer & Colombe 1990a, p. 326; Vandenberghe 1989, p. 410.

and Software Action Group for Europe (SAGE), which attempted to protect these specifications.[333]

Protection of interface specifications thus remains open to court interpretation.[334] This requires an analysis on a case-by-case basis, which substantially reduces certainty. Because of this case-by-case approach, an interpretation that categorically excludes all interfaces from copyrightable expression must be rejected.[335] Conversely, an interpretation according to which interface specifications are *presumed* to constitute copyrightable subject matter, as implicitly offered by the General Court in *Microsoft v. Commission*, is equally unsatisfactory.[336]

Notwithstanding the compromise-character of Article 1(2), however, the provision's explicit reference to interfaces does indicate recognition of the special significance of these parts of a computer program.[337] Indeed, the reference to interfaces could reasonably be interpreted as an indication that interface *specifications* are uncopyrightable ideas.[338] Article 1(2) does not state that there *is* protection for any expression in interfaces but rather that there is *no* protection for ideas and principles, *including* those that underlie interfaces. The ideas and principles underlying the interface could refer to the interface's *specification*, whereas expression in the interface could exist in its *implementation*.[339] An earlier proposal for a directive had suggested that interface *specifications* were not protected *insofar* as they constituted ideas and principles.[340] This was criticized by numerous authors because it implied that there could also be copyrightable expression in interface specifications.[341] The subsequent removal of the reference to specifications could thus be interpreted as an attempt to avoid the suggestion that these specifications might constitute protectable expression. Implicitly, Article 1(2), therefore, may be interpreted as excluding interface specifications from protection.

333. Lake et al. 1989, p. 432.
334. Czarnota & Hart 1991, p. 37; Verstrynge 1993, p. 4.
335. See, for example, Bitan 2006, p. 26; *Computer Associates Int'l* (Tribunal de Commerce de Bobigny 1995), 337; Vivant 2007, p. 126.
336. *Microsoft* (GC 2007), §289. The court presumed, for the sake of argument, that Microsoft's interface specifications were protected by valid intellectual property rights, regardless of whether they were patents, copyrights and/or trade secrets.
337. Sucker 1993, p. 14.
338. See also Menell 1998, p. 708; Samuelson 2008a, p. 21.
339. Goldstein 2001, p. 179; Lai 2000, p. 97.
340. Article 1(3) of the original oroposal suggested that interface specifications *could* constitute expression (rather than ideas), for it read, 'Where the specification of interfaces constitutes ideas and principles which underlie the program, those ideas and principles are not copyrightable subject matter' (Software Directive, Proposal (1989), 13). But see Software Directive, Proposal (1989), §3.11 ('In order to produce interoperative systems it is necessary to replicate the ideas, rules or principles by which interfaces between systems are specified, but not necessarily to reproduce the code which implements them. Ideas, rules or principles are not copyrightable subject matter.')
341. Band & Katoh 1995, p. 230; Cornish 1989, p. 392; Czarnota & Hart 1991, p. 41; Meyer & Colombe 1990a, p. 325; Palmer & Vinje 1992, p. 71; Schelven & Struik 1995, p. 29; Vandenberghe 1989, p. 412; Vinje 1993, p. 48.

An alternative interpretation is that the legislator intended to emphasize that there is no special regime of protection for the intensely debated interface specifications but that, instead, the idea/expression dichotomy should be used to evaluate the copyrightability of these elements in individual cases. If Article 1(2) must indeed be interpreted as a compromise between those groups supporting interoperability and those opposing it, the previously presented distinction between unprotectable interface specifications (as ideas) and protectable interface implementations (as expression) would make little sense because it is solely the copyright protection of the interface *specification* that determines whether interoperability can be achieved.

Article 1(2) thus leaves some room for conflicting interpretations. Nevertheless, a few courts may have found guidance in this provision. In *Iomega v. Societé Nomaï*,[342] the Paris Court of Appeals explicitly relied on Article 1(2) in holding that the data sequence[343] and software used in the communication between Iomega's ZIP drive and the computer were uncopyrightable ideas.[344] In *Navitaire v. EasyJet*, a British High Court offered a broader interpretation of uncopyrightable ideas and principles by relying not only on Article 1(2)[345] but also on the Software Directive's preamble.[346] Recital 11 of the Directive states, *inter alia*:

> to the extent that logic, algorithms and programming languages comprise ideas and principles, those ideas and principles are not protected under this Directive.[347]

Although this provision does not literally state anything more than that ideas and principles are not protected, it could be interpreted as an indication that logic, algorithms and programming languages should generally be regarded as unprotected ideas or principles – similarly to the possible exclusion of interface specifications by Article 1(2). Indeed, the *Navitaire* court noted that the relevant complex user interface commands[348] were not eligible for copyright protection because the commands ought to be regarded as a 'programming language',[349] and, therefore, as uncopyrightable ideas:[350]

---

342. *Nomaï* (Paris Court of Appeals 1997).
343. A data sequence is essentially a 'key', consisting of a code or password that identifies a software or hardware product for use with another product.
344. *Nomaï* (Paris Court of Appeals 1997), 69. See also Belloir 1998.
345. *Navitaire v. EasyJet* (UK High Court of Justice, Chancery Division 2004), §88.
346. Software Directive, Recital 14; *Navitaire v. EasyJet* (UK High Court of Justice, Chancery Division 2004), §87. See also Bainbridge 2006, p. 245.
347. Software Directive, Recital 11.
348. The court defines 'complex commands' as 'commands that have a syntax [or] have one or more arguments that must be expressed in a particular way'. This is very similar to API specifications, which generally also accept certain parameters. See *Navitaire v. EasyJet* (UK High Court of Justice, Chancery Division 2004), §81.
349. But see Bainbridge 2006, p. 246 ('[A] command set is better classified as a user interface than a programming language').
350. *Navitaire v. EasyJet* (UK High Court of Justice, Chancery Division 2004), §85.

> The recitals quoted [recital 11 of the consolidated Software Directive] are said [. . .] to make it clear that 'computer languages are not included in the protection afforded to computer programs'. [. . .] In my view, the principle extends to ad hoc languages of the kind with which I am here concerned, that is, a defined user command interface. It does not matter how the 'language' of the interface is defined. It may be defined formally or it may be defined only by the code that recognises it. Either way, copyright does not subsist in it.[351]

In its original proposal, the Commission had also expressed the view that, where the idea behind an interface can only be expressed in a limited number of ways, ideas and expression would merge, leaving only unprotected ideas.[352] This U.S.-developed merger doctrine was applied to interface specifications, for example, by a British High Court in *TIPS v. Daman.*[353] In continental Europe, however, such restraints on the means by which an author can express his or her work are generally analyzed under the originality standard (see section 3.2.1b).[354]

A strong argument against copyrightability of interface specifications can be found in a systematic interpretation of the Software Directive's provision permitting decompilation for purposes of interoperability (Article 6, further discussed in section 3.2.2). The purpose of Article 6 is ultimately to enable the interoperable developer to create an interoperable program using the interface specifications that have been extracted from the code through decompilation. Because this provision does not provide for an express limitation to use any protected expression in an interoperable program, the argument could thus be made that interface specifications must be considered to constitute non-copyrightable subject matter.[355]

Note that some interfaces may not be eligible as copyrightable expression simply because they are not expressed in the program's (object) code. Although specifications of APIs generally *are* explicit in the distributed object code, many communications and data interface specifications are not.[356] An element of a communications protocol – for instance, a fixed interval between

---

351. *Id.*, §88. Samuelson has similarly observed that Section 102(b) of the US Copyright Act excludes from protection more than abstract 'ideas', but also more concrete systems, processes and methods of operation. Samuelson 2007c. See also section 6.3.1a.
352. Software Directive, Proposal (1989), §3.13. See also Czarnota & Hart 1991, p. 82; Dreier & Hugenholtz 2006, p. 217; Merges et al. 2003, p. 352; *Morrisey v. Proctor & Gamble* (US Court of Appeals, First Circuit 1967); Pilny 1990, p. 439; Samuelson 2007b, p. 215; Schulte 1992, p. 650; Staffelbach 2003, p. 131; Sucker 1993, p. 14; Vinje 1993, p. 79.
353. *TIPS v. Daman* (UK High Court of Justice, Chancery Division 1991), 181. See also Bainbridge 2006, p. 247.
354. Hugenholtz 1989, p. 78. See also Drexl 1994, p. 74.
355. Dreier 1991a, p. 583; Lai 2000, p. 98.
356. Clapes et al. 1987, p. 1562; Pilny 1990, p. 435.

data transmissions – may only be appreciable by studying the functionality performed by the code, rather than from the expression of the code itself. These interface specifications, therefore, are more accurately described as characteristics of the interface or the program rather than as protected expression.[357] In *Navitaire v. EasyJet*, the court provided a coherent analysis of why this type of specifications cannot be considered copyrightable subject matter:

> I do not consider that the individual complex commands are distinct copyright works at all. The corresponding work cannot be identified. As pleaded, they are said to be literary works: that is, they must be written [...]. This aspect of the case turns, it seems to me, on whether and to what extent they have been recorded. [...] [T]he source code records them in the sense that it is possible to analyse the code to ascertain that a machine operating according to that code will 'recognise' [the commands]. But this 'syntax' is recorded without being stated. The reason it is recorded rather than stated is that the reader, in effect, has to turn him- or herself into a machine in order to work out what the machine will recognise when operating according to this program.[358]

In sum, the Software Directive largely relies on the idea/expression dichotomy to distinguish between copyrightable and non-copyrightable elements of a computer program. It was already determined that interface specifications do not necessarily qualify as either ideas or expression. The Software Directive offers little further guidance, although its explicit reference to interfaces as well as logic and programming languages may well have inspired some courts to exclude interface specifications from protection. In any event, it cannot be argued that interface specifications are categorically unprotected subject matter. The possibility of protection, therefore, remains open.

b. Originality

Even if interface specifications were to be regarded as expression rather than idea, the specifications would still require sufficient originality to constitute *copyrightable* expression. Prior to the implementation of the Software Directive, the European Member States applied varying originality thresholds.[359] Such differences risked undermining the objective of harmonizing copyright protection of computer programs.[360] The directive, therefore, sought to harmonize the originality threshold.[361] At the same time, the Commission

357. Clapes et al. 1987, p. 1563. See also section 2.1.2b.
358. *Navitaire v. EasyJet* (UK High Court of Justice, Chancery Division 2004), §83. See also Samuelson 2007c, p. 1946.
359. European Commission 1988, p. 187, §5.6.3–§5.6.7.
360. Software Directive, Proposal (1989), §2.11.
361. Software Directive, 2009, Recital 4; See Czarnota & Hart 1991, p. 9.

intended to have as many programs as possible benefit from copyright protection.[362] To that end, the directive's Article 1(3) provides for a uniform, yet relatively low originality threshold:

> A computer program shall be protected if it is original in the sense that it is the author's own intellectual creation. No other criteria shall be applied to determine its eligibility for protection.[363]

Thus, although mere independent creation does not suffice, aesthetic quality is also not required.[364] Indeed, any criteria other than 'the author's own intellectual creation' are invalid.[365] Trivial programs, however, are not protected.[366] The resulting originality threshold may be regarded as a compromise between the low Anglo-Saxon and higher continental-European standards, particularly in Germany.[367]

Consequently, it must be ascertained whether an interface specification constitutes 'the author's own intellectual creation'. As already noted in section 3.1.1a, this is a difficult inquiry. Still, it appears unlikely – but not impossible – that an interface specification generally meets this standard.[368] Because of the interface's functional constraints and industry standardization, very limited choices are available to a developer with respect to the design of the interface's specification, such that the originality will often be 'low'.[369]

In *Navitaire v. EasyJet*, the court considered the originality of text-based user interface commands used in an airline reservations system, which were, similarly to most API specifications, very brief and descriptive:

---

362. Deene 2007, p. 693. See, for example, Software Directive, Proposal (1989), 18 ('The only criterion which should be applied to determine the eligibility for protection is that of originality, that is, that the work has not been copied').
363. The same standard can be found in the Database Directive. See Database Directive, Article 3(1).
364. European Commission 1988, §5.6.4; Walter et al. 2001, p. 124.
365. Czarnota & Hart 1991, p. 44.
366. Walter et al. 2001, p. 124.
367. Cohen-Jehoram 1994, p. 828; Deene 2007, p. 692; *Inkassoprogramm* (Bundesgerichtshof 1985), 83; Walter et al. 2001, p. 124. A particularly substantial discrepancy existed between the German standard, requiring a degree of originality exceeding that of the average programmer, and the British standard, which essentially required only that the work originate from the author – that is, that it was not the result of copying. See also Lehmann 1989, p. 1059; Pilny 1992; Plana 2007, p. 102. Other countries used a lower standard of originality, in which the same argument was indicative of a computer program's originality. See also Hugenholtz & Spoor 1987, p. 34; Software Directive, Proposal (1989), 9. The second sentence in Article 1(3) ('No other criteria shall be applied to determine its eligibility for protection') has been interpreted as directed mainly at the German legislators; see Drexl 1994, p. 96; Lehmann 1993, p. 8.
368. Lehmann 1989, p. 1059; Lehmann 1992, p. 364; Spoor 1994, p. 1074.
369. See section 3.1.1a.

> Some of the complex codes ('A' for availability, 'G' for grab/sell, 'N-' to name a passenger, '.' for print, 'CC' for calculator, and so on) do not, on their own, seem to me to require much skill or labour.[370]

Similarly, the court observed that commands consisting of single words did not qualify for protection as a Literary Work.[371]

In sum, it appears unlikely (but not impossible) that interface specifications meet the requirement of originality as harmonized by the Software Directive.[372]

c. Conclusion

The Software Directive has left the question as to the copyrightability of interface specifications open to court interpretation, providing negligible guidance. Few courts have indeed interpreted the copyrightability of interface specifications.[373] A first conclusion is, therefore, that, as an *ex-ante* regime, the Software Directive largely fails to provide certainty with respect to this prerequisite to interoperability. This uncertainty generally benefits the rightsholder, which, in addition to factual control over access to this

---

370. *Navitaire v. EasyJet* (UK High Court of Justice, Chancery Division 2004), §47. Note that, although the court examines originality using the British standard 'skill and labour', it is apparent that the court is aware of the prevailing originality standard of the Software Directive. See *Navitaire v. EasyJet* (UK High Court of Justice, Chancery Division 2004), §88.
371. *Navitaire v. EasyJet* (UK High Court of Justice, Chancery Division 2004), §80. See also Bainbridge 2006, p. 245. The Berne Convention also does not recognize protection for titles and other short works. Ricketson & Ginsburg 2006, p. 510.
372. One might consider protecting interface specifications as copyrightable compilations of their parameters. A compilation is copyrightable if its selection *or* arrangement demonstrates originality. Section 3.1.1a already noted that, although the *selection* of parameters cannot be considered original because they follow directly from the function that the interface must perform, there might be some room for subjective choices in the *arrangement* within the parameter list. However, protection for such compilations is generally reserved for databases in which the individual elements do not together form a single entity. This is clearly different for the elements of an interface specification, which do form a single entity. TRIPS, Article 10.2; Database Directive, Article 3(1); Quaedvlieg 2006, p. 160; Reinbothe & Von Lewinski 2002, p. 75; Samuelson et al. 1994, p. 2404; WCT, Article 5. It is, moreover, questionable whether reliance on the compilation theory is justified under the Software Directive. Although the original proposal had referred to the compilation theory (Software Directive, Proposal (1989), §4(b)), the current Software Directive only protects computer programs and their interface specifications as Literary Works under the Berne Convention. Software Directive, Article 1(1). The Berne Convention, in turn, does not expressly recognize copyrights in compilations of works that are not individually protected. Reinbothe & Von Lewinski 2002, p. 72; Ricketson & Ginsburg 2006, p. 489. Complementary to the Berne Convention, Article 10.2 of the TRIPS agreement and Article 5 of the WIPO Copyright Treaty (WCT) do recognize copyright protection for compilations consisting of non-copyrightable material, including in object code form. Gervais 2003, p. 135; Reinbothe & Von Lewinski 2002, p. 72; Ricketson & Ginsburg 2006, p. 514.
373. See also Bainbridge 2006, p. 245.

information (see section 3.2.2), could assert a copyright in her or his interface specifications in order to control their use.[374]

A second conclusion is, nonetheless, that interface specifications generally would not appear to constitute sufficiently original expression. Interface specifications, therefore, rarely will be considered copyrighted subject matter and can thus often be used in interoperable programs. On the normative scale of openness versus control of interface information, the provisions related to use of interface information thus point towards openness, although the possibility of control is not excluded in particular for more complex interface specifications.

The analysis in this section leads to a third conclusion, which is that direct copyright protection of interoperability information is a relatively blunt instrument to strike a meaningful balance between openness and control of such information. Interface information can be either protected or not protected; in the former case, the rightsholder maintains control over the information for the full term of protection (typically 70 years),[375] whereas, in the latter case, the rightsholder would simply have no control over this information. As will be demonstrated, in section 3.2.2, the instruments designed to enable access to interface information could allow for a more subtle balance between openness and control of interface information.

3.2.2 Access

Interoperable program development requires not only use but also access to the relevant interface specifications. Section 3.1.2 already illustrated how copyright protection confers control over access to interoperability information. This section analyzes the Software Directive's reverse engineering provisions designed to limit such control over access in favor of more openness. In the absence of a clear regime addressing the use of such information (see section 3.2.1), these provisions form the pivotal instrument to balance openness and control of interface information.

The Software Directive aims to solve the problem of access to interface specifications primarily through a mechanism whereby competitors' limited ability to reverse engineer the rightsholder's program (section 3.2.2a) should provide an incentive to both parties to negotiate the supply of interoperability information (section 3.2.2b).[376] Because reverse engineering requires substantial time and resources, it does not provide for immediate access to interoperability information, thus allowing some balance to be struck between openness and control of interface information.

---

374. See, for example, *Microsoft* (GC 2007), §272.
375. See also Menell 1998, p. 672.
376. The Software Directive also, in Recital 27, refers to the use of competition law; see Chapter 4.

It will also be demonstrated, however, that, because of a complex and restrictive set of conditions for reverse engineering, which also fail to consider the evolving state of the art in reverse engineering technology (section 3.2.2c), as well as several other restrictive conditions (section 3.2.2d), the Software Directive largely fails to strike an adequate balance between openness and control of interface information.

a. Two Forms of Reverse Engineering

Originally, the Commission had expressed the view that access to information was not a matter of copyright law, and, accordingly, the first proposal for the Software Directive left the problem of access to interface specifications to competition law scrutiny.[377] However, on pressure by ECIS,[378] and notwithstanding substantial opposition by SAGE,[379] the Commission's Amended Proposal did include reverse engineering provisions to enable *ex-ante* access to interoperability information.[380] The interaction between both approaches will be explored in Chapter 4. For present purposes, it suffices to note that the directive's reverse engineering provisions were implemented as a result of competition concerns and may thus be interpreted as *ex-ante* instruments of competition policy.[381]

The directive supports two species of reverse engineering: black-box testing, comprising any external analysis of the target program during normal operation, and decompilation. It was already noted that both forms of reverse engineering differ from a technical perspective black-box testing is limited to an (extensive) observation of the exterior of the 'box' (the computer program), whereas decompilation aims to reconstruct its interior (the source code).[382] This difference also triggers different copyright-relevant acts and is, therefore, addressed by two distinct provisions in the Software Directive. Black-box testing merely entails running the computer program similar to (although more intensely than) running the program for normal use. Article 5(1) of the directive already safeguards the latter reproductions for lawful end-users, and the limitation expressly permitting black-box testing – Article 5(3) – is, therefore, primarily a clarification of this limitation.[383] By contrast, decompilation requires temporary copies to be made for the purpose of analysis and

377. European Commission 1988, §5.5.11, §5.5.12; Lehmann 1992, p. 365; Software Directive, Proposal (1989), 16; Schulte 1992, p. 653.
378. Band & Katoh 1995, p. 232; Meyer & Colombe 1990b, p. 82. See also Spoor 1994, p. 1078.
379. See, for example, Lake et al. 1989, p. 433.
380. Software Directive, Amended Proposal (1990), 3.
381. Samuelson 1994, p. 294; Staffelbach 2003, p. 100.
382. See section 2.1.2b. See also Bainbridge 2006, p. 244; *Navitaire v. EasyJet* (UK High Court of Justice, Chancery Division 2004).
383. See also Cornish 1989, p. 392; Czarnota & Hart 1991, p. 35; Dommering 1992, p. 88; Dreier 1991b, p. 322; Schelven & Struik 1995, p. 88; Spoor et al. 2005, p. 600; Sucker 1993, p. 16.

translation of the program's object code into source code, which is not a limitation already safeguarded for lawful end-users. Article 6, therefore, provides this limitation explicitly.

It was also already observed that black-box testing and decompilation differ from an economic perspective as well: decompilation does, whereas black-box testing does not, normally expose the know-how embedded in the program's source code. This know-how may be considerably more valuable than the actually protected original expression in the code.[384] A substantial source of controversy during the legislative history,[385] exposure of this know-how through decompilation, therefore, is restricted by several conditions in Article 6, which are absent in the limitation permitting black-box testing.[386] However, although most literature and controversy has been devoted to decompilation, the relevance of the black-box testing exemption should not be underestimated, as it could, in some instances, produce a comprehensive set of interfaces, thereby obviating the need for decompilation.[387] Note that neither limitation can be annulled by contract.[388]

Reverse engineering does not provide the interoperable developer with immediate access to the rightsholder's interoperability information. Section 3.1.2a already noted that reverse engineering does not represent an imminent threat of exposure of the rightsholder's know-how because it is significantly time consuming. Indeed, the time and costs required for reverse engineering are important factors in its justification.[389] The rightsholder still enjoys the lead-time between the release of the computer program and successful completion of competitors' reverse engineering efforts. This lead-time for the developer of the original program serves a similar function as the exclusivity period awarded by intellectual property rights.[390] Naturally, the time required for successful reverse engineering not only delays access to the program's know-how but also to the interoperability information contained therein.[391] In other words, a rule permitting reverse engineering does not shift the normative balance of openness versus control of interface information to either full openness or full control. Rather, it should ideally offer a middle ground: the rightsholder can maintain control over its interface information until such time as competitors have managed to reverse engineer it.[392] At that point, the information becomes 'open'.

384. See section 3.1.2a.
385. See, generally, Vinje 1993.
386. See also Walter et al. 2001, p. 216.
387. Dommering 1992, p. 88; Staffelbach 2003, p. 72.
388. Software Directive, Article 8.
389. Samuelson & Scotchmer 2002, p. 1586.
390. Federal Trade Commission 2003, p. 80; Lemley & McGowan 1998, p. 530; Samuelson & Scotchmer 2002.
391. Lemley & McGowan 1998, p. 530; Menell 1998, p. 709.
392. Reichman 1994, p. 2441; Schmidtchen & Koboldt 1993, p. 426. See also Farrell & Saloner 1992, p. 10; Lemley & McGowan 1998, p. 533; Samuelson et al. 1994, p. 2392.

The lead-time created by secrecy of source code and the subsequent ability to reverse engineer this code is, admittedly, not as precisely determined as the fixed term of protection typically offered by intellectual property rights. As such, this lead-time introduces some uncertainty. However, commercial interoperability agreements between firms can remove such uncertainty (see section 3.2.2b).

In conclusion, the Software Directive's limitations permitting reverse engineering for interoperability purposes could, in theory, serve as a basis to balance control versus openness of interface specifications.

b. Reverse Engineering and Negotiations

The main purpose of the reverse engineering provisions of the Software Directive is not to provoke competitors to actually reverse engineer the rightsholder's code but rather to stimulate both parties to negotiate the supply of interoperability information. The limitations allowing reverse engineering essentially impose costs on both the rightsholder and the interoperable developer: the rightsholder is confronted with the possibility that his code, including valuable know-how, could be reverse engineered by third parties,[393] whereas interoperable developers must incur substantial reverse engineering costs to obtain the specifications. From a perspective of total welfare, reverse engineering results in wasteful duplication of resources because it may require the competing developer to invest considerable resources to obtain information that the original developer already possesses.[394] Moreover, both the rightsholder and the competitor are confronted with uncertainty. The competitor may be permitted to reverse engineer the program, yet it is uncertain when reverse engineering will yield results (if any). Conversely, the rightsholder cannot precisely anticipate his or her lead-time. Both confronted with costs and uncertainty, the rightsholder and interoperable developer have an incentive to improve their respective positions by licensing the interoperability information.[395] This obviates the competitor's need to invest in reverse engineering, and it prevents exposure of the rightsholder's know-how. In addition, the agreement improves the uncertainty surrounding reverse engineering. Thus, as Czarnota & Hart note:

> The overriding objective of the Commission and the Council was to provide a mechanism whereby it would be more advantageous to both parties to avoid decompilation. The rightholder, by making information

---

393. See section 3.1.2a.

394. Gibson 2005, p. 197; Samuelson & Scotchmer 2002, p. 1588; Schmidtchen & Koboldt 1993, p. 422. The original proposal for the Software Directive, which lacked reverse engineering provisions, called it a 'lengthy, costly and inefficient procedure' (Software Directive, Proposal (1989), §3.14).

395. Van den Bergh 1998, p. 30; Samuelson & Scotchmer 2002, p. 1589; Schmidtchen & Koboldt 1993, p. 422; Sucker 1993, p. 19; Weiser 2003, p. 548.

available for interoperability, would obviate the need for other developers to explore his program in detail.[396]

Whether reverse engineering is sufficient as an incentive for the rightsholder to enter into negotiations with competitors thus depends on whether reverse engineering, as permitted by the Software Directive, imposes sufficient costs on the rightsholder. This, in turn, depends on several factors, including the state of the art in reverse engineering technology, the legal conditions prescribed by the Software Directive, the resources available to the competitor and the complexity of the target program.[397] The interaction between these factors will be examined in section 3.2.2c.

The pivotal condition linking competitors' abilities to decompile with commercial negotiations is in Article 6(1)(b),[398] which restricts the right to decompile to those situations where 'the information necessary to achieve interoperability has not previously been readily available'.[399] Thus, the rightsholder must make the interoperability information 'readily available' in order to prevent decompilation. Article 6(1)(b) neither specifies when the information is considered to be 'readily available' nor how much information should be made available. Rather, this question is left open to court interpretation.[400]

Because the 'readily available' standard serves a pivotal role in stimulating commercial negotiations between the rightsholder and competitors, it is unfortunate that the standard is so unclear. Commentators disagree, for example, on whether the rightsholder may charge a fee for the information for it to be 'readily available'. Dreier believes a licensing fee to be impermissible

396. Czarnota & Hart 1991, p. 80.
397. See also Samuelson & Scotchmer 2002, p. 1585. See also section 2.1.2b.
398. Czarnota & Hart 1991, p. 80; Staffelbach 2003, p. 117.
399. Schmidtchen & Koboldt 1993, p. 422. It has been argued that the 'readily available' condition is superfluous because the general requirement of indispensability in Article 6 already prescribes that competitors exhaust all non-infringing means to obtain the information first (Dreier & Hugenholtz 2006, p. 231). It would arguably be incompatible with the indispensability condition to require the interoperable developer to use any non-infringing means necessary to obtain the interoperability information but not to request the information from the rightsholder. However, the condition as to 'readily available' could also be interpreted as an exception to the general requirement of indispensability: although decompilation must be indispensable, indispensability does not require a specific request to the rightsholder. In this interpretation, the requirement as to 'not readily available' has independent relevance. Moreover, an earlier proposal, which would have required a specific request for the information to the rightsholder, had expressly been rejected. Vinje 1993, p. 64. See also Dreier 1991b, p. 324; Raubenheimer 1996, p. 636; Spoor et al. 2005, p. 605; Staffelbach 2003, p. 115. But see Czarnota & Hart 1991, p. 80. The 'readily available' standard could, however, also serve as a clarification for rightsholders to stimulate the voluntary supply of interoperability information.
400. Czarnota & Hart 1991, p. 78; Gilbert-Macmillan 1993, p. 259. A court would likely require a developer to disclose as much information as is necessary to establish interoperability as defined in the directive's preamble. See Software Directive, Recital 10.

under Article 6(1)(b),[401] whereas according to Czarnota & Hart, a licensing fee is generally acceptable, subject to competition law.[402] The former position appears to be more persuasive. *Ex-post* litigation is at odds with the purpose of Article 6, which aims to provide an *ex-ante* mechanism stimulating private negotiations.[403] Article 6 was designed, in part, to obviate the need for intervention by competition law. If the rightsholder were *required* to accept a certain licensing fee before conducting decompilation, the intervention of a court could become inevitable, thereby reducing legal certainty and rendering the decompilation right virtually toothless. In the absence of a clear standard for 'readily available', however, rightsholders might be tempted to delay negotiations, or to make available only as much information as would be conceivably required by a minimalist interpretation of the 'readily available' standard. Moreover, there is no mechanism in place to monitor whether the reverse engineering provisions actually stimulate firms to make interoperability information 'readily available'. In Chapter 5, it will be demonstrated that in telecommunications similar concerns about delaying tactics in interconnection negotiations have provoked the use of reference offers as well as regulatory oversight. The reference offer prescribes network operators to state in more detail under which conditions they are prepared to offer interconnection, whereas regulatory oversight of interconnection negotiations offers more insights into the actual conclusion of commercial interconnection negotiations.

Note that negotiated supply of interoperability information does not necessarily preclude the rightsholder's ability to exploit lead-time. Because reverse engineering is time consuming and costly, the rightsholder and the competitor might agree on delayed supply of interoperability information – for instance, three years after the program's initial release. Delayed access could benefit both the rightsholder, who can preserve part of its lead-time, and the interoperable developer, who can still expect less of a delay than in the case of reverse engineering. Generally, if the competitor finds the costs of obtaining a license more favorable than the costs required for the decompilation process, she or he will presumably choose to accept the license. If the competitor finds the terms to be less favorable than the decompilation process, she or he should be free to reject the terms and decompile instead, or renegotiate. The parties, therefore, also might agree on a fee for the information, which is presumably related to the competitor's costs of decompilation.

c. Systematic Difficulties

This section identifies several systematic difficulties in the Software Directive's mechanism of negotiations stimulated by reverse engineering: first, the

401. Dreier 1991b, p. 324; Schricker 1999, p. 1122. See also Staffelbach 2003, p. 119.
402. Czarnota & Hart 1991, p. 80.
403. See also: Raubenheimer 1996, p. 636.

mere passive nature of the reverse engineering instruments, which do not guarantee any results; second, the discrepancy between static legal conditions, on the one hand, and a dynamic state of the art in reverse engineering, on the other; and, third, a number of conditions for reverse engineering that may undermine any results.

First, both forms of reverse engineering supported by the Software Directive are merely passive instruments for obtaining interoperability information. Although their overarching objective may be to stimulate active publication of interface information, the reverse engineering provisions merely remove legal barriers to obtaining this information at the competitors' expense. There is no guarantee that black-box testing or decompilation will actually yield any results, and there is no mechanism in place to safeguard such results should reverse engineering prove impossible or insufficient to obtain access to interface specifications. Indeed, the provision is intended as a 'last resort' or a 'safety valve' to obtain interoperability information.[404] Thus, Article 6 does not impose on the rightsholder an *active duty* to provide interoperability information, and it, therefore, cannot be invoked to force a rightsholder to disclose his or her interface information.[405]

Second, as noted, the Software Directive's reverse engineering provisions – and particularly the decompilation provision – are subject to various conditions. These conditions can complicate a process that is already uncertain of success. Some commentators, notably Czarnota & Hart, express the view that the various conditions in Article 6 of the Software Directive represent a carefully constructed balance of interests, which would be disrupted if conditions were changed or repealed in isolation.[406] One might find support for this view considering the fact that parties supporting and opposing reverse engineering were well represented during the drafting of this provision, while the resulting provision is, indeed, regarded as a compromise between these groups.[407] Nonetheless, this view does not appear persuasive. The effects of a rule permitting reverse engineering are highly dependant on the state of the art of reverse engineering technology, which is anything but static. As reverse engineering technology progresses, so does the ease by which competitors can obtain access to a rightsholder's interface information and know-how.[408] The conditions for lawful reverse engineering in Article 6 may influence the ultimate effect of reverse engineering; however,

404. Software Directive, Amended Proposal (1990), 10; Czarnota & Hart 1991, p. 76; Dommering 1992, p. 88.
405. See also section 3.1.2c. In *Microsoft Decision* (European Commission 2004), §747. The Commission considered forced disclosure through competition law 'consistent' with the purpose of Article 6. See also section 4.1.2d. See also *Pendula* (Voorzieningenrechter Rechtbank Leeuwarden 2005) (with case comment by Koelman).
406. Czarnota & Hart 1991, p. 76.
407. Bartmann 2005, p. 125; Cornish 1993, p. 197; European Commission 2000, p. 20.
408. Bartmann 2005, p. 125; Samuelson et al. 1994, p. 2341.

the conditions being rigid[409] and static and the state of the art being dynamic, these conditions cannot represent a sustainable balance of interests. Although some of the conditions in Article 6 could conceivably be interpreted by a court in such a way as to compensate for the evolving state of the art in reverse engineering technology, the legislative history reveals no basis for such 'dynamic interpretation'. Moreover, several of the conditions in Article 6 appear redundant, too complex or too restrictive, and therefore, cannot contribute to a delicate balance of interests.[410]

Third, several particular conditions further undermine the effectiveness of the decompilation limitation. For instance, an issue not explicitly addressed by Article 6 is the extent to which any protected expression may be used in the interoperable program. To the extent that decompiled interface specifications are copyrightable, the rightsholder would normally be able to prohibit their inclusion in the interoperable developer's code.[411] This would obviously undermine the very purpose of the right to decompile.[412] Yet, Article 6 provides for no express authorization to use such protected expression.[413] Article 6 only explicitly permits reproduction of the target program's code 'to *obtain* [access to] the information necessary to achieve the interoperability [emphasis added]', not to *use* protected expression in the interoperable program. Because it is thus unclear whether protected expression in interfaces can be used after their extraction by decompilation,[414] the possibility that interface information might indeed constitute copyrightable subject matter, which is left open in the Software Directive,[415] is even more problematic. The instruments regarding use and access do not appear to be properly aligned. However, as noted, the absence of an express right to use any decompiled expression necessary for interoperability could also indicate that interface specifications are not considered to constitute original expression.[416]

Furthermore, the phrase 'to achieve the interoperability of an independently created program *with other programs* [emphasis added]' in Article 6 indicates that decompilation may be performed for interoperability with any (complementary or competing) *program*.[417] However, there is no explicit reference to data or hardware interfaces, even though such interfaces can prove crucial to full interoperability.[418]

409. See also Samuelson 1994, p. 292.
410. Stuurman 1995, p. 449.
411. See also section 3.1.1.
412. Staffelbach 2003, p. 130.
413. Band et al. 1992, p. 142; Bartmann 2005, p. 124; Czarnota & Hart 1991, p. 38; Dreier 1991a, p. 583; Koelman 2006, p. 826; Palmer & Vinje 1992. But see Haberstumpf 1993, p. 163; Schelven & Struik 1995, p. 30.
414. Bartmann 2005, p. 125; Dreier 1991a, p. 583.
415. See section 3.2.1.
416. See section 3.2.1a.
417. Czarnota & Hart 1991, p. 78; Dreier 1991a, p. 582; Dreier 1991b, p. 325; Dreier & Schulze 2004, p. 895; Sucker 1993, p. 17; Vinje 1991, p. 5; Vinje 1993, p. 61.
418. Ahn 1999, p. 245; Schulte 1992, p. 654.

Article 6(1)(a) limits the right to decompile to 'a licensee or another person having a right to use a copy of the program, or on their behalf by a person authorized to do so'.[419] This is not normally a prerequisite for copyright limitations; indeed, the purpose of most limitations is to allow certain use in the absence of a license. By expressly requiring a right to use the program, Article 6(1)(a) introduces the theoretical possibility to restrict decompilation by refusing to license the program altogether.[420] The practical effect of this condition appears to be negligible, however, as competitors can typically purchase a 'shrink-wrap license'.[421]

In conjunction with the more contemporary or relative challenges, discussed in section 3.2.2d, these systematic weaknesses undermine the effectiveness of the directive's decompilation provision as a tool to facilitate interoperability.

d. Current Challenges

Thus far, reverse engineering has not proven an effective instrument to stimulate rightsholders to negotiate supply of their programs' interoperability information. The target programs have proven too complex to reverse engineer, their interface specifications have been subject to change, and the conditions for reverse engineering appear too restrictive.[422]

In the *Microsoft* case, which is further discussed in Chapter 4, the Commission and the General Court of the European Union (GC) observed that attempts to reverse engineer the interface specifications of the Windows operating system had failed because of the complexity of the program.[423] A related threat was the possibility for the rightsholder to regularly change the interface specifications.[424] Although there may be legitimate reasons for such changes,[425] they could also undermine the effectiveness of reverse engineering because it requires the process to be repeated.[426]

In the current state of the art, in which reverse engineering is still extremely difficult, numerous conditions in Article 6 also appear too restrictive.

419. See also *Peregrine v. Exa* (District Court The Hague 2002), §3.19. See also Spoor et al. 2005, p. 605.
420. Bay 1993, p. 186. See also Dreier & Schulze 2004, p. 893.
421. van Rooijen 2007b, p. 134.
422. European Commission 2004b, §2.2.1.3; Stuurman 1995, p. 449. The permissibility of reverse engineering is broader in US copyright law. See Samuelson 1994, p. 288.
423. *Microsoft Decision* (European Commission 2004), §685. See also Cifuentes 2001; Lemley & McGowan 1998, p. 529; Mayrhauser & Vans 1994.
424. *Microsoft Decision* (European Commission 2004), §686; Lemley & McGowan 1998, p. 529.
425. Hovenkamp et al. 2002–2007, §12.3e.
426. See Software Directive, Amended Proposal (1990), 12 (noting that in case of a change in interface specifications, the interoperable developer would be permitted to repeat the reverse engineering process 'any number of times'). See also Czarnota & Hart 1991, p. 187; Sucker 1993, p. 18.

For instance, currently, it may be too restrictive to prohibit interoperable developers from sharing the fruits of their reverse engineering efforts – as Article 6(2)(b) does. This effectively prevents multiple competitors from joining their reverse engineering efforts and instead leaves reverse engineering as a viable option only to very large developers.[427] If a certain rightsholder's interfaces have emerged as the *de-facto* standard by tipping of the market, there may well be multiple competitors requiring access to the rightsholder's interfaces, and they might have an interest in sharing this information for the development of their respective programs. If competitors were allowed to share this information, the effective lead-time of the rightsholder would ultimately depend on the time required by the most efficient reverse engineer, which could then recoup its investments in reverse engineering by licensing obtained information to other competitors. In other words, lifting this condition would enable a market for decompilation to emerge.[428] As decompilation technology advances and becomes more widely deployed, there may be less need to share the information with third parties. Furthermore, as will be observed in Chapter 4, competition law also anticipates cooperation between competitors in order to duplicate a dominant competitor's facilities.

Several conditions, such as the need to limit reverse engineering to those parts of the target program related to interoperability (Article 6(1)(c)) and the safeguard against impediment of the rightsholder's 'normal exploitation' (Article 6(3)), further undermine the overarching purpose of the decompilation provision, which is to impose costs on the rightsholder in order to stimulate private negotiations (see section 3.2.2b). If these conditions were literally complied with, the risk of exposure of the rightsholder's know-how would be limited considerably, thus reducing her or his incentive to negotiate the supply of interoperability information in order to preempt decompilation.

Article 6 does not expressly provide for a right to decompile for the purpose of creating future programs.[429] This could prove a substantial constraint in network markets because the success of a standard often depends on *ex-ante* expectations.[430] Competitors may thus need to initiate reverse engineering of a particular program's interfaces if they expect it to emerge as a *de-facto* standard even before they have a sufficiently concrete program that requires interoperability with that standard.

Other conditions in Article 6 further complicate successful decompilation. For instance, the burden of proof for all conditions of lawful decompilation lies with the decompiler,[431] even if it is clearly difficult for the decompiler to prove that, for instance, the interoperability information had *not* been made available

427. Ahn 1999, p. 248, note 831. See also Bently 2006, p. 232; Czarnota & Hart 1991, p. 81; Samuelson & Scotchmer 2002, p. 1586; Walter et al. 2001, p. 226.
428. Van den Bergh 1998, p. 30; Schmidtchen & Koboldt 1993, p. 423.
429. Walter et al. 2001, p. 228.
430. See section 2.2.2c.
431. Czarnota & Hart 1991, p. 77; Verstrynge 1993, p. 8.

to him or her. If, indeed, the purpose of this subsection were to encourage rightsholders to make the information available in advance, it would have been consistent to require the rightsholder to prove that she or he *had* in fact made the information available prior to the – allegedly unlawful – decompilation by the interoperable developer.[432]

Article 6(1)(c) requires that the decompilation process be limited to the parts of the program that relate to interoperability.[433] This can be problematic because it presumes that the engineer has knowledge of the location of such parts in the object code prior to decompilation.[434] Yet, the very purpose of decompilation is to gain an understanding of (the structure of) that object code. Thus, if prior black-box testing has not revealed the approximate location of the relevant interfaces,[435] this condition will be difficult to meet, and should normally not apply.[436]

In sum, technical difficulties as well as restrictive conditions for reverse engineering significantly limit competitors' abilities to access the rightsholder's interoperability information. This, in turn, negatively affects the ability of the reverse engineering provisions to serve as an incentive for negotiations. The Software Directive's mechanism for reverse engineering may, therefore, in theory be a suitable *ex-ante* instrument to balance openness and control of interface information, but a number of issues have been identified that need to be revolved. This will be further explored in Chapters 5 and 6.

3.3. CONCLUSION

Chapter 2 indicated a need for a balance between a developer's ability to control its computer program's interface specifications and competitors' abilities to access and use those specifications through openness thereof. This chapter, therefore, has explored how copyright protection of computer programs affects such control (section 3.1) and openness (section 3.2) of interface specifications, whether this regime strikes a meaningful balance between control and openness of interface specifications and whether it provides for sufficient certainty as an *ex-ante* instrument.

---

432. See also section 6.3.2a.
433. See also Dreier 1991a, p. 582; Staffelbach 2003, p. 122.
434. Meyer & Colombe 1990a. But see, for example, *Creative v. Aztech* (Singapore Court of Appeal 1996), §54.
435. Czarnota & Hart 1991, p. 80; Dommering 1992, p. 88; Staffelbach 2003, pp. 72, 114, 123; Sucker 1993, p. 19; Walter et al. 2001, p. 220.
436. Band & Katoh 1995, p. 252; Dreier & Hugenholtz 2006, p. 231; Schricker 1999, p. 1122; Walter et al. 2001, p. 224. See also *Sega v. Accolade* (US Court of Appeals, Ninth Circuit 1992), 1526 (copying of the entire target program is necessary for the reverse engineering process). See also Goldstein 1993, p. 212; Samuelson 2001, p. 13.

Control of interface specifications is caused by a combination of factors. *Use* of interface specifications may directly be controlled by the rightsholder if the interface specifications constitute copyrightable subject matter. Because copyright law protects computer programs at the level of their written program code, of which interface specifications form a part, these specifications might not be excluded from protection *per-se*. Interface specifications could also meet the strongly objectified originality threshold as applied to software. Furthermore, the free use of interface specifications is impeded by copyright's failure to substantially consider needs to use possibly protected subject matter in the interest of standardization – such as a need to use interface specifications for interoperability. Thus, copyright's protection of functional expression and its failure to consider standardization may impede the free use of interface specifications, which could – in the absence of specific provisions to the contrary – enable the rightsholder to prevent interoperable program development. Moreover, the specifications are not readily *accessible* from the distributed program as they are embedded in its unreadable object code. Copyright law, through a broad reproduction right, limits competitors' abilities to reverse engineer this object code, which could otherwise allow them to access the interoperability information contained therein. In sum, copyright protection of computer programs may confer some control over the use of interface specifications as well as control over access to these specifications.

Openness of interface information is to be achieved through some instruments provided for by the Software Directive, with, however, little success. The Software Directive does not explicitly exclude interface specifications from protection, and it does not provide for a limitation to expressly permit their unauthorized use. Because of copyright's general failure to balance the interests of original expression, on the one hand, and standardized expression, on the other, it may well be difficult to strike a meaningful balance between openness and control of interface specifications in copyright law through direct protection (e.g., subject matter, scope of protection and limitations). This would suggest a preference for striking this balance primarily by regulating access to interface specifications instead (*infra*). Furthermore, the use of open norms on the copyrightability of interface specifications and the lack of a substantial body of case law interpreting these norms impede legal certainty. This primarily affects interoperable developers because, in addition to the costs of obtaining access to these specifications (see *infra*), they cannot be certain whether their use is permitted without authorization.

Access to interface specifications is addressed by limitations that provide for a limited possibility to reverse engineer the rightsholder's computer program in order to achieve interoperability. The primary purpose of these provisions is to stimulate both parties to negotiate. Because reverse engineering requires substantial investments in time and resources and is limited by legal conditions, the rightsholder's initial control over access to interface information (*supra*) is not immediately compromised: control is retained until competitors have successfully managed to reverse engineer the information. This suggests that, indeed, a balance can be struck between control and openness of interface information. However, it has been demonstrated that these provisions pose various difficulties, which can undermine their effectiveness. In addition to various other systematic difficulties, Article 6 of the directive, which contains the decompilation right, fails to take account of the evolving state of the art in decompilation technology. Because the state of the art substantially affects the practical effect of the limitation permitting decompilation, the balance currently fixed by the conditions in these provisions cannot remain valid. Moreover, the conditions may well be too restrictive in the current state of the art. This suggests a need to monitor the state of the art in reverse engineering and to apply its conditions in a more flexible manner in accordance with that state of the art. Such a monitoring mechanism should also shed light on the actual voluntary conclusion of interoperability agreements and, thereby, on the effectiveness of the reverse engineering provisions.

Through its failure to provide for sufficient openness of interface specifications, copyright law can thus impede interoperability between computer programs. By essentially protecting interface specifications under the same regime as the computer program in general – that is, under the idea/expression dichotomy and the requirement of originality, and for the same term of protection – the directive fails to explicitly recognize that, as a result of network effects and standardization, the optimal balance between openness and control of interface specifications may well be different from that of the program at large. Chapter 5 will examine how issues similar to these have been addressed by two other legal regimes concerned with interconnection: design protection and telecommunications law. First, Chapter 4 will examine the *ex-post* competition approach to interoperability.

Chapter 4
Competition Law

Chapter 3 reviewed the *ex-ante* copyright approach to interoperability in computer programs. It demonstrated that the current instruments in European copyright law largely fail to strike a meaningful balance between openness and control of interface information, which, therefore, conflicts with the normative framework suggested in Chapter 2. In addition to this *ex-ante* approach, Chapter 2 already identified a second approach, namely, *ex-post* application of competition laws, which is the focus of the present chapter. Exercising control over interface specifications by a dominant firm may amount to abusive behavior, in which case competition law could be applied to force openness of such information. In comparison to an *ex-ante* approach, competition law has one principal advantage and one principal disadvantage. On the one hand, the competition authority reviews the subject firm's behavior case-by-case and *ex-post* and is, therefore, theoretically in a better position to Judge whether, in the particular case, openness or control of interface specifications is more likely to contribute to innovation and competition. On the other hand, this flexibility reduces the certainty for innovators as to their ability to recoup investments, and for others as regards their ability to compete with the innovator. This may adversely affect innovation and competition.

The twofold purpose of the present chapter is based on these two issues. First, with respect to the instrumental trade-off between an *ex-ante* and an *ex-post* approach to interoperability, section 4.1 demonstrates that, if the *ex-ante* copyright regime strikes a reasonable balance between openness and control of interface specifications, there are strong arguments not to interfere with this balance through *ex-post* competition law. It will be demonstrated that this need for deference to intellectual property rights by competition laws has not yet been extended to copyright's balancing of interface specifications

(Chapter 3). Section 4.1 will argue, however, that the need for deference also applies to copyright's internal approach to balancing openness and control of interoperability information, provided that its shortcomings – which were identified in Chapter 3 – be duly addressed (relevant recommendations are presented in Chapter 6).

Having made the (instrumental) case for limited application of competition rules in addition to an *ex-ante* copyright regime, section 4.2 focuses on the substantive side of the application of competition law to control interface specifications. It demonstrates that competition law is not actually applied with the flexibility it was designed for, and, due in part to this rigidity, does not adequately balance openness versus control of interface information. To that end, it applies the case law on refusals to supply – and particularly refusals to license intellectual property rights – interface specifications. This analysis reveals that competition law fails to expressly balance the benefits of competition in and competition for the market. As already noted in Chapter 2, both forms of competition may be welfare enhancing in a market characterized by strong network effects. Moreover, competition law appears to inadequately analyze incentives to innovate through its new-product test, which, when applied to interface specifications, risks ignoring the *ex-post* value of interface specifications for interoperability and the effects of interoperability on innovation. Section 4.3 concludes.

4.1. COMPETITION LAW AND THE SOFTWARE DIRECTIVE

This section examines the trade-off between the *ex-ante* copyright approach to addressing interoperability, which was studied in Chapter 3, and an *ex-post* competition approach. The preamble of the Software Directive suggests that, in addition to its reverse engineering provisions, competition law could be applicable should a dominant supplier refuse to make interface information available. The copyright control over interface information could thus become subject to competition law scrutiny. As already observed, the directive's reference to competition law predates its reverse engineering provisions.[437] The 17th recital states:

> The provisions of this Directive are without prejudice to the application of the competition rules under Articles [101] and [102] of the Treaty if a dominant supplier refuses to make information available which is necessary for inter-operability as defined in this Directive.

The relationship between the Software Directive's reverse engineering provisions and the competition rules in the Treaty on the Functioning of the

437. See section 3.2.2a.

European Union (TFEU) is, however, more complex than suggested by this recital. The following sections examine the relationship between copyright and competition law from a European Union (EU) law (section 4.1.1) and from a more substantive perspective (section 4.1.2). Section 4.1.3 concludes that, in the presence of an adequate *ex-ante* mechanism in copyright law, balancing openness and control of interface specifications, competition law should only have a limited additional role.

4.1.1. EU Law Perspective

The EU law perspective focuses on the relationship between national intellectual property rights and the TFEU's competition *laws*, rather than their substance or effects. A conflict between competition law and copyright law may arise if competition law is applied to a refusal to supply interface specifications of copyrighted software. This conflict is not expressly resolved in the TFEU.[438]

Within the EU, two conflicting principles complicate the legal relationship between the Software Directive and the competition rules of the TFEU. On the one hand, European competition law, embedded in the TFEU, is necessarily superior to the Software Directive, which is secondary EU legislation. Thus, the directive, much less its implementations in the Member States' national laws, cannot override the TFEU's competition rules. In principle, therefore, Article 102 applies regardless of the directive's 17th recital and any limitations contained therein. Recital 17 would have a mere declaratory purpose.[439]

On the other hand, Article 345 (ex 295) of the TFEU provides that '[t]his Treaty shall in no way prejudice the rules in Member States governing the system of property ownership'. In *Consten and Grundig v. European Commission*, the European Court of Justice (ECJ) implicitly applied Article 345 to intellectual property rights.[440] Consequently, the TFEU's competition rules cannot normally interfere in the (intellectual) property allocation determined by (the laws of) the Member States. This principle has prompted courts to invoke the existence/exercise doctrine, which originated from case law on the free movement of goods within the Communities,[441] in refusals to license

438. Schovsbo 1998, p. 523.
439. Haratsch et al. 2006, p. 130. In the *Microsoft* case, the argument was advanced that the application of Article 102 depends on the directive's definition of *interoperability*. See *Microsoft Decision* (European Commission 2004), §749; *Microsoft* (GC 2007), §211. On appeal, the GC noted that the Software Directive's definition of *interoperability* cannot override the application of competition laws. *Microsoft* (GC 2007), §227. See also Software Directive, Proposal (1989), 16; Stuurman 1995, p. 449; Vinje 1993, p. 44.
440. *Consten and Grundig v. European Commission* (ECJ 1966), 345; Korah 2006, p. 3; Sucker 1993, p. 21.
441. Craig & de Búrca 2003, p. 1108; Govaere 1996, pp. 62, 112; Schovsbo 1998, p. 520.

intellectual property rights. According to this doctrine, the existence – or the specific subject matter[442] – of intellectual property rights, could, in accordance with Article 345 of the TFEU, not be reviewed by European courts.[443] However, notwithstanding the *existence* of an intellectual property right, its *exercise* could prove anticompetitive in certain cases and thus be subject to competition law scrutiny.[444] Applying the existence/exercise doctrine, the ECJ in *Volvo v. Veng* held that Volvo's reliance on its design rights in spare parts to prevent garages from marketing those parts for repair purposes could not, by itself, constitute abusive behavior. However, in accordance with Article 345, the exercise of these rights could, under certain, additional circumstances, constitute an abuse.[445]

There are, however, two caveats to the application of Article 345 to the Software Directive. First, it is questionable whether Article 345 should apply to intellectual property rights in the first place, as the original rationale of the article appears to have been merely to safeguard Member States' freedom to opt for public or private ownership of coal and steel enterprises. This has little to do with the allocation of intellectual property rights.[446] Second, Article 345 should arguably not apply to harmonized intellectual property rights,[447] such as copyright for computer programs as harmonized by the Software Directive, as such harmonized intellectual property rights have not been defined by the Member States' national legislators.

Moreover, the distinction between the existence and exercise of an intellectual property right is somewhat artificial.[448] As Korah observes, 'the existence of a right comprises all the ways in which it may be exercised'.[449] The ECJ's rather abstract definition of the specific subject matter of different intellectual property rights is of little help in distinguishing between the existence and exercise of these rights in individual cases.[450] In the area where tensions between intellectual property rights and competition law are most apparent – namely, where a rightsholder refuses to license an intellectual property right to a competitor – the ECJ currently applies a more elaborate *exceptional circumstances* test. This test is examined in some detail and applied to a refusal to provide interface information in section 4.2.

The need for a more elaborate test already indicates that tensions between intellectual property rights and competition rules are difficult to resolve by

442. Bath 2002, p. 138; Schovsbo 1998, p. 520.
443. Turney 2005, §28.
444. Dolmans et al. 2007, p. 112; Whish 2003, p. 758.
445. See also sections 4.2.1c and 5.1.
446. Hugenholtz et al. 2006, p. 8; Vinje 1992, p. 398. See also Calliess & Blanke 2002, p. 2455; Cornish & Llewellyn 2007, p. 741, note 26.
447. Hugenholtz et al. 2006, p. 14; Walter et al. 2001, p. 53.
448. Craig & de Búrca 2003, p. 1119; Govaere 1996, pp. 70, 113.
449. Korah 2006, p. 3.
450. On the concept of specific subject matter, see Govaere 1996, p. 79.

simply declaring one as superior to the other.[451] The application of competition law should be based on a comprehensive assessment of all the relevant circumstances.[452] In order to get a full picture, these circumstances necessarily include any relevant intellectual property rights. This important aspect of the relationship between the two laws is largely ignored in the simple assessment under the EU law approach.[453]

4.1.2. Economic Perspective

In this section, it will be demonstrated that, from a more substantive perspective, intellectual property rights and competition laws – whether national or EU rights – essentially serve complementary purposes (section 4.1.2a), albeit with different instruments (section 4.1.2b). Competition law interference with intellectual property rights is, therefore, justified only in exceptional cases. It shall be examined how, according to these insights, tensions between copyright law and competition law must be resolved (section 4.1.2c), in particular with respect to control over standards and interface specifications (section 4.1.2d).

a. Substantive: Complementary Goals

Both intellectual property rights and competition laws are essentially concerned with promoting consumer welfare by stimulating and balancing static efficiency (price competition) and dynamic efficiency (innovation). They, therefore, largely serve complementary purposes, although several nuances can be pointed out.

Competition laws are concerned with safeguarding the competitive process.[454] The competitive process generally stimulates both static and dynamic efficiency:[455] as firms compete for customers, they are forced not only to reduce costs and price, which contributes to an optimal dissemination of goods and services among consumers (static efficiency),[456] but also to innovate, or to replace older technologies by newer ones (dynamic efficiency).[457] Where the competitive process is structurally harmed – for

---

451. See also Turney 2005, §65.
452. Larouche 2000, p. 122.
453. Nonetheless, the conceptual distinction between the existence of rights and their exercise remains relevant in the scope of application of competition law, as competition law only interferes in the exercise of rights (abuse) and not in mere possession of market power (existence). See section 5.2.2a.
454. See, for example, *Continental Can* (ECJ 1973), §25.
455. Craig & de Búrca 2003, p. 936; Drexl et al. 2006, §6; European Commission 2005, §4; Merges et al. 2003, p. 989; Whish 2003, pp. 3, 4.
456. Striving for lower costs (static efficiency) also leads to productive efficiency, or the creation of goods using the fewest possible resources. Dommering et al. 2001b, p. 17.
457. Korah 2006, p. 135. See also section 2.2.4.

instance, through a dominant firm's refusal to supply essential resources to other firms – competition law interferes, for example, by forcing a dominant firm to supply to other firms. Competition laws thus safeguard the competitive process, *inter alia*, by supervising firms' exercise of proprietary control over their respective resources.[458] In short, competition law's ultimate purpose is to maximize consumer welfare by safeguarding the competitive process, which, in turn, should stimulate a balanced mix of static and dynamic efficiency.[459]

Intellectual property rights are similarly concerned with stimulating and balancing static and dynamic efficiency. An intellectual property right provides the rightsholder with a temporary right of exclusivity, during which she or he can recoup investments in innovation. This, in turn, should enable and encourage rightsholders to innovate, and thus stimulates dynamic efficiency. However, this exclusivity enables the rightsholder to increase the price above the marginal costs of production, which impedes the dissemination of the innovation. Moreover, it enables the innovator to preclude any follow-on innovation, or innovation that relies on the protected subject matter. The dynamic efficiency, stimulated by the exclusivity awarded by intellectual property rights, thus conflicts with the purpose of stimulating static efficiency and follow-on innovation. Because the duration of the exclusivity period is limited, however, intellectual property rights ensure that, upon expiration of this right, competition and follow-on innovation are fully reinstated.[460] Thus, intellectual property rights, through a limited term and scope of protection, similarly balance the interests of, on the one hand, dynamic efficiency, and on the other hand, static efficiency as well as follow-on innovation.[461]

It can be concluded that competition and intellectual property laws are complementary regimes: the rationale of both competition law and intellectual property rights is to promote consumer welfare by stimulating a balanced mix of static and dynamic efficiency.[462] The competitive process, safeguarded by competition laws, accomplishes this goal by *stimulating* firms to innovate and price lower, and, where necessary, by sanctioning anticompetitive behavior *ex-post*. Intellectual property laws accomplish this goal by *enabling* firms to recoup their investments in innovation during a temporary period of exclusivity, granted *ex-ante*.[463] As the European Commission has observed:

> Intellectual property rights promote dynamic competition by encouraging undertakings to invest in developing new or improved products and processes. So does competition by putting pressure on undertakings to

458. Weber Waller 2008, p. 2.
459. Katz & Shelanski 2005, p. 2. On different interpretations of *consumer welfare*, see Drexl 2004, p. 803; Katz & Shelanski 2007, p. 7; Turney 2005, §11.
460. See also section 2.2.4.
461. Kaufmann 1982, p. 217; Scotchmer 2004, p. 114; Valkonen & White 2007, p. 374.
462. Dreier 2001, p. 312; Drexl 2004, p. 791; Hovenkamp et al. 2002–2007, p. 1.3a; Whish 2003, p. 734.
463. Ullrich 2001, p. 373.

> innovate. Therefore, both intellectual property rights and competition are necessary to promote innovation and ensure a competitive exploitation thereof.[464]

This modern view of the relation between competition and intellectual property laws is to be contrasted with the now largely obsolete view of two regimes in conflict with each other. According to the latter view, intellectual property law creates monopolies, whereas competition law aims to prevent monopolies.[465] However, this seemingly obvious conflict is incorrect. Competition laws do not *prohibit* monopolies; rather, they sanction *abuse* of monopoly power.[466] Monopoly power itself may well be the result of superior business acumen. Competition law should not be concerned with sanctioning the winner of the competitive process; this is what drives competition in the first place.[467] In other words, competition law should not 'remove the jackpot from the lottery'.[468] However, the abuse of monopoly power to structurally impede competition *is* a cause of concern.

Moreover, intellectual property rights, for their part, do not *create* monopolies: the limited exclusivity granted by these rights generally allows for ample competition within the same market and, therefore, does not generally give rise to a monopoly in the (entire) market.[469] For example, the copyright in a computer program may generally confer some market power as it enables the rightsholder to prevent copying of that program,[470] but it does not lead to *substantial* market power, as the market normally allows for numerous competing computer programs. Thus, as the ECJ recognized in *Deutsche Grammophon*,[471] mere ownership of an intellectual property right does not give rise to a finding of a dominant position; a dominant position, instead, must be established by showing a lack of sufficient competitive restraints from other suppliers.

Due to their complementary goals, competition law interference with intellectual property law is thus normally unnecessary.[472] As A-G Jacobs observed in *Bronner*:

> Where such exclusive [copy]rights are granted for a limited period, that in itself involves a balancing of the interest in free competition with

---

464. European Commission 2004a, p. 7.
465. Korah 2006, p. 1; Landes & Posner 2003, p. 372; Lévêque & Méniere 2004, p. 82; Merges et al. 2003, p. 992; US Department of Justice & Federal Trade Commission 2007; Ullrich 2001, p. 365.
466. See section 4.2.1a.
467. Craig & de Búrca 2003, p. 992. See also *Trinko* (US Supreme Court 2004), 407.
468. Ullrich 2001, p. 382.
469. Bechtold 2007, p. 68; Drexl et al. 2006, §6; Lévêque & Méniere 2004, p. 83; Merges et al. 2003, p. 997; *Magill* (ECJ 1995), §46. See also *Illinois Tool Works v. Independent Ink* (US Supreme Court 2006).
470. The intellectual property right may not confer any market power if the protected subject matter fails to attract any demand. Drexl 2008, p. 4.
471. *Deutsche Grammophon* (ECJ 1971), §16, §17. See also *Magill* (ECJ 1995), §46; *Sirena* (ECJ 1971), §16. See also Drexl 2008, p. 3; Govaere 1996, p. 111.
472. Dolmans et al. 2007, p. 114; Schovsbo 1998, p. 523.

that of providing an incentive for research and development and for creativity.[473]

Rather, it should be assumed that intellectual property laws are tailored to serve their intended purpose of stimulating innovation while leaving ample room for competition. Whereas A-G Jacobs' reference to the limited duration of intellectual property rights is one example of this principle,[474] intellectual property rights contain other, sometimes more relevant limitations to their scope.[475] For instance, copyright protection generally does not extend to the functionality of the computer program, which enables others to duplicate this functionality as long as their expression thereof does not infringe.[476] Similarly, one can often 'invent around' a patent to compete with the patent holder in the same market.[477] As observed, in Chapter 3, the primary purpose of the Software Directive's reverse engineering provisions is to encourage innovation in computer software by enabling recoupment of the underlying investments, while at the same time encouraging competition, in particular by enabling competitors to create interoperable programs by discovering the original program's interface specifications. Thus, the anticompetitive problems caused by withholding interface information have, to some extent, been internalized in software copyright law.[478] Similarly, European design protection laws are limited in scope to prevent protection of interconnections, which would have enabled the rightsholder to control the markets for complementary products.[479] These limitations of the scope of design protection laws are further examined in Chapter 5.

However, not all, or even most, intellectual property rights are indeed curtailed to allow for sufficient competition, while existing limitations may prove insufficient.[480] In other words, not all intellectual property rights strike an adequate balance between innovation and competition. This is due in part to the variety of objectives that intellectual property rights fulfill; serving consumer welfare is only one of those objectives.[481] Many continental European copyright systems, for instance, are not primarily rooted in economic theory.[482]

---

473. Opinion A-G Jacobs in *Bronner* (ECJ 1998), §62. See also Derclaye 2003, p. 700. But see Ritter 2005, p. 288.
474. See also Dreier 2001, p. 305; Turney 2005, p. 181.
475. Cotter 1999, p. 230; Dreier 2001, p. 307; Geiger 2008, p. 467; Hovenkamp et al. 2002–2007, p. 1.3.
476. See section 3.1.1a.
477. Drexl et al. 2006, §15, §22; Koelman 2006, p. 825.
478. See also Bay 1993, p. 186; Dreier & Schulze 2004, p. 893; Koelman 2006, p. 826; van Rooijen 2007b, p. 132; Schovsbo 1998, p. 531; Sucker 1993, p. 21.
479. See, generally, Schovsbo 1998.
480. Turney 2005, §3.
481. Grosheide 1986, p. 128.
482. Ullrich 2001, p. 372. See also European Commission 1988, §5.2.10 ('It has also been claimed that "proprietary standards" distort competition in the software markets, but the degree of distortion is difficult to measure because data about software activities are notoriously poor').

Indeed, A-G Jacobs' reference to the limited term of copyright protection (*supra*) is arguably one example of a particularly ill-suited balancing act: the general term of copyright protection is seventy years,[483] which, in many industries, exceeds the commercial life of the protected subject matter by a considerable margin.[484] Moreover, the Software Directive's reverse engineering provisions, discussed in some detail in Chapter 3, although clearly instituted for competition considerations, appear inadequate to allow for sufficient competition.[485]

Competition law, for its part, has been applied not only to stimulate consumer welfare but also to achieve other (policy) objectives. Some of these objectives can squarely interfere with the interests of stimulating welfare through safeguarding the competitive process. For instance, competition law has in the past been applied to protect smaller, less efficient firms against competition from larger firms.[486]

Indeed, although, from an economic perspective, both intellectual property rights and competition rules should aim to stimulate and balance static and dynamic efficiency, there has been a steady expansion of intellectual property rights without due regard to economic necessity. Competition policy has much more explicitly been based on economic principles, although it has arguably focused somewhat more on price and output competition (static efficiency) than on dynamic efficiency.[487] This can create a *substantive tension* between intellectual property rights and competition rules in particular instances.

b. Instrumental: *ex-ante* versus *ex-post*

Although the purpose of intellectual property rights and competition laws should thus be largely complementary, their respective instruments differ. Intellectual property rights determine in advance (*ex-ante*) what is protected and under which conditions. This should provide the *certainty* to potential innovators that they can recoup their investments in innovation, but, because of a lack of flexibility, introduces the risk that the balance struck *ex-ante* produces suboptimal outcomes in particular instances.[488] By contrast, competition rules enable a competition authority to review a firm's behavior case-by-case and after-the-fact (*ex-post*)[489] and to impose tailor-made remedies.

---

483. Term Directive, Article 1.
484. Kroes 2008. See also section 3.1.1a.
485. See section 3.2.2.
486. Korah 2006, p. 135; Turney 2005; Whish 2003, p. 19.
487. Drexl 2008, p. 13; Lévêque & Méniere 2004, p. 85. See also Shelanski & Sidak 2001, p. 11.
488. Dolmans et al. 2007, p. 136; Drexl 2008, p. 13; Drexl et al. 2006, §7B, §12; Kovacic & Reindl 2005, p. 1065.
489. Ullrich 2001, p. 383.

This provides the authority with the *flexibility* to take all circumstances into account.[490] Because the competition authority is armed with significantly more information about each individual case than the *ex-ante* legislator,[491] the authority is, in theory, able to strike a more accurate balance between static and dynamic efficiency: it can consider the effects of control over subject matter, or consider such control in context. However, this flexibility necessarily reduces the very certainty that intellectual property rights aim to provide to their rightsholders, and, thereby, the very incentives to innovate.[492] Moreover, should remedies be imposed that stretch far into the future,[493] the information advantage is largely lost.

Thus, innovation requires sufficient certainty as to the ability to recoup the underlying investments. Such certainty clearly cannot be created by an *ex-post* assessment of whether a particular intellectual creation was, in retrospect, worth protecting but rather must be established *ex-ante*. The legislator has provided for such certainty in the form of intellectual property rights. If the certainty of exclusivity instituted by these rights were fully subject to *ex-post* review by competition law, the very purpose of stimulating dynamic efficiency through a sufficiently certain, *ex-ante* right of exclusivity would be undermined. This would conflict with both intellectual property rights and competition laws, which both aim to stimulate innovation. Thus, in view of the complementarity of intellectual property rights and competition laws, there is a strong argument for limited *ex-post* interference with intellectual property rights that have already been curtailed *ex-ante*.[494] It follows that the competition authority should not conduct a full review of the optimal balance between static and dynamic efficiency in any given case but, instead, must provide some deference to the *ex-ante* balance already established within intellectual property rights by intervening only in exceptional cases. The scope of the intellectual property right as expressly granted by the legislator is, therefore, to some extent relevant in the application of competition law.[495]

Naturally, this deference to the balance struck within intellectual property rights is in some tension with the flexible approach of competition rules. There is a certain rigidity involved because the presence of an(y) intellectual property right automatically prevents the competition authority from scrutinizing the balance between static and dynamic efficiency already struck in that particular intellectual property right. The need to provide deference to an *ex-ante* balance between static and dynamic efficiency in intellectual property

490. Karjala 1999, p. 186; Ritter 2005, p. 287.
491. See also Cooter & Ulen 2007, p. 373.
492. Lévêque 2005, p. 80; Lévêque & Méniere 2004, p. 87.
493. Pitofsky 2001, p. 547.
494. Lévêque & Méniere 2004, p. 87.
495. Cornish & Llewellyn 2003, p. 755; Drexl et al. 2005, p. 453.

rights thereby introduces the risk that any deficiencies in such an *ex-ante* approach could be 'imported' into the application of *ex-post* competition law.

A related consequence of this deference to intellectual property rights in competition law is that, for firms attempting to control a secondary market, it has become more important to base their control on an(y) intellectual property right. Compared to control of a secondary market without an intellectual property right, such control is less likely to be held in violation of competition laws. Intellectual property rights may thus function as a 'safe harbor' for control of secondary markets.[496] Copyright law is a particularly attractive candidate for this task. Because of its low threshold for protection, copyright law is increasingly being used to protect sole-source information essential to competitors.[497] Its lack of any formal registration requirements makes it a suitable tool to claim protection after-the-fact.[498] Indeed, firms have become more resourceful in finding copyright claims in the instruments they use to control secondary markets. In *New York Mercantile Exchange (NYMEX) v. InterContinentalExchange*, for example, NYMEX, who operated an exchange for energy derivatives, sought to preclude competition from the newly created, online Intercontinental Exchange. It did so by claiming a copyright in its settlement prices – data that was, of course, essential to operating a competing exchange. NYMEX's idea of claiming a copyright in its settlement prices was certainly more original than the alleged copyrighted subject matter itself. Indeed, the court observed that NYMEX had advanced no counterarguments to Intercontinental's allegation that the prices did not constitute copyrightable subject matter because their determination was 'mechanical and formulaic, not creative or original'.[499] In the European cases of *Magill*, *IMS Health* and *Microsoft*, which are examined in section 4.2, copyrights similarly played a central role. These cases highlight the importance of internally limited intellectual property rights.

The structural, *ex-ante* nature of intellectual property rights and the case-by-case, *ex-post* nature of competition rules have certain further implications for their respective roles. Broad, structural issues are preferably addressed *ex-ante*: these rules provide the certainty to firms to coordinate their behavior with a generally optimal balance between static and dynamic efficiency. Structural barriers to entry, such as interconnection in telecommunications, are also preferably addressed *ex-ante*.[500] By contrast, exceptional cases require flexibility to account for the particular circumstances of the case and are, therefore, better addressed through the flexible, case-by-case, *ex-post* scrutiny of competition law. The competition authority's focus on the

496. See also Bechtold 2007.
497. Hugenholtz 1989, pp. 165, 177; Koelman 2006, p. 831.
498. See section 3.1.1a. See also section 6.3.2c.
499. *NYMEX* (US District Court, S.D. New York 2004), 562.
500. Dommering et al. 2001b, pp. 34, 35; Koelman 2006, p. 836. See also section 5.2.2.

particular case before it also means that the authority is less suited to strike a broader, structural balance for other cases, which, after all, are characterized by different fact patterns.[501] As Ullrich notes:

> [T]he safeguards for the functionality of intellectual property must be built into the system itself [. . . .] [Antitrust remedies] may help in some singular cases as emergency (or escape) solutions, but they will never really compensate on a broad scale for the inefficiencies of a system of intellectual property protection, let alone guarantee the efficiency of a faulty system.[502]

By the same token, the allocation of rights and resources (such as property rights) that contribute to (substantial) market power are preferably addressed *ex-ante*, whereas abuse of substantial market power is better addressed *ex-post*, through competition law. The preceding section already observed that competition law does not sanction substantial market power *per-se* because such market power may well be the result of superior business acumen. Consequently, competition law is only concerned with exceptional circumstances, or *abuse* of substantial market power. Indeed, this is one objection against application of the essential facilities doctrine, which is further discussed in section 4.2: this doctrine of competition law appears less concerned with abusive behavior and more with structural ownership issues.[503] Such issues are preferably addressed *ex-ante*. However, substantial market power may well be a concern if it was not acquired through superior business acumen but instead through an inefficient, *ex-ante* allocation of rights, such as intellectual property rights that have been defined too broadly, or from the privatization of a publicly owned, national telecommunications operator.[504] If, for instance, the law were to allow broad, 200-year patents, the substantial market power of the relevant rightsholders would not necessarily be the result of their superior business acumen but rather of the inefficient, *ex-ante* patent rights. Such market power would deserve scrutiny, even if it were not necessarily based on any abusive behavior on the part of that firm. Consequently, the preferable approach appears to be within the corresponding *ex-ante* rules – in this example, the relevant patent statute. This is, indeed, confirmed by competition law itself: in the area where sudden and substantial increases in market power are foreseeable, namely, in merger review, competition law relies on an *ex-ante* approach. The market power caused by the merger is reviewed before rather than after – the fact. This enables the competition authority to impose *ex-ante* conditions with a view to preventing any harm to the competitive process caused by the merging parties' combined market power.

---

501. Turney 2005, §69.
502. Ullrich 2001, p. 383. See also Lévêque 2005, p. 91.
503. See section 4.2.
504. van Rooijen 2008, p. 80. See also section 5.2.2a.

An *ex-ante* intellectual property approach is also more suitable to address policy objectives, which are defined here as trade-offs between static and dynamic efficiency that do not necessarily coincide with an economically optimal balance between static and dynamic efficiency. In such instances, one often seeks a trade-off towards more static and less dynamic efficiency. For example, one might regard interoperability between computer programs or interconnection between telecommunications networks as desirable from a policy perspective rather than merely from a perspective of total welfare. Providing for *ex-ante* interconnection rules is one of the main purposes of telecommunications law, which will be discussed in Chapter 5. Although the competition authority has some discretion in executing competition rules, its mandate is generally limited to safeguarding the competitive process. Therefore, there may be less room for policy considerations in the application of competition law than there is in *ex-ante* rulemaking.[505] Note that where such policy adjustments are made *ex-ante*, the relevant *ex-ante* rules and *ex-post* competition laws no longer necessarily serve as complementary regimes. In the extreme case, *ex-ante*, sector-specific regulation can serve as an *alternative* to the competitive process rather than as a complement to it.[506]

The flipside of the policy coin is that legislators also tend to be more driven by political motivations and more sensitive to lobbying efforts.[507] Consequently, the *ex-ante* intellectual property rights may become 'less the product of a rational decision-making process than of lobbying by stakeholders'.[508] Lobbying efforts are known to have contributed significantly to the Software Directive[509] and the limitation on the European design protection of spare parts.[510]

In reality, the distinction presented in this section between the certainty of *ex-ante* intellectual property rights and the flexibility of *ex-post* competition laws is not so clear-cut. Indeed, the distinction may be little more than a theory of the ideal role of intellectual property rights and competition laws. In practice, intellectual property rights do not necessarily provide the certainty that they ideally should provide. Chapter 3 already observed how the vague norms of copyright law make it difficult to assess whether interface specifications constitute copyrightable subject matter.[511] Such issues are, therefore, often ultimately determined *ex-post* by a court rather than *ex-ante* by the legislator.[512]

---

505. Helberger 2005, p. 189. See also Larouche 2000, p. 124.
506. Larouche 2000, p. 363. See also Baldwin & Cave 1999, p. 9.
507. Cooter & Ulen 2007, p. 373.
508. Hugenholtz 2008, p. 498.
509. See section 3.2. See also Band & Katoh 1995, p. 227; Czarnota & Hart 1991; Vinje 1993.
510. See section 5.1.1.
511. Many patents (46%) are also invalidated in *ex-post* litigation. Lemley & Shapiro 2005, p. 8.
512. Note, however, that this type of *ex-post* determination of the scope of an intellectual property right is quite different from the *ex-post* analysis by competition authorities: in the former case, the (civil) court must construct *ex-post* what the *ex-ante* legislator had intended for all cases. In the latter case, the *ex-post* competition authority must assess the optimal outcome for the particular case before it.

Furthermore, adequate *ex-ante* anticipation is not always feasible or desirable, in particular at an international level. Legislators are also known to be slow and not always equipped with the relevant technical expertise, which can make it difficult to timely adapt intellectual property rights to a quickly evolving competitive and technological landscape. A more responsive *ex-ante* approach may be possible through a regulatory authority, which can act quicker and with more sector-specific expertise than the legislator. Chapters 5 and 6 demonstrate that this solution has been used both in telecommunications law and in the protection of technical protection measures, and that it may also be useful to regulate reverse engineering for interoperability *ex-ante*.

Competition law, for its part, is not always applied with the flexibility for which it was designed. As demonstrated in section 4.2, European courts tend to apply a rather rigid analytical framework to cases involving an abuse of a dominant position. The courts thereby arguably risk conducting an inadequate analysis of the specific case before them. Furthermore, EU competition law is increasingly characterized by the use of Commission guidelines, which aim to resolve competition issues structurally and *ex-ante* rather than merely *ex-post* and case-by-case.[513]

In theory, nonetheless, it may be concluded that the case-by-case approach of competition law reduces the certainty that intellectual property rights aim to establish, whereas, conversely, the rigidity of intellectual property rights may in some instances prove to strike a suboptimal balance between static and dynamic efficiency. This causes an *instrumental tension* between these two regimes.

c. Resolving Tensions

The preceding sections have demonstrated that intellectual property rights and competition rules serve similar purposes (section 4.1.2a), using different instruments (section 4.1.2b). Tensions between intellectual property rights and competition rules, nonetheless, may arise where the scope of intellectual property rights is too broad, thus over-stimulating innovation at the expense of competition. This section extrapolates the analyzes of the previous sections for unresolved tensions between intellectual property rights and competition rules. It examines who should resolve such tensions (the legislator, *ex-ante*, or the competition authority, *ex-post*) and how these respective institutions should go about striking the appropriate balance.

In deciding whether the balance between static and dynamic efficiency should be struck *ex-ante*, within intellectual property rights, or *ex-post*, by applying competition law,[514] the observations in the previous two sections ultimately lead to a parameter of structural foreseeability.[515] Circumstances

513. See, for example, European Commission 2009.
514. Dreier 2001, p. 303; Kovacic & Reindl 2005, p. 1067; van Rooijen 2008, p. 78.
515. Drexl 2006, p. 653.

that are structural and foreseeable should ideally be anticipated within intellectual property rights, whereas circumstances that cannot be foreseen or are not structural should be scrutinized on a case-by-case basis, by applying competition rules.[516] The following table demonstrates these approaches.

		Legislator *(ex-ante)*	Competition authority *(ex-post)*
1	Foreseeable + structural, anticipated	(Adjust balance for future cases if necessary)	X Deference to *ex-ante* balance
2	Foreseeable + structural, not anticipated	Balance for future cases	(Balance for this case if necessary)
3	Unforeseeable or not structural (exceptional)	X Cannot be anticipated	Balance for this case
4	Optimal balance	X	X

It follows that, naturally, no action is required where the optimal balance is already struck; there is simply no problem (row 4). Some action *is* required where the balance is not optimal (rows 1–3) – either *ex-ante*, by the legislator, *ex-post*, by the competition authority, or by both. Thus, where an intellectual property right has anticipated a situation but, nonetheless, strikes a suboptimal balance in the particular case, deference should be granted to this *ex-ante* solution (row 1). As already noted, there is a risk of importing any deficiencies in the intellectual property system into the application of competition law.[517] If the problem appears likely to reoccur, it may be worthwhile fine-tuning the scope of the *ex-ante* intellectual property right (row 1). By contrast, where the *ex-ante* intellectual property right results in a suboptimal balance that was not structural or foreseeable, and, therefore, exceptional, competition law could be used to alter the balance *ex-post* (row 3).[518] A more difficult situation arises where a suboptimal balance was structural and foreseeable but had not actually been anticipated by the *ex-ante* legislator (row 2).[519] In such cases, the foreseeability of the problem points to addressing the problem by an *ex-ante* balancing act. Nonetheless, this does not discharge the competition authority from resolving the particular case before it *ex-post* (row 2).[520]

516. Note that structural foreseeability also implies that the optimal balance is reasonably clear; if the effects of either control or openness are highly ambiguous, the balance is less easily fixed in an *ex-ante* intellectual property right.
517. See section 4.1.2b.
518. Dreier 2001, p. 312; van Rooijen 2008, p. 78.
519. See, for example, *Magill* (ECJ 1995). See also section 4.2.1b.
520. Cotter 1999, p. 214; Drexl et al. 2006, §12; Drexl et al. 2005, p. 452; Katz 2002, p. 351; Kovacic & Reindl 2005, p. 1067; Lévêque 2005, p. 80; Lévêque & Méniere 2004, p. 87; Posner 2001, p. 931; van Rooijen 2008, p. 78; Schovsbo 1998, p. 524; Sucker 1993,

It follows that *ex-post* scrutiny of *ex-ante* intellectual property rights is ideally only warranted in exceptional circumstances and that an exceptional circumstance must be defined as a suboptimal balance between static and dynamic efficiency (the substantive aspect) that is not structural and cannot be foreseen (the instrumental aspect).[521] This is the situation described in row 3. In other instances, the balance should be or should have been anticipated *ex-ante*. As demonstrated in section 4.2, however, the European competition authorities and courts have not limited themselves to this proposed definition of exceptional circumstances. Instead, they have permitted competition law to interfere in situations that *were* foreseeable, although not actually anticipated in the relevant intellectual property rights (row 2), and, moreover, in cases that *had* been foreseen and anticipated – notably, by the reverse engineering provisions in the Software Directive (row 1).

Ex-post competition authorities thus regularly correct for intellectual property rights that are too broad. This may well be an indication that the importance of *ex-ante* anticipation of competitive problems in intellectual property rights is not yet sufficiently recognized.[522] Naturally, where intellectual property rights have not (yet) been sufficiently curtailed for competition considerations, the argument for deference to such rights remains fragile (row 2). Conversely, the argument for deference to intellectual property rights becomes stronger as competition considerations become part of the legislative agenda (row 1).

In the light of the foregoing, *ex-post* scrutiny of intellectual property rights places competition courts before a difficult task: on the one hand, they must generally respect the *ex-ante* balance between static and dynamic efficiency already anticipated in the relevant intellectual property rights.[523] On the other hand, they must determine whether exceptional circumstances are present that justify an *ex-post* correction of that balance, and they must subsequently strike the appropriate balance in the case before them. The problem thus consists of two components: first, determining whether the suboptimal balance at issue was anticipated by an applicable intellectual property right. Second, if it was not, the court must determine *ex-post* what the optimal balance is.

The first (instrumental) part of this test – determining whether the situation at issue was anticipated in an intellectual property right – requires the court or authority to assess whether there is an intellectual property right involved and whether the situation at issue was anticipated in that right. The presence of the intellectual property right itself should normally be pointed out by the

p. 21; Turney 2005, p. 196; Ullrich 2001, p. 383. But see Beier 1994, pp. 860, 862; Cornish & Llewellyn 2003, p. 755; Ritter 2005.

521. See also Drexl et al. 2005, p. 453. But see Beier 1994, p. 863.

522. Koelman 2006, p. 831. See also Cornish & Llewellyn 2003, p. 755 ('In a period when intellectual property rights are being rapidly expanded, it must be wise for competition authorities to retain some ultimate means of curbing their range in egregious cases, which, in the scramble to satisfy industrial lobbies, legislatures may not have sufficiently cogitated').

523. See section 4.1.2b.

rightsholder. It may be more difficult to determine whether that intellectual property right had anticipated the suboptimal balance that is before the court or authority, and, indeed, as demonstrated, *infra*, this analysis is often neglected. The legislative history may be a useful starting point for this analysis.[524] The second (substantive) part – determining the appropriate balance between static and dynamic efficiency – draws upon the primarily economic expertise of the relevant institution.

Different courts in different jurisdictions have adopted different approaches to this problem, although few have expressly addressed both sides of the issue.[525] In the United States, the Federal Circuit has adopted a near *per-se* legality rule, according to which the use of an intellectual property right is nearly always lawful.[526] This approach essentially leaves no room for any *ex-post* corrections, thus ignoring the second prong of the problem. In *Data General*, the First Circuit adopted a presumption of legality, according to which the exercise of an intellectual property right is a rebuttable, but presumptively valid business justification.[527] This approach recognizes the *ex-ante* balance struck in intellectual property rights (although it fails to inquire whether the suboptimal balance was anticipated by the intellectual property right), while leaving some room to analyze the second prong, or the optimal balance between static and dynamic efficiency.

The European courts, then, have adopted the so-called new-product test, which will be further examined in section 4.2.2. For present purposes, it suffices to note that this test consists of only one component (whether the refusal to license prevents the emergence of a new product), which must, however, serve as a proxy for both of the components identified, *supra*: instrumentally, obstructing development of a new product must be interpreted as a circumstance unforeseen by the *ex-ante* intellectual property legislator, and, substantively, it must serve as a proxy for a suboptimal balance between static and dynamic efficiency. The instrumental aspect of the test will be examined here, whereas its substantive aspect (its suitability as a proxy for consumer welfare) will be analyzed in section 4.2.2.

Instrumentally, the new-product test does not appear to accurately distinguish between foreseeable and exceptional cases. The prevention of new-product development is not necessarily exceptional because most intellectual property rights do not protect products as such, but rather certain aspects thereof, such as innovative technology or creative expression. Thus, technology protected by a patent is not necessarily tied to any specific product but rather to technology that may be incorporated in different products.[528]

524. The legislative history of the Software Directive, for example, contains some clues as to the situations that had been foreseen by the legislator. See also section 4.1.2d.
525. See also Hovenkamp et al. 2005.
526. *In re ISO Antitrust Litigation* (US Court of Appeals, Federal Circuit 2000).
527. *Data General* (US Court of Appeals, First Circuit 1994). See also van Rooijen 2008, p. 74.
528. See also Merges 1999, p. 17.

Similarly, the copyright in a protects the original expression in its plot, which may also extend to translations or even a film or play based on that plot. Although the film may be a new product, it clearly falls within the intended scope of the rightsholder's exclusive rights. The new-product test may thus well cover foreseeable and even anticipated cases, and, therefore, appears to be an unsatisfactory test to isolate exceptional circumstances.

Yet another approach to the interface between intellectual property rights and competition law was offered in *United States v. Microsoft*.[529] In this case, the Court of Appeals for the DC Circuit appeared unwilling to grant any deference to intellectual property rights at all, suggesting that these rights were subject to full competition scrutiny. The court observed:

> [Microsoft] claims an absolute and unfettered right to use its intellectual property as it wishes: '[I]f intellectual property rights have been lawfully acquired,' it says, then 'their subsequent exercise cannot give rise to antitrust liability.' That is no more correct than the proposition that use of one's personal property, such as a baseball bat, cannot give rise to tort liability. [citation omitted][530]

The excerpt from the court's opinion contains two opposite and equally unpersuasive positions. Microsoft's position, not surprisingly, amounts to a *per-se* legality rule for the exercise of intellectual property rights, similar to that of the Federal Circuit. Such a rule was already rejected, *supra*: exceptional circumstances *can* warrant *ex-post* review of a firm's exercise of intellectual property rights, in particular as long as intellectual property rights have not yet been sufficiently curtailed to allow for sufficient competition. However, it is submitted that the court's comparison to one's property rights over a baseball bat and the simultaneous possibility of tort liability is equally unpersuasive. Unlike intellectual property laws and competition laws, property laws and tort liability do not generally fulfill complementary purposes. Consequently, there are strong arguments that one's exercise of property rights should be fully subject to scrutiny by tort law, as the court suggests. In other words, there is no deference from tort law to property rights. The complementary relationship between intellectual property rights and competition laws, however, introduces a strong argument that one's use of intellectual property should be subject to only limited review by competition law.[531] The court appears to ignore this crucial difference.

Nonetheless, the DC Circuit's baseball bat can fulfill a useful role to illustrate the relationship between *ex-ante* intellectual property rights and *ex-post* competition rules, and particularly to demonstrate the role for *ex-ante* legislation of addressing market power, and of *ex-post* competition law to

529. *United States v. Microsoft* (US Court of Appeals, DC Circuit 2001).
530. *Id.*, 63.
531. See sections 4.1.2a and 4.1.2b.

sanction abusive behavior.[532] If the *ex-ante* rules of the baseball game allowed for only one particular person to handle the baseball bat, this would foreseeably prevent other people from playing the game. Such an *ex-ante* rule would structurally impede access to the game (the 'competitive process'), and, because the result is entirely foreseeable, should be addressed by a change in these *ex-ante* rules. However, if a player used the baseball bat to physically attack and exclude the other players from the game, this would quite clearly amount to the type of abusive, unforeseeable and exceptional behavior that deserves *ex-post* scrutiny.

As to the *ex-ante* balancing act in intellectual property rights, anticipation could involve a change in the scope or term of protection. Legislators may be well advised to coordinate their balancing efforts with competition authorities, perhaps supported by a sector-specific observatory body.[533] This is particularly relevant as the competition authority may often be confronted with competitive problems caused by a broad scope of intellectual property protection earlier and in more detail than the legislator. In other words, what is structural and foreseeable could change with experience. Indeed, the ECJ's judgment in *Volvo v. Veng*,[534] in which a car manufacturer refused to license design rights in spare parts to independent garages, has provoked specific limitations and exclusions in European design protection laws. These provisions will be examined in some detail in Chapter 5. From the General Court's *Microsoft* judgment, one might similarly conclude that the scope of copyright protection for computer programs is too broad because it also effectively protects the program's interface information (see section 4.1.2d).

d. Application to Control Over Standards and Interface Specifications

The previous section presented a general framework to resolve the question of whether the balance between static and dynamic efficiency should be addressed by *ex-ante* intellectual property rights or by *ex-post* application of competition law. Based on this framework, this section seeks to determine whether control over standards and interface specifications should be addressed *ex-ante* or *ex-post*.

Intellectual property protection of standards poses special challenges to the complementary relationship between intellectual property rights and competition rules. Chapter 2 already noted that standards often exhibit strong network effects: as the market adheres to a certain standard, the value of the standard increases. If a standard is used by a significant share of market players, its network effects may be sufficiently substantial for the market to tip in favor of that standard. Once tipping occurs, the market may not tolerate any

---

532. See section 4.1.2b.
533. Drexl et al. 2005, p. 653; Kovacic & Reindl 2005.
534. See section 4.2.1c.

alternative standards: the benefits of standardization outweigh those of variety.[535] Consequently, if one firm holds the intellectual property rights protecting that standard, these rights can be a source of substantial market power and possibly harm to competition.

Against the background of section 4.1.2c, one can attempt to answer the question of whether intellectual property control of standards should be addressed *ex-ante*, within intellectual property rights, or *ex-post*, by applying competition rules. On the substantive side, it could be argued that indiscriminate intellectual property protection of standards creates substantial market power more often than ownership of other subject matter. The rightsholder may preclude competitors from entering the market through its ownership of the essential standard, which may ultimately harm competition.[536] On the instrumental side, it is questionable whether issues of standards ownership are necessarily foreseeable.[537] In particular, it may be difficult to anticipate which types of subject matter are likely to be 'elevated' to a *de-facto* or *de-jure* standard. The consequences of an *ex-ante* approach to standards for dynamic and static efficiency, therefore, are difficult to anticipate. If it is difficult to foresee what subject matter can become a standard, the case for a change in *ex-ante* intellectual property rights becomes weaker, and the argument to correct for ownership of standards using an *ex-post* competition law approach becomes stronger. Under an *ex-post* approach, the effects of control over standards can be assessed in context. It may thus be inevitable to deal with control over standards through *ex-post* competition law.

As noted in section 2.1.2b, interface specifications exhibit many characteristics of standards: the computer programs they form part of may be subject to very strong network effects, and intellectual property control of these specifications, therefore, may result in substantial and sustainable market power, in particular after tipping has occurred. However, this market power may also serve as a strong incentive to innovate, whereas adherence to an existing standard limits variety. Substantively, the effects of control over interface specifications are thus similar to that of control over standards in general.[538]

Instrumentally, the assessment of the effects of control over interface specifications may require both flexibility and certainty. There is a need for flexibility because the effect of control over a particular set of interface specifications can significantly depend on the circumstances of the case. For example, it may be relevant to determine whether the market has already tipped in favor of a single set of interface specifications, whether tipping is or is not likely to happen and what the rate of innovation in the market is. Such

535. This issue will be explored in more detail in section 4.2. See also Drexl et al. 2006, §7B, §19; European Commission 2005, §230; Farrell 1989, p. 47; Turney 2005, p. 197.
536. See sections 4.1.2a and 2.2.4.
537. Drexl 2006, p. 652; Koelman 2006, p. 837.
538. See section 2.2.4.

considerations cannot be fixed in a detailed *ex-ante* instrument but can only be established through an *ex-post* assessment. In other words, these circumstances are not foreseeable.

However, a more certain *ex-ante* approach to control over interface specifications may also be necessary. Significantly, the need for interoperability and access to interface specifications in the software industry is more structural than it is exceptional.[539] Ideally, competitors, therefore, should not be required to wait until a competition authority has established *ex-post* that openness of interface specifications is desirable. As long as intellectual property rights structurally impede interoperability, for example, by durable protection of interfaces, the use of competition law may represent too high a burden to facilitate interoperability in the many instances in which it is likely to be beneficial, and one should, therefore, arguably not have to rely on pursuing litigation under competition law to obtain interoperability. In other words, despite possible differences in each case, a default rule in favor of more *ex-ante* openness of interfaces may be preferable over structural application of competition law. Telecommunications law, which similarly regulates an industry in which there is a structural need for interconnection, also relies on *ex-ante* interconnection duties.[540]

Conversely, to the extent that the temporary control over interface specifications enables the rightsholder to exploit proprietary network effects, which, in turn, can serve as an incentive to innovate,[541] it may be important for the rightsholder to have some certainty as to the conditions under which it can actually control its interface specifications. It is submitted that the fact that control over interface specifications could, in individual cases, yield either positive or negative effects does not in itself obstruct an *ex-ante* approach. Intellectual property rights strike a balance between control and openness for many intellectual creations that, considered individually, may or may not actually be worth protecting. Yet, this has not prevented legislators from protecting certain subject matter by *ex-ante* intellectual property rights, and the same could be argued for control over interface specifications.

Furthermore, unlike the more general notion of standards, interface specifications are considerably more concrete and more straightforward to identify. Consequently, the case for an *ex-ante* approach to ownership of interface specifications may be stronger than for standards in general.

During the drafting of the Software Directive, the European legislator originally sought to address the protection of interface specifications *ex-post*, through competition law. However, it was later persuaded to adopt reverse engineering provisions in the Software Directive, which aim to facilitate the task of obtaining access to such specifications *ex-ante*. These instruments were examined in section 3.2.2, which also concluded that they are

539. See section 2.1.1.
540. See section 5.2.
541. See section 2.2.2d.

insufficient to strike an appropriate balance between openness and control of interface information. When reverse engineering proves prohibitively difficult, this *ex-ante* copyright approach to interoperability leaves rightsholders with too much control over interface specifications, which may result in sustainable and substantial market power.

The question is whether this suboptimal balance must be resolved *ex-ante*, within copyright, or on a case-by-case basis, through *ex-post* competition law. The Software Directive's preamble, in its 17th recital, appears to suggest that both could be used. This also appears to be the Commission's view. In the *Microsoft* case, which will be discussed in further detail in section 4.2, the Commission was confronted with the weaknesses of the Software Directive's reverse engineering provisions. Microsoft's operating systems appeared too complex to reverse engineer.[542] The Commission, therefore, viewed an *ex-post* competition approach to access to Microsoft's interface specifications as justified. To Microsoft's argument that the problem of access to interface information was already addressed *ex-ante* by the Software Directive's reverse engineering provisions, therefore precluding an *ex-post* competition approach, the Commission responded:

> Article 6 of the Software Directive thus limits a copyright-holder's rights in favour of interoperability, whether the copyright-holder is dominant or not. In view of Microsoft's extraordinary market strength as well as the other exceptional circumstances in this case, this Decision establishes that Microsoft has an obligation to *actively* supply interface information to other work group server operating system vendors. While thus being consistent with the Software Directive as regards the balancing of intellectual property rights and interoperability, this Decision establishes a disclosure obligation for Microsoft under Article [102] of the Treaty which goes beyond mere passivity in the face of de-compilation of its software code for interoperability purposes.[543]

The Commission thus suggests that the cumulative, *ex-post* application of competition law to force a dominant firm to supply its interface specifications is consistent with the *ex-ante* approach in copyright law, through which these competitors are permitted to reverse engineer the same information at their own expense. This perspective is in some tension with the framework established in this section, which instead suggests a need to distinguish between foreseeable cases – to be addressed in *ex-ante* intellectual property rights – and exceptional cases, which may be addressed through *ex-post* application of competition law. Therefore, it would appear relevant to determine whether the European legislator had anticipated the difficulty and complexity of reverse engineering certain computer programs, or whether such difficulties must instead be characterized as exceptional.

542. *Microsoft Decision* (European Commission 2004), §685.
543. *Id.*, §744, §745, §747.

However, it appears that the problem of access to interface specifications of a copyright-protected and complex computer program was anticipated in the Software Directive. As observed in Chapter 3, the directive's reverse engineering provisions were expressly adopted with a view to obviating the need to invoke competition law. Moreover, the difficulty of reverse engineering, which, in *Microsoft*, proved a major obstacle to obtaining interface specifications, also appears to have been foreseen by the legislator.[544] In other words, the difficulty of reverse engineering was arguably anticipated and, therefore, not exceptional. This would imply a need to grant some deference to this *ex-ante* balancing mechanism.

However, Chapter 3 also demonstrated that the current instruments permitting reverse engineering under the Software Directive appear too restrictive. By, *inter alia*, preventing firms from sharing their reverse engineering efforts, the Software Directive arguably and foreseeably falls short of providing an adequate *ex-ante* approach to obtaining interface specifications for interoperability. As observed, in section 4.1.2c, if the *ex-ante* approach is deficient, as the reverse engineering provisions in the Software Directive arguably are, the argument for deference to such an *ex-ante* balancing mechanism is weaker. Nevertheless, rather than a structural application of *ex-post* competition law to correct for this suboptimal balance, the more appropriate course of action would appear to be an adjustment to the *ex-ante* reverse engineering instrument. This is, indeed, the approach that will be studied in more detail in Chapter 6.

4.1.3. Conclusion

This section examined the relationship between an *ex-ante* copyright approach and an *ex-post* competition law approach to addressing interoperability.

An EU law perspective on the relationship between national intellectual property rights and the competition rules of the TFEU was rejected as too simplistic: this approach does not account for the effects that intellectual

544. In the original proposal for the Software Directive, the Commission had dismissed decompilation as a viable means to obtain interface specifications, describing it as a 'lengthy, costly and inefficient procedure'. Nevertheless, it was subsequently persuaded to include detailed black-box testing and decompilation provisions in the Amended Proposal. Still, it chose to permit decompilation only under stringent conditions. Being at least somewhat familiar with the difficulty involved in decompiling a computer program, it could have chosen less stringent conditions, such as a lower burden of proof or the ability to decompile the entire program rather than only the parts necessary for interoperability. Changes in interface specifications, which can add to the difficulty of reverse engineering, were also anticipated. See Software Directive, Amended Proposal (1990), 12 (noting that in a case of interface changes, the interoperable developer could repeat the reverse engineering process 'any number of times'). See section 3.2.2b. See also Czarnota & Hart 1991, p. 80; Software Directive, Article 6(1)(c); van Rooijen 2007b.

property rights have on innovation and competition. The two bodies of law are intertwined, and the EU law perspective ignores this substantive aspect.

The more substantive perspective recognizes that intellectual property rights and competition rules largely serve complementary purposes: both aim to stimulate and balance innovation and competition. Intellectual property rights accomplish this through an *ex-ante* approach, which provides more certainty to rightsholders and their competitors. Competition law accomplishes this through *ex-post* scrutiny of abusive behavior. Because a full *ex-post* review of *ex-ante* intellectual property rights reduces the very certainty that these intellectual property rights aim to provide to innovators, any structural deficiencies in the *ex-ante* allocation of intellectual property rights, such as copyright control over interface information, should – to the extent foreseeable – ideally be anticipated *ex-ante*. Competition law should be applied to unforeseeable and, therefore, exceptional cases. It follows that, in the application of competition law, there is a need to grant a certain degree of deference to the balance between innovation and competition already struck within the relevant intellectual property rights. Because the Software Directive's reverse engineering provisions already strike a balance between openness and control of interface information, this would imply a need for competition law to grant some deference to this balance and to review this balance only in situations not already anticipated by this *ex-ante* approach.

However, this section also identified several nuances to the theory of complementarity. *Ex-ante* intellectual property rights do not always provide the certainty they ideally should provide, and *ex-post* competition law is not always applied with the flexibility it was designed to offer. Copyright law, for example, provides little more than vague guidelines as to the protected subject matter, including whether interface specifications qualify for protection. Moreover, *ex-ante* intellectual property rights are not always properly curtailed to strike an appropriate balance between innovation and competition that would deserve *ex-post* deference. Indeed, Chapter 3 observed that the Software Directive's reverse engineering provisions are too restrictive and arguably leave rightsholders with too much control over their computer programs' interoperability information. The general lack of an adequate *ex-ante* balancing act in many intellectual property rights may well have prompted competition authorities to apply competition law to correct for such inadequate balances. From the perspective of the theory of complementarity, however, it appears preferable to adjust the *ex-ante* approach in intellectual property rights rather than to apply competition law to adjust for such structural deficiencies. Thus, it may similarly be preferable to adjust the Software Directive's instruments addressing use of and access to a computer program's interface specifications. If intellectual property rights are more adequately curtailed to balance innovation and competition for foreseeable cases, the application of competition law can be limited to the role it was designed for – namely, addressing abusive behavior and exceptional circumstances in situations not already anticipated by these *ex-ante* instruments. These situations may also include abuses of market power that is not caused and anticipated by copyright law.

Based on approaches in design protection and telecommunications law, which are studied in Chapter 5, Chapter 6 will consider possibilities to improve the balance between openness and control of interface specifications in copyright law *ex-ante*. The remainder of this chapter will examine the application of competition law to refusals to supply interface information to competitors.

4.2. REFUSALS TO SUPPLY INTERFACE INFORMATION

Thus far, this chapter has examined the instrumental relationship between an *ex-ante* copyright approach to interoperability and an *ex-post* competition approach, suggesting a limited role for competition law in favor of a strong(er) approach in copyright law. This *ex-ante* approach was examined in Chapter 3 and will be further developed in Chapter 6. This section examines how *ex-post* application of competition law can affect the balance between openness and control of interface information through application of the 'essential facilities' doctrine. Under this doctrine, a dominant firm could be forced to share certain resources that prove essential to competitors.

Section 4.2.1 first examines the essential facilities doctrine as a basis for mandatory sharing of interface specifications under competition law. In particular, it demonstrates that, even if the European courts have applied the essential facilities doctrine to an increasingly varied array of facilities and circumstances, including control over interface specifications, they have done so using a single, rather rigid analytical framework. In section 4.2.2, then, it will be demonstrated why it may be particularly inappropriate to apply this rigid analytical framework to refusals to supply interface specifications.

4.2.1. Competition Law and Control of Interface Information

This section examines the essential facilities doctrine under European competition law because this doctrine serves as the primary legal basis for forcing a firm to share its interface specifications with competitors under competition law (section 4.2.1a). It will also discuss some general points of criticism of the essential facilities doctrine (section 4.2.1b). Finally, this section will demonstrate the rigidity of the application of the doctrine in the case law of the European courts (section 4.2.1c).

a. European Competition Law and Essential Facilities

The body of European competition law is developed mostly in the case law of the ECJ and the GC, which is based on a limited number of articles in the European Union's primary statute, the TFEU.[545] The TFEU recognizes, *inter alia*, two primary and partly contrasting threats to the competitive process: *collusion* and *exclusion*.[546] Collusion, sanctioned by Article 101 of the TFEU, concerns the cooperation between multiple firms that should instead be competing. By forming agreements or *cartels*, they can reduce competition, thereby provoking higher prices and possibly less innovation.[547] By contrast, exclusion concerns single-firm (*unilateral*) acts that can structurally harm (exclude) competition. This category, the topic of study in this chapter and addressed by Article 102 of the TFEU, is also known as abuse of dominance. As this phrase indicates, dominance *per-se* is not unlawful. Because a dominant position may well be the result of superior business acumen,[548] one may – to a certain extent[549] – lawfully enjoy a monopoly position. However, this position may not be abused.[550] Article 102 lists a number of examples of abusive behavior or *foreclosure*.[551] This list is not exhaustive: Article 102 prohibits any abuse by a dominant undertaking, which, in theory, leaves the courts with considerable flexibility to scrutinize abusive behavior.[552]

The conduct enumerated under subsection (b) of Article 102 ('limiting production, markets or technical development to the prejudice of consumers') is of particular importance to this chapter.[553] Under this heading, competition authorities and courts have held some so-called refusals to deal by dominant firms as abusive behavior. Generally, firms in the European Union's internal market, even dominant ones, are free to choose whom they contract with and

545. Larouche 2000, p. 119.
546. European Commission 2009; *Continental Can* (ECJ 1973), 23; Geradin & Kerf 2003, p. 11; Nihoul & Rodford 2004, p. 330.
547. Licensing of interoperability information could fall under scrutiny of Article 101. This issue will not be explored in this study. See Lemley 2002; Shapiro 2000; Stuurman 1995, p. 323.
548. See section 4.1.2a.
549. Article 102(a) of the TFEU refers to *exploitative abuses* – that is, maintaining 'unfair selling prices'. Because a monopolist by definition charges a monopoly price, a monopolist's conduct is arguably abusive under Article 102(a). Craig & de Búrca 2003, p. 993. See also Whish 2003, p. 195.
550. *Microsoft Decision* (European Commission 2004), §542; Craig & de Búrca 2003, p. 1006; Temple Lang 2005, p. 58.
551. See also European Commission 2009, §19.
552. Doherty 2001, p. 422; Nihoul & Rodford 2004, p. 348; Whish 2003, p. 194. For the general concept of *abusive behavior*, see *Akzo* (ECJ 1991), §69. See also Govaere 1996, p. 249; Whish 2003, p. 194.
553. Larouche 2000, p. 167. A duty to deal on non-discriminatory terms may also arise from subsection (c). This duty will not be described in this chapter. See Temple Lang 2005, p. 59.

under what terms.[554] This freedom necessarily incorporates the freedom to *refuse* to contract.[555] The freedom to (refuse to) contract or to deal is a critical element of the competitive process in a free market economy.[556] However, under certain exceptional circumstances, the refusal by an undertaking to provide competitors access to an input can structurally harm the competitive process – especially when that 'facility' is 'essential' for competitors to compete in a downstream market, such that effective competition in that market likely will be eliminated as a result of the refusal. The exclusion of effective competition in a market can result in higher prices and (although more controversially) less innovation. As a remedy for this abuse, the firm may be forced to provide competitors access to its facility on reasonable and non-discriminatory terms, known as a *duty to deal*. This has become known as the *essential facilities* doctrine, or, more generally, as the concept of *refusals to deal*.[557]

Originating from the United States, the essential facilities doctrine was first applied to the leveraging of market power from one market to another through a refusal to provide downstream competitors access to rather unique, physical infrastructural works, such as bridges and seaports.[558] However, both in Europe and the United States, the doctrine has more recently been invoked to scrutinize foreclosure of horizontal, rather than only vertical, competitors[559] and to limit control over many other types of 'facilities', including information products, software and, indeed, interface specifications of computer programs.[560] In general, the scope of the doctrine has been expanded to apply not only to tangible property but also to intellectual property rights and information. Application of the essential facilities doctrine to interface specifications could thus change a state of control over interface specifications to openness thereof *ex-post*. The crucial question for this chapter is whether this balance is struck with considerations of the indirect effects of control over interface specifications on innovation and competition (Chapter 2).

554. Faull & Nikpay 1999, p. 151; Whish 2003, p. 663.
555. European Commission 2009, p. 75.
556. Whish 2003, p. 663.
557. See, generally, Areeda 1990; Derclaye 2003; Doherty 2001; Dolmans et al. 2007; Furse 1995; Geradin 2004; Larouche 2000, p. 165; Lipsky Jr. & Sidak 1999; Pitofsky et al. 2002; Temple Lang 1994; Werden 1987. Although some commentators distinguish between refusal-to-deal and essential facility cases, the two terms are used interchangeably here. A refusal to deal is illegal only if it relates to a facility indispensable to competition; hence, the element of essentiality is incorporated in both concepts. See also Doherty 2001, p. 435; Whish 2003, p. 667.
558. *Terminal Railroad* (US Supreme Court 1912); Whish 2003, p. 667. See also Frischmann & Weber-Waller 2008; Opinion A-G Jacobs in *Bronner* (ECJ 1998).
559. Doherty 2001, p. 425; Pitofsky et al. 2002, p. 458; Whish 2003, p. 664. See also Hovenkamp et al. 2005, p. 19; Marquardt & Leddy 2003, p. 850.
560. *IBM Undertaking* (European Commission 1984); *Microsoft* (GC 2007). See also Areeda 1990; Glazer & Lipsky Jr. 1995.

b. Criticism of the Essential Facilities Doctrine

Application of the essential facilities doctrine remains controversial.[561] Four main points of general criticism are discussed here. More specific concerns related to application of the essential facilities doctrine to interface specifications will be analyzed in section 4.2.2.

First, imposing a duty to deal under the essential facilities doctrine could impede incentives to invest. Firms invest in facilities to gain a competitive advantage over their rivals. If they were forced to share these facilities with competitors, it is feared that this might reduce incentives to invest in such facilities in the first place; competitors might not invest either because of the prospect of forced access.[562] It is generally procompetitive to allow firms to control the facilities they have created and to permit forced access only when absolutely necessary to prevent structural harm to the competitive process. The 'essentiality' or 'indispensability' threshold of the doctrine is, therefore, an important policy lever; a 'doctrine of convenient facilities' should be avoided.[563] The ECJ in *Bronner* recognized that the indispensability threshold must indeed be substantial (see section 4.2.1c). Because of its effect on incentives to invest, the freedom to refuse access is especially relevant where the facility that the competitor seeks access to comprises an intellectual property right.[564] Exclusivity is the very essence of an intellectual property right. Forced access to competitors undermines the very certainty that intellectual property rights aim to create. The result could be a substantial impediment to incentives to innovate.[565] Consequently, a refusal to license an intellectual property right may require an even higher threshold than a refusal to supply tangible resources.[566] As section 4.2.2b will demonstrate, incentives to invest also play a role in a duty to supply interface specifications, yet the incentives are different from many other cases because of the involvement of network effects.

A second argument against application of the essential facilities doctrine is that this doctrine appears less related to abusive behavior, which is the

561. Indeed, some US commentators and cases suggest abandoning the doctrine altogether. See Areeda & Hovenkamp 1994; *Trinko* (US Supreme Court 2004). See also Weber Waller 2008.

562. European Commission 2009, §75; Geradin 2004, p. 1539; Korah 2006, p. 135; van Rooijen 2008, p. 77; Whish 2003, p. 670. See also *Trinko* (US Supreme Court 2004), 407.

563. Forrester 2005, p. 951.

564. Gual et al. 2005, p. 44; Hovenkamp et al. 2005, p. 20; Kovacic & Reindl 2005, p. 1065; Marquardt & Leddy 2003, p. 856; Turney 2005, §18. But see Ritter 2005.

565. Gilbert & Shapiro 1996; Hovenkamp et al. 2005, p. 17; Katz & Shapiro 1998, p. 39; Lévêque 2005, p. 80; Lipsky Jr. & Sidak 1999, p. 1218; Marquardt & Leddy 2003, p. 857; Opinion A-G Jacobs in *Bronner* (ECJ 1998), §62; Shapiro & Teece 1994, §VI; Turney 2005, §25.

566. Temple Lang 2005, p. 65. See also Hovenkamp et al. 2005, p. 14. But see Ritter 2005. See also section 4.1.2c.

primary concern of Article 102,[567] than it is to structural ownership issues. Many essential facilities cases arguably arise from inefficient *ex-ante* allocation of rights and resources rather than abusive behavior.[568] For example, these cases involve refusals to provide access to facilities constructed or sanctioned by the government, such as telecommunications networks and other infrastructure,[569] or to intellectual property rights that were defined too broadly, such as the copyrights in *Magill* and *IMS Health*, or the design rights in *Volvo* (see *infra*).[570] In such instances, the competitive problems arguably arise from the *ex-ante* allocation of rights and resources rather than any particular abusive behavior. The 'abusive behavior', after all, consists of nothing more than a refusal to provide access to a right allocated to the dominant firm. Having allocated these (intellectual property) rights and resources to these undertakings, it may well have been entirely foreseeable that they would refuse access to competitors. This foreseeability would point to an *ex-ante* change in the allocation of (intellectual property) rights, rather than *ex-post* application of competition law to correct for such structural ownership issues.[571] The competition authority or the court is no more (and probably less) equipped to deal with broader, structural ownership issues than the *ex-ante* legislator.[572] The *Volvo* judgment, therefore, has led to an *ex-ante* limitation of the design right for the free use of spare parts for repair purposes, which will be examined in section 5.1, while telecommunications law provides for *ex-ante* interconnection duties.[573] Indeed, section 4.1.2d already hinted that the protection of interface specifications should also be addressed through an *ex-ante* adjustment in copyright law.[574]

A third problem with forcing access to a tangible good or intellectual property right is the difficulty of determining and monitoring the terms of access.[575] Based on the unwillingness of the parties to do so, a court or competition enforcer must formulate appropriate remedies and terms itself and must also monitor compliance with these terms. To this end, Regulation 1/2003 authorizes the Commission to impose behavioral remedies in addition to fines to sanction abusive behavior.[576] However, the Commission and courts must proceed with caution when making use of this flexibility because it

567. Larouche 2000, p. 212. See section 3.1.
568. van Rooijen 2008.
569. See section 5.2.2.
570. Frischmann & Weber-Waller 2008, p. 32; van Rooijen 2008, p. 80; Turney 2005, §61, §62.
571. See section 4.1.2c.
572. See section 4.1.2b.
573. See section 5.2.
574. See also Chapters 3 and 6.
575. Doherty 2001, p. 432; Geradin 2004, p. 1543; Korah 2006, p. 135; Lévêque 2005, p. 87. *Microsoft*'s terms, including the price for the specifications and the monitoring system, were intensely litigated. *Microsoft* (GC 2007), §D.
576. Regulation 1/2003. See, for example, *Microsoft Decision* (European Commission 2004). See, generally, Whish 2003, p. 254.

increases legal uncertainty.[577] Furthermore, it is questionable whether courts or competition authorities are capable of this task and whether it is desirable to have these terms imposed by a central authority.[578] Setting 'fair and reasonable' terms will be difficult, especially in the case of new and emerging technologies, where no market precedent exists[579] – for instance, where interface specifications of a new platform computer program have not previously been supplied. It is also questionable whether the court or antitrust enforcer is equipped to monitor compliance with the terms.[580] The more complex the details of the remedies are, the more likely compliance with the terms will be litigated. Imposing a duty to supply interface specifications may be particularly complex: a court will need to determine not only the price for the interoperability information but also the amount of information to be provided, the frequency at which the information is to be made available and so on.[581] Indeed, one commentator has argued that courts should refrain from imposing a duty to deal altogether where compliance with the consent decree is difficult to monitor.[582] Nonetheless, a sector-specific regulatory authority could assist in the monitoring process.[583] Still, it altogether appears preferable to incentivize the parties to negotiate access privately. This is, indeed, the ultimate purpose of the Software Directive's reverse engineering provisions[584] and the preferred method in interconnection regulation under telecommunications law.[585]

A fourth argument against application of the essential facility doctrine, in its more traditional role of preventing the leverage of market power from one market to another, lies in the *Single Monopoly Theorem* and related arguments attributed to the Chicago school. These arguments have already been discussed in section 2.2.3b. Essentially, these arguments entail that leveraging market power from one market to another does not make economic sense (and is not harmful to consumers) because the monopoly rent, which can already be extracted from the first market, cannot be increased simply by monopolizing the adjacent market. There are several caveats to this theory, however – most

577. The Commission is bound by the general principle of proportionality. See TFEU, Article 5(3); Regulation 1/2003, Recital 12; Ortiz Blanco 2006.

578. Faull & Nikpay 1999, p. 202.

579. See generally Swanson & Baurnol 2005. Although courts' experience with infringement cases may be helpful, designing forward-looking terms may well be more complicated than designing remedies for past harm. See US Department of Justice & Federal Trade Commission 2007, p. 23.

580. Turney 2005, §27.

581. *IBM Undertaking* (European Commission 1984) and *Microsoft Decision* (European Commission 2004) may serve as precedents.

582. Areeda 1990, p. 853. Indeed, the system for monitoring compliance with the Commission's *Microsoft* decision, which comprised an independent monitoring trustee, was rejected by the GC. See *Microsoft* (GC 2007), §D.

583. Areeda 1990, p. 853. See section 6.3.2b.

584. See section 3.2.2b.

585. See section 5.2.3b.

notably that it only applies to perfectly complementary goods.[586] More importantly, application of the essential facilities doctrine is no longer limited to leveraging market power from one market to another.[587] In Europe, the *IMS Health* judgment appears to have opened the door to essential facility claims among horizontal competitors (see section 4.2.1c).

c. Concretization in the Case Law

Even if the essential facilities doctrine's scope of application has been expanded, the European courts have effectively applied the same analytical framework to all of these cases. Instrumentally, this rigidity is in some tension with competition law's role as a flexible instrument to assess abusive behavior by dominant firms (see section 4.1.2b).[588] Substantively, application of a single analytical framework to all cases of refusals to deal may also lead to inadequate analyzes.[589] Indeed, in section 4.2.2, it will be demonstrated why the usefulness of this single framework is particularly questionable for cases involving refusals to supply interface specifications.

The TFEU is not to blame for the rigid application of the essential facilities doctrine. Article 102 itself, in relevant part, merely provides that 'any abuse by one or more undertakings of a dominant position within the internal market or in a substantial part of it shall be prohibited' and that '[s]uch abuse may, in particular, consist in [. . .] (b) limiting production, markets or technical development to the prejudice of consumers'. These open norms enable the competition authority to consider all the circumstances relevant to the behavior under scrutiny, which corresponds to the use of competition law as a flexible instrument to assess exceptional cases.[590] According to Larouche, it is, indeed, the application of competition law's broad, open norms to the particular circumstances of the case that forms the legitimacy for intervention on such broad terms.[591]

However, in the case law, little has remained of the flexibility offered by Article 102. In a series of cases involving refusals to deal, the European courts have determined and reiterated the set of circumstances that constitute an unlawful refusal to deal, and, therefore, abusive behavior under Article 102(b).

The European incarnation of the essential facilities doctrine can be traced back to the 1974 case of *Commercial Solvents*.[592] This case involved the

586. See, for example, *Microsoft Decision* (European Commission 2004), §767.
587. See also Glazer & Lipsky Jr. 1995, p. 757.
588. See also Larouche 2000, p. 212.
589. See also Glazer & Lipsky Jr. 1995, p. 763 (similarly arguing for US case law that, 'analysis of unilateral refusals to deal suffers primarily from the failure to recognize that not all of the myriad fact patterns that arise in specific cases can be fit into one procrustean framework').
590. See section 4.1.2b.
591. Larouche 2000, p. 122.
592. *Commercial Solvents* (ECJ 1974).

termination of a supply of raw materials by Commercial Solvents, a dominant company, to Zoja, a downstream manufacturer of the derivative product ethambutol. The ECJ observed that there were no alternative sources for the raw material than Commercial Solvents. Thus, as a consequence of Commercial Solvents' termination, Zoja risked being eliminated.[593] Commercial Solvent's refusal to supply, therefore, constituted abusive behavior. Without substantial (economic) analysis, the ECJ noted:

> [A]n undertaking being in a dominant position as regards the production of raw material and therefore able to control the supply to manufacturers of derivatives, cannot, just because it decides to start manufacturing these derivatives (in competition with its former customers) act in such a way as to eliminate their competition [. . .].[594]

Elimination of effective competition is easily conceivable if a software developer refuses to supply interface specifications of a successful program to competitors. As noted, markets with strong network effects, including many markets for computer programs, are subject to tipping. When tipping occurs, competitors must offer interoperable programs in order to compete viably; non-interoperable competitors are excluded from the market.[595] Achieving interoperability is not possible without the interface specifications. Therefore, it is generally not difficult to prove a likelihood of elimination of effective competition if access to interface specifications of a tipped product is refused.[596] Indeed, in *Microsoft*, the GC noted that network effects contributed significantly to the elimination of competition on the separate market for workgroup server operating systems.[597]

In subsequent cases, the ECJ concretized the concept of an unlawful refusal to deal to a more specific set of conditions. In *Bronner*,[598] the ECJ clarified that a refusal to deal is not unlawful unless it relates to a facility that is indispensable to competitors in a downstream market.[599] The *Bronner* case originated from a dispute between Mediaprint, a large Austrian newspaper company controlling a nationwide distribution network, and Oscar Bronner, a small publisher. Arguing that 'it would be entirely unprofitable for it to organise its own home-delivery service',[600] Bronner claimed that Mediaprint abused its dominant position in home-delivery services by not including Bronner's publication in the delivery process. Following an influential opinion by A-G Jacobs, the ECJ disagreed with Bronner, noting that there were no:

593. *Id.*, §25.
594. *Id.*
595. See section 2.2.2d.
596. Lévêque 2005, p. 84.
597. *Microsoft* (GC 2007), §562.
598. *Bronner* (ECJ 1998).
599. See also Doherty 2001, p. 423; Helberger 2005, p. 164; Turney 2005.
600. *Bronner* (ECJ 1998), §8.

> technical, legal or even economic obstacles capable of making it impossible, or even unreasonably difficult, for any other publisher of daily newspapers to establish, alone or in cooperation with other publishers, its own nationwide home-delivery scheme and use it to distribute its own daily newspapers.[601]

The stringent *Bronner* test for indispensability addresses a significant concern of the essential facilities doctrine: if access to competitors' facilities were too straightforward, there would be little incentive to create these facilities in the first place, whereas the outlook of forced access would cause others to wait and free-ride rather than to invest themselves.[602]

The indispensability test can be applied to interface specifications. Generally, competition does not necessarily require interoperability with the target program, let alone access to its interfaces.[603] Following *Bronner*, the interoperable developer normally would be required to develop its own platform product to compete in the downstream application (sub)market. *Bronner* entailed a similar obligation: in order to compete in the (downstream) market for daily newspapers, Bronner could not rely on Mediaprint's (upstream) distribution facilities, but instead had to offer both.

However, as already demonstrated in section 2.2, there may be no possibility to compete if a market contains strong network effects and has tipped in favor of a single firm's product, while the competing product is not interoperable with the dominant firm's product.[604] Thus, whereas consumers would be indifferent to multiple newspapers and journals being distributed to their homes by multiple distribution networks, as envisaged in *Bronner*, they are unlikely to switch to a non-interoperable alternative computer program that does not allow them to interoperate with other users.[605] This, in turn, requires access to that product's interoperability information. Indeed, in *Microsoft*, the GC held that the ability to interoperate on an equal footing with the Windows operating systems was vital to compete.[606]

In addition to these criteria of elimination of competition and indispensability, the European courts have consistently held that a refusal to deal does not constitute an abuse if it is objectively justified,[607] and, indeed, economic theory recognizes several procompetitive motivations for foreclosure.[608] With equal consistency, however, the courts have rejected various objective justifications. Consequently, it is largely unclear what justifications an

601. *Id.*, §44.
602. See section 4.2.1b.
603. See also Hovenkamp et al. 2002–2007, p. 12.8.2; McGowan 1996, p. 834.
604. Drexl et al. 2006, §15; European Commission 2005, §230.
605. See section 2.2.2a. See also *Microsoft* (GC 2007), §421.
606. *Id.*
607. See, generally, Craig & de Búrca 2003, p. 1030; Dolmans et al. 2007, p. 134; European Commission 2009, §28; Loewenthal 2005.
608. See section 2.2.3b. See also Bechtold 2007, pp. 62, 66; Geradin 2004, p. 1540.

undertaking may rely on.[609] In *Microsoft*, the Commission and, subsequently, the GC, rejected a number of objective justifications related to vertical, but not to horizontal, foreclosure. Before the Commission, Microsoft had raised the *Single Monopoly Rent* theory in its defense:[610] it claimed that leveraging its market power from client PC operating systems to workgroup server operating systems would not make economic sense because it could already extract its monopoly profits from the former market.[611] The Commission rejected this argument relying on post-Chicago school theories.[612] The Commission was concerned that Microsoft's conduct raised entry barriers for competitors.[613] Furthermore, the Commission noted that Microsoft's conduct allowed it to leverage its currently strong position in client PC operating systems to dominate a future market for server-oriented computing.[614]

One well-recognized justification is limited capacity of the facility. Where access to a facility by third parties would introduce security problems or would otherwise compromise the integrity of the facility, a refusal may be justified.[615] In this respect, it is important to recall that access to interface specifications enables the creation of interoperable systems. As more components from different vendors interoperate, the system can become more vulnerable to attacks and capacity problems. Within the context of a refusal to provide interface information about a platform product, the undertaking could thus legitimately fear that access to competitors would introduce security risks or harm to the platform's reputation.[616]

In *Volvo v. Veng*,[617] the ECJ was first confronted with the refusal to license intellectual property rights, rather than the more traditional refusal to supply access to a tangible facility. *Volvo* concerned the refusal by a car manufacturer to license design rights in spare car parts to garages, which risked foreclosing all competition in the secondary repairs market.[618] The ECJ held that the exclusion of others to use the registered design constituted the specific subject matter of the intellectual property right.[619] Consequently, such exclusion could not by itself amount to an abuse of a

---

609. Doherty 2001, p. 428; Turney 2005, §48. See generally, Loewenthal 2005. The ECJ essentially requires that any objective justification be proportionate to the abuse. Thus, the positive effects of the refusal to deal must outweigh its negative effects. *British Airways* (ECJ 2007), §86; *United Brands* (ECJ 1987), §158. See also Craig & de Búrca 2003, p. 1030.
610. See section 2.2.3b.
611. *Microsoft Decision* (European Commission 2004), §765.
612. See, generally, section 2.2.3.
613. *Microsoft Decision* (European Commission 2004), §768.
614. *Id.*, §770.
615. Doherty 2001, p. 431; Lévêque 2005, p. 80; Temple Lang 1994, p. 513; Whish 2003, p. 677.
616. Jones II & Turner 1997, p. 389; Samuelson 2008a. See also section 2.2.3b.
617. *Volvo* (ECJ 1988).
618. See also Doherty 2001, p. 407; Schovsbo 1998, p. 517.
619. *Volvo* (ECJ 1988), §8. See also section 4.1.1.

dominant position.[620] The court mentioned examples of 'additional circumstances' that could amount to an abuse[621] but did not provide a test to determine which circumstances could generally be found abusive.[622] Thus, *Volvo* provided some deference to intellectual property rights by recognizing that a refusal to license an intellectual property right could never by itself amount to abusive behavior. However, the judgment also left some flexibility for an assessment of exceptional circumstances that could justify an *ex-post* correction of the balance struck by *ex-ante* intellectual property rights – as suggested by section 4.1.2c.

Magill, then, shed more light on what might constitute 'additional circumstances', and this was also the first case in which a dominant intellectual property rightsholder was actually forced to license its (copy)rights. Magill was a magazine publisher that intended to create a new, comprehensive TV guide, obviating the then-existing need for consumers to combine the individual TV schedules from the three main broadcasters. However, because these schedules were protected by copyrights, the three broadcasters could prevent Magill from using their information and thereby from developing a competing, comprehensive TV guide. In judging whether the broadcasters' conduct amounted to an abuse of their joint dominant position, the court first referred to *Volvo*, noting that refusing to license an intellectual property right cannot by itself – in the absence of exceptional circumstances – constitute an abuse.[623] Unlike in *Volvo*, however, the court found such exceptional circumstances to be present in this case:

> The appellants' refusal to provide basic information by relying on national copyright provisions thus prevented the appearance of a new product, a comprehensive weekly guide to television programmes, which the appellants did not offer and for which there was a potential consumer demand.[624]

Whereas A-G Gulmann had sought to allow a duty to license only if this license would not result in horizontal competition with the rightsholder,[625] the ECJ appeared to accept a broader duty to license through the new-product test: although a new product could be a product in a different market, it could also compete directly with the rightsholder's product.

The relevance of *Magill*'s new-product condition for refusals to license intellectual property rights was confirmed in *IMS Health*.[626] In this case, copyrights protected a geographical map used to collect and analyze sales data in the German pharmaceutical industry (a 'brick structure', in pharmaceutical

620. *Id.*
621. *Id.*, Recital 9.
622. See also Govaere 1996, p. 113; Turney 2005, §31.
623. *Magill* (ECJ 1995), §49. See also Govaere 1996, p. 145.
624. *Magill* (ECJ 1995), §54.
625. Opinion A-G Gulmann in *Id.*, §96. See also Turney 2005, §37.
626. *IMS Health* (ECJ 2004).

parlance). IMS' brick structure had become a standard among doctors and other stakeholders, due in part to their early involvement in its design.[627] IMS' refusal to license the structure to competitor NDC thus precluded direct, horizontal competition in the market for analyzing pharmaceutical sales data because it meant that NDC had to arrange its data according to a different, non-standard format.[628] Citing *Magill*, the ECJ held that, because the brick structure was copyrighted subject matter, NDC had to prove that the refusal to license the structure obstructed the development of new products or services. The court observed:

> [T]he refusal by an undertaking in a dominant position to allow access to a product protected by an intellectual property right [. . .] may be regarded as abusive only where the undertaking which requested the licence [. . .] intends to produce new goods or services not offered by the owner of the right and for which there is a potential consumer demand.[629]

The ECJ left the application of this principle to the national court.[630] It was difficult to see how the condition would be met because NDC intended to offer essentially the same services as IMS Health.[631] Indeed, the ECJ's adherence to the new-product test was arguably ill founded because the brick structure had become a standard in the industry. The function of the new-product test for control over standards, including interface specifications, will be studied in further detail in section 4.2.2.

Indeed, the ECJ in *IMS Health* also disposed of the requirement that the refusal to deal eliminate competition on a secondary market. Following the A-G's opinion, the ECJ accepted that a hypothetical market or even a separate production stage sufficed to meet this condition.[632] The court identified such a hypothetical market for IMS' brick structure. In this interpretation, there obviously is a hypothetical market for almost anything. More importantly, the court, by accepting 'hypothetical markets', allowed for a situation in which the firm controlling the relevant input is nearly automatically dominant on the hypothetical market, which is often not the case if a real market were identified.[633] In a case involving a refusal by a dominant software developer to provide interface specifications, one could envisage identifying the creation of interfaces and their specifications as a separate production stage. Access could thus be granted for both horizontal and vertical competitors.[634]

In sum, the ECJ has held that a refusal to deal constitutes an abuse under Article 102 if it concerns a facility that is *indispensable* to competition, such

627. *Id.*, §5. See also Opinion A-G Tizzano in *IMS Health* (ECJ 2004), §7; Turney 2005, §58.
628. See also Turney 2005, §55.
629. *IMS Health* (ECJ 2004), §49.
630. *Id.*, §50.
631. Drexl 2004, p. 800; Temple Lang 2005, p. 72.
632. *IMS Health* (ECJ 2004), §45. See also Turney 2005, §47, §59, §84.
633. Drexl 2004, p. 564.
634. See also Drexl et al. 2006; Geradin 2004, p. 1530.

that effective competition is likely to be *eliminated* if access is refused. If the facility comprises an intellectual property right, the refusal to license the intellectual property right must, in addition, obstruct the development of a *new product*. Notwithstanding these conditions, a refusal to deal or to license may be *objectively justified*.

These four conditions (or three, if the facility does not comprise an intellectual property right) have essentially been applied in all recent cases involving refusals to deal and thus form a rather rigid framework. The rigidity of this framework has been questioned.[635] There has, indeed, been an ongoing discussion as to the relevance of any other circumstances that could be important in refusals to deal. In particular, it has been questioned whether the obstruction of new-product development should be the only parameter that determines whether the refusal to license an(y) intellectual property right constitutes abusive behavior, or whether other exceptional circumstances could also be considered.[636]

In the light of the complementary relationship between intellectual property rights and competition rules, this is a highly relevant question. As noted in section 4.1, competition authorities should not structurally review the balance between static and dynamic efficiency already struck in intellectual property rights but should instead allow intervention only in exceptional circumstances, or circumstances that were not anticipated *ex-ante*. Section 4.2.2 observed that it is questionable whether the new-product test can serve as an adequate parameter to distinguish foreseeable from exceptional cases, and it may, therefore, be useful to consider other parameters.

Indeed, in *Volvo v. Veng*, the first case about a refusal to license an intellectual property right, the ECJ did not mention the new-product condition (see *supra*). Although the court offered examples of additional circumstances that could render a refusal to license an intellectual property right as abusive, none of the court's examples included the obstruction of new-product development. In *Magill*, the court first introduced the new-product factor (see *supra*), yet it failed to clarify whether this was only relevant to that particular case or whether it constituted a cumulative condition for all refusals to license intellectual property rights. Because *Magill* was based on *Volvo*'s observation that there had to be some additional element for the refusal to license to be a violation of Article 102, and because *Volvo* did not mention obstruction of new-product development as an example of such additional elements, the reference to new product in *Magill* should arguably be read as a mere case-specific factor rather than a cumulative condition.[637] In *IMS Health*,

---

635. See, for example, European Commission 2005, §4; Gual et al. 2005, p. 3; Ullrich 2001, p. 397.
636. See also Derclaye 2003, p. 689; Drexl 2004, p. 799; Korah 2006, p. 139; Temple Lang 1997, p. 729; Turney 2005, §33. This debate is similar to the discussion in US antitrust law between those favoring *rule-of-reason* and those favoring *per-se (il)legality* approaches.
637. See also *Microsoft Decision* (European Commission 2004), §557.

the ECJ, nonetheless, held that it was necessary for this condition to be met.[638] In its *Microsoft* decision, which was issued shortly prior to the ECJ's judgment in *IMS Health*, the Commission had argued:

> [T]here is no persuasiveness to an approach that would advocate the existence of an exhaustive checklist of exceptional circumstances and would have the Commission disregard *a limine* other circumstances of exceptional character that may deserve to be taken into account when assessing a refusal to supply.[639]

In the light of competition law's primary role as an instrument to review unforeseeable, exceptional behavior, this position appears persuasive indeed.[640] Nevertheless, the Commission's all-circumstances approach was not embraced by the GC. On Microsoft's appeal, the GC followed *IMS Health* by reiterating the four-part exceptional circumstances test, including the new-product condition.[641]

In sum, the European courts have developed a rigid framework for assessing essential facility claims. This rigidity is in some tension with the use of competition law for exceptional cases of abusive behavior.[642]

4.2.2. Application to Interface Specifications

Section 4.2.1 demonstrated how application of the essential facilities doctrine could serve as a basis to balance openness and control of interface specifications *ex-post*, with – in theory – consideration of the particular circumstances of the case. It was already demonstrated, however, that this flexibility is largely lost in the rigid set of requirements of the European essential facilities doctrine. The present section demonstrates that application of this rigid framework risks ignoring the particular issues that arise when access is sought to standards and particularly interface specifications. The balance between openness and control of interface specifications is, therefore, struck without consideration of factors particularly relevant to interoperability and standardization, which were identified in Chapter 2, and may, therefore, not

---

638. *IMS Health* (ECJ 2004), §49. See Ahlborn et al. 2005, p. 1127; Temple Lang 2005, p. 71. However, the court also and somewhat confusingly observed that it was 'sufficient' if the four conditions discussed *supra* – including new product – were met. *IMS Health* (ECJ 2004), §38.
639. *Microsoft Decision* (European Commission 2004), §555. See also Bechtold 2007, p. 111.
640. See section 4.1.2b.
641. Still, the GC failed to explicitly reject the relevance of other factors, noting that the established four factors were 'in particular' relevant. *Microsoft* (GC 2007), §332. The court also considered some of the Commission's additional factors under the established four-part test. For instance, the GC, like the Commission, noted that non-disclosure of interface specifications was contrary to industry practice and constituted a disruption of previous levels of supply. *Microsoft* (GC 2007), §702.
642. See section 4.1.

be adequate. The two leading cases are *IMS Health* and *Microsoft*, which both concerned control over standards or interface specifications.[643]

Two particular issues arise when the previously described rigid framework for essential facilities is applied to a refusal to supply interface specifications. First, firms may refuse access to interface specifications in order to compete for the market. In comparison to the more common competition in the market, competition for the market has different, yet not necessarily harmful, effects on consumer welfare (see Chapter 2). The framework for essential facilities, however, is largely focused on safeguarding competition in, rather than for the market, and thus ignores any positive welfare effects of the latter type of competition (section 4.2.2a).

Second, competition law is (rightfully) concerned about impeding incentives to innovate caused by mandatory sharing of intellectual property rights. It safeguards the incentive function of intellectual property rights through the new-product-test, which represents a higher threshold for refusals to license intellectual property rights than for refusals to supply other facilities. However, the primary concern of a dominant software developer may well be that, by being forced to supply its interface specifications, it can lose its exclusivity over a *de-facto* proprietary network. The generally low innovative value of the interface specifications themselves is disproportionate to the significant effect of their control on market power, innovation and competition. By, nonetheless, focusing on the incentives to innovate driven by the intellectual property rights in the interfaces themselves, rather than their function of controlling access to a *de-facto* proprietary network, competition law risks ignoring both the relevant incentives and harm to competitors (section 4.2.2b).

a. Competition in or for the Market

The suggested balance between control and openness of interface specifications in software markets described in Chapter 2 was based in part, on the one hand, on a trade-off between the relative efficiencies of having firms compete *for* the market by exploiting a proprietary network during a period of temporary dominance (controlled interfaces), and, on the other hand, having multiple firms compete *in* the market through interoperable programs (open interfaces). A combination of both forms of competition could be welfare enhancing. This section demonstrates that competition law inadequately balances these two forms of competition.

The basic starting point of competition law appears to be similar to that of intellectual property laws, including copyright law: independent competition is superior to sharing between competitors because such sharing will reduce incentives to innovate.[644] Applying this principle to a network market, such as

643. *Microsoft Decision* (European Commission 2004); *IMS Health* (ECJ 2004); *Microsoft* (GC 2007).

644. See section 4.2.1a.

a software market, competitors are, therefore, in principle free to withhold their interface information, which jeopardizes interoperability. Chapter 2 already noted that, as a result of non-interoperability, firms may (horizontally) tend to compete for the market. Ultimately, the effect of competition law's basic premise against mandatory sharing in the software industry is thus competition for the market. However, this is not the end of the inquiry. As already noted in section 4.2.1b, the essential facilities doctrine represents an exception to this general rule against mandatory sharing. If a firm's refusal to supply risks excluding effective competition, there may be a duty to share the essential facility – for instance, relevant interface specifications. This, in turn, facilitates interoperability, which may stimulate competition in the market.

The result of competition law's basic premise against mandatory sharing, which leads to competition for the market, and application of the essential facility doctrine, which can lead to competition in the market, is a somewhat uncomfortable mix of competition for and in the market. It is uncomfortable because the trade-off between these two forms of competition is not expressly made, let alone on sound considerations. Rather, the primary criterion is whether a refusal to deal risks excluding effective competition. In a network market, elimination of competition is a natural result of the process of tipping,[645] such that the condition of exclusion of competitors will easily be met.[646] Chapter 2 established, however, that the choice of competition for or in the market, which could both be efficient, depends on other factors, such as the rate of innovation in the industry, coordination costs, strength of network effects, necessary investments and other entry barriers. The crucial question is whether there is any room for such considerations in the rigid framework for essential facilities, as established by the European courts. Following Article 102 of the TFEU, there are two levels at which the type of competition (in or for the market) could be assessed: the analysis of dominance and of abusive behavior. Dominance will be examined first.

Only a dominant firm can be forced to share its resources, such as copyrights protecting interface specifications, under the essential facility doctrine. Therefore, it is relevant to determine how a dominant position is established[647] and, in particular, whether dominance is established only in relation to current competitors (competition in the market) or also to successive competitors (competition for the market). In the latter case, a currently high market share may not necessarily amount to a dominant position based on the competitive pressure from subsequent competitors. This enables a consideration of any efficiencies of competition for the market. However, there appears to be little room for such considerations.

645. See section 2.2.2d.
646. See also section 4.2.1b.
647. The inquiry into dominance is a mainly factual analysis in which the European Commission, as the competition authority for the Union's internal market, enjoys considerable discretion. See, for example *Microsoft* (GC 2007), §23–§35, §87.

A dominant position equals a position of significant market power on a given market.[648] The purpose of this inquiry is to examine whether the subject firm is under sufficient competitive restraints in relation to its market.[649] Therefore, the first step in the analysis is the determination of the relevant market.[650] The second step is the determination of the firm's market power on that market and, particularly, whether such market power suffices to qualify as a dominant position.

Determining the relevant market essentially comprises an inquiry into the interchangeability of goods and suppliers.[651] This process typically consists of an analysis of demand-side substitutability, of supply-side substitutability and of entry barriers or competitive restraints.[652] Demand-side substitutability relates to the interchangeability of products from a consumer perspective. If products are interchangeable, they are generally part of the same market as their respective suppliers compete for the same consumers. Supply-side substitutability relates to the interchangeability of suppliers: more suppliers may be attracted to a given market if prices were to increase, and these suppliers, therefore, may need to be considered. Traditionally, demand- and supply-side interchangeability is measured primarily by determining the effects of price increases.[653] In network markets, however, prices may not be an accurate or

648. *United Brands* (ECJ 1987), §65 ('a position of economic strength enjoyed by an undertaking which enables it to prevent effective competition being maintained on the relevant market by giving it the power to behave to an appreciable extent independently of its competitors, customers and ultimately of its consumers'). See also European Commission 2009, §10.
649. European Commission 2009, §10.
650. Katz & Shapiro 1998, p. 40. In the United States, the concept of technology markets is used to scrutinize competition in innovation independent of concrete product markets. Katz & Shelanski 2005.
651. As already noted, this critical analysis may risk being largely ignored in the application of the essential facilities doctrine if a market is defined for access to the relevant facility. See section 4.2.1c.
652. European Commission 2005, §18; Helberger 2005, p. 123; Whish 2003, p. 24.
653. If a small price increase would cause consumers to switch to another product, that product is part of the market definition. If a small price increase would cause additional suppliers to join the market, those suppliers are also part of the market definition. In both cases, the hypothetical small price increase is thus unprofitable for the subject firm because it would cause consumers to switch to rival products or invite other suppliers. Conversely, the subject firm is confronted with sufficient competitive restraints from those other products and suppliers. This test is known as the *hypothetical monopoly test* or *SSNIP* test, which is short for Small but Significant, Non-transitory Increase in Price. An important caveat to the SSNIP test is that, within the context of monopolization cases, this test may result in an overly broad market definition due to the so-called *Cellophane Fallacy*, named after a US case involving a cellophane manufacturer. Because the subject firm, if it is indeed a monopolist, already charges supra-competitive (monopoly) prices, a further price increase would automatically be unprofitable, such that, following the SNIPP test, additional products and geographical areas could (erroneously) be added to the market. European Commission 2005, p. 7; Schaerr 1985; Schotter 2003, p. 383; Whish 2003, pp. 30, 194. See, for example, *Microsoft Decision* (European Commission 2004), §388.

sufficient parameter for the relevant market because these markets may demonstrate lower sensitivity to price increases in favor of network benefits and standardization.[654]

The faster the innovation cycles in a given market, the more the focus of market definition should shift from current to future market conditions.[655] Scrutiny of structural entry barriers can provide some insight into future market conditions.[656] Competitive pressure on the incumbent could be higher if entry barriers are lower.[657] Conversely, if entry barriers are high, or technological change occurs less rapidly, a currently high market share may be more indicative of a sustainable dominant position.[658]

Once the relevant market has been determined, one must examine the market power of the subject firm on that market. In the light of the necessity to balance the interests of competition in the market, through interoperability and open interface specifications, and competition for the market, through non-interoperability and controlled interfaces, the crucial question is thus whether a currently high market share – which can be the natural result of competition for the market – can be put in perspective through an analysis of competitive restraints from future competitors.

In theory, the Commission accepts that market shares are only a proxy for market power, which is recognized as the decisive factor.[659] In practice, however, there appears to be little room to counter a currently high market share. The Commission and the ECJ consider a high market share (40%) to be strongly indicative of significant market power.[660] Consequently, there appears to be little room to counterweigh a high market share by considering the effects of competitive pressure from subsequent competitors.[661] Indeed, in its *Microsoft* decision, the European Commission rejected Microsoft's arguments relating to the relative unimportance of current dominance in a model

654. Prices may initially be kept artificially low in order to drive demand for the platform, while profits could be realized at a later stage – for instance, by selling compatible add-on products. Katz & Shapiro 1998, pp. 11–13; Shapiro & Varian 1999, p. 273. See also section 2.2.3.
655. Katz & Shapiro 1998, p. 13; Katz & Shelanski 2005, p. 10; Katz & Shelanski 2007, p. 15; Turney 2005, §8. See also Helberger 2005, p. 122. See also section 2.2.2d. For example, the 'old' markets for individual word processing, spreadsheet and presentation programs has been replaced by one for office suites. Previously, the separate markets for desktop operating systems and graphical user interfaces had been replaced by a single market for desktop operating systems.
656. Katz & Shelanski 2005, p. 9; Katz & Shelanski 2007, p. 15; US Department of Justice & Federal Trade Commission 1992.
657. See section 2.2.2d. See also Schotter 2003, p. 383; Turney 2005, §76.
658. See also Drexl 2004, p. 796.
659. European Commission 2009, §13.
660. European Commission 2005, §31; *Hoffmann-La Roche* (ECJ 1979), §39 ('The existence of a dominant position may derive from several factors which, taken separately, are not necessarily determinative but among these factors a highly important one is the existence of very large market shares').
661. See also Van Loon 2008, p. 221.

of competition for the market.[662] Although it did thoroughly inquire whether Microsoft's *present* market power was curtailed by sufficiently low entry barriers, including the possibility of reverse engineering under the Software Directive,[663] it was less prepared to consider *future* market conditions:

> Even if it were to be the case that a dominant position might be limited in time, this does not in itself constitute a limitation to the *present* market strength of the dominant company.[664]

Additionally, there is some uncertainty as to the concept of *superdominance* – that is, market shares substantially higher than the 40% threshold. Although the courts and the Commission have not explicitly referred to superdominance,[665] they have alluded to this concept – including in the *Microsoft* case.[666] If there is indeed a more stringent set of rules applying to superdominant companies, this could be very relevant to the situation in which a rightsholder refuses to provide interface information of its platform products to competitors. As noted, tipping in network markets could, indeed, result in the emergence of a superdominant undertaking.[667]

The Commission also appears to acknowledge the role of entry barriers in innovation markets. It recognizes that, if entry barriers are low, or if technological change emerges rapidly, a finding of a high market share may not be determinative of sustainable dominance because a price increase would attract other suppliers and follow-on innovators.[668] Nonetheless, it appears to view entry barriers primarily as a confirmation of market power. In its Guidance Paper, the Commission recognizes that network effects may constitute a significant barrier to entry.[669] In *Microsoft*, the presence of network effects was similarly found to contribute significantly to Microsoft's (sustainable) market power.[670]

By contrast, the Commission's 2002 Guidelines for market definition in telecommunications markets are more explicit about possible competitive pressure from future, innovative competitors:

> A finding of dominance depends on an assessment of ease of market entry. In fact, the absence of barriers to entry deters, in principle, independent

662. See, generally, *Microsoft Decision* (European Commission 2004), §5.2.1.4. The US Court of Appeals also rejected Microsoft's claims to this effect. *United States v. Microsoft* (US Court of Appeals, DC Circuit 2001), 49.
663. *Microsoft Decision* (European Commission 2004), §5.2.1.3.
664. *Id.*, §469.
665. Appeldoorn 2005, p. 653.
666. See, for example, *Microsoft Decision* (European Commission 2004), §586, §747; European Commission 2005, §92. See also Appeldoorn 2005, p. 653; Larouche 2008, p. 9.
667. See section 2.2.1. See, for example, *Microsoft* (GC 2007), §31.
668. European Commission 2005, §34.
669. European Commission 2009, §17, §20. See also *Microsoft Decision* (European Commission 2004), §338, §340, §420, §5.2.1.3, §541; Turney 2005, §16.
670. *Microsoft* (GC 2007), §31, §33.

> anti-competitive behaviour by an undertaking with a significant market share. [...] Furthermore, barriers to entry exist where entry into the relevant market requires large investments and the programming of capacities over a long time in order to be profitable. However, high barriers to entry may become less relevant with regard to markets characterized by on-going technological progress. In electronic communications markets, competitive constraints may come from innovative threats from potential competitors that are not currently in the market. In such markets, the competitive assessment should be based on a prospective, forward-looking approach.[671]

In conclusion, the concept of dominance under Article 102 of the TFEU appears primarily focused on a more traditional assessment of competitive restraints from current competitors, rather than competitive pressure from subsequent follow-on competitors. This approach to dominance, therefore, largely focuses on competition in the market, and may risk ignoring any benefits of competition for the market.

Also, even if a firm is dominant, Article 102 only sanctions abuse of a dominant position; it does not sanction dominance *per-se*. As observed in section 4.2.1, one form of abuse is a refusal to supply access to a tangible facility or an intellectual property right that risks eliminating effective competition (the essential facilities doctrine). Exclusion of competitors is, however, a natural result if firms compete for the market – for instance, by offering non-interoperable computer programs in an attempt to tip the market and to capture the network benefits of their respective proprietary networks.[672] In network markets, the process of tipping can eliminate competitors in favor of a single standard, causing exclusion of non-interoperable developers. However, section 2.2.2d concluded that such tipping could have pro- as well as anticompetitive effects. Thus, the mere fact that a single firm is likely to eliminate effective competition is, in a network market, not necessarily sufficient to prove consumer harm. Exclusion of competitors could be inefficient in a model of competition in the market, but it is not necessarily inefficient if a monopolist were better able to serve a network market than are multiple competitors. It follows that, as in a situation in which elimination of effective competition is caused by an intellectual property right, an additional test is necessary because it remains to be demonstrated that the dominant firm's exclusionary conduct causes harm to consumers.[673]

One could consider the effects of exclusion on software network markets within the analysis of exclusionary behavior, conducted under the conditions of indispensability and elimination of competition (see section 4.2.1b).

---

671. European Commission 2002, §80. See also section 5.2.
672. See section 2.2.2d.
673. Drexl et al. 2006, §16; Katz & Shelanski 2005, p. 7; Lévêque 2005, p. 85. See section 2.2.2d.

Access to interface specifications might not be considered indispensable to compete if a competitor can compete with a different but non-interoperable technology.[674] In *Microsoft*, however, the Commission and the court primarily viewed the presence of network effects as an indication that access to Microsoft's interface specifications *was* indispensable to compete – apparently, to compete not for, but in the market.[675]

Another approach is to analyze the effects of exclusion under objective justifications. As already noted, however, objective justifications are rarely accepted.[676] It is, moreover, for the dominant firm to raise such justifications,[677] which may be difficult after exclusionary conduct has already been established.[678]

In sum, according to the European case law on refusals to deal, a dominant firm's refusal to provide access to a facility to competitors is normally considered contrary to Article 102, if that facility is indispensable to competitors and, therefore, risks eliminating them. This leaves any positive effects of such exclusionary behavior to be analyzed under objective justifications.[679] However, courts and competition authorities often do not appear to accept objective justifications for exclusionary behavior. There thus appears to be a strong preference for safeguarding competition in rather than for the market under the application of Article 102, such that any benefits of competition for the market risk being ignored.

b. Balancing Incentives to Innovate and Free Competition

This section demonstrates that application of the European essential facilities framework to a refusal to supply interface specifications risks inadequately balancing relevant incentives to innovate. This is essentially caused by a focus on interface specifications as such (their *ex-ante* or direct value), rather than their indirect (*ex-post*) value for controlling market power caused by network effects.

Under the European case law on essential facilities (see section 4.2.1b), the new-product test represents a higher threshold for a duty to supply access to facilities that comprise intellectual property rights: the Commission must demonstrate that, in addition to the risk of exclusion, the refusal to license obstructs the emergence of a new product. Thus, access to interface specifications protected by intellectual property rights (e.g., copyright law) can only be imposed if the interoperable product is 'new'.

674. DeSanti & Cohen 2001, p. 334; Turney 2005, §81. See also Shapiro & Varian 1999, p. 196.
675. *Microsoft Decision* (European Commission 2004), §5.3.1.2.3; Larouche 2008, p. 8.
676. See section 4.2.1b.
677. *Microsoft* (GC 2007), §688.
678. Larouche 2008, p. 12; Lévêque 2005, p. 79.
679. See section 4.2.1b.

In part, application of a more stringent test for a refusal to license an intellectual property right appears justified in the light of the complementary nature of intellectual property rights and competition rules. Recall that, instrumentally, intellectual property rights granted *ex-ante* should only be subject to limited review by *ex-post* application of competition law: ideally, only in unanticipated, exceptional circumstances.[680] Section 4.1.2c already observed that it is questionable whether the new-product test can serve as an accurate parameter to instrumentally distinguish anticipated cases from exceptional ones.

Moreover, the question remains whether, substantively, the new-product test can adequately balance static and dynamic efficiency in such exceptional cases not already anticipated *ex-ante*. The substantive need for an additional parameter in the case of a refusal to license an intellectual property right could, *inter alia*, be explained as follows. The loss in static and dynamic efficiency caused by the exclusion of competitors through the intellectual property right could be outweighed by the interests in dynamic efficiency of allowing the dominant firm to exercise its intellectual property right.[681] On balance, the elimination of effective competition through a refusal to license, therefore, might not decrease welfare, indicating a need for an additional check. It appears questionable whether the new-product test can adequately fulfill this role, however, in particular when applied to a refusal to supply interface specifications.

The requirement that a new product be prevented from entering the market could indeed be interpreted as a balancing mechanism. The test would balance the interests of the dominant firm in exercising its intellectual property right against competitors' incentives to innovate through new-product development. Exclusion of effective competition by an intellectual property right would only be contrary to Article 102 if it prevents follow-on innovation (new-product development).[682]

This test, however, appears to be as accurate as it is sophisticated. Applying this new-product test, the courts will always assume that obstruction of new-product development outweighs the negative effects caused by a duty to license the intellectual property right, regardless of the nature of that intellectual property right, or, for that matter, the nature of the new product. Indeed, economists are skeptical about the new-product test as a proxy for consumer welfare. As Lévêque notes:

> From an economic perspective what is important is not whether some consumers would like the improvement being made but what their willingness to pay for it is, and whether it outweighs the costs of improvement.[683]

---

680. See section 4.1.
681. See section 4.1.2. See also Dolmans et al. 2007, p. 119; Drexl et al. 2006, §14; European Commission 2005, §237; Stuurman 1995, p. 348. But see Ritter 2005.
682. Ahlborn et al. 2005, p. 1132; Drexl 2004, p. 801; Drexl 2008, p. 14; Drexl et al. 2006, §17; Lévêque 2005, p. 76; Van Loon 2008, p. 262; *Microsoft* (GC 2007), 659.
683. Lévêque 2005, p. 76.

This decision – whether consumers' willingness to pay for innovation outweighs its costs – is arguably preferably left to the market rather than courts or antitrust enforcers. Thus, rather than having courts determine whether consumers are prejudiced by the hindrance of a 'new product', it may be more economically sound to investigate whether firms have sufficient incentives to innovate. After all, firms will generally take the opportunity to innovate if consumers are willing to pay for the innovation and if there are sufficient incentives to innovate.[684]

Furthermore, the term *new product* is inherently vague, and neither *Magill* nor subsequent cases have been particularly helpful in defining its scope.[685] The vagueness of the term *new product* means that it is unclear what exactly the refusal to license is balanced with in the first place. The broader one interprets 'new product', the easier it is to impose a compulsory license; the narrower 'new product' is interpreted, the higher the threshold.[686] Moreover, the term *new product* lacks economic relevance. As Lévêque notes:

> In modern microeconomics, a given product is just a specific bundle of characteristics [. . .]. Preferences of consumers are attached to characteristics and not to the product itself.[687]

The new-product test may be more persuasive as a legal normative balancing mechanism than as an economic test to safeguard dynamic efficiency.[688]

In case of a refusal to provide a computer program's interface information to a competitor, the adequacy of the new-product condition appears even more questionable. As already observed, the value of control over interface specifications lies not primarily in the innovation in interface specifications as such (their *ex-ante* value), but rather in their function of *de-facto* control over the network effects of the underlying product, such as an operating system or a

684. *Id.*
685. See also Bechtold 2007, p. 110; Geradin 2004, p. 1531; Lévêque 2005, p. 73; Turney 2005, pp. 189, 193. See also *IMS Health* (ECJ 2004), §49 (A product is new if 'the undertaking which requested the licence does not intend to limit itself essentially to duplicating the goods or services already offered on the secondary market by the owner of the intellectual property right, but intends to produce new goods or services not offered by the owner of the right and for which there is a potential consumer demand'); Van Loon 2008, p. 287.
686. Ahlborn et al. 2005, p. 1147, suggests that a product is new if it expands the market at current prices, that is, if the product 'satisfies potential demand by meeting the needs of consumers in ways that existing products do not'.
687. Lévêque 2005, p. 75.
688. In *IMS Health*, the A-G's opinion appears to have interpreted the new-product condition as a legal, normative balancing mechanism, which balances the rightsholder's freedom to refuse to license, on the one hand, and free competition, on the other. The latter only prevails if consumers are deprived of a new product entering the market. Opinion A-G Tizzano in *IMS Health* (ECJ 2004), §62. See also Drexl 2004, p. 801.

popular application program (their *ex-post* value).[689] Yet, the new-product test is invoked not because of the high *ex-post* value of the interfaces but rather because the interface specifications as such may be protected by intellectual property rights. Thus, the test prescribes that, as soon as interface specifications constitute subject matter protected by intellectual property rights, the Commission, in order to find an infringement of Article 102, must demonstrate obstruction of new-product development. The test must be met regardless of how much the dominant firm has invested in the network or platform behind the interface specifications, and regardless of whether the firm has or has not yet been able to benefit from a tipped position. By focusing on the former, *ex-ante* value of interface specifications and treating them on an equal footing with any other intellectual property right – without regard to their indirect function for control over networks or platforms – the new-product test risks ignoring the relevant incentives. Instead, it erroneously focuses on the very modest negative effects of decreased incentives to innovate in interface specification development on the one hand, and the positive effects of a new product compatible with the dominant vendor's network, on the other.

Thus, on the one hand, the rightsholder may have invested significantly in a platform or standard, expecting to extract the network benefits of its technology as the market tips in his or her favor. The interface specifications essentially form the key to extraction of that platform's substantial network benefits.[690] The market power caused by this network value represents the primary incentive to innovate for the dominant firm. The incentives may thus largely coincide with the market power resulting from winning competition for the market (see section 4.2.2a). On the other hand, the mandatory supply of these specifications to competitors limits the rightsholder's ability to exploit proprietary network effects, which represent a considerably more substantial reduction in incentives than any decreased incentives to innovate in interface specifications. If competitors are able to introduce a new yet also interoperable product based on mandatory disclosure of the rightsholder's interfaces, the latter is no longer able to fully extract the network benefits of her or his platform or standard because the competitor's new product offers the same network benefits as the dominant firm's products. The compulsory license of interface specifications could thereby decrease the market power that may contribute to incentives to innovate.[691] It follows that the incentives to innovate on the part of the dominant undertaking can be significantly chilled. Ultimately, consumers, therefore, are not guaranteed to be better off by the new products. Although static efficiency might be stimulated as

689. See section 2.2.1. See also Turney 2005, §82.

690. Merges 1999, p. 4. See also Hovenkamp et al. 2005, p. 25 (noting that some ip-protected telephony network components are only incidental to such networks). See also section 2.2.3a.

691. See also Weiser 2003, p. 603.

the new interoperable product could provoke price competition in the market, it may reduce the dominant firm's incentives to innovate and, hence, risks impeding dynamic efficiency. This is, however, not true for all markets; a market analysis must shed light on whether such competition for the market drives incentives to innovate and whether these incentives are beneficial to consumer welfare. For present purposes, it suffices to recall that the incentives driven by exclusivity in the standards and interface specifications as such are to be distinguished from those of *de-facto* exclusivity of the network effects behind those standards and interface specifications, and that which of these two incentives is relevant in the market under scrutiny depends on the circumstances of the case.

However, maintaining the new-product condition may be too high a threshold if the previously described exploitation of a network can no longer or not at all contribute to dynamic efficiency. This was arguably the case in *IMS Health*.[692] IMS' copyrighted brick structure in this case had become a *de-facto* standard for conveying pharmaceutical sales data of the German pharmaceutical industry, such that IMS' refusal to license the structure to horizontal competitor NDC prevented horizontal competition. The (*ex-post*) value of IMS' brick structure was primarily derived from the number of pharmaceutical professionals using it (namely, all of them), rather than from any inherent qualities of the brick structure (its *ex-ante* value). The market did not accept an alternative, non-standard brick structure because any benefits of a new structure would be greatly outweighed by the advantages of communicating all sales information in the same (existing) format.[693] IMS' brick structure thus benefited from strong network effects. This enabled IMS to leverage its copyright in that format to sustain substantial market power among horizontal competitors, such as NDC.[694] By insisting on meeting the new-product condition, the ECJ failed to recognize that follow-on innovation was not possible due to a strong need for standardization and that allowing IMS to maintain control over the standard could not stimulate competition for the market because the market for pharmaceutical sales data was, unlike some markets in the software industry and the pharmaceutical industry itself, hardly characterized by a quick rate of innovation.[695] Imposing the new-product condition, therefore, could not achieve its goal of safeguarding dynamic efficiency. Moreover, imposing the new-product condition amounted to a substantial burden for NDC's attempt at competing with IMS horizontally. Consequently, imposing the new-product test in *IMS Health* not only failed to stimulate dynamic efficiency but also risked impeding static efficiency.[696] Ignoring the effects of standardization in *IMS Health* through application of the existing framework for refusals to license

692. See also section 4.2.1b.
693. Drexl 2004, p. 802; Drexl et al. 2005, p. 654.
694. See also Turney 2005, §63.
695. See also section 2.2.2d.
696. Drexl 2004, p. 803.

intellectual property rights, the ECJ essentially issued a judgment that appears to conflict directly with competition law's purpose of stimulating and balancing both static and dynamic efficiency.

In *Microsoft*, the GC appeared more aware of the risks of a strict application of the new-product test in a standardization case. Sun requested access to Microsoft's interface specifications of its Windows series of server operating systems, which had become a *de-facto* standard because of network effects. Because the interface specifications were presumptively protected by intellectual property rights,[697] Sun had to demonstrate obstruction of new-product development. Similar to the case of *IMS Health*, this was a difficult task: Sun actually sought to compete with Microsoft in the same market.[698] The court had, indeed, established that, in order to compete, Sun's server operating systems had to interoperate with those of Microsoft on an 'equal footing', such that a Microsoft server in a network could be replaced by a Sun server.[699] Even through Sun sought to offer features not present in Microsoft's software,[700] it was difficult to qualify Sun's operating system as a 'new product'.

On the other end of the innovation balance were Microsoft's incentives to innovate. Unlike the sales data market in *IMS Health*, the markets for operating systems at issue in *Microsoft* may well have been characterized by innovation through competition for the market. In *Microsoft*, incentives generated by winning competition for the market may thus have been more relevant to dynamic efficiency than in *IMS Health*. An analysis of such incentives, however, is mostly absent in the GC's decision. Instead, the GC largely used the relatively low *ex-ante* or direct value of the interface specifications as a proxy for Microsoft's incentives to innovate, concluding that a duty to share these interface specifications could not result in a substantial impediment to incentives to innovate.[701] In its earlier decision in *Microsoft*, the Commission similarly observed that Microsoft's interface specifications constituted 'basic information'[702] and, to some extent, were mere variations of public domain interfaces.[703] The meager inquiry into Microsoft's incentives to innovate appears to be due in part to the GC's determination of the burden of proof. The GC observed that Microsoft's incentives were to be analyzed under

---

697. *Microsoft* (GC 2007), §289.
698. Forrester 2005, p. 945.
699. *Microsoft* (GC 2007), §421.
700. *Microsoft Decision* (European Commission 2004), §695.
701. *Id.*, §5.3.1.4.1.1; *Microsoft* (GC 2007), §110. See also *Microsoft* (GC 2007), §695 ('it is inherent in the fact that the undertaking concerned holds an intellectual property right that the subject-matter of that right is innovative or original. There can be no patent without an invention and no copyright without an original work'.).
702. *Microsoft* (GC 2007), §276.
703. *Microsoft Decision* (European Commission 2004), §244. Similar observations were made in earlier US interoperability cases. Merges 1999, p. 5; *Sega v. Accolade* (US Court of Appeals, Ninth Circuit 1992).

objective justifications.[704] It also noted that it was for Microsoft to raise such objective justifications, but that Microsoft had failed to do so, other than to point at its intellectual property rights.[705] By placing the burden of proof for incentives to innovate on Microsoft, this crucial element of the effects of any alleged abusive behavior may well have been left out of the analysis.[706]

On balance, however, it may well have been efficient to enable Sun to develop interoperable software. It appeared that, even if incentives generated by dominance and competition for the market might have been relevant to dynamic efficiency, Microsoft had, nonetheless, already benefited from a position of significant market power for quite some time, suggesting that its incentives to innovate may well have been ample. Indeed, due to this apparent sustainable significant market power and a converse lack of competitive pressure, Microsoft's incentives to innovate may actually have been reduced, as the Commission suggested.[707] The same lack of competitive pressure might also have caused higher prices and, therefore, have impeded static efficiency. In such conditions, maintaining the new-product condition for a duty to license intellectual property rights could adversely affect both static and dynamic efficiency, as it similarly did in *IMS Health*.[708]

Perhaps aware of this danger, the GC expanded the meaning of 'new product' considerably. Rather than the more stringent interpretation of 'new product' in *Magill* and *IMS Health*, the GC instead interpreted the condition as equivalent to the statutory language 'prejudice to consumers' in Article 102(b):[709]

> The circumstance relating to the appearance of a new product, as envisaged in Magill and IMS Health [. . .] cannot be the only parameter which determines whether a refusal to license an intellectual property right is capable of causing prejudice to consumers within the meaning of Article [102(b) TFEU]. As that provision states, such prejudice may arise where there is a limitation not only of production or markets, but also of technical development.[710]

Under this broader definition, it was accepted that Sun's new features amounted to a new product. Although the court was careful to formally follow the new-product condition of *Magill* and *IMS Health*,[711] it follows from this excerpt that the new-product test, as applied in these cases, has actually been expanded. However, the GC did not expressly limit this expansion to

704. *Microsoft* (GC 2007), §659.
705. *Id.*, §688, §689.
706. See also Larouche 2008, p. 12.
707. *Microsoft Decision* (European Commission 2004), §725.
708. Drexl 2006, p. 654; Koelman 2006, p. 829.
709. Larouche 2008, p. 10.
710. *Microsoft* (GC 2007), §647, §665.
711. *Id.*, §665 ('The Court therefore finds that the circumstance relating to the appearance of a new product is present in this case.')

the case-specific presence of network effects. Consequently, its broader interpretation of new product could potentially be invoked in any refusal to license an intellectual property right – not merely in refusals to license interface specifications or other standards. Therefore, it has become easier to force a dominant firm to license its intellectual property rights.

In its earlier decision in the same case, the Commission had applied an incentives balancing test to replace the 'new-product' condition.[712] Applying this balancing test, it found that non-disclosure of Microsoft's interface specifications would chill competitors' incentives to innovate because they had no access to the information necessary to create innovative but interoperable products,[713] and Microsoft's incentives would also be deterred as, without competition, there was insufficient pressure to innovate.[714] Although a test based on incentives to innovate is theoretically a more accurate proxy for prejudice to consumers,[715] such a test introduces more uncertainty and is difficult to apply accurately in cases presenting complex fact patterns, such as *Microsoft*.[716]

Not persuaded by the exhaustive nature of the new-product test, the Commission in its 2004 decision had also taken into account other circumstances that it considered relevant to the abuse.[717] Among these circumstances, the Commission noted the fact that Microsoft's refusal to supply interface specifications was contrary to industry practice[718] and that it constituted a disruption of a previous level of supply.[719] Indeed, an initial availability of interface information followed by a refusal to continue to supply the information may help to establish network effects based on wide support for the platform, with the subsequent possibility to fully exploit the platform's popularity by the rightsholder.[720] Some commentators similarly interpret *Commercial Solvents* to be limited to the termination of a supply, rather than a refusal to start supplying.[721]

In sum, the European courts maintain a higher threshold for a duty to deal if the facility comprises an intellectual property right. The purpose of this additional condition is to safeguard the incentives to innovate created by

---

712. See also Bechtold 2007, p. 112.
713. *Microsoft Decision* (European Commission 2004), §695.
714. *Id.*, §725. See also Drexl 2004, p. 796; Lévêque 2005, p. 78.
715. Lévêque 2005, p. 76.
716. *Id.*, p. 80.
717. European Commission 2005, §242 (identifying refusals to supply interoperability information as a separate category of abuses, deserving special treatment).
718. *Microsoft Decision* (European Commission 2004), §5.3.1.4.1.2.
719. *Id.*, §5.3.1.1.3.2. See also Appeldoorn 2005, p. 656.
720. Geradin 2004, p. 1535; Lévêque 2005, p. 83.
721. See European Commission 2005; Geradin 2004, p. 1535. See also Ritter 2005, p. 284 (noting that such a distinction would chill incentives to start supplying an input. US case law on refusals to deal also focuses on terminations of existing supplies); Whish 2003, p. 667. See, for example, *Aspen Skiing* (US Supreme Court 1985); *Trinko* (US Supreme Court 2004). See also Drexl 2004, p. 790.

intellectual property rights. However, this rather mechanical approach to balancing incentives to innovate may not be accurate. This is in part because of the questionable adequacy of the new-product test as a proxy for incentives to innovate, in particular for cases involving control over standards and interface specifications. On the one hand, the new-product test may be too high a threshold for refusals to license intellectual property rights protecting standards, such as interface specifications. This may impede both static and dynamic efficiency. On the other hand, the new-product test fails to consider the more important function of interface specifications as a means to control access to the substantial network benefits of a successful computer programs, which may provide considerably more substantial incentives to innovate.

4.3. CONCLUSION

This chapter has reviewed the use of competition law as an instrument to balance openness versus control of interface specifications *ex-post*. In contrast to an *ex-ante* approach in copyright law, as studied in Chapter 3, the case-by-case competition approach allows for a consideration of all the relevant circumstances of the case, which, in theory, should result in a more optimal balance between openness and control of interoperability information.

Section 4.1 first reviewed the instrumental trade-off between an *ex-ante* intellectual property and an *ex-post* competition law approach to control over interface specifications. Based on the complementary nature of intellectual property rights and competition rules, it demonstrated that, ideally, intellectual property rights should provide for a balance between openness and control of interoperability information that is generally adequate in structural and foreseeable conditions. The role of competition law should ideally be reserved for exceptional circumstances, which were described as misbalances between control and openness not anticipated within the *ex-ante* intellectual property approach. A more expansive role for competition law could risk impeding the very certainty through which these intellectual property rights aim to provide incentives to innovate. Nonetheless, as long as the *ex-ante* copyright approach remains deficient, as is arguably the case for the Software Directive's mechanism for access to interface specifications, the argument for such deference remains weak because it would cause the structural deficiencies in the copyright system to be imported into the application of competition law. The following chapters will, therefore, examine how the current *ex-ante* approach to control over interfaces in software copyright law could be improved, relying in part on interconnection mechanisms in design protection and telecommunications law.

Section 4.2 focused on how application of Article 102 TFEU could substantively affect the balance between control and openness of interface specifications. It demonstrated that competition law is not actually applied with the flexibility it was designed for, as the European courts have developed a rather static set of conditions for an unlawful refusal to deal. This introduces the risk that individual cases are not examined on their merits. Indeed, this rigidity poses a particular risk to the adequacy of cases in which a dominant firm refused to license intellectual property rights protecting a standard, including interface specifications: these cases may inappropriately be analyzed under the same analytical framework as cases involving control over non-standards.

Section 4.2.2 focused on how competition law affects the form of competition (competition in or for the market) and how it analyzes incentives to innovate. As regards the form of competition, competition law generally, through its basic premise against mandatory sharing, appears to rely on a role model of independent competition. In such independent competition, mandatory sharing obligations between competitors can substantially reduce incentives to invest and, therefore, mostly should be avoided. This is reflected by a stringent application of the essential facilities doctrine, which constitutes an exception to the general rule against mandatory sharing. However, in industries characterized by stronger interdependency, such as the software and telecommunications industries, there can be a greater necessity to have access to interface specifications and other *de-facto* standards controlled by competitors. This could conflict with a stringent interpretation of Article 102. It was also demonstrated that, even if it may also be welfare enhancing to have software firms temporarily compete independently for the market by controlling interface specifications, as suggested in Chapter 2, competition law does not expressly balance the relative benefits of competition in and for the market under the essential facilities doctrine, such that an important part of the analysis is ignored in a case of a refusal to license interface specifications.

With respect to incentives, the new-product test used to assess refusals to license intellectual property rights largely ignores the particular incentives that arise when such rights are used to control standards and in particular interface specifications. The new-product test focuses primarily on the incentives to innovate as directly affected by the duty to share the interface specification as such. It is not a helpful test to assess the indirect effect that intellectual property protection of interface specifications can have on interoperability, and thereby, on innovation and competition. If intellectual property rights protect a standard or interface specifications, the new-product test may prove either too low or too high a threshold for competitors, and may, therefore, inadequately analyze incentives to invest.

Thus, incentives to develop interface specifications themselves are barely necessary and are not necessarily reduced by a duty to share them. It is rather the *ex-post* value of control over interface specifications or standards that determines their significance: widespread (*de-facto*) use of these interface specifications or this standard, strengthened by network effects, could make control thereof a source of substantial market power.

On the one hand, this market power may be what drives firms to compete for the market in the first place by establishing a large installed base for their network product. In markets characterized by such competition for the market, the new-product test could prove too low a threshold for competitors. If competitors are allowed to obtain a compulsory license for interface specifications, in order to develop a new, yet interoperable product, their new product's network benefits are equal to those of the new entrant, even if only the new entrant might have invested substantially in order to build her or his installed base. The new entrant could free ride on the incumbent's efforts in building an installed base, which could reduce incentives to invest in new software platforms. Compulsory licensing for new-product development could thus reduce innovation and competition in network benefits.

On the other hand, if dynamic efficiency is not driven by such competition for the market through non-interoperable products (*IMS Health*), or if the incumbent has already benefited from a *de-facto* exclusivity over his or her network for a considerable time (*Microsoft*), application of the new-product test may amount to a substantial burden for competitors of the dominant firm. Consumers may have a direct interest in more competition in the market through interoperable products from different vendors. In such instances, requiring the competitor to develop a new product before it is eligible to obtain a compulsory license may prove too high a threshold, which could risk impeding both static and dynamic efficiency.

In sum, this chapter demonstrated that, instrumentally, the role of competition law in regulating control versus openness of interface specifications should be a limited one, provided that the *ex-ante* copyright approach to interoperability and control over interface specifications is improved. Substantively, it demonstrated that competition law does not yet appear to sufficiently consider the issues of network competition in the software industry. By analyzing refusals to supply interface information under the same framework as other intellectual property rights, competition law ignores the indirect effects of control over interface specifications on interoperability, innovation and competition. As already noted in the context of copyright protection of software (Chapter 3), control of interface specifications should not be treated on an equal footing with other subject matter.

Chapter 5

Ex-Ante Interconnection Rules

Thus far, Chapters 3 and 4 have demonstrated that the primary regimes responsible for interoperability of computer programs – *ex-ante* protection by copyright law and *ex-post* control of abuse of dominance by competition law – actually fail to sufficiently facilitate interoperability, thereby risking to impede competition, innovation and a realization of network effects in software. Chapter 3 demonstrated that interface information is not necessarily excluded from copyrightable subject matter, whereas copyright's limitations permitting reverse engineering may not suffice to obtain access to these specifications in all or even in most instances. Rightsholders can thus maintain control over interoperability with their computer programs by exercising control over use of and access to its interface specifications. Chapter 4 by competition law can be insufficient or inappropriate to limit market power conferred by copyright law. Article 102 TFEU only sanctions abusive *behavior* and not market power *per-se*. If copyright law confers sustainable market power through control over interoperability information, these structural entry barriers are not necessarily tied to any abusive behavior. Adjusting the *ex-ante* allocation of (copy)rights may thus be preferable to the use of *ex-post* competition law to correct for such allocation. Moreover, competition law, like copyright law, does not fully consider the significant indirect effects of control over interface specifications and other standards on innovation and competition.

With a view to adjusting the *ex-ante* instruments for interoperability in software copyright law, this chapter examines two other legal regimes in which these weaknesses of competition law have led to *ex-ante* interconnection instruments, thus obviating the need to establish abusive behavior *ex-post* in accordance with Article 102 TFEU. First, design protection law, a species of intellectual property law, contains specific exclusions and limitations of the design right in order to limit a rightsholder's market power in the adjacent markets for interconnecting products and replacement body parts (section 5.1). Second, telecommunications law, which is primarily sector-specific regulation, provides for *ex-ante* interconnection duties monitored by a regulatory authority. Telecommunications law thereby maximizes networks effects of telecommunications infrastructure (section 5.2).

Both approaches to interconnection will be examined symmetrically along the two scales identified in Chapter 2: first, along the *normative* scale of openness versus control, and second, against the *instrumental* scale of flexibility versus certainty. A third subsection will examine their specific legal instruments used to provide for interconnection.

First, sections 5.1.1 and 5.2.1 will examine the normative balance between openness versus control for design protection and telecommunications, respectively. Chapter 2 demonstrated that control over interface information can confer sustainable market power in relation to both vertical competitors (section 2.2.3) and horizontal competitors, through network effects (section 2.2.1). These concerns of vertical and horizontal market power are also recognized in design and telecommunications law, respectively. Thus, in design protection law, the legislator primarily aims to limit market power in the *adjacent* markets for complementary products and replacement parts, whereas in telecommunications law, the (fixed line) interconnection rules aim to limit the control of interconnection with horizontal competitors within the *same* market. Both forms of control may similarly need to be addressed *ex-ante* in software copyright law.

Second, sections 5.1.2 and 5.2.2 will analyze the instrumental trade-off between flexibility and certainty. In both design protection and telecommunications law, there have been debates as to whether the market power (*supra*) should be curtailed by *ex-ante* rules or by *ex-post* application of competition law. These debates have primarily leaned towards the use of *ex-ante* interconnection rules. Both debates can provide insights into the relative advantages of *ex-ante* instruments over *ex-post* instruments to limit market power caused by control over interface specifications in computer programs.

Third, in sections 5.1.3 and 5.2.3, it will be examined whether the instruments that aim to prevent market power in design protection and telecommunications law are of value to an *ex-ante* approach to use of and access to interface information in software copyright law. In design protection, the specific exclusion of protection for elements necessary for interconnections and the limitation allowing reproduction of spare parts provide more certainty than the application of general subject matter requirements to software interface specifications under copyright law. In telecommunications law, which is based on a model of regulation, the instrument of interconnection negotiations and the reference offer, and particularly regulatory oversight thereof, may also prove useful to facilitate interoperability in computer programs. These instruments offer more flexibility than the rigid reverse engineering provisions in the Software Directive. Section 5.3 concludes.

5.1. DESIGN PROTECTION

Chapter 3 concluded, *inter alia*, that copyright law leaves uncertainty with respect to the copyrightability of a computer program's interface specifications. Protection of these specifications can, however, confer substantial and sustainable market power on the rightsholder *vis-à-vis* vertical competitors, which, in the absence of additional, abusive behavior, is difficult to correct through competition law. In design protection law, similar concerns about market power in adjacent markets for complementary products and replacement parts have led to specific, *ex-ante* exclusions of and limitations to the design right. This section demonstrates that the rationale of this *ex-ante* approach, as well as its specific instruments, can serve as a model for the exclusion of interface specifications in copyright law.

European design protection laws offer protection for the appearance of two- and three-dimensional objects that are new and demonstrate individual character (see section 5.1.3). Unlike copyright laws, design laws can provide protection even against independent creation, albeit for a shorter term of protection.[722] Design protection is, therefore, highly relevant to industries where appearance is a decisive factor in consumer preferences, such as in the consumer appliances, fashion and automotive industries.[723] However, as copyright law might (indirectly) protect the interface specifications of a computer program,[724] thereby providing the rightsholder with control over the secondary market for complementary computer programs, design protection can likewise protect the appearance of individual parts of a complex design or elements of the appearance necessary for interconnection with complementary products. Design protection can, therefore, similarly lead to substantial and sustainable market power in the secondary markets for replacement parts and complementary products. Section 5.1.1 will examine this normative balance between openness and control.

Section 5.1.2 will demonstrate that the flexible, *ex-post* approach of competition law did not suffice to address these normative concerns, provoking an *ex-ante* approach within design protection laws.

Section 5.1.3 will examine the specific legal instruments of this *ex-ante* approach in design protection. These instruments – an exclusion of interconnection elements and a limitation allowing reproduction of replacement parts – also appear useful for interface specifications under copyright law.

---

722. The regulation and directive both provide for a maximum term of protection of twenty-five years, which still exceeds the average commercial life of many objects covered by the right, including cars and their spare parts. See Articles 12 and 10, respectively. See also Gemeenschappelijk Commentaar 2002, p. 4; Horton 1994, p. 55.
723. Govaere 1996, p. 221; Proposal amending Directive 98/71/EC (2004), 4.
724. See section 3.1.

5.1.1. Openness Versus Control

Similar to interoperability in the Software Directive, the issue of control of secondary markets through design protection has been fiercely debated by lobbying organizations, or, as the Commission refers to them in more neutral terms, 'interested circles'. Amidst the most interested of circles are the car manufacturers, which, due in part to their design rights, by and large control the aftermarkets for replacement parts. The car manufacturers, therefore, would prefer to maintain this market power through continued *control* of these parts; competitors in the repairs industry would prefer *openness* so as to use these parts to offer repair services.

Similar to the development of software, the appearance of a product is often the result of substantial investments in design, while the result can easily be copied in the absence of legal protection.[725] A limited design right provides the rightsholder with temporary exclusivity (control) in order to recoup investments in the design process, while allowing others to use the design once the period of exclusivity has expired (openness). Although such protection confers temporary market power on the rightsholder, it does not normally lead to a monopoly because there is ample room for variation in design within the same market.[726] However, this does not necessarily hold true for certain aftermarkets. Generally, there are two categories of objects or elements, the protection of which could enable complete control of the relevant (after)market: must-fit parts (section 5.1.1a) and must-match parts (section 5.1.1b). Consequently, protection of both must-fit and must-match parts can create lock-in effects or induce systems competition: consumers could be limited to purchasing complementary products or replacement parts from the rightsholder.[727]

a. Must-Fit Parts

Similar to copyright protection of a computer program's interface specifications,[728] protection of elements of a design that are necessary for interconnection with other objects would allow for control of the aftermarket for complementary products because competitors would be unable to reproduce the appearance necessary for interconnection. Thus, whereas, for instance, protection of an operating system's interface specifications could enable control of the markets for application programs, protection of the appearance of a laptop port would give the rightsholder control over accessory devices, such as mice.[729] In design protection law, these parts are

725. European Commission 1991; Reichman 1994, p. 2460. See also section 3.1.1a.
726. COM(1993) 342 final (1993), 8.
727. Bechtold 2007, p. 67; Schovsbo 1998, p. 516.
728. See section 2.2.1. See also Horton 1994, p. 54.
729. Bently & Sherman 2004, p. 620.

called *must-fit* parts.[730] Protection of must-fit elements could thus allow for control over a potentially endless array of complementary products that rely on interconnection.[731] As discussed in section 3.2.1, this was a very controversial issue in computer programs, which, however, did not result in an explicit exclusion of interface specifications from copyrightable subject matter. The exclusion of interconnections from design protection laws, by contrast, stimulates component competition more than systems competition.[732] Like interface specifications of computer programs, the innovative value of design interconnections bear no relationship with the market power they can contribute to *vis-à-vis* vertical competitors. There is, in other words, a similar discrepancy between the direct and the indirect value of these interconnections. When regarded as a trade-off between providing sufficient incentives to invest in design, on the one hand, and allowing for sufficient competition in complementary products, on the other,[733] an exclusion of these elements of a design might, therefore, not be very controversial.

b. Must-Match Parts

In some instances, however, the concern is not (merely) the interconnection with another product as much as an identical appearance in the case of repairs.[734] This category of products is called the *must-match* category.[735] Although this type of control is not directly related to interoperability or interconnection, it is nonetheless discussed here because of its more general relevance of control of secondary markets through intellectual property protection. The must-match category is especially relevant in the market for car repairs. For instance, on damage to a car door, repair would call for a replacement unit with the exact same shape and dimensions. Protection of such parts by an exclusive right gives the rightsholder control of the aftermarket for replacement parts.[736] Although the protection of the design of parts of a complex product required for repair, such as a side-view mirror or hood of a car, only limits competition in the relevant market for repairs, and not, as with must-fit parts, in the broader variety of markets for complementary products, this market for repairs is nonetheless concrete

---

730. Bechtold 2007, p. 79; Bently & Sherman 2004, p. 671; Govaere 1996, p. 221; Horton 1994, p. 55; Posner 1995, p. 125; Schovsbo 1998, p. 513.
731. European Commission 1991, p. 63; Posner 1995, p. 125; COM(1993) 342 final (1993), 15.
732. See section 2.2.3.
733. See, for example, Horton 1994, p. 54; Posner 1995, p. 125.
734. Bently & Sherman 2004, p. 656; Govaere 1996, p. 291; Horton 1994, p. 55; Posner 1995, p. 126; Schovsbo 1998, p. 529.
735. Bechtold 2007, p. 79; Bently & Sherman 2004, p. 673; Govaere 1996, p. 221; Proposal amending Directive 98/71/EC (2004), 3; Schovsbo 1998, p. 513.
736. European Commission 2004c, p. 13.

and substantial. Moreover, this market is currently controlled by the car manufacturers, which makes the must-match category a controversial type of limitation.[737]

Whereas this discussion has thus far implicitly assumed that there is indeed a separate aftermarket for spare parts, this position has been contested. Relying on the *systems* or package deal theory, some have argued that there is a single market for primary products and replacement parts, rather than two separate markets.[738] This assumption, originating from the Chicago school, is based on the complementary nature of cars and their replacement parts: consumers generally require cars and repair parts to fully benefit from their purchase, thus making the combined price more relevant than the individual elements. It has been counterargued that, following the *costly information theory*, consumers cannot predict, with any degree of certainty, the quantity of parts they will require at the time of purchase of the primary product, and that, therefore, the cars and parts are not regarded as constituting a single market.[739] Consumers, therefore, find themselves locked into buying parts from their car manufacturer. Although it is indeed unlikely that consumers would regard the markets for cars and their spare parts as a single one, it does not follow that the same holds true for manufacturers. Rather, it seems plausible that car manufacturers are aware of the average life cycle consumption of spare parts and, in any event, of the total income generated from parts in the aftermarket and of the prices charged by competitors.[740] Because not all car owners require repair parts and because the demand for car parts is less elastic (i.e., less sensitive to a price increase) than the demand for cars, it may be economically sound to compensate the price of new cars for the expected total income from spare parts so as to offer cars and parts at a competitive price in relation to each other and in relation to the competition.[741] A prerequisite for this type of competition is that the systems market is competitive, and, indeed, the *Extended Impact Assessment* confirms that the automotive industry is highly competitive. Conversely, if the latter market were to be liberalized through an exclusion to or limitation of the design right protecting these parts, it is to be expected that prices of cars rise.[742] Of course, the mere fact that car manufacturers generate part of their development costs for cars from the aftermarket for repairs does not imply that they would be *unable* to recoup all investments from the primary market, and, indeed, many have suggested that this ought to be the case (see *infra*). In general, section 2.2.3b

737. Gemeenschappelijk Commentaar 2002, p. 4. See, generally, European Commission 2004c. See literature in Drexl et al. 2005, p. 448, note 3.
738. Bartmann 2005, p. 129; Schovsbo 1998, p. note 9.
739. Bartmann 2005, p. 130; Bechtold 2007, p. 71, note 280; Drexl et al. 2005, p. 450; Govaere 1996, p. 237; Schovsbo 1998, p. 516. See also section 2.2.3b.
740. Govaere 1996, p. 226. See also section 2.2.3b.
741. This is known as *Ramsey* pricing (see section 2.2.3b). See Shapiro & Teece 1994, §IV.C. But see Bechtold 2007, p. 71.
742. European Commission 2004c, pp. 8, 16.

already demonstrated that control of secondary markets could have both pro- and anticompetitive effects.

Car manufacturers have furthermore expressed concerns about the quality and safety of replacement parts should these parts be marketed by third parties.[743] Inferior car parts could damage their reputation, which, although marketed by third parties, nonetheless, may be associated with the car manufacturers themselves. Indeed, independent part suppliers may have less of an incentive to produce quality parts in order to maintain a reputation in the primary market, in which, after all, these suppliers do not compete.[744] It was already established that such reputational damage could have welfare-deterring effects, even though some have argued that quality and safety issues are not the proper subject matter of design protection laws but rather of trademark law and of specialized directives in the field of automotive safety.[745] Note that this problem appears to be less relevant to software markets because a software product – even if it is fully interoperable with another (platform) program – will generally less easily be associated with the latter's developer.

The European legislator appears primarily concerned about fragmentation of the markets for spare parts caused by design protection. Because of differences in the design protection of spare parts, independent part suppliers are unable to reach the economies of scale that might lead to price competition and more choice.[746] The Commission also observes that, not surprisingly, spare parts protected by design protection are generally more expensive than parts not protected by intellectual property laws.[747] Furthermore, it argues that the innovation-incentive function of design laws would not be jeopardized if spare parts were excluded from design protection. Studies have demonstrated that no positive correlation exists between protection for spare parts and increased innovation in these parts.[748] Similar to the recoupment of investments in interface specifications,[749] car manufacturers might well be able to recoup all their investments in the primary market, namely, the sale of the new car. A related argument that has been advanced is the limited costs of innovation in

743. Beier 1994, p. 873; European Commission 2004c, p. 22; Proposal amending Directive 98/71/EC (2004), 9; Schovsbo 1998, p. 517.
744. Govaere 1996, p. 225; Schovsbo 1998, p. 517.
745. Drexl et al. 2005, p. 456; European Commission 2004c, p. 31; European Parliament 2007, p. 13; Proposal amending Directive 98/71/EC (2004), 9. See also section 2.2.3b.
746. European Commission 2004c, p. 34; European Parliament 2007, p. 12; Posner 1995, p. 127; Proposal amending Directive 98/71/EC (2004), 2. Moreover, it is inaccurate to refer simply to the aftermarket for spare parts, as each car model requires different and specially designed parts for the particular model in case of repairs. See also Shapiro & Teece 1994, §III.
747. European Commission 2004c, p. 24 (Table 3); Proposal amending Directive 98/71/EC (2004), 2. See also Schovsbo 1998, p. 526.
748. Schovsbo 1998, p. 526. See also Govaere 1996, p. 219.
749. See section 2.2.4.

the design of these parts.[750] Recall that this argument is also relevant to the development costs of software interface specifications.[751] Finally, liberalization of the market for must-match parts is believed to increase employment opportunities, particularly with small and medium sized enterprises.[752]

The Commission notes, however, that the effective control of the aftermarket for repairs by car manufacturers is not exclusively caused by design protection, and that, indeed, car manufacturers continue to demonstrate substantial market power in countries where the aftermarket for parts has already been liberalized, such as the United Kingdom.[753] This problem also resembles the protection of interface specifications in computer programs: regardless of the protection by intellectual property rights, an interoperable developer will still need to obtain access to the specifications because they are not readily available from the distributed program.[754] In the car industry, the manufacturers can naturally produce the spare parts from the molds already used for the production of the car in the primary market, whereas independent suppliers are forced to reverse engineer the shape of the parts. This is exacerbated by the precision engineering (and limited tolerance for error) in modern car manufacturing. Furthermore, minor design revisions in these parts force the independent suppliers to repeat their reverse engineering process[755] – a problem that, as noted, also exists in the software industry.[756] Finally, third-party suppliers often do not enjoy the same high reputation as the original car suppliers, and consumers, therefore, may be reluctant to obtain spare parts from such suppliers.[757]

The protection of must-match parts also has its equivalent in computer programs, namely, with respect to error correction and maintenance of programs. As repair of a complex product may require reproduction of a protected design, such as a car door, maintenance and error correction for computer programs similarly require the making of temporary copies of the computer program. Such copies cannot be made without authorization of the rightsholder, who would, therefore, maintain complete control of the relevant aftermarket. To prevent such control, the Software Directive provides for an error correction exception in Article 5(1), thereby similarly preventing lock-in effects for maintenance and warranty.[758]

---

750. Bechtold 2007; Proposal amending Directive 98/71/EC (2004), 8.
751. See section 2.2.1.
752. Bartmann 2005, p. 131; Bechtold 2007, p. 70; Drexl et al. 2005, p. 455; European Commission 2004c, p. 28; Govaere 1996, p. 222; Proposal amending Directive 98/71/EC (2004), 8.
753. In the United States, car manufacturers do not benefit from protection of spare parts at all, yet they still enjoy an 85% share of the market for spare parts. See European Commission 2004c, p. 19.
754. See section 3.1.2.
755. Bechtold 2007, p. 68; Proposal amending Directive 98/71/EC (2004), 5, 8.
756. See section 3.2.2d.
757. Bartmann 2005, p. 132.
758. See also section 3.1.2a. See also Bechtold 2007, p. 77; Sucker 1993, p. 22.

5.1.2. Flexibility Versus Certainty

This section demonstrates that the normative balance between openness and control in design protection, described in section 5.1.1, should preferably be created by *ex-ante* instruments. The *ex-post* application of general competition law cannot achieve the same results due to its case-by-case approach, the absence of any particular abusive behavior and the risk of undermining the certainty that design protection rights aim to create with a view to providing incentives to innovate.

In *Volvo v. Veng* and the similar case of *CICRA v. Renault*,[759] the ECJ essentially rejected the *ex-post* approach to limiting a design rightsholder's market power in the secondary market for repairs. As already examined in Chapter 4, the ECJ held that the exclusive right conferred by national design laws to prohibit others from marketing a product incorporating a protected design constituted the very subject matter of such rights.[760] Absent additional circumstances, such use of a design right, therefore, could not by itself amount to an abuse of a dominant position and could not be sanctioned by competition laws.[761] In the case of *Volvo*, this meant that a car manufacturer could prohibit independent service providers from offering repair parts for its car models, which effectively conferred on the car manufacturer complete control of this secondary market. Although the *Volvo* case concerned must-match parts, must-fit elements must similarly be reproduced in order to market complementary products. Protection of such elements, therefore, creates similar problems for application of competition law.

The *Volvo* judgment appears consistent with the complementary relationship of competition and design protection laws, as well as with their instrumental function (see section 4.1). As already noted in Chapter 4, Article 102 TFEU only sanctions *abuse* of a dominant position and not dominance as such. This is due in part to the fact that a dominant position may well have been obtained through the type of superior business acumen that competition law aims to promote. In *Volvo*, however, the design right itself conferred market power (dominance) in the secondary repairs market (the *existence* of the right),[762] whereas the *exercise* of these rights did not involve any abusive behavior.[763] Thus, as observed in *Volvo*, abusive behavior may well be absent in the case of a bare refusal to license the design protection right.[764] In the absence of abuse behavior or abusive exercise of design rights,

---

759. *Volvo* (ECJ 1988); *Renault* (ECJ 1988). §16
760. *Volvo* (ECJ 1988), §8.
761. *Id.* See also COM(1993) 342 final (1993), 9; Schovsbo 1998, p. 520.
762. Drexl 2006, p. 653; Drexl 2008, p. 8; Drexl et al. 2005, p. 453; Govaere 1996, p. 227; Schovsbo 1998, p. 524. See also van Rooijen 2008, p. 81.
763. *Volvo* (ECJ 1988), §9; Drexl 2006, p. 653.
764. Drexl 2006, p. 653.

the court could not impose a duty to license under Article 102 TFEU even if the refusal resulted in elimination of all competition.[765]

The *Volvo* judgment was based on the existence/exercise doctrine. Recall that in section 4.1.1, the existence/exercise doctrine was questioned as a proper analytical tool to scrutinize the unlawful exercise of intellectual property rights by a dominant undertaking. This approach was deemed too simplistic, due in part to the very general terms by which the ECJ tended to distinguish the two concepts (the 'specific subject matter' of the relevant intellectual property rights).[766] The primary reason for heightened scrutiny of intellectual property rights by competition rules, it was argued, lies not in the Member States' supremacy as to their intellectual property rules (based on Article 345 of the TFEU) but rather in the complementary relationship of intellectual property and competition laws.[767]

The existence/exercise distinction might, nonetheless, prove a useful concept, not for scrutinizing abusive *exercise* of intellectual property rights on the part of undertakings but rather to emphasize the role of the state in defining the *existence* of these rights. If it is accepted that, in a competitive market, undertakings should only be held accountable for the abusive exercise of their rights (Article 102) and not for the existence of these rights as such, then, conversely, there appears to be a responsibility for the state not to allow for rights to come into existence of which the exercise structurally and foreseeably leads to harm to the competitive process. In other words, because Article 102 only concerns undertakings' abuse of market power, as the market power itself is presumptively acquired by superior business acumen, there is arguably a responsibility for the state not to create market power artificially by granting intellectual property rights that are too broad. Again, this is illustrated by the problems arising from broad copyright grants in *Magill* and *IMS Health* (see section 4.2.1b).

The role of the legislature in shaping the competitive process is illustrated by legislative changes to the design right after the *Volvo* judgment. By altering the scope of the design protection rights *ex-ante*, the legislator can accomplish something the competition courts cannot, namely, preventing such market power in secondary markets without the need to establish particular abusive behavior. This approach provides rightsholders and competitors with more *ex-ante* certainty about the scope of the design rights. Certainty is particularly important in the context of intellectual property rights because rightsholders rely on these rights to calculate their investments in innovation. Conversely, structural limitations to the right should not be concluded on an *ad-hoc*

765. *Volvo* (ECJ 1988), §9. See also *Renault* (ECJ 1988), §16. The *Volvo* court did not define 'abusive behavior', although it did provide several examples.

766. *Volvo* (ECJ 1988), §8 (the specific subject matter of the design right is 'the right of the proprietor of a protected design to prevent third parties from manufacturing and selling or importing, without its consent, products incorporating the design').

767. See sections 4.1.1 and 4.1.2.

basis but are preferably to be anticipated within the design right itself. This approach contributes to – rather than conflicts with – the certainty that the design rights aim to provide. A related argument against application of competition law is that its case-by-case approach and high threshold for a duty to license an intellectual property right conflict with the use of competition law to address structural ownership issues. The market power caused by design protection in the repairs market is not exceptional but foreseeable, suggesting an *ex-ante* approach. A similar *ex-ante* approach can be found in telecommunications law (section 5.2.2).

Some commentators, however, disagree with the need for an *ex-ante* approach.[768] Their arguments are essentially twofold. First, there is an argument of lack of flexibility: the *ex-ante* exclusion of protectable subject matter excludes a variety of designs from protection, while such protection would only be harmful, if at all,[769] in a smaller subset of situations. Competition law could limit a duty to license to those particular circumstances in which design protection actually caused economic harm, thereby conversely mitigating the reduction in incentives to innovate for rightsholders. As already noted, however, it is still questionable whether competition law could, indeed, correct for such effects because the exercise of the design right in the form of a 'bare' refusal to license does not necessarily involve any abusive conduct.[770] Moreover, as demonstrated in the next section, both the limitation for spare parts (must-match parts) and the exclusion of interconnecting elements of a design (must-fit parts) have been curtailed to fairly specific circumstances, thus causing only a limited decrease in incentives to innovate. Second, opponents of an *ex-ante* approach argue that a limitation or exclusion for certain markets deprives the rightsholder of the essence of his or her rights: unlike interconnection elements (which are functional rather than aesthetic), it is the very aesthetic value of designs in spare parts that is excluded from protection.[771] Nonetheless, it remains questionable how much investments in design go into the spare parts individually, as opposed to the car in its entirety. Indeed, it appears plausible that much of the design of spare parts follows from the overall design of the car, which is eligible for its own design protection.

In sum, if one subscribes to the notion that market power in secondary markets caused by design protection laws ought to be limited, an *ex-ante* approach, involving altering the scope of the exclusive design right, appears superior to an *ex-post* approach, which relies on competition law. An *ex-ante* approach provides for more certainty, consistent with the incentive function of

768. Beier 1994, p. 860; Horton 1994, p. 54; Straus 2005, p. 391.
769. Opponents also argue that, following the *package deal theory*, there is no harmful control of market power because there is no separate market for spare parts. This argument relates to the normative balance between openness versus control, and has already been discussed in section 5.1.1b.
770. Drexl et al. 2005, p. 452.
771. Beier 1994, p. 862; Straus 2005, p. 399.

the design protection right. Moreover, it obviates the need to establish particular abusive behavior and to address a structural issue case-by-case in accordance with competition law.

5.1.3. Instruments

The previous section demonstrated that there are strong arguments to limit the market power caused by design protection *ex-ante* rather than *ex-post*. This section demonstrates that, at an instrumental level, such an *ex-ante* limitation of market power caused by design protection laws required explicit exclusions to and limitations of the design right. These instruments could serve as a model to limit protection of software interface specifications under copyright law.

Recall that copyright law could hinder the free use of a computer program's interface information for interoperability largely based on two factors: first, its protection of functional expression, which includes interface specifications, and, second, its failure to balance the relative benefits of original expression and the type of standardized expression required for interoperability. In section 5.1.3a, it will be demonstrated that both causes are also present in design protection laws. Neither must-fit nor must-match parts are, therefore, generally excluded from protection. However, in response to the concerns of sustainable market power (section 5.1.1), design protection laws contain an explicit exclusion for must-fit parts (section 5.1.3b) and a limitation permitting use of must-match parts (section 5.1.3c). These sections will explore whether these provisions could be of use to similar exclusions or limitations in copyright protection of computer programs.

The must-fit exclusion and must-match limitation have been pursued at two levels: the European Community Design Regulation 6/2002 (hereinafter the regulation), which aims to offer EU-wide protection for designs, and Directive 98/71 (the directive), which seeks to harmonize Member States' national design laws in order to align them with the EU design protection system.

a. Protection of Functional Designs and Promotion of Variety

It will first be demonstrated that, similar to copyright law, design protection may extend to functional designs, including interconnections. In addition, it promotes variety in designs, which, as noted, may conflict with the interests of standardization.[772] Indeed, similar to possible copyright protection of interface specifications, the general subject matter requirements of design

772. See section 3.1.

protection law, and particularly those related to parts of complex products, individual character and technical function, do not necessarily exclude must-fit and must-match parts from protection. This explains the necessity of the exclusion for must-fit parts (section 5.1.3b) and the limitation for must-match parts (section 5.1.3c).

Similar to copyright law, design protection is not limited to aesthetic designs, but also extends to functional designs. Design protection is generally available to two- and three-dimensional appearances that are new and that demonstrate individual character.[773] However, according to Article 8(1) of the regulation and Article 7(1) of the directive, neither EU design protection nor national protection exists for designs dictated solely by a technical function. Unlike must-match parts, which are not primarily defined by technical requirements but rather by the aesthetics of the complex product,[774] must-fit elements clearly serve a technical function, and their protection could thus possibly be prevented under Article 8(1) or 7(1). Although the term *technical function* is not defined, this concept is familiar in European patent law.[775] Protection of the appearance of products dictated by technical requirements would hamper technical development by offering patent-like protection without the stringent requirement as to novelty and inventive step, which is safeguarded by patent law.[776] The exclusion for elements dictated by a technical function could be considered a more specific application of the general requirement that the design demonstrate individual character.[777] The regulation's Article 6(2) and the directive's Article 5(2) specify that, in evaluating the individual character of a design, the degree of freedom of the designer shall be considered. Thus, to the extent the designer was constrained by external requirements, including technical ones, the degree of individual character is necessarily lower. It follows that a 'design', for which the creator had no design freedom because of technical requirements, should not be awarded protection under design laws.[778] It could be argued that, under this narrow, so-called mandatory approach, the exclusion for technically dictated designs serves no added purpose over the consideration of the freedom of the designer and is thus redundant.[779]

---

773. Community Design Regulation, Article 4; Directive 98/71/EC, Article 3.
774. Bartmann 2005, p. 133. But see Beier 1994, p. 856; Posner 1995, p. 126.
775. Bently & Sherman 2004, p. 618. See also Pinckaers 2007, p. 259; Quaedvlieg 1987, p. 39.
776. Beier 1994, p. 851; Bently & Sherman 2004, p. 618; Directive 98/71/EC, Recital 13; Gielen 2007, p. 153. But see Koschtial 2005, p. 307. Similar considerations have played a role in confining the scope of copyright protection for computer programs. See Samuelson 2007c, p. 1944.
777. The articles read: 'A design right [or Community design] shall not subsist in features of appearance of a product which are solely dictated by its technical function'. See, generally, Koschtial 2005, p. 297; Pinckaers 2007. See also COM(1993) 342 final (1993), 14.
778. Beier 1994, p. 851. See also Bently & Sherman 2004, p. 618; Pinckaers 2007, p. 270.
779. Bently & Sherman 2004, p. 619.

In a different interpretation, one might construe the exclusion more broadly. Under this so-called causative approach, elements of the appearance of a product would be excluded from design protection if they were designed solely with technical considerations in mind – even if the same technical effect would allow for various appearances.[780] Notwithstanding the attractiveness of this causative approach – even if solely for its added value over the exclusion with respect to freedom of the designer – the mandatory approach appears to prevail. A causative approach, which essentially seeks to ignore the freedom that the designer has had in implementing a technical solution as not eligible for design protection, would conflict with the rationale of European design laws. As in copyright law,[781] aesthetic value judgments should not play a role in determining novelty and individual character of a design. The difficult distinction between designs with an arbitrary and designs with a more functional nature was to be avoided, and 'functional designs' were also to be protected.[782] In *Philips v. Remington,*[783] A-G Colomer concluded that *trademark law* could not provide for protection of Philips' iconic three-part shaver heads because this configuration was 'necessary' to accomplish a technical function – namely, superior shaving.[784] The A-G then contrasted this *necessary*-standard to the *dictated-by* standard for exclusion of technical effects in design protection law and concluded that the latter implied a stricter causative relationship between appearance and technical function than did the former.[785] The A-G's opinion thus points towards applying the mandatory approach. The mandatory approach is also reflected in the regulation's Explanatory Memorandum:

> In extremely rare cases, the form follows the function *without any possibility of variation.* In such cases, the designer cannot claim that the result is due to personal creativity. The design has, in fact, no individual character and cannot attract protection. [emphasis added][786]

Thus, the Explanatory Memorandum suggests that the scope of the exclusion for technically dictated elements is indeed quite limited.[787] Under this mandatory interpretation, the exclusion of technical effects does not appear to preclude protection of must-fit parts[788] because an interconnection may

780. *Id.*, p. 618; Gielen 2007, p. 153; Koschtial 2005, p. 307.
781. See section 3.2.1b.
782. Beier 1994, p. 842; Bently & Sherman 2004, p. 612; European Commission 1991, p. 59; Posner 1995, p. 125.
783. *Philips v. Remington* (ECJ 2002). But see Gielen 2007, p. 153.
784. Opinion A-G Colomer in *Philips v. Remington* (ECJ 2002), §20. See also *Case T-270/06 (Lego)* (GC 2008), §43; Pinckaers 2007, p. 269.
785. Opinion A-G Colomer in *Philips v. Remington* (ECJ 2002), §34. See also Bently & Sherman 2004, p. 619; Quaedvlieg 1987, p. 45.
786. COM(1993) 342 final (1993), 14. See also Beier 1994, p. 856; Horton 1994, p. 54.
787. Bently & Sherman 2004, p. 618; Horton 1994, p. 54; Koschtial 2005, p. 307.
788. Horton 1994, p. 54. But see Beier 1994, p. 856.

often, similar to a software interface specification,[789] function equally in a number of different forms or configurations. It follows that the functionality performed by the interconnection does not typically dictate any single configuration,[790] and that, under the mandatory approach, the exclusion for functionally dictated designs does not prevent protection of must-fit parts.[791] This is similar to the protection of an interface specification under copyright law: because interface specifications can typically be expressed in a (wide) variety of different, yet functionally equal expressions, the specifications might still be eligible for protection.[792] Under design protection law, a more explicit exclusion, therefore, is needed to prevent protection of must-fit parts.

The second problem is that, similar to copyright law, design protection fails to generally balance the benefits of new and distinctive designs, on the one hand, and the use of standardized designs on the other. Like copyright law, design protection laws promote variety in designs. This obviously conflicts with standardization: rather than adhering to the interconnections of a primary product, a complementary product maker would be required to develop a new design for an interconnection, while a spare parts manufacturer would be required to design new spare parts rather than using those of the car model. Except for the specific must-fit and must-match provisions, discussed *infra*, design protection is not generally concerned with balancing the promotion of variety in designs with the interests of standardization, such as standardization in repair parts or in interconnecting elements.

Both must-fit and must-match parts are generally parts of a larger product. European design protection laws offer protection for parts of these 'complex' products to the extent that the parts themselves meet the requirements of novelty and individual character and, in addition, remain visible during normal use of the complex product. The term complex product is primarily intended to cover motor vehicles,[793] and the exclusion of elements not visible during normal use was primarily introduced to exclude engine parts from protection.[794] Accordingly, there is no concern of control of the markets

---

789. See section 3.1.1a.
790. Some interconnections cannot be considered to serve a solely technical function. Hence, the exception for interconnecting elements would not be entirely redundant even under the causative approach. See Beier 1994, p. 856; Posner 1995, p. 125. The latter author, however, also labels the must-fit exception 'redundant' in addition to the exception for elements dictated by a technical function; see Beier 1994, p. 857.
791. However, the appearance of an interconnecting element may still fail to demonstrate sufficient individual character, particularly when the degree of freedom of the designer is taken into consideration – as required by Article 6(2) of the regulation and Article 5(2) of the directive. See also Kur 1999, p. 627.
792. See section 3.1.1a.
793. Bently & Sherman 2004, p. 616.
794. Gemeenschappelijk Commentaar 2002, p. 13; Kur 1999, p. 624. On the term *normal use*, see [Author: Add to Refs?] Gemeenschappelijk Commentaar 2002, p. 14; Koschtial 2005, p. 311.

for these 'internal' parts through design protection.[795] This is to be contrasted with copyright law, which does not require its subject matter to be aimed at communication with humans (as the protection of computer programs demonstrates),[796] but can also protect 'invisible' parts (source code and interfaces) of those works (computer programs).[797] It would appear that some must-fit elements might well be visible during normal use, as many interconnections are mounted on the surface of the product.[798] Must-match parts are necessarily visible during normal use, as this visibility provokes the demand for an identical appearance in the case of repairs. It is because of these aesthetic considerations that consumers refuse alternative designs and thus are locked into buying those parts from the car manufacturer, who typically owns the rights to their design.[799]

In sum, the general subject matter requirements of design protection laws do not necessarily preclude protection of must-fit elements and must-match parts.

b. Must-Fit Parts

In the light of the possibility of protection for must-fit parts under general subject matter requirements (*supra*), a specific exclusion for these parts was considered necessary.[800] Article 8(2) of the regulation and Article 7(2) of the directive provide:

> A[n] [EU] design right shall not subsist in features of appearance of a product which must necessarily be reproduced in their exact form and dimensions in order to permit the product in which the design is incorporated or to which it is applied to be mechanically connected to or placed in, around or against another product so that either product may perform its function.

This *must-fit* provision thus provides for an explicit exclusion to design rights to the extent elements of the appearance of a product are necessary for interconnection with other products. This is not a limitation in favor of the certain use of what is otherwise considered protected subject matter, but rather an exclusion of must-fit parts from protected subject matter. Unlike must-match parts (section 5.1.3c), must-fit parts are simply not protected by design laws. It is the nature of these elements itself, rather than their use, that causes a need

795. Beier 1994, p. 844; Gielen 2007, p. 150.
796. See section 3.1.1a.
797. See section 3.1.
798. Of course, if the two products are interconnected during normal use – such as a coffee mug and lid – then the interconnections will typically be covered and, hence, invisible during normal use.
799. Bently & Sherman 2004, p. 656.
800. See, for example, COM(1993) 342 final (1993), 15.

for their reuse. A more specific carve-out of the design right for interconnections, therefore, would be difficult to conceive.[801]

Similar considerations are relevant for interface specifications of computer programs: these specifications, if protected, can also preclude competition in a variety of complementary markets.[802] One argument against a similar exclusion of interface specifications from the copyright protection of computer programs, however, was the difficulty of defining the term *interface specification*. Opponents of such an exclusion argued that any part of a computer program could qualify as an interface, thus considerably reducing the scope of protection if interfaces were excluded.[803] Similar concerns were raised within the context of the previously mentioned exclusion for interconnections under design protection. An exclusion of interconnections in modular products, in which interconnections can be an important aspect of the design, was believed to amount to too substantial a reduction in incentives to innovate.[804] A complementary subsection, therefore, limits the scope of the exclusion for interconnections of modular products.[805]

Although both copyright and design protection laws can thus extend to functional creations, in part because of the difficulty of distinguishing aesthetic from functional subjective design choices, design protection law demonstrates that it may, nonetheless, be possible to identify and exclude interconnections. Because of their specific purpose, interconnections and interfaces can more easily be identified than 'purely' functional aspects of a design or copyrighted work. Unlike the treatment of software interfaces in the Software Directive,[806] the previously described exclusion provides for considerable legal certainty.[807] The must-fit exclusion obviates the need to assess design protection claims in individual circumstances. The exclusion does not demand a complex inquiry as to whether the appearance of the product was constrained by external (compatibility) requirements,[808] which would leave the possibility of protection open in individual cases but examines whether interconnection with other products would require exact reproduction of the relevant elements. If this is the case, then the elements are not protected, notwithstanding the fact that they could otherwise be eligible for protection under the requirements of novelty, individual character and technical function.[809] The must-fit exclusion does not appear to substantially

801. See also European Commission 1991, §5.4.10.3.
802. See section 2.2.4.
803. See section 3.2.1. See also Lake et al. 1989, p. 432.
804. Some commentators suggest that this exception served primarily to prevent the Lego bricks from losing protection. See Beier 1994, p. 857; Bently & Sherman 2004, p. 622. See also Levin & Richman 2003, p. 113.
805. Gemeenschappelijk Commentaar 2002, p. 15; COM(1993) 342 final (1993), 15.
806. See section 3.1.1. See also Dreier 1991a, p. 583.
807. See also Stuurman 1995, p. 458.
808. See section 5.1.3a.
809. See also Schovsbo 1998, p. 519.

lessen incentives to innovate because innovators can recoup any investments in interconnections from the sale of the complex product.[810] A similar, specific subject matter exclusion could be useful to exclude interface specifications from protection. This would mitigate the current uncertainty surrounding the protection of interface specifications under copyright's idea/expression and originality doctrines.[811]

c. Must-Match Parts

As noted, another controversial issue in design protection was a possible limitation for use of must-match or spare parts, which would, *inter alia*, reduce the market power of the car manufacturers in the respective after-markets for those parts. Section 5.1.3a already demonstrated that, similar to the must-fit parts, the more general subject matter provisions in design protection law did not suffice to exclude must-match parts from protection. The exclusion of must-fit elements (see section 5.1.3b) was also insufficient to prevent protection of must-match parts. Although many of these body parts, such as a car door, often interconnect with the complex product (the car), customers' demand for an identical appearance relates to the aesthetic features of these body parts rather than their interconnections.[812] A specific limitation, therefore, was considered necessary.

After a temporary, so-called freeze plus compromise,[813] the Commission, in 2004, issued a proposal to amend the directive on the spare parts issue,[814] which read:

> Protection as a design shall not exist for a design which constitutes a component part of a complex product used within the meaning of Article 12(1) of this Directive, *for the purpose of the repair of that complex product so as to restore its original appearance*. [emphasis added][815]

This proposal is currently under consideration.[816] Although this language may suggest otherwise, the proposal is not intended to exclude spare parts from

810. Bartmann 2005, p. 131.
811. See section 3.1.1.
812. Beier 1994, p. 856.
813. Directive 98/71/EC, Article 18. See also Straus 2005. Pursuant to this provision, Member States were to preserve any existing exceptions for spare parts (*freeze*). However, they could introduce further limitations to liberalize the market for spare car parts (*plus*).
814. The proposal also addresses reputational concerns of rightsholders, by enhancing transparency as to the origin of the spare parts. Article 14(2) of the proposal provides that '[m]ember states shall ensure that consumers are duly informed about the origin of spare parts so that they can make an informed choice between competing spare parts'. Consequently, inferior spare parts would less easily be associated with the primary product maker, thus preventing damage to the latter's reputation. Bechtold 2007, p. 82; Proposal amending Directive 98/71/EC (2004), 10.
815. Proposal amending Directive 98/71/EC (2004), Article 1.
816. See, for example, European Parliament 2007.

protection altogether.[817] Spare parts are still eligible for protection to the extent that they meet the general requirements of design protection for parts of complex products (see *supra*). Unlike the must-fit provision, the must-match provision is, in other words, a *limitation* of the design right rather than an *exclusion*. This corresponds to the cause of the underlying standardization problem, which lies not primarily in the nature of these designs but rather in their use. An exclusion of spare parts was therefore not considered justified or possible.[818] The proposal instead enables a more precise limitation of market power because the exclusive right itself is left intact, whereas reproduction of spare parts without authorization is only allowed for a particular purpose (repairs).[819] A rightsholder can still exercise protection for spare parts in situations other than the ones covered by this provision, thereby recouping investments in the design process. For instance, BMW might enforce design rights in a particular side-view mirror against imitation by Volkswagen but cannot prevent an independent parts supplier from marketing an identical side-view mirror for repair purposes. The limitation thus, through the language emphasized previously, effectively distinguishes between a primary market for the initial sale of the part in the complex product and a secondary market for repairs to the appearance of that product. Consequently, the design right does not compromise the incentives to invest in the design of these parts, whereas third parties can freely reproduce the parts for repair purposes. In the context of interface specifications under copyright protection of computer programs, a limitation – rather than an exclusion – could similarly enable use of the relevant specifications without authorization only insofar as they were successfully reverse engineered. Such a limitation would preserve the rightsholder's ability to prevent the use of any specifications eligible for protection that had not been reverse engineered but somehow otherwise obtained.

Prior to the 2004 proposal, the Commission had examined several alternative solutions to the spare parts issue, including a shorter term of design protection and a remuneration system.[820] A shorter term of protection for spare parts would enable rightsholders to benefit from protection in the aftermarket for a limited time, thereby providing a short-term opportunity to recoup investments in the aftermarket, while enabling more competition on expiration of that term. A difficult question raised by this alternative was the appropriate duration of the protection for spare parts, in particular in relation to the commercial life of motor vehicles and other complex products affected

817. Gemeenschappelijk Commentaar 2002, p. 4; Gielen 2007, p. 177; Proposal amending Directive 98/71/EC (2004), 10 ('The repairs clause does not limit the right of design right holders, it prevents the existence of monopolies on the spare parts market. The design right on the appearance of a primary product will not be extended to the product in the secondary market.').
818. Drexl et al. 2005, p. 451.
819. Bently & Sherman 2004, p. 616.
820. European Commission 2004c, p. 15.

by the right.[821] An initial proposal had contemplated a term of seven years, which was criticized for coinciding with the entire commercial life of most cars.[822] In other words, protection for spare cars would not expire until a time at which consumers would no longer have an interest in replacing any parts in the first place. A later proposal, therefore, provided for a more limited protection of three years.[823] This proposal, then, was criticized for the opposite reason: repairs would not be required during these first three years after the sale of the car, thus providing the car manufacturers with no effective right at all.[824] The rejection of the option for a shorter period of protection demonstrates the difficulty of codifying *ex-ante* competition concerns in the law. It is next to impossible to fix a single, appropriate term of protection for spare parts in the car industry, let alone for all other industries affected by this limitation.[825]

The remuneration system would provide the rightsholder with a reasonable compensation for the use of its designs in the secondary market. It would, therefore, continue to enable rightsholders to recover part of their investments in the aftermarket for spare parts.[826] However, similar to imposing a duty to license under competition law, it remains difficult to determine the appropriate compensation, making the remuneration option costly to administer.[827] Furthermore, remuneration appears unnecessary because rightsholders can recoup their investments in the design of these parts from the primary market.

5.2. TELECOMMUNICATIONS

This section demonstrates the importance of addressing the strong network effects and the corresponding need for interoperability in the software industry in an *ex-ante* rather than *ex-post* manner, using telecommunications law as a model. Telecommunications law deserves scrutiny in this study because it is a discipline in which legislators and regulators have long accumulated experience in addressing network effects and interdependent competition – issues that also underlie the software industry – in an *ex-ante* manner. Chapter 3 demonstrated that the copyright regime that should stimulate investments in software development largely fails to facilitate interoperability, thereby failing to maximize network effects for consumers and risking impeding competition and innovation. Telecommunications law more explicitly balances incentives to invest in infrastructure with an optimal

821. Posner 1995, p. 126.
822. Horton 1994, p. 55.
823. COM(1993) 342 final (1993), Article 23.
824. Beier 1994, p. 862; Proposal amending Directive 98/71/EC (2004), 7.
825. See also Dreier 2001, p. 305.
826. European Commission 2004c, p. 29.
827. Bartmann 2005, p. 133; European Commission 2004c, p. 37. See also section 4.2.1b.

realization of network effects. Telecommunications law strikes this balance, *inter alia*, by regulating the extent to which network operators can exercise control over their infrastructure: this control is, in particular, limited by interconnection obligations. This balance between openness and control is examined in section 5.2.1. Section 5.2.2 focuses on the rationales for an *ex-ante* approach to interconnection (as opposed to an *ex-post* competition approach), and section 5.2.3 on its instruments, of which regulatory oversight and the reference interconnection offer also appear useful instruments for use within software copyright law.

A few side notes are relevant to the comparison made in this section between interconnection in telecommunications and interoperability in computer programs. First, interconnection and interoperability can both be a precondition to maximizing network effects, but they are only comparable to a certain extent. As noted in section 2.1.2b, interconnection is simpler and takes place at a lower, physical level. Interoperability is more complex and occurs at a higher, logical level. In telecommunications, interconnection (at the physical level) can be a necessary precondition for interoperability between higher-level telecommunications services. Second, interconnection in telecommunications regulation primarily applies to direct, horizontal network effects, whereas, as noted in section 2.2.2b, network effects in software are often of an indirect, vertical nature. Third, as the purpose of this section is primarily to demonstrate the importance of an *ex-ante* approach to *horizontal* interoperability and network effects for computer programs, it suffices to focus on the relatively simple problem of horizontal interconnection regulation between voice telephony networks. More complex issues of interconnection in mobile communications and of vertical interconnection (e.g., between a network and a service provider) are left aside. Finally, the study of telecommunications law takes the interoperability issue outside the realm of intellectual property rights, demonstrating that, regardless of how interoperability is controlled – be it through intellectual property rights protecting interfaces, or by controlling physical access to premises and telecommunications equipment – firms may have various incentives and means for refusing to interconnect with rivals. Obstacles to interconnection in telecommunications primarily lie in physical access, pricing and related issues rather than in intellectual property rights protecting network technology. Logical access in telecommunications is greatly facilitated by extensive use of standards. Accordingly, the central analogy in the present comparison is not how the exclusivity conferred by intellectual property rights negatively affects competitors' ability to interconnect, but rather how telecommunications law positively stimulates competing network operators to achieve the *result* of interconnection. The present comparison with interconnection regulation is, in other words, more relevant to the problem of *access* to interface specifications (which may also require cooperation from the target program's developer) than to *use* of interface specifications.

5.2.1. Openness Versus Control

This section demonstrates how, unlike in copyright protection of computer programs, network effects and interconnection have long been central issues on the telecommunications agenda.

In Chapter 2, it was demonstrated that, where products are subject to network effects, it is important to maximize their network benefits. Although computer programs were identified as being subject to strong network effects, Chapter 3 demonstrated that copyright law fails to adequately address the maximization of network effects in software, as it fails to substantially facilitate interoperability. Perhaps this is based on the fact that the need to stimulate investments in software development through strong copyright protection was recognized earlier and more explicitly than the need to address interoperability, which would have required limiting such protection – at least for the programs' interfaces. Ignoring the special relevance of interface specifications for interoperability, copyright law essentially enables rightsholders to control their computer programs' interface specifications to the same generous extent as the program at large, thereby effectively denying competitors access to these specifications. It thereby impedes interoperability and risks obstructing a maximization of network effects in software.

In contrast to the copyright regime addressing protection of computer programs, telecommunications law has long recognized that maximizing network benefits was critical in the telecommunications industry, where it is also known as any-to-any connectivity. More so than in computer programs, it was clear that consumers would gain little from innovative and low-cost telephones that did not connect to many other users. In other words, telecommunications infrastructure has, from the beginning, been regarded as a network, whereas computer programs have primarily been regarded as individual products. The recognition of network effects in telecommunications law can be attributed to the fact that the telephone is the textbook example of a product subject to network effects: unlike computer programs, which typically offer some stand-alone benefits, the only function of the telephone is to connect to other subscribers.[828] It can also be attributed to concerns over access to telephony for the public: soon after its invention, the telephone was recognized as an essential public utility, both for consumers and as a backbone for economic activity, thus warranting a degree of regulatory oversight.[829] Software has not yet been considered a public utility, although this could change over time.[830]

Telecommunications law, therefore, has aimed at maximizing network benefits for subscribers, while stimulating the creation of telecommunications

828. Larouche 2000, p. 365.
829. European Commission 1987. See also Bouwman et al. 2004, p. 13; Larouche 2000, p. 362.
830. See, for example, Carr 2008.

infrastructure, by regulating the extent of proprietary control over telecommunications networks. Chapter 2 demonstrated that network effects could be maximized both by relying on a (temporary) monopoly serving all subscribers and by competition between multiple, interconnected rivals in the market. The relevance of these models for maximizing network benefits is also reflected in telecommunications law, which, through time, has relied on both. It has evolved from initial models relying on regulated monopolist operators to the more recent model of competition in the market by rival operators. In that last and current model of competition in the market, interconnection obligations are critical because they safeguard any-to-any connectivity between the rival operators and, thereby, stimulate a maximization of network effects. These obligations form the core of the present study on telecommunications (section 5.2.1b). First, section 5.2.1a will briefly examine the model of monopoly regulation as well as the rationales for its abandonment.

a. Controlled Access and Monopoly Regulation

Until the 1980s, telephone networks were largely operated by monopolist carriers, which were regulated by the state. A monopolist carrier could help to maximize network benefits or demand-side economies of scale because all users were connected to the same network and could call each other.[831]

Arguments for having the networks operated by a single firm were also found in supply-side economies of scale. In the light of the considerable investment necessary for such networks, particularly for the local loop, telephone networks were considered to be natural monopolies, or a good most efficiently exploited by a single entity. The investments in infrastructure were considered prohibitively high in relation to the negligible marginal costs of serving each additional customer.[832] The telephone network was, therefore, only viable with a very large number of subscribers that contribute to the costs of construction.[833] An obvious solution to these difficulties was to have a single entity (a monopolist) operate the telephone service. However, this would necessarily result in supra-competitive prices because the monopolist, by definition, sought to

---

831. Larouche 2000, p. 381. Bell had raised this argument in its attempt to become the regulated monopolist in the United States, after expiration of its initial telephone patents had caused fierce competition from independent carriers. Benjamin et al. 2006, p. 704. See also section 2.2.1. According to Mueller, this competition for the market had helped to quickly establish a comprehensive telecommunications infrastructure, in which network benefits were maximized because each carrier attempted to connect as many subscribers as possible. Mueller 1993, p. 365. Similar forms of independent competition were present in Europe. Dommering et al. 1999, p. 36.
832. Angel 2001, p. 58; Baldwin & Cave 1999, p. 10; Benjamin et al. 2006, p. 706; Correa 2001, p. 24; Dommering et al. 1999, p. 23; Koenig & Loetz 2002, p. 364; Ottow 2006, p. 46; Schotter 2003, p. 369.
833. Constructing a second network would entail a duplication of the fixed costs, while consumers are equally well served by the first network. Both operators would need to raise their price to recoup investments in their respective networks, which is inefficient.

maximize profits in the absence of competition. Moreover, the monopolist might not bother to serve certain consumers – for instance, because their remote location rendered infrastructure too costly. Consequently, regulators were also called on to control prices and availability.[834] This became known as *universal service*: affordable, quality telephone service for all citizens, implemented through a system of cross-subsidies among the monopolist's revenue streams from different customer groups.[835] European governments thus granted exclusive rights to state-regulated entities for the construction and exploitation of telephone networks,[836] while Bell became a regulated monopolist in the United States.[837]

However, the monopoly regulation model became redundant in the 1980s. Based in part on technological advances that significantly reduced the costs of infrastructure, the natural monopoly argument underlying the model of monopoly regulation became weaker, and it appeared that, instead, private firms could bear the costs of telephony infrastructure.[838] Moreover, monopoly regulation was costly, whereas investments in new infrastructure under this model proved insufficient.[839] Policy makers, therefore, contemplated liberalizing the telecommunications industry, allowing for multiple carriers to compete within the market. In Europe, a 1987 Green Paper initiated the abandonment of monopoly regulation in telecommunications.[840]

b. Open Access and Competition in the Market

Liberalization of the monopoly regulation model required more than merely removing the monopolist's privileges to exclusively supply telephone service.[841] In particular, interconnection obligations were central to the new model of competition in the market,[842] for two purposes: first, safeguarding

834. Baldwin & Cave 1999, p. 10; Benjamin et al. 2006, p. 708; Geradin & Kerf 2003, p. 6; Ottow 2006, p. 48; Schotter 2003, p. 380.
835. Benjamin et al. 2006, p. 708; Dommering et al. 1999, p. 36; Mueller 1993. See also Benjamin et al. 2006, p. 768; Geradin & Kerf 2003, p. 6; Schotter 2003, p. 394.
836. Larouche 2000, p. 1; Shelanski 2002, p. 22. See also Dommering et al. 1999, p. 36.
837. Benjamin et al. 2006, p. 713.
838. Dommering et al. 1999, p. 39; European Commission 1987, p. 29; Geradin & Kerf 2003, p. 7; Koenig & Loetz 2002, p. 364; Larouche 2000, p. 4.
839. European Commission 1987, p. 44. See also Dommering et al. 2001b, p. 25; Drexl 2004, p. 797; Geradin & Kerf 2003, p. 7; Nihoul & Rodford 2004, p. 66.
840. European Commission 1987.
841. Removal of legal entry barriers included abandoning exclusive exploitation rights and privatization of national telephone operators. Furthermore, their regulatory role was separated from their business operations. Dommering et al. 2001b, p. 34; European Commission 1987, p. 73; Nihoul & Rodford 2004, p. 73. See also Correa 2001, p. 40; Dommering et al. 1999, p. 123; European Commission 1987, pp. 69, 95; European Commission 1998, §89; Geradin & Kerf 2003, p. 8; Koenig & Loetz 2002, p. 367.
842. Benjamin et al. 2006, p. 774; Bouwman et al. 2004, p. 19; Correa 2001, pp. 25, 51; Koenig & Loetz 2002, p. 365; Larouche 2000, p. 365.

any-to-any connectivity (maximizing network effects), and, second, removing entry barriers for competition with the former monopolists (the incumbents).

First, because telephony service would be operated by different carriers in competition rather than by a single monopoly, any-to-any connectivity (a maximization of network effects) was no longer self-evident, as competing operators might refuse to connect each other's calls.[843] Interconnection duties, therefore, aim to safeguard any-to-any connectivity, or a maximization of network effects.[844] Interconnection is similar to interoperability in software, which enables data exchange between users of different vendors:[845] customers are not limited to calling other customers of their own provider; rather, customers can exchange conversations with subscribers of any interconnected provider.

Interconnection for any-to-any connectivity need not necessarily be imposed. If multiple telecommunications providers exploit a network, interconnection can serve each provider's interests because it increases the network effects for their respective subscribers.[846] In such instances, the interests of the competitors and their consumers coincide and the competitors have an incentive to interconnect. Nonetheless, drawing on the similar problem of market-driven standardization, Larouche demonstrates that, although competing operators may often have strong incentives to interconnect,[847] firms may also have various incentives not to interconnect with rivals.[848] Any-to-any connectivity is, therefore, inherently at risk, and safeguarding any-to-any connectivity may thus require mandatory interconnection. The interconnection instruments are examined in section 5.2.3.

One argument against competition by interconnected networks is the problem of coordination costs.[849] As in computer programs, interconnection and other forms of access between operators can be complicated as a result of the use of different interfaces, thus frustrating a maximization of network effects.[850] One answer to this problem is, of course, to avoid interconnection and to rely on a monopoly.[851] Modern telecommunications law instead relies on commercial negotiations and the use of *de-facto* and *de-jure* standards and reference offers to facilitate interconnection.[852]

The competition in the market driven by interconnection obligations first maximizes network effects because it prevents any particular network

843. Correa 2001, p. 40; Larouche 2000, p. 365. See also section 5.2.1a.
844. See section 2.2.1. See also Bouwman et al. 2004, p. 13.
845. See section 2.2. Indeed, similar calls for mandatory interoperability have been made for software. Frischmann & Weber-Waller 2008, p. 55; Goldberg 2005; Lemley et al. 2000, p. 1.
846. See section 2.2.2. See also Dommering et al. 1999, p. 114; Gijrath 2006, p. 48; Larouche 2000, p. 198.
847. Larouche 2000, p. 382.
848. *Id.*, p. 383. See also Ofcom 2006. See also section 2.2.2d.
849. See section 2.2.2c. See also Benjamin et al. 2006, p. 705.
850. Dommering et al. 2001b, p. 40; Neumann 2002, p. 622. See also section 2.2.2c.
851. See also section 2.2.2d.
852. Dommering et al. 1999, p. 167; Framework Directive, Article 17.

operator from exploiting its proprietary network effects, or the size of its network relative to other networks. Compared to competition for the market, competition in the market stimulates relatively more static efficiency than dynamic efficiency because there is less of an opportunity to extract monopoly rents by building a more extensive network than competitors and tipping the market.[853] This arguably corresponds to the public-utility rationale of telecommunications policy, which places relatively more emphasis on any-to-any connectivity and ubiquitous availability. However, in order to maintain incentives to invest in infrastructure, other incentives must be created. Such incentives are instituted, *inter alia*, by interconnection charges: an operator has stronger incentives to invest in a large network if interconnection fees are high.[854] In the context of software, interconnection fees would translate to mandatory licensing of interoperability information for a fee based on the program's number of users.[855]

The second rationale for interconnection is the more specific problem of the historical advantage of the incumbents over any new entrants. Upon liberalization of monopoly regulation, the incumbents, who inherited the full subscriber bases from monopoly regulation, could be particularly eager to refuse to connect calls from new entrants because this would shield them from any such competition based on the very strong network effects in telecommunications.[856] New entrants would not attract any subscribers because customers switching to the new entrants would be unable to call the incumbent's subscribers.[857]

853. See section 2.2.2d.
854. By contrast, lower access fees tend to stimulate price competition. Benjamin et al. 2006, p. 826; Correa 2001, p. 41; Geradin & Kerf 2003, p. 46.
855. See, for example, Koelman 2006, p. 834.
856. The incumbents also inherited key infrastructure, such as the local loop, which introduced risks of foreclosure of competitors. Rules regulating access to the incumbents' facilities, most notably the local loop, obviate these problems. Geradin & Kerf 2003, p. 10; Larouche 2000, p. 324; Ottow 2006, p. 50; Shelanski 2002, p. 28. In addition, these rules facilitating access to the infrastructure of incumbents also serve to facilitate entry for horizontal competitors that do not necessarily seek to invest in entirely new infrastructure, as required for competition by interconnection (see *supra*). Thus, in contrast to interconnection, rules permitting unbundled access to and resale of the incumbent's network assets enable competition by operators without a comprehensive proprietary infrastructure. This, in turn, intensifies price competition, thereby providing more immediate appreciable benefits to consumers upon liberalization. Bouwman et al. 2004, p. 14; Dommering et al. 2001b, p. 42; Larouche 2007b, p. 11; Maxwell 2002, pp. 1.3–25 (§11); Ottow 2006, p. 51; Shelanski 2002, p. 26. An alternative approach is functional separation: the incumbents' infrastructure could be separated from their service activities. While still rejected in the New Regulatory Framework (NRF), current reviews of the regulatory framework do hint at this possibility. Geradin & Kerf 2003, p. 57; Larouche 2007b, p. 21. Unlike interconnection, the concern of access to incumbent's facilities is not directly related to network effects and will not be discussed in further detail.
857. Another cause of switching costs is the numbering system: users may find it prohibitively burdensome to change their number in order to switch to a new provider. See, generally, Angel 2001, p. 70; Geradin & Kerf 2003, p. 9; Shapiro & Varian 1999, p. 114.

This translates into prohibitive entry barriers for the new entrants.[858] In the absence of mandatory interconnection, competition with incumbents, therefore, would not be viable, and the very goal of liberalization would be at risk. In addition to the objective of any-to-any connectivity, interconnection thus also serves to remove entry barriers for competition with incumbents.[859]

5.2.2. Flexibility Versus Certainty

The preceding section has demonstrated how, in attempting to maximize network effects, telecommunications law has evolved from a model of monopoly regulation to a model of competition in the market, which is, in particular, sustained by interconnection obligations. The focus of regulation has thereby shifted from actively determining the monopolist's output – essentially as a *substitute* for the competitive process – towards ensuring and monitoring interconnection between operators, thus *supporting* the competitive process as *ex-ante*, sector-specific competition law.[860] The present section will demonstrate why an *ex-ante* approach to software interoperability is to be preferred over an *ex-post* competition approach, using telecommunications law's *ex-ante* approach to interconnection as a model.

The need for an *ex-ante* approach to the problem of copyright's threat to interoperability (Chapter 3) can conceptually be split into two subproblems. First, the *cause* of copyright's impediment to interoperability is the scope of protection: this scope is arguably too broad because it effectively protects a computer program's interface specifications. This problem – that of a correction for intellectual property rights that have been defined too broadly – resembles that of the privatization of incumbent telecommunications operators: in both situations, there is an inefficient *ex-ante* allocation of rights that foreseeably and structurally harms competition by awarding too much market power to a single party. Telecommunications law, therefore, contains specific provisions aimed at correcting for the incumbents' significant market power (section 5.2.2a). Second, the *result* of copyright's broad protection of interface specifications is an impediment to interoperability. Telecommunications law demonstrates that the use of *ex-ante* interconnection regulation to safeguard the similar issue of interconnection is to be preferred over a competition law approach, as, due to very strong network effects, the need for interconnection is of a structural, rather than an incidental nature, and,

858. See also Ofcom 2006, §1.1. In Europe, any-to-any connectivity is also considered a means to develop the internal market (TFEU, Article 154). Framework Directive, Article 8(3)(B). See also Gijrath 2006, p. 117; Stuurman 1995.
859. Benjamin et al. 2006, p. 773; Gijrath 2006, p. 52; Koenig & Loetz 2002, p. 365; Shelanski 2002, p. 26.
860. Benjamin et al. 2006, p. 693; Koenig & Loetz 2002, p. 363.

therefore, cannot be sufficiently safeguarded by an *ex-post*, case-by-case approach (section 5.2.2b).

a. Interconnection and Incumbents

Competition law necessarily applies to the telecommunications industry,[861] even if only due to its foundation in primary EU law.[862] Similar to a refusal to supply interface information of a computer program, it is conceivable that an incumbent telecommunications operator's refusal to interconnect its network with that of a new entrant would amount to an abuse of the incumbent's dominant position under Article 102 TFEU.[863] This is, indeed, the view expressed by the Commission in its Access Notice, which discusses the Commission's interpretation of the application of the TFEU's competition rules to the telecommunications sector.[864]

However, relying on an *ex-post* approach to facilitating competition with incumbents appears to be a questionable course of action. Both instrumentally and substantively, competition law appears ill suited to address the specific concerns of the incumbents' historical advantage in telecommunications markets. It was already noted that competition law does not normally sanction monopoly power (as enjoyed by the incumbents) *per-se* because it can be a natural result of superior competition in a competitive market. Thus, only abuse of a dominant position gives rise to competition law scrutiny.[865] Moreover, in order to stimulate the competitive process and to safeguard incentives to invest, competition law applies a high threshold for a duty to deal, such as a duty to interconnect. Such sanctioning of abusive *behavior* under competition law functions best if the market is effectively competitive.[866]

In telecommunications, however, the central concern is precisely the fact that the incumbents obtained their dominant position, including their substantial client base and key network facilities, not from the competitive process but, indeed, from being shielded from competition. The historical background is thus different from the competitive situation presumed in competition law,[867] and the rationales for protecting (private) investments in a competitive market do not necessarily apply. Rather than any abusive *behavior* on the part of the privatized incumbents, the problem arguably lies primarily in the *ex-ante allocation* of all resources to these incumbents – including the

861. *British Telecom* (ECJ 1985); Dommering et al. 1999, p. 149; Nihoul & Rodford 2004, p. 485.
862. Geradin 2004, pp. 1546, 1549.
863. See, generally, section 4.2. See also *MCI v. AT&T* (US Court of Appeals, Seventh Circuit 1983).
864. European Commission 1998.
865. See section 4.2.1a. See also Craig & de Búrca 2003, p. 1130.
866. Dommering et al. 2001b, p. 19.
867. Koenig & Loetz 2002, p. 366.

full subscriber base – and the consequent foreseeable and structural entry barriers that this allocation causes for new entrants.[868]

Thus, the *ex-ante* allocation of all market power to the incumbent, combined with strong network effects, enables the privatized incumbent to preclude all competition from new entrants by refusing to interconnect such new networks. The effects of privatization of a telecommunications incumbent are similar to the *ex-ante* grant of a 200 year patent to a single firm,[869] or, for that matter, the grant of intellectual property rights in a computer programs' interface specifications: in all three situations, the broad *ex-ante* allocation of these rights foreseeably and structurally leads to substantial market power and possibly harm to the competitive process. However, it is difficult to characterize the firms' exercise of these rights as abusive behavior *ex-post*: similar to a 'bare' refusal to license an intellectual property right, a simple refusal to interconnect – as opposed to a termination of existing interconnection arrangements – may not amount to clearly abusive behavior under competition law.[870] Rather, harm to competition is primarily caused by the inefficient *ex-ante* allocation of the rights, and it, therefore, appears more appropriate to address these structural inequalities first – that is, using an *ex-ante* approach.[871] The flexible, case-by-case approach to abusive behavior is more sensible if such abuse originates from unforeseeable behavior or circumstances on an otherwise competitive market.[872] These rationales for an *ex-ante* correction of significant market power of telecommunications incumbents should also apply to the similar problem of correcting for the broad scope of copyright protection in interface specifications of computer programs: this scope is preferably addressed by an *ex-ante* adjustment in the scope of these rights, rather than through *ex-post* application of competition law.

Thus, the central problem is that substantial market power itself can cause harm to the competitive process even in the absence of any particular abusive behavior, especially when such market power does not stem from superior competition but is, instead, artificially created by a generous *ex-ante* allocation of exclusive rights to a single firm.[873] The absence of any particular abusive behavior makes it difficult to sanction the firm's actions under Article 102, which, after all, only concerns abuses.

However, the problem of harm to the competitive process caused by *ex-ante* allocation of exclusive rights is recognized in EU law under the rubric of Article 106(1) (ex Article 86(1)), which deals with public undertakings and undertakings to which special privileges have been granted. In the so-called *eo ipso* cases,[874] the ECJ recognized that, by granting exclusive rights to

868. van Rooijen 2008, p. 83.
869. See also section 4.2.1b.
870. Larouche 2000, p. 204; van Rooijen 2008. See also Gijrath 2006, p. 101.
871. Ottow 2006, p. 51; van Rooijen 2008, p. 78.
872. Dommering et al. 2001b, p. 34.
873. Craig & de Búrca 2003, p. 1126.
874. See, for example, *ERT* (ECJ 1991); *Höfner* (ECJ 1991); *Merci* (ECJ 1991).

certain undertakings, a state can organize such undertakings so as to hold significant market power and, moreover, so as to unavoidably (*eo ipso*) exercise these rights in breach of the competition rules.[875] This is prohibited by Article 106(1).[876] Although the existence of substantial market power caused by the exclusive rights is,[877] by itself, still not unlawful under Article 106(1),[878] the fact that exercise of the relevant privileges would unavoidably amount to an abuse under Article 102, or would very likely (foreseeably) induce the relevant undertaking to exercise them so as to commit an abuse, *does* make such allocation unlawful.[879] It is no surprise, then, that Article 106 has, in the past, served as the cornerstone for the liberalization of the telecommunications market, which, after all, was characterized by the presence of incumbents with exclusive rights to exploit telephony.[880]

The addressee of Article 106(1) is the Member State, not the undertaking.[881] It follows that Article 106 holds the Member State responsible for the *ex-ante* allocation of exclusive rights to an undertaking if such rights induce that undertaking to exercise these rights, thereby harming the competitive process, and that the Member State can have an obligation to correct this.[882] Article 106 thereby essentially complements Article 102 and other TFEU competition provisions directed at undertakings. Read together, these provisions underscore that both undertakings and the state have an obligation to safeguard the competitive process, by, respectively, refraining from abusive behavior and by preventing the creation of rules, rights or privileges that instigate such abuse.

One could argue that too broad intellectual property rights effectively shield the beneficiary firms from competition similar to the exclusive rights covered by Article 106, and can, therefore, similarly harm the competitive process.[883] In *Inno v. ATAB*, however, the ECJ held that Article 106 does not

875. Note, however, that the dividing line between market power *per se* and abusive behavior is a fine one, and this is apparent from both the application of Article 102 and Article 106. See, for example, Craig & de Búrca 2003, p. 1127; Larouche 2000, p. 317.
876. Craig & de Búrca 2003, pp. 1126, 1129. See, generally, Buendia Sierra 1999.
877. On the difference between 'exclusive rights' and a dominant position, see Faull & Nikpay 2007, p. 602.
878. *Merci* (ECJ 1991), §16.
879. Craig & de Búrca 2003, p. 1136; Jones & Sufrin 2001, p. 440; *Merci* (ECJ 1991), §17. On the difference between the 'unavoidable', 'lead to' and 'induce' standards, see *ERT* (ECJ 1991), §37 ('led to'); Jones & Sufrin 2001, p. 442; *Höfner* (ECJ 1991), §34 ('cannot avoid'); *Merci* (ECJ 1991), §19 ('induce'). Jones and Sufrin observe that any undertaking with significant market power will be induced to use that market power to compete, such that allocating such market power by way of exclusive rights can foreseeably result in an abuse. Jones & Sufrin 2001, p. 444.
880. See, generally, Larouche 2000, p. 37. See also Jones & Sufrin 2001, p. 435.
881. Ehlermann 1993, p. 65; Faull & Nikpay 2007, p. 596; Jones & Sufrin 2001, p. 432.
882. Craig & de Búrca 2003, p. 1125 ('The rationale is that where the State has relieved an undertaking wholly or partially from the discipline of competition, it must bear responsibility for the consequences.').
883. See also Buendia Sierra 1999, p. 70 §2.27.

apply to intellectual property rights because these rights are not generally granted to undertakings at the State's discretion but rather follow from the undertaking's own actions.[884] In other words, intellectual property rights are not 'exclusive' rights in the sense of Article 106 because any undertaking can obtain them.

It is, of course, one thing to hold Member States directly accountable for intellectual property rights that prove to have been too broadly defined. This could well be too intrusive and contrary to the ECJ's interpretation of Article 345 TFEU, which prescribes that the Member States' national rules of property ownership are not to be overridden by the TFEU.[885] It is quite another thing, however, to emphasize that it is ultimately the legislature's responsibility to define these intellectual property rights and that, in fulfilling this task, legislatures should be alarmed that defining these rights too broadly can shield the beneficiaries similarly to the 'true' exclusive rights that are covered by Article 106. Based on the principles underlying Article 106, one could, therefore, argue that the *ex-ante* legislature, rather than the competition authorities, should take responsibility for the problem of too broad intellectual property rights – such as copyright protecting software interface specifications and design laws protecting interconnections.

The idea that an undertaking cannot be sanctioned for substantial market power *per-se*, but only for abuse of substantial market power, arguably comes close to accepting a doctrine of existence/exercise,[886] which is indeed the formal way in which EU law distinguishes between undertakings' mere possession of market power and abuse thereof.[887] Thus, one could reconcile the three concepts of too broad intellectual property rights, the *eo ipso* case law based on Article 106(1), and the existence/exercise doctrine, by accepting that, if undertakings' exercise of an intellectual property right would structurally and foreseeably lead to harm to the competitive process (an abuse), then the existence of that right should ideally be redefined by the state.

Returning to the application of Article 102 to telecommunications, it must be observed that use of the essential facilities doctrine in the bottleneck type of cases, including the incumbents' substantial client base and key network facilities, also raises instrumental questions as to the legitimacy of using competition law for this purpose. According to Larouche, structural use of Article 102 to force interconnection with incumbents, in particular under the essential facilities doctrine, can lead to an analysis in which the 'essentiality' of the relevant facility, based on 'more or less informed assumptions about how the market could be structured', replaces a more thorough analysis of the relevant market, dominance, and particularly abusive behavior in the

884. *Id.*, p. 71, §2.33; Faull & Nikpay 2007, p. 603; Jones & Sufrin 2001, p. 435; *Inno v. Atab* (ECJ 1977), §41.
885. See also section 4.1.1.
886. See also sections 4.1.1 and 5.1.2.
887. Craig & de Búrca 2003, p. 1126.

specific case.[888] This would entail stretching the application of Article 102 beyond its legitimate basis, which, after all, lies in the application of the law to these case-specific circumstances.[889]

Consequently, in accordance with the concerns of market power caused by the historical client base and ownership of unique network facilities, rather than any particular abusive behavior, the European Regulatory framework-provides for an *ex-ante* approach to interconnection with incumbents that corrects for their market power without the need to establish abusive behavior. Thus, unlike competition law, a mere finding of significant market power – which may be caused, *inter alia*, by a substantial subscriber base or by ownership of network facilities that are difficult to duplicate – can give rise to access obligations. These access duties may entail both interconnection with facilities-based competitors and access to the incumbents' network facilities for service-based competitors.[890] By tying these access duties to possession of significant market power, rather than additional abusive behavior, the Regulatory frameworkis more suitable to remove the structural entry barriers in the market. The determination of market power as well as the type of access obligations best suited to correct for such market power both require judgments to be made in individual cases. This requirement of flexibility has led to a substantial role for a sector-specific regulatory agency. The National Regulatory Authority (NRA) has the necessary discretion in assessing both the continued need for sector-specific obligations and the nature of such obligations.[891]

This transformation process might be considered complete when new entrants have gained sufficient market power of their own, for example, by attracting a subscriber base and by investing in their own facilities.[892] This temporary element is embedded in the European Regulatory Framework. By tying access obligations to the dynamic concept of significant market power, the New Regulatory Framework (NRF) anticipates an increasingly limited role for *ex-ante*, sector-specific intervention as competition progresses and as the market power of the incumbents decreases.[893] Thus, to the extent the incumbents continue to enjoy significant market power, they are subject to more extensive access duties (see *supra*), which should eventually limit their market power in favor of a level playing field. Once this phase has been reached, the specific significant market power (SMP) obligations will terminate automatically and the market is effectively left to *ex-post* review by

888. Larouche 2000, p. 212.
889. *Id.*, p. 122.
890. Access Directive, Article 12(1).
891. *Id.*, Articles 8 and 12.
892. See section 5.2.1b. See also European Commission 2002, §78; Koenig & Loetz 2002, p. 365; Shelanski 2007, p. 69.
893. European Commission 2002, §19.

general competition law.[894] This temporary approach corresponds with its purpose of transforming the market from a monopolistic to a competitive one.

b. Interconnection and Any-to-Any Connectivity

As already observed in section 5.2.1b, interconnection is not only relevant to enable competition with the incumbents but also will remain a vital condition for effective competition in the market even after the incumbents have lost their historical advantage. Even if the market has *become* effectively competitive, there is no guarantee that it will *remain* effectively competitive.[895] It was already observed that there is a particular risk of instability and monopolization in network industries because such markets can tip in favor of a single firm in the absence of mandatory interconnection.[896] Consequently, even if the incumbents have lost their historical advantage to make way for a level playing field, the market can remain inherently unstable. It follows that mandatory interconnection remains relevant even after the incumbents have lost their historical advantage.[897] Drawing on the experience of the competition between Bell and the independents in the United States,[898] Shelanski observes:

> [S]ome sector-specific laws, even if not a specific regulatory agency, are necessary for competitive telecommunications. The most important of these laws would be non-discriminatory interconnection of competing networks for the purpose of exchanging calls among their respective subscribers. [. . .][899]

In the Access Directive (see section 5.2.3a), the general interconnection obligations for all network operators in Article 4 apply regardless of the presence of operators with significant market power. This suggests that, unlike the interconnection and access rules for SMP operators (see section 5.2.2a), the general interconnection rules are not of a temporary but of a permanent nature.[900]

---

894. Access Directive, Article 8(2); European Commission 2002; Framework Directive, Article 16(3), 16(4). See also Dommering et al. 2001b, p. 19; European Commission 1999, p. 19; Geradin & Kerf 2003, p. 119; Koenig & Loetz 2002, p. 365; Larouche 2000, p. 363. But see Dommering et al. 2001a, p. 186; Larouche 2000, p. 321.
895. Dommering et al. 2001b, p. 30.
896. See section 2.2.
897. Larouche 2000, p. 397. But see May & Levine 2005.
898. See section 5.2.1a. See also Mueller 1993.
899. Shelanski 2002, p. 23. See also Larouche 2000, p. 397; Shelanski 2007, p. 68.
900. This is also the view reflected in the EU's 1999 Review, which contemplates the contours of the current regulatory framework. The Review regards interconnection regulation as a 'minimum level of regulation' for telecommunications. European Commission 1999, p. 30.

Because of the very strong network effects in telecommunications, the possibility to interconnect with other networks thus remains a crucial condition for viable entry and competition even after the incumbents have lost their historical advantage. In order to stimulate entry and competition, therefore, there must be sufficient certainty about the ability to connect the new network's subscribers to those of the existing networks.[901] Similar to investment decisions based on intellectual property rights,[902] certainty about the possibility to interconnect cannot be created by *ex-post* competition law but must necessarily be addressed *ex-ante*.[903] The same certainty about the ability to interoperate is relevant in software because this industry is similarly characterized by strong network effects. Furthermore, competition law can only remedy abusive behavior in particular instances. Based on this case-by-case approach and the substantial threshold for a duty to deal or interconnect (*supra*), competition law appears less suited to structurally alter the market-wide entry barriers caused by refusals to interconnect in telecommunications.

Moreover, the relevant bottlenecks for interconnection with other networks can be readily identified, thus significantly facilitating anticipation through an *ex-ante* approach.[904] As already noted, the same holds for software interface specifications.

A strong rationale for permanent interconnection duties in telecommunications, which is not necessarily relevant to software, can also be found in the public-utility character of telecommunications services.[905] The public-utility character may require not merely incentives to interconnect but also actual safeguards that any-to-any connectivity is not at risk. Larouche observes that competition law can only safeguard the competitive process, not its results. Sector-specific regulation *can* safeguard such results, for instance, by imposing interconnection obligations where parties lack the incentives to negotiate interconnection privately.[906]

Where operators do not have incentives to interconnect, it is also questionable whether, substantively, interconnection can be sufficiently safeguarded through competition law. Competition law's current focus on stimulating independent competition and innovation appears difficult to reconcile with the more substantial need for interdependency, coordination and standardization in the telecommunications industry.[907] In the context of software interoperability, it was already observed that application of the essential facilities doctrine under competition law is reserved for exceptional circumstances, *inter alia*, because it is believed that a duty to deal diminishes

901. *Id.*, p. 27.
902. See section 4.1.2.
903. Dommering et al. 2001b, p. 26.
904. Koelman 2006, p. 836. See also section 4.1.2c.
905. See section 5.2.1b.
906. Larouche 2000, p. 363. See also section 5.2.3c.
907. See also section 4.2.2a.

incentives to innovate.[908] In particular, the *Bronner* test for indispensability places high burdens on competitors of a dominant undertaking to invest in their own network before resorting to the dominant firm's resources.[909] The effects of a duty to deal (i.e., mandatory interconnection) may well be different, however, in an industry characterized by strong network effects, interdependency and standardization, such as the software and telecommunications industries. In such industries, a degree of standardization (interconnection or interoperability) can be critical to stimulate competition in the market and follow-on innovation. *Bronner*'s high indispensability threshold for a duty to deal, therefore, appears to conflict with a more structural application of competition law to safeguard interconnection in the market. The inaptness of using competition law to safeguard interoperability in computer programs thus also applies to safeguarding interconnection in telecommunications.[910] Recall that, moreover, the *Bronner* test is an objective standard, making it less suited to accommodate smaller new entrants.[911]

5.2.3. Instruments

The previous section demonstrated the advantages of an *ex-ante* over an *ex-post* approach to limiting market power in telecommunications, in particular for interconnection. This section examines the specific instruments for interconnection under European telecommunications law, as well as their potential relevance for access to interface information within software copyright law. The focus of this section lies on general interconnection regulation for any-to-any connectivity, rather than specific interconnection rules for SMP operators. Thus, section 5.2.3a first outlines the European Regulatory frameworkfor interconnection. Section 5.2.3b subsequently analyzes the instrument of commercial interconnection negotiations. Telecommunications law demonstrates that, in the trade-off between the flexibility of *ex-post* competition law and the certainty provided by *ex-ante* legislation, there is an important intermediate solution – namely, *ex-ante* regulation by a sector-specific agency. Within statutory limits, the regulator can use its discretion and expertise in assessing whether the *ex-ante* regime functions appropriately or requires facilitation in particular instances. Section 5.2.3c demonstrates that this mechanism, in conjunction with commercial negotiations, appears particularly suitable to address the complexity of interconnection arrangements – not only in telecommunications but also in software. Finally, section 5.2.3d studies the reference interconnection offer.

---

908. See section 4.2.2b.
909. See section 4.2.1b. See also Larouche 2000, p. 385; Shelanski 2007, p. 101.
910. See section 4.2.2.
911. See section 4.2.1a. See also Helberger 2008, p. 1137; Larouche 2000, p. 195.

a. Regulatory Framework

The current European Regulatory frameworkfor electronic communications comprises, *inter alia*, the 2002 framework and Access Directives. The framework and Access Directives are part of the NRF, which replaces an older set of directives.[912] The Framework Directive contains general provisions about the objectives and limitations of telecommunications regulation, the role of the Commission and of the NRAs therein, and the procedures for market analysis and standardization. The Access Directive contains the specific rules for access to networks.

The NRF is characterized by a market-driven approach, in which intervention is only warranted if the market does not produce the desired outcome. A related characteristic is that it is technologically neutral: the NRF applies to whichever technology is used for electronic communications.[913] It also refrains from favoring certain technologies over others because the market is considered to be better suited to determine the optimal technology.[914] An exception to the technological neutrality is the standardization-framework, which is not further discussed here.[915]

It was already noted that telecommunications law aims to address two types of interconnection: temporary problems of interconnection with incumbents and more permanent interconnection between all networks. This dual structure is reflected in the Regulatory framework, which contains rules for operators with significant market power and rules for telecommunications operators in general. Rules for incumbents were briefly described in section 5.2.2a. The latter type of rules, the interconnection rules for all operators, appear more relevant for software interoperability and, therefore, are discussed later.

b. Interconnection Negotiations

The interconnection obligations for all operators require certainty and flexibility at the same time. Because of very strong network effects, certainty about the possibility of interconnection with established networks is crucial for entry. In order to allow for such certainty, interconnection obligations in the NRF do not normally require action by the NRA but rather apply directly to operators of public communications networks. Notwithstanding this need for certainty, there is still some need for flexibility. Similar to interoperability in computer programs, interconnection in telecommunications is a complex task. It involves high coordination costs, caused by a need to synchronize

912. Note that the current regulatory framework (NRF) is currently being reviewed.
913. Ottow 2006, p. 111.
914. See also Gijrath 2006, p. 103.
915. See Framework Directive, Article 17.

numerous technical and financial matters.[916] Anticipating such issues under detailed, *ex-ante* interconnection obligations appears difficult and undesirable.[917] Recall, moreover, that the NRF prefers a market-driven and technology-neutral approach to detailed *ex-ante* regulation.

In accordance with these requirements, Article 4(1) of the Access Directive provides that interconnection is first and foremost to be arranged by commercial negotiations between operators, in which the resulting obligations thus follow from a private contract rather than an obligation imposed by the NRA.[918] Note that this is similar to the instrument for access to interfaces in software copyright law: the actual purpose of the reverse engineering provisions is to stimulate both parties to negotiate terms of access to interoperability information.[919] Negotiating interconnection generally allows both parties to safeguard their respective interests and to coordinate the complex issues that need to be resolved for interconnection.[920]

Whereas Article 4(1) prohibits an operator from refusing to negotiate altogether, it does not *guarantee* access on viable terms.[921] Similar to reverse engineering provisions in the Software Directive, the instrument for achieving interconnection is available, yet its outcome is not guaranteed.[922]

c. Intervention by NRA

Unlike the Software Directive, however, the NRF recognizes that incentives or even an obligation to negotiate may be insufficient to guarantee interconnection – in particular for incumbents and operators with significant market power.[923]

Thus, unlike the reverse engineering provisions in the Software Directive, which are intended as a 'last resort' for obtaining interoperability information,[924] the NRA can intervene in interconnection negotiations and can even impose interconnection obligations if negotiations develop slowly or fail to materialize entirely.[925] The NRA may intervene in negotiations by issuing binding guidelines for further negotiations. In addition, the contract that emerges from commercial negotiations can be enforced through an action

---

916. See section 2.1.
917. See also European Commission 1999, p. 11.
918. Koenig & Loetz 2002, p. 432; Maxwell 2002, pp. 1.3–3 (§5.1).
919. See section 3.2.2b.
920. Gijrath 2006, p. 264.
921. *Id.*, p. 271; Maxwell 2002, pp. 1.3–5 (§5.3); Nihoul & Rodford 2004, p. 206.
922. See section 3.2.2.
923. See section 5.2.2b. For instance, Ofcom, the NRA in the United Kingdom, observed in 2006 that incentives to negotiate did not suffice to guarantee interconnection on the part of incumbent British Telecom, which had considerably more subscribers than new entrants. See Ofcom 2006, §2.18, §3.21, §4.3. See also section 5.2.1b.
924. See section 3.2.2c.
925. See Gijrath 2006, p. 214.

before the NRA.[926] The NRA may also impose substantive binding amendments to interconnection agreements if necessary[927] and can impose interconnection duties on operators controlling access to end-users if such obligations are necessary and justified.[928] In sum, the NRA can *ensure* that interconnection is actually accomplished.[929]

Telecommunications law thus essentially aims to maximize network benefits and enable competition in the market in the same manner as attempted for software interoperability – namely, through connecting the networks or programs of different rivals. Unlike the copyright protection regime applying to computer programs, however, which fails to exclude interface specifications from the effective scope of protection, telecommunications law explicitly limits the proprietary control over a network's interconnection with other networks, and even provides for affirmative obligations to interconnect.

Note that the NRA's role in imposing SMP obligations (see *supra*, section 5.2.2) is of a different nature than its role in general interconnection regulation (discussed here). In its former role, the NRA conducts, on its own initiative, complex economic analyzes and relies on its sector-specific expertise to impose forward-looking obligations, with a view to transforming the market from a monopolistic into a competitive one.[930] In this role, the NRA itself must determine which obligations are appropriate to achieve the NRF's policy objectives. By contrast, in its latter role, the NRA merely facilitates the interconnection negotiations between operators, primarily at the request of either operator. The objective – interconnection – is specifically defined, and it is not normally for the NRA to assess whether interconnection is appropriate. Rather, it is merely required to examine whether commercial negotiations suffice to achieve interconnection, and if not, which obligations might facilitate this process. In other words, the former role of the NRA is more akin to that of a case-by-case competition law approach, whereas the latter role is primarily aimed at safeguarding the proper functioning of the *ex-ante* interconnection regime.

The latter, more limited role of a facilitator of the *ex-ante* instrument of commercial interoperability negotiations could be of value to software interoperability. As observed in Chapter 3, the reverse engineering provisions in the Software Directive enable a competitor to obtain another developer's interface specifications at its own expense in order to create an interoperable program. Similar to the interconnection negotiations in telecommunications law, it is, however, not guaranteed that reverse engineering will be successful.

926. *Id.*
927. Access Directive, Article 5(4).
928. *Id.*, Article 5(1)(A). See also, regarding the older Open Network Provisions (ONP) Directive, Koenig & Loetz 2002, p. 399.
929. Note, however, that the NRA's power may also induce parties to be less reasonable in their negotiations, expecting the NRA to resolve the problem instead.
930. European Commission 2002, §22. See also Ottow 2006, p. 130.

In telecommunications, this might be due to substantial differences in bargaining power. In software, some programs might be too complex to reverse engineer, while, in addition, a change in specifications could render previous efforts fruitless. Moreover, the success of reverse engineering and the effect of the restrictions for reverse engineering depend significantly on the evolving state of the art in reverse engineering technology.[931] The effect of the instrument of reverse engineering is, therefore, technology-dependent. Under current law, this may preclude the competitor's ability to achieve interoperability because the reverse engineering provisions are a 'last resort' for obtaining interoperability information.[932] Moreover, if reverse engineering constitutes no actual threat to exposure of the rightsholder's know-how,[933] it will also fail to produce incentives for the rightsholder to make interoperability information available in order to avoid reverse engineering.[934] It was already noted that these factors might require a judgment to be made in specific cases as to the effectiveness of reverse engineering. This is not necessarily a subjective inquiry into the ability of the particular competitor to reverse engineer a particular computer program, but rather an objective inquiry of the possibility of reverse engineering in the light of the state of the art. Against this background, a sector-specific authority might well fulfill a useful role in monitoring the effectiveness of reverse engineering for purposes of interoperability in computer programs. It is conceivable that an observatory or a regulatory authority, on the request of an interoperable developer, determine the restrictions on reverse engineering in accordance with the state of the art – for instance, allowing multiple competitors to share their reverse engineering efforts. The ability of the NRA to determine restrictions could be tied, for instance, to the publication of a reference offer for interoperability information (see section 5.2.3d). As in telecommunications, the authority could also monitor whether commercial interoperability agreements are actually concluded. Chapter 6 will elaborate further on how a regulatory authority could facilitate software interoperability.

d. Reference Offer

For purposes of interoperability in software, an important additional instrument is the reference offer, publication of which can be requested by the NRA. In both software and telecommunications, the complexity of interconnection causes transaction costs, which can be used strategically to delay negotiations and, ultimately, interconnection and realization of network effects.[935] This problem also persists in the Software Directive's mechanism of negotiations

931. See section 3.2.2.
932. In very specific cases, competition law might offer a remedy. See section 4.2.
933. See also section 3.1.2a.
934. See section 3.2.2.
935. See sections 2.2 and 5.2.1b.

stimulated by reverse engineering. Recall that in order to stimulate private negotiations, the Software Directive's decompilation provision is only available if the interoperability information has not previously been made 'readily available'. It was already observed, however, that the vagueness of the 'readily available' standard may provoke disputes about whether this standard has been met,[936] which, in turn, can undermine the purpose of the decompilation provision as a mechanism to stimulate interoperability negotiations.

In telecommunications, similar problems are addressed in part by the reference offer. The reference offer contains the conditions under which an (SMP) operator is prepared to offer interconnection or access to its facilities to other undertakings. The purpose of the reference offer is to promote transparency and non-discrimination, while accelerating negotiations.[937] The reference offer reduces transaction costs because it provides competitors with the practical information they need to obtain access. If the offer is sufficiently detailed, acceptance by a competitor may even suffice for a private contract to be concluded.[938] Because the NRA has the power to determine the precise information that must be made available in the reference offer,[939] this instrument provides the NRA with some control over the negotiations process. The reference offer could serve a similar function for interoperability of a computer program. The rationale of the reference offer is precisely to overcome issues of deliberate attempts to slow down negotiations by providing competitors with a more concrete and detailed offer. Although a direct duty to publish a reference offer might not be appropriate within the context of copyright protection, a regulatory authority (see section 5.2.3c) could consider the publication of a reference offer in its assessment of the feasibility of reverse engineering.

5.3. CONCLUSION

This chapter has reviewed two legal disciplines that expressly recognize a need to interconnect with a competitor's product in order to prevent sustainable market power and harm to competition: design protection and telecommunications law. As observed in Chapter 3, (in)direct copyright protection of interface specifications in a computer program may risk creating sustainable market power in relation to horizontal competitors through control over network effects, and *vis-à-vis* vertical competitors through control over adjacent markets. The latter concern of foreclosure in adjacent markets was also present in design protection law: design protection could enable exercise of

936. See section 3.2.2c.
937. Gijrath 2006, p. 351; Maxwell 2002, §7.1.1; Nihoul & Rodford 2004, p. 230. See also Lloyd & Mellor 2003, p. 97.
938. See, generally, Gijrath 2006, p. 310.
939. Access Directive, Article 9(3); Nihoul & Rodford 2004, p. 231.

market power in adjacent markets for complementary products and replacement parts. The former concern of control of network effects is eminent in telecommunications law, where the value of a communications network is directly dependent on its number of subscribers. This gives the former monopolist telecommunications operators, as well as other operators with large client bases, a significant advantage over smaller new entrants. Both design protection and telecommunications interconnection regulation expressly deal with the vertical and horizontal interdependency in their respective industries by providing for appropriate interconnection instruments. These laws could be regarded as *ex-ante* competition policy. Both disciplines provide for *ex-ante* interconnection instruments in part based on the instrumental and substantive weaknesses of competition law in addressing interconnection problems *ex-post*. Design protection and telecommunications law, therefore, could serve as models for an *ex-ante* approach to the similar issues in software interoperability.

The study of interconnection rules in both disciplines can shed light on the rationales for an *ex-ante* approach to interoperability in computer programs. These rationales can be split in two: first, the *cause* of copyright's impediment to software interoperability, which lies in an arguably too broad a scope of protection and, therefore, requires a correction, and, second, the *result* of this broad scope of protection, which is an impediment to interoperability.

First, the *cause* of the problem of copyright's impediment to software interoperability lies in its broad scope of protection, which, it was argued, resembles the problems arising from the privatization of telecommunications incumbents. In both instances, the *ex-ante* allocation of too much market power to a single party foreseeably introduces harm to the competitive process, which cannot necessarily be characterized as an abuse of a dominant position. Telecommunications law, therefore, provides for *ex-ante* rules to limit the market power of the incumbents, *inter alia*, through incumbent-specific access duties. As demonstrated in section 5.2.2a, this rationale – correcting for or safeguarding against a too broad *ex-ante* allocation of market power – also underlies the ECJ's *eo ipso* case law, based on Article 106, and the existence/exercise doctrine. It is also found in the limitations to the design protection right, which was studied in section 5.1. In particular, the *Volvo* judgment of the ECJ recognized that, instrumentally, competition law is not the appropriate approach to limiting the market power of design rightsholders in adjacent markets. A rightsholder may refuse to license his or her design rights without committing an abuse. It is thus the market power conferred by the design right itself (the existence), rather than any particular abusive behavior (the exercise), that can cause harm to the competitive process. If harm to competition is caused by a broad allocation of rights or resources – such as design protection for spare parts, the client base of a former state-governed telecommunications operator, or copyright protection for software interfaces – the refusal to provide access to these rights should preferably be addressed by a change in the *ex-ante* allocation of these rights. An *ex-ante* approach, rather than an *ex-post* competition approach, also supports the incentive function of design protection rights. This incentive function requires legal certainty. A similar need for legal certainty is present in telecommunications law: without a sufficient level of certainty about the ability to interconnect with incumbents, new entrants cannot be certain that their new, isolated network will attract any subscribers. These concerns can also be eminent in computer programs, where access to a *de-facto* standard may be a *sine-qua-non* for entry and competition. Thus, the broad allocation of copyrights in computer programs, which effectively protects the programs' interface specifications, should arguably also be addressed *ex-ante* rather than through competition law.

The second problem is the *result* of copyright's broad scope of protection, which is an impediment to interoperability. The study of telecommunications law takes the interoperability issue outside of the realm of intellectual property rights, demonstrating that, regardless of how interoperability is controlled – be it through intellectual property rights protecting interfaces, or by controlling physical access to premises and communications equipment – firms may have various incentives not to interconnect with rivals. In other words, it is questionable whether the competitive process alone suffices to safeguard interconnection. Telecommunications law, therefore, recognizes that the similar problem of interconnection in telephony is preferably addressed in an *ex-ante* manner. As the study of telecommunications demonstrates, such structural concerns are difficult to address by competition law because of its case-by-case approach and its substantial thresholds for a duty to deal. Even in individual cases, it is questionable whether interconnection could be enforced through competition law because it maintains a very substantial and objective threshold for a duty to deal. Finally, the public-utility character of telecommunications networks justifies an approach that guarantees (rather than merely stimulates) interconnection for purposes of any-to-any connectivity. With the exception of the public-utility character, these rationales for an *ex-ante* interoperability approach also apply to computer programs.

Turning to the specific instruments for interoperability or interconnection, Chapter 3 observed that software copyright law does not provide for sufficient instruments to enable competitors to use and access the interface specifications of a copyright-protected computer program, which they need in order to establish interoperability with that program. Alternative instruments that could facilitate the *use* of interface specifications were found in design protection law, whereas the regime of interconnection regulation in telecommunications law might offer perspectives on facilitating the *access* to the interface specifications.

First, the problem of the possible protection of functional expression in copyright law, such as interface specifications, is, in design protection law, addressed by more explicit exclusions and limitations. Unlike the treatment of a computer program's interface specifications under copyright law, the relevant must-fit and must-match provisions provide for considerable legal certainty. Although these provisions do limit the rightsholder's ability to control certain secondary markets, they do not appear to significantly impede the incentive function of design protection laws in the primary market. Both the exclusion of must-fit parts and the limitation permitting use of must-match parts were designed with the aim of sufficiently preserving incentives to invest in new designs. Similar exclusions or limitations could prevent protection of interface information in copyright law on similar considerations.

Second, problems similar to the various weaknesses of the Software Directive's mechanism of interoperability negotiations stimulated by reverse engineering are, in telecommunications law, addressed by a regulatory authority. Whereas both software copyright and telecommunications law primarily rely on commercial negotiations to stimulate interoperability and interconnection, telecommunications law provides for more safeguards that such negotiations produce actual results. The regulatory authority can 'fine-tune' the *ex-ante* instrument to stimulate negotiations so as to ensure that interconnection arrangements are actually concluded, while also monitoring the conclusion of such interoperability agreements. This more flexible instrument of regulatory intervention appears particularly suited to address the complex technical issues involved in interconnection negotiations. Similar technical issues can arise within software copyright law, as the state of the art of reverse engineering evolves and may require a highly factual and technical appraisal as to the feasibility of reverse engineering in the light of the state of the art. It is thus conceivable that a regulatory authority be provided with the more flexible power to determine conditions for reverse engineering *ex-ante*. Such conditions could be based, *inter alia*, on whether the rightsholder has published a reference offer for the interface specifications. The next chapter will consider whether these *ex-ante* interconnection rules are of value to a redesign of copyright law to allow for use of and access to software interfaces.

Chapter 6

Conclusion: Rethinking the Interface

Against the background of the normative framework established in Chapter 2, Chapters 3 and 4 sketched a fairly grim picture of how copyright and competition laws address the control of interface specifications in computer programs. However, the study of *ex-ante* interconnection rules in design law and telecommunications regulation (Chapter 5) offered some perspectives for possible improvements. The present chapter aims to combine these findings in order to draw conclusions (sections 6.1 and 6.2) and discuss recommendations (sections 6.3 and 6.4).

To that end, this chapter will follow the three-layer approach adopted in this study thus far. Section 6.1 will first conclude on the normative balance between openness and control of a program's interoperability information. Based on its indirect effect on interoperability and market power, the optimal balance between openness and control for interface specifications is different from that of other subject matter. This differentiation is not yet reflected in copyright and competition law. Subsequently, section 6.2 will conclude on the trade-off between a more flexible, *ex-post* and a more certain, *ex-ante* approach to implementing this balance. As observed in Chapters 4 and 5, there are strong arguments for addressing interoperability concerns primarily *ex-ante*. Competition law, nonetheless, can fulfill a role as a safety valve, particularly in those circumstances in which a refusal to supply interoperability information was not anticipated by an *ex-ante* (copyright) regime. This trade-off is not reflected in the current relationship between copyright and competition law, in which an inadequate copyright approach to interoperability effectively demands a more structural role to be played by competition law.

In the light of the preference for a stronger *ex-ante* approach to software interoperability and the insufficient *ex-ante* instruments in current copyright law, the main focus of the recommendations lies in section 6.3, which explores alternative instruments that could facilitate achieving interoperability with a copyright-protected computer program. These instruments are drawn directly from the analysis of current copyright instruments in Chapter 3, which were found to be insufficient, as well as the alternative instruments to limit market power in design law and telecommunications regulation (Chapter 5).

Section 6.4 will briefly present some recommendations for the application of competition law to cases in which a dominant rightsholder refuses to supply interface specifications. Essentially, it is recommended that the current, rigid analytical framework be abandoned in favor of more flexibility. The 'mandatory' application of, particularly, the new-product test may require reconsideration. Section 6.5 concludes with a brief outlook on software interoperability and the law.

6.1. OPENNESS VERSUS CONTROL

Throughout this study, the central normative issue has been whether openness or control of interface specifications is more beneficial to competition and innovation. Chapter 2 concluded that, depending on the circumstances, both openness and control of interface specifications can be beneficial to consumer welfare, innovation and competition.

Chapter 2 demonstrated that the control over interface specifications could have a dual function: a direct and an indirect one. The direct function of control over interfaces is similar to that of control over other subject matter: to provide a right of exclusivity over interface technology, through which a developer can recoup its investments in interface innovation. This could stimulate innovation in interface technology. However, in particular with respect to interface *specifications*, it was demonstrated that such incentives are barely necessary because the relatively limited investments in creating interface specifications can be recouped from selling or licensing the computer program that the specifications form part of.

The more profound indirect function of control over interface specifications is to enable control over interoperability with other computer programs. Control over interoperability, in turn, serves as a tool to control access to a computer program's network effects, or to control access to vertically interoperable components. As such, control over interface specifications may indirectly serve to establish substantial market power – either *vis-à-vis* horizontal competitors, through *de-facto* control over a computer program's network effects, or *vis-à-vis* vertical competitors, through *de-facto* control over access to complementary products or components. In other words, control over interface specifications – and many other technical standards – could be compared to a password for extracting substantial network benefits or access to complementary product markets. As with passwords, it is not the (direct) value of the password itself but rather the value for what is behind the password that makes control over the password valuable. The difference between the direct and the indirect function of control over interfaces is critical for an understanding of the effects of how the law addresses such control.

Chapter 2 also demonstrated that in particular the latter, indirect effects of control over interface specifications can significantly affect the type of competition and innovation in the software industry. Rather than the more conventional competition in the market, control over interfaces may stimulate competition for the market, or systems competition. The more substantial market power that could emerge from either form of competition may be the prize that firms compete for, and this competition may induce substantial innovation and penetration pricing efforts. On the one hand, some control over interfaces may, therefore, ultimately benefit consumers – not primarily due to advances in interface technology (the direct function), but rather due to its effects on the type of competition and innovation in the industry (its indirect function). On the other hand, openness of interface specifications enables interoperability, which can stimulate competition in the market and increase network effects based on a greater supply of interoperable products produced by different manufacturers. The software industry is normally characterized by a substantial degree of interdependency, in which openness of different vendors' interface specifications permits different programs and components to function in seamless cooperation with each other. Chapter 2, furthermore, related openness and control of interface specifications to the trade-off between standardization and variety: open interface specifications can stimulate standardization and a maximization of network effects, whereas control of interface specifications can induce variety. Both standardization (realizing network effects) and variety can have welfare-enhancing effects. In sum, both control over interfaces – stimulating competition for the market or systems competition as well as variety – and openness of interfaces – stimulating competition in the market or component competition as well as standardization – may ultimately benefit consumers.

Chapter 2, therefore, suggested that a balance should be struck between openness and control of interface specifications. Based primarily on the indirect effects on standardization and network effects, control over interface specifications and many other technical standards has different effects on static and dynamic efficiency than control over other, regular subject matter. The optimal balance between openness and control of interface specifications in the law, therefore, should be different accordingly. In particular, Chapter 2 suggested that, in comparison to other subject matter, such control should generally be substantially shorter in order to counteract for the amplifying effect that control over standards can have on market power. Thus, market power may be significant and, therefore, should be limited in time. Depending on the legal approach to this control (*ex-post* or *ex-ante*), the balance between openness and control of interface specifications, however, may be struck with, respectively, more or less consideration of the particular circumstances of the case. Section 6.2 will conclude on this trade-off between flexibility and certainty.

In the subsequent analyzes of the two principal legal regimes balancing control and openness of interface specifications – namely, copyright law (Chapter 3) and competition law (Chapter 4) – it became clear that these laws largely fail to recognize the previously described indirect effect of control over standards, and control over interface specifications in particular. By addressing control over standards and interface specifications in essentially the same manner as other intellectual creations, these laws essentially ignore this important indirect effect of control over interface specifications on interoperability, innovation and competition in the industry. Thus, by addressing use of and access to interface specifications under largely the same regime as applied to the rest of a computer program's code, copyright law fails to explicitly recognize that, due to network effects and standardization, the optimal balance between openness and control of interface specifications may well be different from that of the program at large. Although, in the end, interface specifications may fail to attract copyright protection based on insufficient originality, they are not necessarily unprotected subject matter because they are part of the program's code, which is eligible for copyright protection. Moreover, copyright law places substantial restrictions on obtaining lawful access to these specifications. Similarly, in the application of competition law, European courts appear to apply the same so-called new-product test to refusals to license interface specifications as to refusals to license other intellectual property. Accordingly, in their respective balancing acts between control and openness, current copyright and competition laws fail to distinguish between standards such as interface specifications and 'regular' subject matter. Instead, copyright and competition laws essentially stimulate firms to innovate and compete independently, thus ideally developing their own, original interface specifications, independently from those of others, while a duty to share this information is presumed to result in the same impediment to incentives to innovate as a duty to share other intellectual property. Copyright and competition laws thus largely ignore the indirect effects of control over interface specifications on interoperability, and, thereby, for competition and innovation in software. It follows that the current legal approach to control over interface specifications in copyright and competition laws deserves reconsideration, and the following sections contain recommendations to that end.

The comparative study in Chapter 5 demonstrated that, unlike in software copyright law, the importance of standardization and network effects was recognized in design protection and telecommunications law. Thus, design protection laws isolate and exclude interconnections from design protection, thereby preventing a design rightsholder from exercising control in a manner that prevents innovation and competition in complementary products. Under telecommunications law, network operators can exercise proprietary control over their respective networks but, because of interconnection obligations enforced by a regulatory authority, cannot preclude interconnection with other networks. Similar to open interface specifications in computer programs, these interconnection obligations ensure a maximization of network effects among all network operators and enable competition in the market.

Whereas the current treatment of control over interface specifications by copyright and competition law is thus unsatisfactory because of their undifferentiated approaches to standards, on the one hand, and normal subject matter, on the other, one should be careful not to make the same error in attempting to correct this balance. Rather, interface specifications and standards should, where possible, be isolated from normal subject matter and be treated differently. Although there are strong arguments for more limited control over interface specifications and other standards, these arguments do not necessarily apply – or can at least not be supported by the analysis in this study – to other intellectual creations. Thus, one should similarly avoid shifting the balance between openness and control towards more openness for all subject matter in an attempt to solve the specific problem of too much control over interface specifications and other standards. Applying a lower level of protection to all subject matter can thus impede incentives to innovate. In copyright law and other intellectual property laws, these risks are imminent in proposals to adopt a general *ex-ante* standardization exception.[940] Because of the difficulty of defining and isolating standards *ex-ante*, there is a risk that normal subject matter (non-standards) erroneously become subject to a lower level of proprietary control, thereby impeding incentives to innovate. This risk is imminent because it was demonstrated that, outside the context of some very specific uses and subject matter, such as interface specifications in software copyright law and interconnections in design protection law, it might be prohibitively difficult to clearly isolate standardization issues *ex-ante*. In competition law, the same risk lures in the General Court's broadening of the new-product test in *Microsoft*, which not only affects the threshold for a refusal to license interface specifications but also and erroneously for other intellectual property. The court, thereby, failed to address the standardization problem in isolation and lowered the threshold for a duty to license intellectual property rights in general.[941] Such approaches thus conflict with Chapter 2's recommendation of applying a differentiated approach to standards and particularly to interface specifications. As will be demonstrated in section 6.2, the need to isolate interface specifications and other standards in order to apply a different level of protection has implications for the legal approach to such control.

A final and related observation is that, by more explicitly addressing the balance between openness versus control of interface information within an intellectual property right, such as copyright, with a view to allowing the rightsholder to enjoy a position of temporary market power, one implicitly accepts widening the 'gap' between such statutory exclusive rights and market power. Intellectual property rights are necessarily designed to enable

940. See section 6.3.1b.
941. See section 4.2.2b.

some market power because this market power should enable recoupment of the investments in innovation.[942] However, this market power is often fairly closely linked to the protected subject matter itself. For instance, a patent often quite directly links market power to the precisely claimed subject matter.[943] The more demand there is for the patented (claimed) subject matter, the more market power the rightsholder can achieve. This market power is directly related to the demand for the claimed subject matter. Similarly, the market power caused by copyrights in a novel is quite closely linked to the demand for the very original expression in that novel that copyright law protects. With interface specifications, however, the market power is not directly – or even remotely – linked to the demand for the protected interface specifications, but rather it is caused by demand for the computer program or the platform relying on such interfaces. Other factors, such as the number of other users and their expectations, determine the demand for the computer product. Moreover, as already observed in Chapter 2, network effects could amplify this market power. There is thus a considerable discrepancy between the effectively protected subject matter (the original expression in interface specifications) and the market power effectively provided for through this protection (see *supra*). In other words, the potential control that copyright – through protection of interface specifications – awards to the rightsholder is arguably disproportionate to the subject matter actually protected by copyright law.[944] This could be considered undesirable. It could be counterargued that these arguments also apply to the protection of computer programs under copyright in general: copyright's protection of original expression in the computer program's source and object code bears little relationship to the market power conferred by such rights because the market power is caused by the demand for the functionality offered by the program. Copyright law does not protect this functionality.[945] Thus, the direct relationship between exclusive rights and market power was, in the context of computer programs, already abandoned. Moreover, as demonstrated in Chapter 2, either alternative to the suggested middle-ground to protecting interface specifications – denying any proprietary control over interface specifications and permitting protection of interface specifications under the same conditions as the computer program at large – appear undesirable.[946] Both copyright protection of computer programs and the treatment of interoperability within copyright law must primarily be justified by their economic effects on innovation and competition, rather than as a property claim following from a 'natural' right (see *supra*). It will also be recalled that copyright control over interface specifications need not necessarily be effectuated through direct protection of these specifications; rather, copyright

942. Drexl 2008, p. 2.
943. If the patented component is only part of an end product, the gap between the patented subject matter and the market power may be larger.
944. Merges 1999, p. 4.
945. See section 3.1.1a.
946. See section 2.2.4.

law can indirectly regulate access to interface specifications.[947] This indirect form of protection thus corresponds to the indirect economic effects of such protection. Moreover, the substantial network benefits of successful platform computer programs may be difficult to protect otherwise.

6.2. FLEXIBILITY VERSUS CERTAINTY

Chapter 2 identified an instrumental trade-off between two complementary legal approaches to addressing the previously concluded normative balance between openness and control of interface specifications: a more flexible *ex-post* approach (Chapter 4) and a more rigid *ex-ante* approach, providing more certainty (Chapter 3).

Section 4.1 further examined this instrumental trade-off between an *ex-ante* and an *ex-post* regime of control over subject matter in general. It established arguments to address the control over subject matter *ex-ante* in structural, foreseeable cases, whereas competition law could be used to review control in cases not anticipated in an *ex-ante* regime. Innovation and competition require certainty for market players as to their ability to recoup investments in innovation and to compete with others. An *ex-ante* regime can more easily establish such certainty than the case-by-case, *ex-post* regime of competition law. Conversely, these anticipated circumstances should be respected by the *ex-post* competition authority so as to prevent undermining the very certainty that these *ex-ante* regimes aim to create. For the application of *ex-post* competition law, this implies a need to grant a certain degree of deference to the balance between openness and control already struck within an *ex-ante* intellectual property right: this balance should not be reviewed in full but should only be reviewed in exceptional circumstances. Exceptional cases, in other words, are cases that are not structural and that have not been anticipated in an *ex-ante* regime, such as copyright law.

It was also observed that making this distinction between foreseeable and exceptional cases, or cases that should ideally be addressed *ex-ante* and cases that should be addressed *ex-post*, may not always be self-evident.[948] The legislative history of the particular *ex-ante* (intellectual property) regime may provide insight into whether the regime was designed with competition considerations in mind, and, if so, which particular situations and circumstances the legislator had anticipated. The legislative histories of the European Software

947. See section 3.1.3.

948. In *Trinko*, for example, the U.S. Supreme Court noted that telecommunications operator Verizon was not under a duty to deal under general competition law, *inter alia*, because it already had such a duty under telecommunications law. *Trinko* (US Supreme Court 2004), 411 ('the indispensable requirement for invoking the [essential facilities] doctrine is the unavailability of access to the "essential facilities" – where access exists [by virtue of the 1996 Telecommunications Act], the doctrine serves no purpose'). See also Larouche 2007a.

and Design directives, for example, demonstrate the competition considerations underlying the provisions related to interface specifications and interconnections, respectively.[949]

This distinction between anticipated and exceptional cases is also reflected in design protection of spare parts and interconnections (section 5.1.2) and interconnection regulation in telecommunications law (section 5.2.2), in which structural, foreseeable situations of too much control over designs and telecommunications networks, respectively, have led to *ex-ante* limitations to such control. Design protection laws limit the scope of the design right in the secondary markets for interconnecting products and replacement parts.[950] Telecommunications law addresses the specific structural problems caused by the difficulties of competing with the large, former monopolist operators, and by possible refusals to interconnect between operators in general.[951] Both design and telecommunications laws thereby obviate the need to invoke competition law in order to correct for such structural and foreseeable cases.

Applying this trade-off between foreseeable and exceptional cases to control over standards, it became apparent that issues of standardization are often not generally foreseeable and, therefore, may not be straightforward to anticipate in an *ex-ante* intellectual property regime. Which subject matter or which uses made of subject matter must be made in the interests of standardization often only become apparent well after the creation of such subject matter (*ex-post*). Moreover, the effects of standardization on innovation and competition may vary per market. It was also noted, however, that it may well be possible to anticipate *specific* standards *ex-ante*. In particular, interface specifications can more easily be identified as subject matter that could foreseeably evolve into a standard, similar to the foreseeability of control over interconnection with a network operator's infrastructure in telecommunications and the foreseeability of control over interconnections through design protection. The case for an *ex-ante* approach to control over interface specifications, therefore, is stronger than for standardization issues in general. An *ex-ante* approach provides both rightsholders and competitors with more certainty as to the scope of the relevant intellectual property rights in interfaces[952] and can thus stimulate competition and innovation.

However, the suggested distinction between foreseeable and exceptional problems of control over interface specifications is not yet reflected in current copyright and competition laws. The current *ex-ante* copyright approach to interoperability appears insufficient, by providing for instruments that foreseeably result in too little openness of interface information. In particular, copyright law imposes substantial restrictions on lawful reverse engineering, which can preclude a competitor's ability to extract the interface specifications of a

949. See, generally, Vinje 1993.
950. See section 5.1.
951. See section 5.2.
952. See also Stuurman 1995, p. 456.

computer program.[953] Copyright law thereby effectively demands a more substantial role in addressing interoperability from *ex-post* competition law – that is, even in foreseeable instances. Conversely, competition authorities could be tempted to apply competition law beyond exceptional circumstances. Section 6.3 suggests possible changes that would result in a more substantial role for copyright law in addressing interoperability *ex-ante*, thereby simultaneously reducing the role of *ex-post* application of competition law.

In the light of the limited applicability of competition law, this study thus suggests a more substantive role for addressing interoperability between computer programs by copyright law. Yet, some might object to a further fine-tuning of copyright law to address the particular difficulties raised by issues of competition through interoperable program development. In particular, strong supporters of a *droit d'auteur* or author's rights tradition in copyright law, which is typically associated with the Continental European copyright systems,[954] might object that issues of competition policy are not the proper subject matter of copyright law.[955] This view is, however, in obvious tension with the theory of complementarity (*supra*). Moreover, as Chapter 3 observed, copyright protection for computer programs has effectively served as a *sui generis* approach since its beginning:[956] the focus lies on preventing *access* to valuable know-how in the source code of the program, rather than protecting *use* of the know-how as such. The existence of software-specific provisions, such as the right to decompile in Article 6 of the Software Directive, only emphasizes the *sui generis* nature of copyright protection for computer programs.[957] There is, therefore, a strong argument that current European copyright law, notwithstanding its primary foundation in an author's rights tradition, has already been adapted to accommodate the specific needs of protection of computer programs. The approach suggested in section 6.3, merely requires further improvements to this system; it does not necessarily require substantial changes.

Notwithstanding the suggested, more substantial role for *ex-ante* copyright law in addressing software interoperability, competition law should fulfill a valuable role in cases not anticipated by the *ex-ante* copyright approach to interoperability. This may be the case where the complexity of reverse engineering under the current state of the art precludes any practical result, such that *ex-ante* regulation of reverse engineering, as suggested in section 6.3.2b, cannot serve to enable interoperability. These may also include incidents of more clearly abusive behavior and cases in which market power was caused by factors other than copyright. Section 6.4 will suggest related recommendations.

---

953. See section 3.2.2.
954. Dreier 2001, p. 298; Goldstein 2001, p. 8; Lewinski 2008, p. 33.
955. See also Samuelson 1994, p. 294.
956. See section 3.1.
957. See section 3.2.2a.

6.3. INSTRUMENTS WITHIN COPYRIGHT LAW

The present section examines instruments to address use of and access to interface specifications that could be implemented within software copyright law, and that would align the balance between openness and control of such specifications more closely with the normative framework established in Chapter 2. Because current copyright law was identified as enabling too substantial control over use of and access to interface specifications by the rightsholder, thus, conversely, insufficient openness from a perspective of competitors, the instruments explored in this section all aim to reduce the rightsholder's control over these specifications. The instruments examined here are drawn directly from some of the weaknesses identified in the current instruments available under copyright law (Chapter 3) as well as those available for interconnection under design and telecommunications law (Chapter 5). These instruments are divided based on instruments affecting *use* of interface specifications (section 6.3.1) and *access* to interface specifications (section 6.3.2).

6.3.1 USE

Section 3.1.1 already described how copyright protection of computer programs could enable control over use of interface specifications: to the extent that these specifications constitute original expression, they cannot be reproduced without authorization from the rightsholder. It was demonstrated that, indeed, copyright law could still protect interface specifications – particularly more complex ones – and, therefore, may provide for substantial control over such specifications. This control can interfere with the more balanced approach to access to interface specifications under copyright law, which will be studied further in section 6.3.2. Accordingly, this section examines instruments to limit protection of interface specifications.

Before proceeding to these suggested instruments, it is important to recall the two principal causes for the tension between copyright protection of computer programs and the free use of interface specifications for interoperability, which were examined in Chapter 3. First, the interface specifications are part of the concrete program code that is eligible for protection as a literary work under copyright law. Although interface specifications clearly constitute functional expression, such functional expression has not been excluded from copyright law *per-se*.[958] Consequently, interface specifications are not necessarily uncopyrightable subject matter. Second, copyright law does not balance the benefits of original expression, which it promotes, and identical expression, which it does not promote.[959] Using identical expression, however, may be

958. See section 3.1.1a.
959. See section 3.1.1b.

necessary in the interests of standardization, such as the use of identical interface specifications for purposes of interoperability.

These two factors – protection of functional expression and promotion of originality rather than standardization – thus mean that there are at least two broader approaches to excluding interface specifications from protection. First, one could exclude highly functional expression, such as expression in interface specifications, from copyright protection (section 6.3.1a). Second, one could permit the use of identical expression without authorization in the interests of standardization (section 6.3.1b). In addition to these two broader approaches, section 6.3.1c considers a more specific exclusion of interface specifications from copyrightable subject matter. These approaches are outlined in the accompanying diagram.

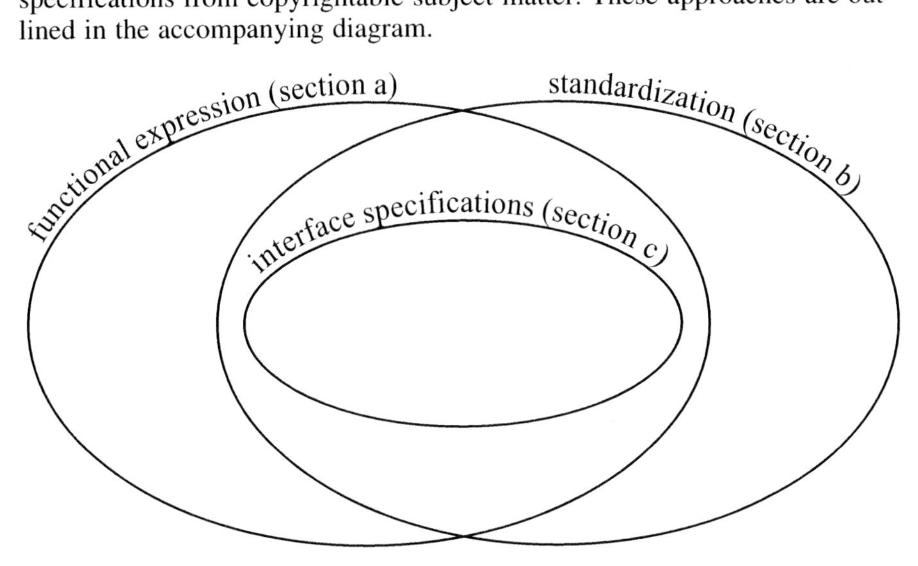

a. Interfaces under a Subject Matter Approach

Chapter 3 already observed how the concreteness of interface specifications may contribute to copyright protection as they may be considered part of the computer program's expression in the code, and why the highly functional nature of interface specifications does not preclude copyright protection. This section, nonetheless, considers excluding such highly functional expression, including interface specifications, from copyrightable subject matter.

Traditionally, a work's eligibility for copyright protection is primarily analyzed under the idea/expression doctrine and the originality requirement in copyright law. If a work constitutes original expression, it is generally found to be eligible for copyright protection. The traditional approach to the idea/expression dichotomy in copyright law distinguishes between abstract, unprotectable ideas and concrete, protectable expression. Because interface specifications are highly concrete and, furthermore, can be the result of a modicum of original choices, they could thus qualify as original, copyrightable expression.[960]

However, there is a continuing debate on whether the idea/expression and originality doctrines of copyright law should be the only parameters for copyrightability. Some commentators argue, and various cases appear to support their position, that certain subject matter ought not to be protected under copyright law at all, regardless of whether that subject matter might be considered original expression.[961] Rather, some commentators describe this approach simply as the 'unprotectable/protectable' distinction.[962] The excluded subject matter primarily concerns systems, process and methods of operation, and could also encompass interface specifications and, in short, other highly functional expression. The rationale for this exclusion is that such technical elements belong to the domain of patent law. The difference between the two approaches is illustrated in the accompanying diagram.

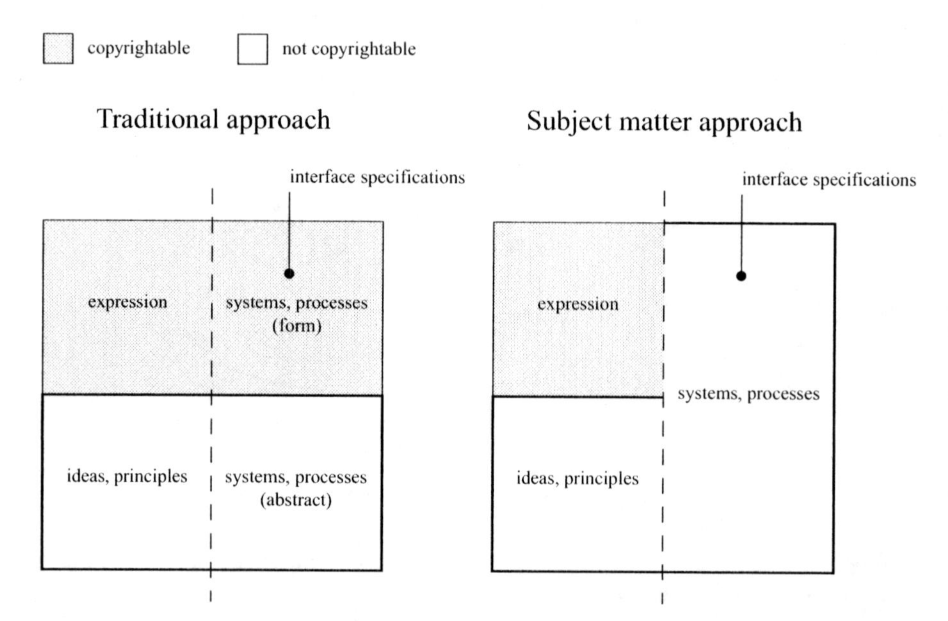

This section examines some possible sources of the subject matter approach in U.S. copyright law: the Supreme Court case *Baker v. Selden* and its

960. See section 3.1.1a.
961. Arguing from 'within' copyright law, other commentators note that the distinction between abstract ideas and concrete expression is, in fact, quite arbitrary; courts simply qualify subject matter as ideas if they do not believe copyright protection is appropriate, and as expression if they believe protection is appropriate. See, for example, Hugenholtz 1989, p. 74. See also Weinreb 1998, p. 1169.
962. Samuelson 2007c, p. 1923. See also Hugenholtz 1989, p. 73; Newman 1999.

codification in Section 102(b) of the U.S. Copyright Act. Section 102(b) has eventually found its way into the TRIPS agreement and the WIPO Copyright Treaty, which could make it directly relevant to the copyright laws of European Member States (see *infra*).

Section 102(b) of the U.S. Copyright Act complements Section 102(a). Whereas Section 102(a) describes the subject matter that *is* eligible for protection, Section 102(b) excludes certain subject matter from protection:

> In no case does copyright protection for an original work of authorship extend to any idea, procedure, process, system, method of operation, concept, principle, or discovery, regardless of the form in which it is described, explained, illustrated, or embodied in such work.

Section 102(b) does not necessarily exclude highly functional expression from protection. This depends on one's interpretation of this provision, and Section 102(b) can be read in at least two interpretations. One is that the words 'regardless of' in this provision distinguish between, on the one hand, *unprotectable* ideas, procedures, methods, processes and the like, and on the other hand ('regardless of'), the *protectable* form in which they are embodied. Their form *is* copyrightable. This is essentially the traditional distinction between abstract ideas and concrete expression (left square in the diagram).[963] The second interpretation is that not only the procedures, processes and the like are unprotectable but also ('regardless of') the form in which they are embodied – that is, regardless of the freedom the creator has had in choosing an original form for the process, system, method etc. Their form *is not* copyrightable. This would amount to a subject matter exclusion (right square in the diagram).

A similar question of interpretation arises from the Berne Convention's exclusion of news of the day:[964] is this exclusion merely a restatement of the idea/expression dichotomy (the facts and ideas in the news story are not protectable, whereas its form is) or does it exclude not merely the facts and ideas in the news story but also its particular form?[965] The Berne Convention's exclusion for news stories will be briefly examined in section 6.3.1c.

Essentially the same question arose within the context of design protection laws, which exclude elements from protection that are solely dictated by a technical function. It was observed that, under the prevailing 'mandatory' interpretation, this exclusion does not preclude protection of functional design as long as the designer has had any freedom in implementing their form, even

963. Nimmer & Nimmer looseleaf, §2.03[D] ('It would, then, be a misreading of Section 102(b) to interpret it to deny protection to "the expression" of a work, even if that work happens to consist of an "idea, procedure, process, etc." Thus, if a given "procedure" is reduced to written form, this will constitute a protectible work of authorship [. . .]'). See also section 3.1.1a.
964. Berne Convention, Article 2(8).
965. Ricketson & Ginsburg 2006, p. 498.

if that form was predominantly based on a technical function.[966] Under the alternative, 'causative' interpretation, elements of a design having a primarily technical function would have been excluded from design protection. It was also observed that trademark law offers no protection for marks that are predominantly dictated by a technical function.[967] In other words, highly functional creations, in which there is, nonetheless, some freedom of choice, are precluded from trademark protection but not necessarily from design protection.

Section 102(b) of the U.S. Copyright Act is a codification of the seminal 1879 U.S. case of *Baker v. Selden*,[968] which might thus provide insights into the proper interpretation of Section 102(b). Unfortunately, *Baker v. Selden* can be read in the same two interpretations as Section 102(b) (see *infra*). In *Baker v. Selden*, Selden had designed a new bookkeeping system with accompanying forms and explanation. Selden had published the explanation and the forms in a book. Baker subsequently began marketing and using essentially the same bookkeeping system, using a different explanation and forms with a different layout.[969] Selden alleged that Baker's similar bookkeeping system amounted to an infringement of his copyright in the bookkeeping system.[970] The Supreme Court ruled for Baker, holding that Selden could not, through a copyright in his *book*, obtain protection for his accounting *system*.[971] The explanation and illustration of such a system, however, was eligible for copyright protection but was not copied. The rationale resembles that of the more limited exclusion of technical elements from design protection: applying the relatively low standard of copyright or design protection to functional works would enable the rightsholder to circumvent the higher thresholds of patent law.[972] In the words of the U.S. Supreme Court, such backdoor-protection would be a 'fraud upon the public'.[973]

Baker thus involved three elements: first, the bookkeeping system; second, the forms used to practice the system; and third, the explanation of the system. Uncontroversially, *Baker* can be read as holding that the bookkeeping system is beyond the scope of copyright protection, whereas the explanation thereof is not.[974]

---

966. See section 5.1.3a.
967. See section 5.1.3a.
968. *Baker v. Selden* (US Supreme Court 1879). See also Goldstein 1986, p. 1124; Samuelson 2007c, p. 1944.
969. *Baker v. Selden* (US Supreme Court 1879), 100 ('The defendant uses a similar plan so far as results are concerned, but makes a different arrangement of the columns, and uses different headings').
970. *Id.*
971. *Id.*, 102. See also Samuelson 2007b, p. 208.
972. *Baker v. Selden* (US Supreme Court 1879), 102; Menell 1998, p. 671.
973. *Baker v. Selden* (US Supreme Court 1879), 102.
974. Weinreb 1998, p. 1173. See, for example, *Baker v. Selden* (US Supreme Court 1879), 104 ('The use of an art is a totally different thing from a publication of the book explaining it. The copyright of a book on book-keeping cannot secure the exclusive right to make, sell, and use account-books prepared upon the plan set forth in such book.').

However, it is less clear whether the forms in *Baker* were held uncopyrightable, like the bookkeeping system, or copyrightable, like the explanation of the system. For purposes of interoperability and protection of interface specifications, the copyrightability of the forms according to *Baker* is crucial. Similar to interface specifications, the forms of Selden's bookkeeping system are concrete expressions serving a highly functional purpose. If Selden's forms were held uncopyrightable, so too would interface specifications be uncopyrightable, thus facilitating interoperability. The crucial question, therefore, is whether *Baker* can be read as holding that Selden's forms were uncopyrightable like his accounting system, permitting their exact duplication, or whether the uncopyrightability of Selden's system left the possibility of a copyright in his forms intact, thus preventing literal copying of Selden's forms. Indeed, *Baker v. Selden* could be read in two different interpretations, which essentially correspond to the subject matter approach and the idea/expression dichotomy. The difference in interpretations is critical to the protection of highly functional expression, including interface specifications, and, therefore, to interoperability.

Under one interpretation, embraced by Samuelson & Weinreb, the Supreme Court held that Selden's forms did not constitute copyrightable subject matter, being a necessary incident to the accounting system.[975] Several passages in *Baker* indeed appear to hint that Selden's forms are uncopyrightable, like the bookkeeping system, and can thus be duplicated verbatim.[976]

If the forms are uncopyrightable as necessary incidents to the bookkeeping system, it follows that the concreteness of these forms is immaterial to a qualification as copyrightable expression and that any freedom Selden has had in designing these forms (originality) should be disregarded as unworthy of copyright protection. This, in turn, implies a need to distinguish between

975. Samuelson 2007c, p. 1974; Weinreb 1998. See also *Lotus v. Borland* (US Court of Appeals, First Circuit 1995), 816 ('Our holding that "methods of operation" are not limited to mere abstractions is bolstered by *Baker v. Selden*').

976. *Baker v. Selden* (US Supreme Court 1879), 103 ('where the art it [the book] teaches cannot be used without employing the methods and diagrams used to illustrate the book, or such as are similar to them, such methods and diagrams are to be considered as necessary incidents to the art.'); *Id.*, 104 ('And, of course, in using the art, the ruled lines and headings of accounts must necessarily be used as incident to it.'); *Id.*, 107 ('The conclusion to which we have come is, that blank account-books are not the subject matter of copyright, and that the mere copyright of Selden's book did not confer upon him the exclusive right to make and use account-books, ruled and arranged as designated by him and described and illustrated in said book.'). The court added that the fact that Selden's uncopyrightable system was practiced using paper forms, rather than the more common use of inventions in 'concrete forms of wood, metal, stone, or some other physical embodiment', did not change the analysis; 'the principle is the same in all'; *Id.*, 105. One could interpret this passage as meaning that Selden's system and its forms, even if practiced on paper, was still a system and, therefore, did not constitute copyrightable, but, if at all, patentable subject matter. Samuelson 2007c, p. 1935.

such works as Selden's forms, which may be concrete and modestly original but also highly functional and, thus, uncopyrightable, and those that exhibit originality and are primarily non-functional. Indeed, the court seems to make precisely this distinction:

> Of course, these observations are not intended to apply to ornamental designs, or pictorial illustrations addressed to the taste. Of these it may be said, that their form is their essence, and their object, the production of pleasure in their contemplation. This is their final end. [. . .] On the other hand, the teachings of science and the rules and methods of useful art have their final end in application and use [. . .].[977]

The distinction made by the court resembles that suggested by Quaedvlieg in distinguishing functional from non-functional works by reference to the test (aesthetics or efficiency) that the creator applies to evaluate her or his work.[978] The tests apparently suggested by the *Baker* court and by Quaedvlieg, however, suffer from the same weakness: they are arguably too subjective and uncertain to be useful in many instances.[979] An alternative test might be to consider whether the work is intended for communication with humans (rather than machines). This test, however, was already rejected by admitting object code to the copyright domain.[980]

Under another interpretation, embraced by Nimmer, *Baker* did not hold that Selden's forms were uncopyrightable.[981] In this interpretation, the Supreme Court was primarily concerned with not extending any copyright protection in Selden's book to the functionality in his accounting system, which, it sensibly ruled, belonged to the domain of patent law. Whether Baker was permitted to use identical forms to practice that uncopyrightable system was more or less irrelevant to that problem. Indeed, Baker's forms were *different* from Selden's – he was using 'a similar plan as far as results are concerned; but [with] a different arrangement of the columns, and [with] different headings'.[982] The question of whether Baker could use *identical* forms as Selden, therefore, was arguably not before the court, and, therefore, it might be inaccurate to interpret the judgment as, nonetheless, answering this question. Most relevant to the case was that Baker should not be prevented from practicing the bookkeeping system itself; such protection would be a 'fraud upon the public'. If he was not already doing so, forcing Baker to use forms different from Selden's would at most be a minor inconvenience to Baker and hardly the 'fraud upon the public' that the court appears concerned with.[983]

977. *Baker v. Selden* (US Supreme Court 1879), 103.
978. See section 3.1.1a.
979. See also section 5.1.3a on the similar discussion in European design protection laws.
980. See section 3.1.1a.
981. Nimmer & Nimmer looseleaf.
982. *Baker v. Selden* (US Supreme Court 1879), 100.
983. Accordingly, the court's observation that Selden's system was practiced on paper, rather than in a more traditional, physical embodiment, could be interpreted as clarifying, not

Indeed, the fact that Baker and Selden used different looking forms to practice essentially the same system serves as a reminder for why copyright protection of computer programs was not believed to cause substantial harm: one can normally use different code expression to implement the same functionality as a copyright-protected program.[984] A compelling need for exact duplication of the plaintiff's expression, therefore, does not normally arise if the purpose is only to duplicate the rightsholder's functionality (as in *Baker*), but it does arise if the rightsholder's particular expression has become a standard. Standardization is, however, an issue that *Baker* (unlike *Lotus v. Borland*) was not concerned with (see *infra*).[985] The two cases are compared in the diagram below.

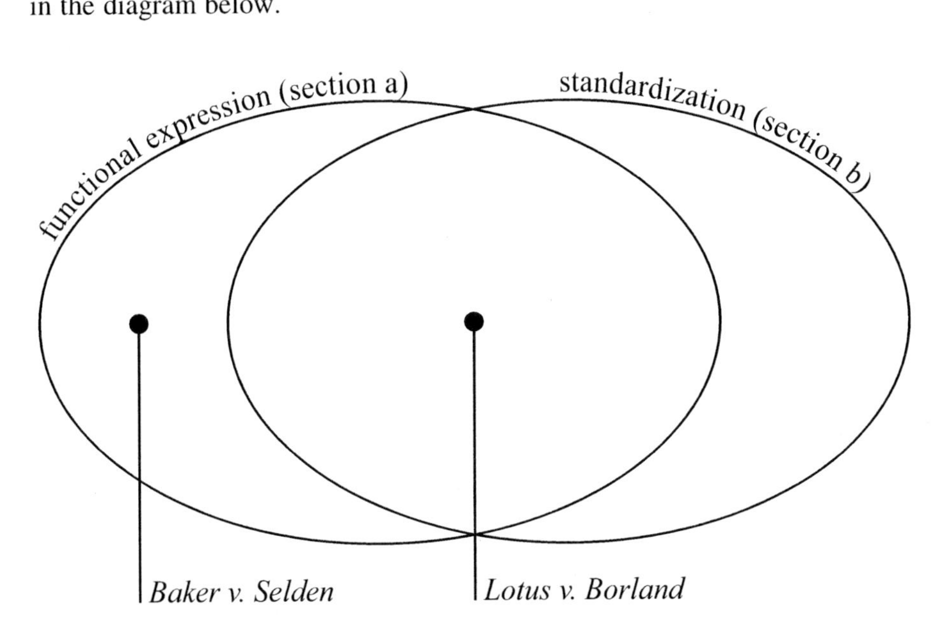

Returning to Section 102(b), it must be concluded that the question as to which of the two interpretations of this provision is the most accurate one appears difficult to resolve by studying its precedent *Baker v. Selden* because this case can be read in essentially the same two interpretations as Section 102(b).

---

that the forms were in fact an uncopyrightable system despite their paper embodiment (see *supra*, note 976), but rather that a possible copyright in Selden's forms used to practice the system on paper should not extend to the underlying bookkeeping system itself. *Id.*, 105 ('But the principle is the same in all. The description of the art in a book, though entitled to the benefit of copyright, lays no foundation for an exclusive claim to the art itself.').

984. See section 3.1.1a.

985. See also *Taylor Instrument* 1943, 100. See also Menell 1998, p. 701. See also section 3.1.1.

Nevertheless, the *Baker v. Selden* doctrine was codified in Section 102(b) of the U.S. Copyright Act primarily in response to concerns about the risks of protection of functionality in computer programs.[986] Section 102(b), therefore, is particularly relevant to the scope of protection in computer programs, including their interfaces.[987] If Section 102(b) is indeed to be interpreted in the first of the two alternatives, it excludes highly functional expression – such as interface specifications – from copyrightable subject matter.[988] Section 102(b) would thus exclude subject matter from copyrightable subject matter that might otherwise be sufficiently concrete and original to qualify as protectable expression. This exclusion would also apply to interface specifications of computer programs and other 'complex and detailed intellectual innovations'.[989]

A legitimate question at this point is what is the relevance of Section 102(b) and *Baker v. Selden* for European copyright law. The answer could lie in Article 9(2) of the TRIPS Agreement[990] and Article 2 of the WIPO Copyright Treaty.[991] Both international instruments contain the following, virtually identical rule:

> Copyright protection extends [TRIPS: shall extend] to expressions and not to ideas, procedures, methods of operation or mathematical concepts as such.

The similarity between these provisions and Section 102(b) of the U.S. Copyright Act is no coincidence: they were, indeed, modeled after Section 102(b).[992] The argument, therefore, could be made that their interpretation should reflect that of Section 102(b), and, ultimately, of *Baker v. Selden.* European Member States, as individually contracting parties to the TRIPS agreement and WCT, may well be obliged to implement these exclusions. This could ultimately make *Baker v. Selden* relevant to copyright law in European Member States. Alternatively, it is conceivable that national courts interpret their national laws' implementation of the Software Directive's Article 1(2) in accordance with such an interpretation of the relevant provisions in TRIPS and WCT, thus excluding detailed systems and methods (including interface specifications) from copyrightable subject matter.

---

986. See, generally, Samuelson 2007c. See also Weinreb 1998.
987. Samuelson 1994, p. 297; Samuelson 2007c, p. 1961.
988. Band & Katoh 1995, p. 100; Band et al. 1992, p. 142; Goldstein 1993, p. 208; Samuelson 2007b, p. 196.
989. Samuelson 2007c, p. 1974.
990. See, generally, Gervais 2003, p. 130.
991. See Ficsor 2002, p. 457; Reinbothe & Von Lewinski 2002, p. 45.
992. Article 9(2) of the TRIPS Agreement was modeled after Section 102(b), whereas Article 2 of the WCT was modeled after TRIPS. See Ficsor 2002, p. 459; Gervais 2003, p. 131 ('The inspiration is clearly the United States Copyright Act.'); Reinbothe & Von Lewinski 2002, p. 46 ('Article 2 WCT reproduces the general principle contained in Article 9(2) TRIPs Agreement.').

Traces of both the traditional idea/expression approach and the subject matter approach can already be found in the Software Directive. Whereas Article 1(2) of the directive appears to reflect the traditional distinction between abstract ideas and concrete expression,[993] the directive also, in its 11th recital, states that ideas and principles underlying 'logic, algorithms and programming languages' are not protected under the directive. As noted, in *Navitaire v. Easyjet*, the (British) court interpreted this recital as excluding computer languages from copyrightable subject matter, regardless of the means by which they were expressed or defined.[994] Nonetheless, one could imagine a more explicit reference to the unprotectability of systems, processes and methods, similar to the previously cited provisions.

For three reasons, this study does not, however, recommend relying on a subject matter approach to exclude interface specifications from copyright protection. The first reason is that it is unclear which of the two interpretations of *Baker v. Selden* and Section 102(b) underlies the similar provisions in TRIPS and the WCT. The provisions in the TRIPS Agreement and the WIPO Copyright Treaty may have meant to codify nothing more than the (traditional) idea/expression dichotomy, thus leaving expression of systems and methods (highly functional expression) eligible for copyright protection.[995] Indeed, commentators suggest that the purpose of Article (2) of the TRIPS Agreement and of Article 2 of the WCT was only to codify the 'idea/expression dichotomy', particularly as the Berne Convention does not expressly contain this principle.[996] There is little discussion in the commentaries about how, precisely, this dichotomy should be interpreted. A second reason is that, even if these provisions are interpreted as excluding highly functional expression, this approach may well cause significant uncertainty as to the scope of the exclusion of functional expression. One will need to establish with some clarity what a 'system', 'process' or 'method' is, and how aesthetic (and non-functional) certain expression must be in order to still benefit from copyright protection. Neither the tests mentioned by the court in *Baker v. Selden*, nor that suggested by Quaedvlieg, appear to provide a satisfactory answer to this question.[997] This may

993. See also Lewinski 2008, p. 288.
994. *Navitaire v. EasyJet* (UK High Court of Justice, Chancery Division 2004), §88.
995. On TRIPS, see, for example, Gervais 2003, p. 131. ('In order to comply with [Article 2(2) and 9(1) of the Berne Convention], Article 9(2) [of TRIPS] must be interpreted as clarifying existing exceptions, not instituting new ones.') On the WCT, see Reinbothe & Von Lewinski 2002, p. 46. ('One of the principal features of copyright is that this form of intellectual property extends to creative expressions of ideas or information, but not to the ideas or the information themselves. This is based on the general understanding that ideas, information or mere thoughts as such are in the public domain, and that access to them should not be restricted or even denied completely by vesting one individual with copyright, as a form of property protection, in them.')
996. Lewinski 2008, p. 123; Ricketson & Ginsburg 2006, p. 517.
997. See, for example, Samuelson 2007b, p. 209. See also Hugenholtz 1989, p. 31. Indeed, Samuelson argues that computer programs would be excluded from protection as

ultimately leave the question of the protection of interface specifications unsettled. The third and most important reason, however, is that this approach is potentially much broader than a mere exclusion of interface specifications from copyrightable subject matter, even if that is all that can be supported by this study. The broader exclusion for systems and processes, although welcomed from the perspective of facilitating use of interface specifications, therefore, cannot be supported solely by the framework established in this study.

b. Standardization

Section 3.1.1b already noted that, in addition to the protection of functional expression, the conflict between copyright protection of computer programs and interoperability is also caused by copyright's failure to balance the relative benefits of original and identical expression – particularly for purposes of standardization. Thus, the need to use identical expression in interface specifications, for example, is not generally accommodated under copyright law. Section 3.1.1b mentioned three causes for this failure: first, copyright's primary goal of promoting original expression, rather than the conflicting standardization of expression; second, the difficulties of anticipating standardization issues *ex-ante*; and third, the possible negative effects of a 'standards' exception on copyright's function of providing incentives to innovate.

The first cause, or the promotion of original expression, is in obvious conflict with the needs of standardization: rather than creating original expression, standardization would call for reuse of existing expression. This is also the case for interoperability, which requires reuse of any expression in interface specifications. However, copyright's promotion of original expression is generally beneficial for most other subject matter it protects: in the realm of traditional literary expression, such as novels and plays, originality in expression is generally beneficial to society.[998] It appears undesirable to alter this system for those few works accommodated under copyright law for which this originality may not always be beneficial to society, such as interface specifications of computer programs. The reverse appears more sensible: if certain subject matter benefits less from originality than from standardization, it should arguably not be protected by copyright law at all. Thus, one way to 'address' the standardization issue through copyright policy is to exclude subject matter from copyright protection if that subject matter generally benefits more from standardization than from originality. If such subject matter is not protected by copyright law, no rightsholder can prevent its copying. As interface specifications often need to be copied for standardization (interoperability), one might, therefore, consider excluding interface specifications from the scope of copyright protection (see section 6.3.1c).

---

uncopyrightable processes under Section 102(b) were it not for their explicit protection. Samuelson 2007b, p. 213, note 136.

998. See section 3.1.1b.

The second cause for copyright's failure to consider issues of standardization is that these issues typically rise *ex-post*, rather than *ex-ante*. At the time of creation of the work, which is the moment at which copyright law normally determines the eligibility for protection, it may not yet be known whether certain subject matter is likely to become a standard, or whether certain use of such subject matter will need to be made in the interest of standardization. Save very specific elements – such as interface specifications of computer programs – it cannot generally be ascertained *ex-ante* what subject matter or what use thereof is *a priori* likely to become a standard, as this requires an extensive analysis of the relevant markets and the exclusionary effect of protecting such subject matter, including the availability of alternatives.[999] It follows that a standard cannot generally be accurately excluded *ex-ante*. Moreover, these *ex-ante* standards approaches do not, therefore, provide considerable benefits over *ex-post* review through competition law.[1000] Indeed, allowing *ex-post* considerations to be made within *ex-ante* copyright appears to conflict with the respective roles of intellectual property and competition laws, which were outlined in section 4.1.

Some U.S. courts have, nonetheless, permitted *ex-post* considerations under copyright law in attempts to accommodate standardization needs. In so doing, the courts have relied on the open fair use defense in U.S. copyright law, which offers more *ex-post* flexibility than the generally closed systems of copyright limitations in Europe.[1001] For example, the Second Circuit, in its oft-cited decision in *Computer Associates v. Altai*,[1002] held that Computer Associates' interface specifications were uncopyrightable because interoperable developer Altai, *after* the creation of Computer Associates' software and interface specifications (*ex-post*), had no choice but to copy Computer Associates' exact interface specifications in order to achieve interoperability.[1003] These specifications, therefore, were not eligible for copyright protection *ex-post*. Although these approaches have met with approval from some commentators,[1004] other court decisions have adhered to the more traditional *ex-ante* approach, in which the freedom to use different (original) 'expression' at the stage of creation of the work points to copyright protection.[1005]

999. See also section 3.1.1b.
1000. But see Koelman 2006, p. 836 (noting that, at least, the new-product condition would be disposed of).
1001. See also Samuelson 1994, p. 285.
1002. *Computer Associates v. Altai* (US Court of Appeals, Second Circuit 1992).
1003. *Id.*, 712. See also Menell 1998, p. 689.
1004. See, for example, Menell 1998, pp. 689, 700; Samuelson 2007b, p. 215 (discussing the relevance of the scenes-à-faire doctrine for standards).
1005. *Lotus v. Borland* (District Court Massachusetts 1992); *Lotus v. Paperback* (US District Court, Massachusetts 1990). See also Menell 1998, p. 700. On appeal, *Lotus v. Borland* was solved by the First Circuit by declaring Lotus' command structure as an unprotectable 'method of operation' within the meaning of Section 102(b) of the US Copyright Act. See also Menell 1998, p. 701. See also section 6.3.1a. See also *Apple v. Franklin* (US Court of Appeals, Third Circuit 1983), 1253. See also Band & Katoh 1995, p. 87.

In the Netherlands, a similar debate about the permissibility of *ex-post* considerations within copyright law emerged after the Dutch Supreme Court handed down its *Elwood* judgment.[1006] At issue in that case was the design of a pair of jeans, which was originally protected by trademark law, and, in addition, by copyright law. Some design features of these jeans had become so common in the industry that their trademark protection had expired due to genericness: the distinctive character of these features, which constitutes the primary ground for trademark protection, was lost because of common use in the industry. This notwithstanding, the protection by copyright law remained, and, because copyright law has no 'genericide' doctrine, the rightsholder could presumably still prevent competitors from using these features by relying on copyright law. Commentators disagreed about whether *ex-post* considerations, such as 'genericide' in cumulative trademark protection, should have any bearing on the scope of copyright protection of a work, and even about the question of whether the Supreme Court itself had allowed for such *ex-post* considerations in *Elwood*.[1007] Even if *ex-post* considerations were permissible under *Elwood*, however, it is important to put this debate in perspective: it primarily emerged because of the somewhat unsatisfactory gap that existed based on the combination of a loss of a trademark protection and the cumulative protection of copyright law. It is questionable whether this debate has any relevance beyond this rather specific setting.[1008]

Dutch commentator Koelman has suggested a broader 'standards exception' within intellectual property laws, according to which protected subject matter that has become a 'standard' become subject to a compulsory license.[1009] Substantively, this approach seeks to achieve a result similar to that suggested in Chapter 2: it aims to preserve incentives to invest in standard development by allowing for intellectual property rights in standards, yet enable others to build upon and implement the standard by making the relevant intellectual property rights subject to a compulsory license once the protected subject matter has become a *de-facto* standard.[1010] This approach, therefore, effectively permits for some competition for the market, through some intellectual property protection of standards, while allowing for competition in the market once the standard has become widely accepted in the industry.[1011]

Instrumentally, however, setting terms for a compulsory license is a difficult task. Recall that the difficulty of determining appropriate terms is one of the principal objections against application of the essential facilities

1006. *Elwood* (Hoge Raad 2006).
1007. Cohen-Jehoram 2007; Visser 2007. The Supreme Court was not very clear on this issue. It only held that genericness was not proven; it did not rule that such genericness would have any bearing on the copyright protection of the pair of jeans. *Elwood* (Hoge Raad 2006), §3.313.
1008. Visser 2007. See also Quaedvlieg 1992, p. 24.
1009. Koelman 2006.
1010. *Id.*, pp. 833, 838, 839.
1011. *Id.*, p. 841.

doctrine[1012] and was also rejected in the approach to limiting protection for spare parts in design protection law.[1013] By contrast, the reverse engineering instruments in the Software Directive and the obligation to negotiate interconnection in telecommunications law are aimed at having the parties negotiate the terms of access privately.[1014] Moreover, a central instrumental difficulty remains that standards cannot be clearly defined *ex-ante*.[1015] If standard subject matter or standard use of subject matter cannot be clearly distinguished from regular subject matter *ex-ante*, the effects of such an exception may be broader than standardization, and the exception could have significant negative effects on the objective of intellectual property rights of stimulating innovation.[1016] A 'standards' exception would effectively require extensive *ex-post* scrutiny of what constitutes a standard because only a standard should be subject to compulsory licensing. This impedes the very certainty that intellectual property rights, such as copyright, aim to provide to innovators. Moreover, if extensive *ex-post* considerations are necessary to determine whether intellectual property rights protect a *de-facto* standard, it is unclear what the advantage is over application of competition law.[1017]

c. Exclusion or Limitation for Interface Specifications

The previous sections have considered two approaches to limiting protection of interface specifications: an exclusion of highly functional expression (section 6.3.1a) and a 'standards' exception (section 6.3.1b). Under the first approach, the highly concrete nature of interface specifications would not necessarily lead to copyright protection – as it could under the traditional distinction between abstract ideas and concrete expression – because the subject matter approach would also exclude more concrete yet highly functional elements of a work – such as interface specifications of computer programs – from protection. Under the second approach, the necessity to use any protected interface specifications without authorization would be permitted in the interests of standardization. Both approaches were, however, rejected as being too broad for present purposes and failing to provide certainty about the copyrightability of interface specifications.[1018] Thus, it is unclear what the extent is of an exclusion of highly functional expression, while it is similarly difficult to isolate and exclude all standards from copyrightable subject matter.

1012. See section 4.2.1b.
1013. See section 5.1.3c.
1014. See sections 3.2.2b and 5.2.3b.
1015. Koelman 2006, p. 823 ('A commonly accepted definition of 'standards' does not exist'). See also sections 3.1.1b and 4.1.2d.
1016. See also section 6.1. See also Bartmann 2005, p. 131, noting that limiting the scope of an intellectual property right *ex-ante* is warranted only if the existing scope of protection necessarily creates market power in a secondary market.
1017. But see Koelman 2006, p. 836.
1018. See section 6.3.1a.

Limiting protection via a more explicit reference to interface specifications solves both problems: it provides more certainty and does not exclude more from copyrightable subject matter than supported by this study. The rationale for limiting protection for interface specifications can be based on the broader rationales for excluding highly functional expression, of which interface specifications are a species, and for excluding standards, of which interface specifications are also a species. This section, therefore, considers more specific approaches to limiting copyright protection of interface specifications.[1019]

Naturally, an approach that specifically excludes protection of interface specifications would, by itself, provide for complete openness of interoperability information, rather than the balance between openness and control suggested in Chapter 2. However, it must be recalled that the rightsholder still maintains some control over *access* to interface specifications. An access-based regime could allow for a more balanced approach to control over interface specifications as long as their use is generally permitted.[1020]

A similar approach to an explicit exclusion of interconnections was studied in design protection law. The exclusion of interconnections from design protection, and its limitation permitting use of spare parts, demonstrates that incentives to innovate for such elements need not necessarily be reduced because the rightsholder should typically be able to recoup investments in innovation from the sale of the primary product.[1021] The 'sale' (or licensing) of the computer program may similarly enable the rightsholder to recoup investments in interface specifications.[1022]

However, an exclusion of interface specifications might prove a more significant impediment to innovation than an exclusion of interconnections under design protection laws. Section 3.2.1 already noted that the exclusion of interconnections from design protection might be less problematic than an exclusion of interface specifications from copyright protection because the latter are generally more numerous than the former. Indeed, an exclusion of interfaces was opposed on an earlier occasion based on to its 'accordion-like nature': many parts of a computer program could be named an 'interface', which could thus ultimately result in a strongly reduced level of protection.[1023] Be this as it may, an interface *specification* is still clearly distinguishable from its *implementation*.[1024] Thus, even if all elements of a computer

---

1019. The Japanese copyright act contains an explicit exclusion of 'rules' from copyrightable subject matter, in Article 10(3)(ii), which was indeed, according to some, intended to exclude (*inter alia*) interface specifications from the scope of copyright protection. Band & Durney 1995, p. 3; note 7. The Article notes, '"rule" means a special rule on how to use in a particular program a programming language [. . .]'.
1020. See sections 3.2.1c and 6.3.2.
1021. See section 5.1.1a.
1022. But see Lévêque 2005, p. 79.
1023. Lake et al. 1989, p. 432.
1024. See section 2.1.2b.

program were considered as interfaces, only the lines of code that constituted their specifications would be excluded from protection. Compared to the interface implementation, the specification only comprises a small part of the interface. Consequently, an exclusion of interface specifications should not result in a substantial impediment to innovation.

One could envisage four approaches to limiting copyright protection specifically for interface specifications: first, a 'soft law' instrument providing guidance in interpreting interface specifications as uncopyrightable ideas; second, a limitation or compulsory license permitting use of these specifications without authorization; third, shortening the duration of protection of interface specifications; and fourth, an exclusion of interface specifications from copyrightable subject matter.

Recall that the current Software Directive leaves the protection of interface specifications to be decided by courts in individual cases. In addition to the requirement of originality, Article 1(2) of the directive hands courts as their primary analytical tool the idea/expression dichotomy.[1025] The directive does not provide any guidance on how to judge whether an interface specification constitutes an unprotected idea or a protectable expression. In addition, there is a lack of a substantial body of case law interpreting the copyrightability of interface specifications. This creates legal uncertainty. If, in future cases, courts follow the few precedents established by British and French courts,[1026] they may well conclude that interface specifications are unprotected ideas or principles. As more courts reach this conclusion, the uncertainty about the copyrightability of these specifications will naturally be reduced. However, uncertainty may remain if courts continue to struggle with the difficult question of whether interface specifications constitute copyrightable expression under the Software Directive. The concreteness of interface specifications may tempt courts to accept these specifications as copyrightable expression. Notably, the General Court, in its *Microsoft* judgment, failed to address the question specifically, proceeding instead on a presumption of valid intellectual property claims, including copyright protection, on interface specifications (albeit only for the sake of argument). This suggests that more guidance may well be desirable.

Thus, rather than leaving the application of the idea/expression dichotomy to interface specifications to courts in individual cases, it could be desirable to provide some guidance to courts, stating that interface specifications are generally to be qualified as (unprotected) ideas. This appears to be consistent with the majority of the opinions in the literature as well as the case law.[1027] Guidance could be provided in a separate Guideline or Notice, or, alternatively, in the Software Directive's preamble.[1028] Of course, this solution

1025. See section 3.2.1.
1026. See section 3.2.1a.
1027. See section 3.2.1a.
1028. Interestingly, an initial version of the Original Proposal for the Software Directive contained such a reference in the preamble, although probably erroneously. Rather

would provide less certainty than a more explicit exclusion of interface specifications. Courts might still be persuaded to accept particular specifications as copyrightable 'expression'. Rightsholders could still claim protection *vis-à-vis* interoperable developers. This may cause a particularly chilling effect between large rightsholders and smaller interoperable developers. This approach to limiting interface protection, therefore, is not recommended.

An alternative could be the introduction of a limitation permitting use of interface specifications under certain circumstances. Recall that design protection laws similarly prevent a rightsholder from enforcing design rights in spare parts only for repair purposes.[1029] This approach was preferable because it was not primarily the nature of these designs, but rather the particular use made of them, that justified a lower level of protection.[1030] Moreover, the limitation preserved the incentive function for design of these parts in general because rightsholders could still enforce their rights in spare part designs against imitators.

Ideally, a person having a right to decompile a computer program would thus automatically have a right to reproduce any decompiled interface specifications for purposes of interoperability. Such a limitation would closely align the regimes of use of interface specifications and access to such specifications.[1031] Consequently, there would be no risk of a lack of a right to use any decompiled interface specifications without further authorization. Some commentators already interpret the Software Directive's reverse engineering provisions as necessarily encompassing a right to use the obtained specifications.[1032] Recall, however, that Article 6 does not *explicitly* provide for a right to use any copyrightable expression that has been extracted using decompilation.[1033]

---

than the 'correct' recital published in a later version of the same proposal, which read 'where the specifications of interfaces constitutes ideas and principles, those ideas and principles are not copyrightable subject matter', the erroneous recital, which could be copied verbatim, read 'where*as* the specification of interfaces constitutes ideas and principles; *whereas* those ideas and principles are not copyrightable subject matter [emphasis added]'. COM (88) 816 final – SYN 183, published in the Official Journal and reprinted in Czarnota & Hart 1991, p. 173. In other words, adding two letters ('as') to the preamble of the Software Directive could remove an important barrier to interoperability. The text of Article 1(3) in that same publication, however, as well as the German and Dutch versions of the proposal, reprinted as Vorschlag für eine Richtlinie des Rates über den Rechtsschutz von Computerprogrammen 1989 and in Keuchenius et al. 1990, respectively, all confirm that this version was erroneous.

1029. See section 5.1.3c. Recall, however, that the limitation of the design of spare parts for repair purposes does have a significant effect on the car manufacturer's market power in the aftermarket for repairs. There does not appear to be a separate market for interface specifications as such, although there is of course a considerable market for interoperable programs.

1030. See section 5.1.3c.

1031. Bartmann 2005, p. 125.

1032. See section 3.2.2c.

1033. *Id.*

A problem with such an approach could lie in the subsequent sharing of interface information. A limitation permitting the use of interface specifications only after successful decompilation would only be of help to the decompiler and would not aid other interoperable developers, unless the decompiler could sublicense the interoperability information. Although feasible in theory, a sub-licensing system could well evolve into a complex pattern of unmanageable (sub)licensing arrangements. It could become prohibitively difficult for the rightsholder to ascertain whether use of his or her interoperability information by a third party stems from a valid (sub)license or whether it was obtained in a different manner and, therefore, possibly constituted an infringement.

The option of a shorter term of protection for computer programs or their interface specifications will not be studied in detail. Recall that, based on the difficulty of fixing a single, appropriate term of protection, a similar approach was rejected for replacement parts under design protection laws.[1034] These difficulties would likely arise within the realm of protection of interface specifications. Attempting to influence the dynamics of platform software competition through a single, fixed term of protection for interface specifications similarly appears too detailed an instrument to be effective.[1035] A substantially shorter term of protection might also be considered to be in conflict with the Berne Convention, which prescribes a minimum term of protection of fifty years for literary works.[1036] Moreover, a shorter term of protection specifically for interface specifications would imply that these specifications are indeed protected – which is questionable – and would, by itself, offer no remedy for the more critical problems of access to such specifications (see section 6.3.2).[1037]

The most certain exclusion of interface specifications would be ascertained by an explicit exclusion of these specifications in Article 1 of the directive. Such an exclusion was debated during the legislative history of the directive, but it never materialized.[1038] Although an explicit exclusion from copyrightable subject matter would provide for substantial certainty to the interoperable developer, it could, *a contrario*, suggest that other, similar 'works' *do* constitute copyrightable subject matter. This suggestion could

1034. See section 5.1.3c.

1035. See also Dreier 2001, p. 305.

1036. Berne Convention, Article 7(1). Nonetheless, the Berne Convention is not directly applicable to the protection of computer programs under copyright law; the convention is only incorporated by reference in the WCT and TRIPS, and, by reference, in the Software Directive. Howevere, one could argue that the protection of computer programs as Literary Works has become a state practice – *inter alia*, through the WCT, TRIPS and the Software Directive – thereby perhaps opening the door to direct protection of computer programs as Literary Works under the Berne Convention. See also Goldstein 2001, p. 77; Vaver 1986, p. 607.

1037. Admittedly, the absence of a fixed term of protection creates some uncertainty about the effective term of protection for interface specifications. The effective term instead primarily depends on how quickly competitors are able to reverse engineer the relevant specifications. See also section 6.3.2.

1038. Vinje 1993, p. 48.

easily be overcome, however, by a recital in the preamble articulating the intent of such an exclusion. Indeed, similar 'redundant' clarifications are not unheard of in copyright law. For example, the Software Directive itself, in Article 5(3), explicitly permits for reproductions to be made in the interest of black-box testing, even if this already follows from the right to make reproductions in order to run the program, in Article 5(1).[1039] The Berne Convention's exclusion of news articles similarly clarifies the unprotectability of facts and ideas underlying a news story (see *infra*).

Save the typical exclusions of legislation and court decisions, specific subject matter exclusions are somewhat uncommon in copyright law.[1040] A notable exclusion, however, can be found in Article 2(8) of the Berne Convention, which excludes from copyrightable subject matter news of the day. As noted, there are two interpretations of Article 2(8) of the Berne Convention: one in which Article 2(8) merely reconfirms that facts and ideas underlying a news story are unprotected, while its particular form can still constitute copyrightable expression, and one in which it also denies protection to the particular form (expression) of the news story.[1041] Under the first interpretation, Article 2(8) does not technically state anything more than the idea/expression dichotomy. According to most commentators, this is indeed the most persuasive interpretation of Article 2(8).[1042] This is not to say that there are no arguments supporting the second, broader interpretation of the exclusion in Article 2(8). Similar to interface specifications, there may be some room for original expression in news stories, but the room for originality is generally quite limited. Copyright protection for news stories is, therefore, typically 'thin'.[1043] Moreover, the main purpose of the news story, like that of interface specifications, lies not in the originality of its expression but rather in the unprotected facts or events conveyed by that expression. The main purpose of an interface specification is to provide for a clear, functional format for interoperability. Thus, in both interface specifications and news stories, any originality in the expression is generally subordinate to the underlying purpose of these expressions. However, as in interface specifications, there may well be a need to duplicate the exact form of a news story, rather than its underlying facts and ideas. For instance, the news value of a news photo can lie in the exact expression in that photo rather than its more abstract message or idea.[1044] For interface specifications, the need to copy their exact expression arises from standardization advantages.

1039. See section 3.2.2a.
1040. See also Ricketson & Ginsburg 2006, p. 497.
1041. See section 6.3.1a.
1042. Hugenholtz 1989, p. 83; Lewinski 2008, p. 128; Ricketson & Ginsburg 2006, p. 498.
1043. Hugenholtz 1989, p. 82.
1044. *Id.*, p. 169.

In sum, a specific exclusion of interface specifications from copyrightable subject matter could remove the current uncertainty regarding their free use for interoperability purposes by competitors. Such an approach could take the form of a specific subject matter exclusion, or, alternatively, a limitation permitting the use of interface specifications for purposes of achieving interoperability.

6.3.2. Access

Section 3.1.2 already described that copyright's control over interoperability information originates primarily from control over access to such information. These specifications are normally embedded in the unreadable object code of the computer program. Although they could be extracted from a copy of the program using reverse engineering techniques, these require temporary reproductions to be made, which are covered by copyright's right of reproduction. Although the Software Directive does provide for express limitations to enable reverse engineering, these instruments, in their current form, appear insufficient. The present section explores alternative instruments to allow for improved access to interface specifications. Section 6.3.2a considers a narrower interpretation of the reproduction right in (software) copyright law, which would exclude from the scope of protection the temporary copies required for reverse engineering. Section 6.3.2b considers a solution within the current, broad reproduction right, in which the existing conditions for reverse engineering are interpreted more flexibly, possibly with assistance from a regulatory authority. Section 6.3.2c considers possibilities to require the rightsholder to actively publish interoperability information.

a. Narrower Reproduction Right

Section 3.1.2a already observed that the temporary reproductions required for reverse engineering fall within the exclusive reproduction right of the copyright holder. This enables the legislator to restrict reverse engineering by certain conditions, which, in turn, can hinder the effectiveness of reverse engineering as a tool to obtain access to interface specifications. A narrower interpretation of the reproduction right could place these acts outside of the scope of the rightsholder's control. This would eliminate all legal obstacles to reverse engineering, thereby potentially greatly facilitating access to interoperability information.

A narrower reproduction right has more generally been advocated in relation to digital media, including computer programs. Because the consumption of digital media typically requires reproduction before each individual use – namely, in order to load the media into the memory of a computer or other electronic device – the current reproduction right, which extends to such intermediate or temporary reproductions, enables rightsholders to control consumption of such works in much greater detail than for more traditional, physically embodied works.[1045] These calls have not materialized, however. Quite to the contrary, the more recent protection for technological protection measures illustrates a trend towards even more detailed control over consumption of digital media.[1046]

However, the EU Directive on the harmonization of certain aspects of copyright and related rights in the information society (InfoSoc Directive)[1047] does contain a provision that limits rightsholders' control over reproductions of their works with respect to distribution over electronic communications networks. Article 5(1) of the directive requires Member States to exclude from the scope of the reproduction right the:

> [t]emporary acts of reproduction [. . .] which are transient or incidental [and] an integral and essential part of a technological process and whose sole purpose is to enable:
>
> (a) a transmission in a network between third parties by an intermediary, or
> (b) a lawful use of a work or other subject-matter to be made, and which have no independent economic significance.

The acts named under subsections (a) and (b) primarily refer to uses generally known as *routing* and *caching*, respectively.[1048] Both uses often form an integral part of the transfer of data over a packet-switched, electronic communications network, in which data typically pass through various network *nodes* before reaching the end-user.[1049] The individual reproductions made at each node could give the rightsholder substantial and detailed control over distribution of her or his work, even if such reproductions are not generally individually exploited by rightsholders.[1050] An exclusion of these uses from the reproduction right, therefore, improves legal certainty by expressly permitting what is already a well-recognized practice, thus preventing unexpected copyright claims in such temporary reproductions. Article 5(1) thus prevents rightsholders from controlling the use of their content in too much detail, yet without depriving the rightsholder of control over reproductions that do have independent economic significance.

In a 2004 working paper, the European Commission suggested broadening the application or scope of this provision to other temporary reproductions of digital content, and particularly to running and black-box analysis of

1045. Dommering 1994; Hugenholtz 1998, p. 5; Legal Advisory Board 1995. Indeed, the need to reproduce digital works for every use made of them has inspired Visser to advocate abandonment of the reproduction right altogether. Instead, he argues for a broader role of the right of communication to the public (Visser 1997).
1046. See also section 6.3.2b.
1047. InfoSoc Directive.
1048. *Id.*, Recital 33.
1049. In the case of routing, these reproductions are stored no longer than a few milliseconds.
1050. Hugenholtz 1998, p. 7.

computer programs.[1051] It is questionable, however, whether the rationales behind Article 5(1) can be readily applied to the reproductions involved in running and reverse engineering computer programs. To be sure, the rationales behind Article 5(1) do not apply to the reproductions necessary for decompilation. Section 3.1.2a already examined in some detail that the reproduction right in software copyright law has economic relevance precisely because it enables the rightsholder to control decompilation, which, in turn, enables third parties to access the valuable know-how in the computer program. Thus, the economic significance of the broad reproduction right lies not in the reproductions as such but rather in their facilitation of exposure of know-how. This is all the more relevant because copyright law cannot offer direct protection for such know-how, which generally does not constitute original expression. The rationales behind excluding the reproductions listed in Article 5(1) of the InfoSoc Directive thus do not appear to be applicable to the reproductions required for decompilation of a computer program, and application of Article 5(1) to decompilation does not, therefore, appear to be a recommendable (or even a possible) course of action.

Some commentators have suggested narrowing (the interpretation of) the reproduction right specifically in the context of computer programs.[1052] The approaches suggested by Lehmann & Schneider would limit the reproduction right to those temporary copies that enable increased, concurrent use of the computer program.[1053] Such reproductions would include copying a program to a(nother) disk or another computer in a network. The temporary reproductions made in RAM required to *run* the program do not allow for such increased concurrent use and, therefore, would not be covered by this reproduction right. However, neither author explicitly addresses the question of whether black-box testing or decompilation should fall within this narrower reproduction right. It is, therefore, unclear how these approaches would affect access to a computer program's interface information through reverse engineering.[1054]

Regardless of the exact legal implementation, however, a principal objection to narrowing the reproduction right remains the subsequent inability to impose conditions on reverse engineering. It is conceivable that reverse

1051. European Commission 2004b, §2.1.3.2. See also Visser 1997, pp. 45, 79.
1052. See also Hugenholtz & Spoor 1987, p. 52.
1053. Lehmann 1991, p. 331; Schneider 1990, p. 503. See also *Betriebssystem* (Bundesgerichtshof 1990), 85 ('[. . .] zu beachten [. . .], daß bei der Benutzung von Computerprogrammen rein technisch verschiedene tatsächliche Vervielfältigungsvorgänge anfallen können, die nicht uneingeschränkt vom Vervielfältigungsrecht nach §16 UrhG erfaßt werden'); Dreier 1991a, p. 579.
1054. Although not applicable to computer programs under the Software Directive, the making of temporary copies could perhaps be permissible under a limitation for private use or private study. Even then, however, the commercial nature of reverse engineering does not appear to be reconcilable with private use. See also *Creative v. Aztech* (Singapore Court of Appeal 1996), 504; Hugenholtz & Spoor 1987, p. 52.

engineering could become a significant threat to effective protection of computer programs if the state of the art were to enable reverse engineering with only trivial efforts.[1055] This would support at least some legal restrictions on reverse engineering.[1056] If, however, the reproduction right is interpreted narrowly, thus excluding the temporary acts necessary for reverse engineering from the scope of copyright protection, there remains no possibility for the legislator to permit reverse engineering only under certain conditions and no possibility to consider the state of the art in reverse engineering technology.

Moreover, if decompilation cannot be restricted to purposes of interoperability, as it currently is,[1057] it may also be employed for purposes other than achieving interoperability. Some commentators have, indeed, advocated permitting a broader application of reverse engineering techniques. This would, for instance, enable decompilation for purposes of access to the unprotected ideas and principles of a computer program.[1058] As this study is limited to interface information, however, it cannot by itself support a broader right to reverse engineer.

In sum, a narrower reproduction right eliminates the ability to regulate reverse engineering, and leaves the balance between openness and control of interface information, as well as the effective protection of computer programs by copyright law, entirely to the state of the art in reverse engineering technology. A narrower reproduction right, therefore, is not recommended.

b. More Flexible Approach to Reverse Engineering

This section considers resolving the balance between control and access to interface specifications via a more flexible reverse engineering rule, in which conditions for reverse engineering are changed *ex-ante* in response to the evolving state of the art.

Section 3.2.2 concluded that the current instrument for access to interface specifications under copyright law – reverse engineering – is, in theory, suitable to maintain a balance between openness of interface information and control of such information. Control of interface information is factually accomplished through its embedding in unreadable object code, whereas openness of interface specifications can be achieved by successful reverse engineering. Because reverse engineering requires time and is restricted by legal conditions, the rightsholder effectively retains control over this information for some time, thus allowing for a balance between control and openness of interface specifications. However, section 3.2.2c also identified various difficulties, particularly with the right to decompile in Article 6 of the Software Directive. These problems can make reverse engineering

1055. See section 2.1.2b.
1056. Samuelson et al. 1994, p. 2392.
1057. Software Directive, Article 6(2)(a).
1058. See, for example, Bartmann 2005, p. 125. See also Samuelson 1994, p. 288.

prohibitively difficult, thus effectively leaving the rightsholder with substantial and sustainable control of his or her program's interface information. First, several conditions in Article 6 appear to hinder *any* successful decompilation. These shortcomings must be addressed.[1059] Second, the rigid nature of the conditions in Article 6 does not appear to be reconcilable with the evolving state of the art in reverse engineering. This will be the focus of the remainder of this section.

Section 3.2.2c noted that the effects of reverse engineering are highly dependant on the state of the art in reverse engineering technology. Rather than fixing the conditions for reverse engineering in detail, as they currently are, it may, therefore, be useful to apply a more flexible *ex-ante* reverse engineering regime, in which conditions can be changed in response to the evolving state of the art in reverse engineering technology. In addition to more flexibility, section 3.2.2c suggested a need to monitor the voluntary conclusion of interoperability agreements.

Chapter 5 noted that similar concerns in telecommunications interconnection regulation have led to a supervisory role for a regulatory authority. The regulatory authority provides for *ex-ante* flexibility by intervening in cases where the statutory *ex-ante* interconnection instrument (e.g., mandatory interconnection negotiations) fails to produce results. The authority also monitors the conclusion of interconnection agreements. In this section, it will be demonstrated that a similar regulatory mechanism has been created in another area closely related to software copyright law: the legal protection of technical protection measures (TPMs). Based on this model, a similar role for a regulatory authority will be discussed to execute and monitor a more flexible *ex-ante* reverse engineering regime for software interoperability. Later, it will be demonstrated, first, what TPMs are and how they compare to reverse engineering of computer programs; second, why their legal protection required a degree of regulatory flexibility, rather than fixed statutory rules; and, third, why this model of *ex-ante* flexibility appears useful to the regulation of reverse engineering for purposes of software interoperability.

TPMs are typically digital measures, such as passwords and encryption systems, that are deployed to enable detailed control over access to copyrighted works in order to prevent their unauthorized use.[1060] Quite similar to the distribution of computer programs in object code form, which, as noted in section 3.1.2, also effectively restricts access to the know-how in the program, TPMs thus aim to add a protective shell around a copyrighted work. Such restricted access was considered necessary to effectively enforce copyrights in new, so-called on-demand business models used for distribution of media over the internet.[1061] The individual use made of copyrighted works in such on-demand models called for more detailed control than effectively enabled by

1059. See section 3.2.2c. See also Bartmann 2005, p. 125.
1060. Guibault et al. 2007, p. 76.
1061. *Id.*, p. 71.

copyright law itself, which would require tracing infringements in individual cases and in the private sphere.[1062]

TPMs are not merely factually deployed. Similar to the legal restrictions on reverse engineering of a computer program's object code, the law protects rightsholders against the circumvention of and trafficking in TPMs, thus providing for legal protection of this shell around the copyrighted work.[1063] The international obligations on TPMs, arising from the WCT and the WIPO Performances and Phonogram Producers Treaty (WPPT), have, in Europe, been implemented and harmonized in Article 6 of the InfoSoc Directive.[1064]

Legal protection of TPMs raised concerns, however, about the end-user's ability to benefit from certain uses permitted under statutory copyright limitations: if access to copyrighted works was digitally controlled through TPMs, and the circumvention of these TPMs amounted to an unlawful act, there might not be any means for end-users to enjoy the free use of the work under these copyright limitations, such as the right to make a copy for private use, or to use non-copyrightable content.[1065] This is particularly relevant for the implementation of TPM protection under the InfoSoc Directive because this directive does not appear to relate the legal protection of TPMs to the scope of intellectual property rights for the underlying content.[1066] This could result in overprotection of content by TPMs. However, too little protection for TPMs was believed to undermine the purpose of stimulating on-demand business models,[1067] while it also proved technically difficult to implement TPMs that accurately and adequately permitted end-users to benefit from copyright limitations.[1068] Protection of TPMs covering copyrighted works thus introduced a need to balance under- and overprotection of this shell in order to align this protection with the scope of copyright protection of the underlying works. This need to balance over- and underprotection of the 'shell' also exists in the legal conditions for reverse engineering: preventing reverse engineering may limit end-users' ability to access and use unprotected ideas and principles of a computer program, as well as its interface specifications,[1069] yet an overly permissible approach to interoperability would chill incentives to innovate.

Thus, the legal protection of TPMs, similar to the legal restrictions on reverse engineering of software, effectively enabled protection of the shell around the copyrighted work, which could result in overprotection. In the case of software, such 'overprotection' was partly intentional because copyright

1062. Note that this view starkly conflicts with calls to limit copyright law's reproduction right in the digital environment based on the increased level of detail at which rightsholders could control the use of their works. See section 6.3.2a.
1063. InfoSoc Directive, Article 6; Guibault et al. 2007, p. 73.
1064. Guibault et al. 2007, p. 76.
1065. *Id.*, p. 102; Zittrain 2008, p. 115.
1066. Guibault et al. 2007, p. 79. But see European Commission 2007, p. 7.
1067. Guibault et al. 2007, p. 102.
1068. *Id.*, p. 103.
1069. See section 3.1.2a.

law, with its focus on the protection of literal expression in the source code, could not provide for effective protection of the more valuable know-how in the computer program.[1070] However, the legislator also intended to enable competitors to access the interface specifications required for interoperability, which would be difficult if all reverse engineering were fully covered by the rightsholder's reproduction right. Protection of TPMs could similarly preclude end-users from benefiting from statutorily granted copyright limitations or from access to uncopyrightable content.[1071] In short, the legal protection of TPMs, like the legal restrictions on reverse engineering, introduces issues of how to safeguard lawful access to the underlying work.

As already observed, copyright law does not normally address concerns of access to works, as it merely entails a right to prohibit copying of subject matter, which is normally necessarily disclosed.[1072] The same laws that introduced the legal protection of TPMs thus also had to balance this protection with end-users' interests in access to the underlying copyrighted works in order to benefit from certain use permitted under copyright limitations.[1073]

A significant complication to implementing this balance between over- and underprotection of TPMs, like the regulation of reverse engineering, lies in a quickly evolving technology and a lack of substantial knowledge of the effects of this relatively new form of legal protection.[1074] These factors obstruct a detailed *ex-ante*, statutory approach. However, a failure to address these problems *ex-ante* results in considerable uncertainty for both rightsholders and end-users or competitors.[1075] Consequently, rather than fixing this problem of access in detailed statutory provisions, several European Member States have chosen to leave the *ex-ante* execution of this balance to a specialized regulatory authority.[1076]

The balance addressed by these *ex-ante* instruments is thus comparable to that of access to interface specifications of a computer program through reverse engineering. In both situations, the rightsholder's exclusive copyrights have already been curtailed *ex-ante* to allow for certain use without authorization (i.e., making a copy for private use or use of unprotected interface specifications). Copyright law has already structurally balanced the interests of rightsholders and end-users through a limited scope of protection. The authority need not revisit this balancing act. However, the authority must ascertain whether this balance can actually be effectuated to the benefit of the public as protection of the 'shell' (i.e., the TPM or the ability

1070. See section 3.1.2.
1071. Guibault et al. 2007, p. 79.
1072. See section 3.1.2.
1073. Guibault et al. 2007, p. 104. The IViR Report observes that not all copyright limitations are accounted for; see Guibault et al. 2007, p. 109.
1074. Guibault et al. 2007, p. 124.
1075. *Id.*
1076. *Id.*, p. 109.

to reverse engineer) may prevent lawful access to the work.[1077] The only question is whether, given (legal protection of) the shell around the work, the public can factually obtain access to the copyrighted work in order to benefit from the free use of that work provided for by certain copyright limitations. Thus, the authority's task lies in ensuring that there are no technical obstacles to effectuating the *ex-ante* balance between control and openness already provided for by copyright law.

In the context of TPMs, the regulatory authority can have both rulemaking and dispute resolution powers.[1078] Rulemaking powers may enable the authority, for example, to grant end-users a right of 'self-help' to circumvent TPMs in order to benefit from use permitted under copyright law. Dispute resolution powers may be necessary to quickly resolve highly factual conflicts between rightsholders of TPMs and end-users. The primary role for a regulatory authority in reverse engineering similarly appears to be in *ex-ante* rulemaking:[1079] which conditions are appropriate for decompilation by competitors depends significantly on the evolving state of the art. These conditions thus require some flexibility: they must be adjusted for all cases with the evolution of reverse engineering technology and must be based on considerable technological and contemporaneous expertise.

In practice, execution of this rulemaking task could mean, for instance, that the authority lift the ban on sharing of decompiled data among competitors.[1080] Lifting the condition on sharing of decompiled code would enable sharing of decompilation efforts, recoupment of decompilation costs, and, generally, decompilation by the most efficient and specialized firms.[1081] This, in turn, could significantly increase rightsholders' costs resulting from the risk of exposure of their know-how, and, thereby, their incentives to negotiate the supply of interoperability information.[1082] The authority might also permit competitors to commence decompilation even before they have sufficiently developed their own computer program,[1083] or it might shift the burden of proof for availability of the interface information to rightsholders. In judging which conditions for decompilation are appropriate, the authority might consider whether

1077. *Id.*, p. 102.
1078. *Id.*, p. 125.
1079. In addition to rulemaking powers, dispute resolution could also prove useful – for example, where a rightsholder and a competitor disagree as to the interface information that must be made available in order to prevent decompilation, or on the competitor's compliance with the conditions set by the authority. Recall that the regulatory authority overseeing interconnection in telecommunications also has dispute resolution powers in order to resolve disagreements about privately concluded interconnection agreements. See section 5.2.3c.
1080. Software Directive, Article 6(2)(b). See also section 3.2.2d.
1081. Van den Bergh 1998, p. 30; Schmidtchen & Koboldt 1993, p. 422.
1082. See section 3.2.2b.
1083. See section 3.2.2d.

rightsholders issue sufficiently detailed reference offers for their interface specifications, as used in telecommunications regulation.[1084]

Note that, because the authority would only execute a balance between control and openness already provided for *ex-ante* in copyright law, the authority need not itself strike a balance based on the circumstances of each individual case. Rather, it must assess whether, in order to allow this *ex-ante* balancing mechanism to function properly in all cases, more or less stringent conditions should be imposed for reverse engineering in the light of the current state of the art. Similar also to the regime of interconnection regulation in telecommunications, the inquiry is further unrelated to any market-specific analyzes.[1085] The authority need not define a relevant market or determine whether a lack of access would result in elimination of effective competition. Accordingly, the authority's expertise should be of a more technical than economic nature.[1086]

In both rulemaking and dispute resolution capacities, regulatory authorities have several advantages over, respectively, the legislator and the courts: they tend to be more cost efficient, quicker, better suited to closely observe technological development and more specialized in their specific field.[1087] The rationale of specialization is of particular importance to reverse engineering: the complexity of this matter is amplified by the evolving state of the art, which may be difficult for general legislators or courts to monitor. If, in the absence of a regulatory authority described *supra*, a court would need to determine appropriate conditions for reverse engineering in each individual case, this would effectively defeat the purpose of an *ex-ante*, legislative reverse engineering instrument: the conditions would ultimately be determined *ex-post* in each individual case. By contrast, the regulatory authority can broadly determine conditions *ex-ante* based on its contemporaneous knowledge of the state of the art in reverse engineering.

Notwithstanding the rulemaking and dispute resolution powers of the TPM observatories, it should be noted that, like the reverse engineering provisions of the Software Directive and the obligation to negotiate interconnection in telecommunications law,[1088] the InfoSoc Directive first and foremost aims to stimulate rightsholders to solve the problem of access to their TPM-protected content voluntarily.[1089] Member States can only impose obligations on rightsholders if they fail to take measures voluntarily.[1090] The authority's

1084. See also section 5.2.3d.
1085. See section 5.2.3c.
1086. Such expertise might be available at European telecommunications standards institutions CEN, CENELEC and ETSI. Framework Directive, Article 17(1); Neumann 2002, p. 665; Nihoul & Rodford 2004, p. 736.
1087. Guibault et al. 2007, p. 125. See also Samuelson 2007a, p. 569. See also sections 4.1.2b and 5.2.3c.
1088. See sections 3.2.2b and 5.2.3b, respectively.
1089. Guibault et al. 2007, p. 107.
1090. InfoSoc Directive, Article 6(4).

powers must, therefore, ultimately stimulate voluntary action by the parties. This is equally important in software interoperability: the primary purpose of the reverse engineering exception is for rightsholders to make the interoperability information available voluntarily. However, for this incentive mechanism to work, the costs of a failure to act voluntarily must be sufficiently high.[1091] A regulatory authority can adjust the costs *ex-ante*, thus ultimately achieving the goal of stimulating voluntary measures. The authority could also accelerate the subsequent commercial negotiations process by stimulating the use of reference offers for interface information, similar to those used in interconnection regulation.[1092]

In addition to their rulemaking and/or dispute resolution powers, TPM authorities, like the regulatory authorities in telecommunications,[1093] also function as monitoring agencies, collecting information on the effects of TPMs, their legal protection and voluntary measures taken by rightsholders. The monitoring function of the authority reinforces its status as a specialized agency, which, in turn, can improve the quality of its decision making. Monitoring can be particularly helpful to assess whether the incentive mechanism, based on the possibility of intervention by the authority, actually results in satisfactory conclusion of voluntary interoperability agreements (*supra*). If it does not, then the incentive mechanism arguably requires adjustments. In the context of reverse engineering, this would translate into loosening the restrictions for lawful decompilation. Furthermore, the TPM authorities are presumably well suited to advise policy makers on future courses of action.[1094] For these reasons, the monitoring function could also be valuable in the context of reverse engineering.

Furthermore, the monitoring function could make the authority well suited to serve as a bridge between the application of competition law and the *ex-ante* copyright instruments for interoperability. The informed opinion of the regulatory authority could be considered by the competition authority in considering whether the *ex-ante* copyright approach to interoperability is sufficient in the light of the state of the art, such that the problem of access to interface specifications can, in the particular case, be considered to have been anticipated *ex-ante*. In other words, it could determine whether the difficulty of reverse engineering is anticipated or exceptional. If it is anticipated, the balance between openness and control of interface information is thus already struck *ex-ante*, possibly obviating the need for intervention based on competition law. If it is exceptional, this argument of limited intervention by competition law within intellectual property rights based on the latter's internal balance does not apply, and competition law could be used.[1095] To the

1091. See section 3.2.2b.
1092. See section 5.2.3d.
1093. See section 5.2.3c.
1094. Guibault et al. 2007, p. 125. See also section 4.1.2b.
1095. See section 4.1.

extent application of competition law results in a duty to supply interface specifications that requires compliance monitoring, this task could also be fulfilled by the regulatory authority.

In sum, an adequate approach to an *ex-ante* balance between openness and control of interoperability information through reverse engineering requires some flexibility to respond to an evolving state of the art. Similar considerations in the legal protection of TPMs have led to the institution of a regulatory authority, which has the necessary rulemaking, dispute resolution and monitoring powers. This form of flexible, *ex-ante* and expertise-based rulemaking appears suitable to introduce more flexibility in the Software Directive's reverse engineering instrument. Furthermore, the monitoring function appears useful as an instrument to enhance and update the authority's expertise of reverse engineering and voluntary measures, and to inform competition authorities and policy makers of the effects of the reverse engineering instrument on openness and control of interoperability information.

c. Affirmative Disclosure Requirements

This section considers means to impose affirmative duties on rightsholders of computer programs to disclose their interface specifications, other than the incentive to disclose this information arising from competitors' ability to reverse engineer the computer program.

A recurring theme in this study is that reverse engineering is a difficult and costly method of obtaining access to a computer program's interoperability information.[1096] Although the difficulty and costs of reverse engineering may decrease over time, the advances in reverse engineering technology could perhaps be outrun by an even faster growing complexity of computer programs.[1097] If this is the case, reverse engineering may never become a viable option to obtain the rightsholder's interface specifications. In this scenario, rightsholders of computer programs would thus retain full control over their interoperability information, notwithstanding substantial loosening of legal restrictions on reverse engineering. The regulation of reverse engineering would prove an inadequate instrument to maintain a balance between openness and control of interface information.

An alternative could be an affirmative duty to disclose interface specifications.[1098] Of course, immediate publication of interface information would shift the balance between openness and control of interface information

---

1096. See sections 2.1 and 3.2.2a.

1097. Compare, for example, the centralized 1959 Sabre airline reservation system developed by American Airlines, comprising 1 million lines of code, and today's copies of Microsoft Windows, which is installed on most PCs and consists of approximately 40 million lines of codes. See also Carr 2008, p. 50; *Microsoft Decision* (European Commission 2004), note 423.

1098. See also Bartmann 2005, p. 125; Kroes 2008, p. 3.

to complete openness. At first sight, this would, therefore, appear inconsistent with the normative framework established in Chapter 2, which rather suggested a middle ground between openness and control. However, as the Commission observed in its *Microsoft* decision, the implementation of a set of interface specifications for a highly complex computer program in an interoperable program may require significant time in and of itself – that is, even without the time otherwise invested in obtaining the information through reverse engineering.[1099] This suggests that, even if this information were to become available directly upon release of the computer program, the rightsholder would still enjoy lead-time to exploit network effects while competitors developed their implementation of the interface specifications. For highly complex programs, even immediate availability (openness) of interoperability information, therefore, may provide sufficient lead-time. The need for a balance between openness and control of this information would thus become obsolete because the difficulty of implementing the specifications itself provides for lead-time.

Mandatory publication of interface specifications conceivably could be implemented in public law, possibly through intervention by a regulatory authority. A similar approach is adopted in telecommunications law, in which a regulatory authority generally has the power to impose interconnection obligations on operators of telecommunication networks.[1100] The obligation to supply interface specifications thus would be imposed on the developer in her or his capacity of a creator of computer programs, rather than as an intellectual property rightsholder. In this scenario, there would be an affirmative duty to supply interoperability information arising from public law. This is to be contrasted with the 'obligation' to supply interface information under the limitation permitting reverse engineering,[1101] or the 'obligation' to provide end-users with abilities to benefit from copyright limitations in the presence of TPMs. In the latter two models, the obligation is no more than an incentive arising from the threat of a reduced level of protection. Thus, if the rightsholder fails to take voluntary measures, he or she may be confronted with reverse engineering of his or her computer program,[1102] or end-users could be armed with a right of 'self help' to circumvent TPMs.[1103] It is submitted that the latter incentive approach appears preferable over the former public law approach. The public law approach would necessarily entail adding a third dimension to the complementary relationship between intellectual property rights and competition law.[1104] It appears preferable to address interoperability concerns within the framework of the latter

1099. *Microsoft Decision* (European Commission 2004), §721.
1100. See section 5.2.3c. See also Koelman 2006, p. 833; Weiser 2003, p. 549.
1101. See section 6.3.2b.
1102. See section 6.3.2b.
1103. Guibault et al. 2007, p. 106.
1104. See section 4.1.

two regimes, rather than by resorting to a third regime of public law. Moreover, a risk of a substantial reduction in (copyright) protection normally should be sufficient an incentive for the rightsholder to disclose interface information.

Thus, if reverse engineering does not prove sufficient an incentive to supply interface specifications,[1105] another incentives-based approach might be to subject copyright protection of the computer program to registration of its interface specifications. However, an interface registration requirement would likely meet with considerable resistance. Unlike design protection,[1106] patent and trademark law,[1107] copyright law does not require, and, indeed, prohibits, any formal conditions – such as registration, notice or deposit – as a precondition to copyright protection. This well-established principle of automatic copyright protection, known as the prohibition on formalities, has long been codified and safeguarded by the Berne Convention, and, by reference, in other copyright treaties.[1108] More recently, however, Van Gompel has suggested that, at least from a historical perspective, the prohibition on formalities in copyright law is not a 'sacred cow'. This could perhaps open the door to a reintroduction of formalities.[1109]

Indeed, various commentators have suggested reintroducing some formal requirements to copyright protection, based on different rationales. For instance, a copyright registration system lowers transaction costs for copyrighted material. It thereby mitigates the risk that a licensee be unable to locate the rightsholder in order to secure a license, while also informing the public about the delimitations of the protected work.[1110] Mandatory registration is also likely to expand the public domain because not all potential rightsholders will bother complying with the registration requirement and associated fees.[1111] Consequently, not all works eligible for copyright protection would actually be protected, thus expanding the public domain. Within the realm of computer programs, some commentators have suggested registration of the program's source code as a *quid-pro-quo* for protection: in return for copyright protection, the rightsholder would need to disclose the protected subject matter.[1112] This enables others to benefit more effectively from the rightsholder's copyrighted

1105. See section 6.3.2b.
1106. See section 5.1.
1107. See section 6.5.
1108. TRIPS, Article 9(1); Berne Convention, Article 5(2); WCT, Article 1(4), 3. See also Reinbothe & Von Lewinski 2002. Note, however, that the Berne Convention is only indirectly applicable to the protection of computer programs under copyright law. See note 1036.
1109. Van Gompel forthcoming.
1110. Landes & Posner 2003, p. 477; Lévêque & Méniere 2004, p. 105; Sprigman 2004, p. 485. Indeed, transaction costs can be prohibitively high if the rightsholder of a copyrighted work cannot be found at all. This is the problem of the so-called *orphan works*. See Van Gompel forthcoming.
1111. Samuelson 2007a, p. 562; Sprigman 2004, p. 502.
1112. See, for example, Gibson 2005. See also section 3.1.2c.

subject matter. Indeed, for this reason, the disclosure requirement is a central element of the patent system.[1113]

Indeed, registration requirements are common in most regimes of industrial property rights, although the respective functions of these registration requirements admittedly vary. Registration requirements are also contained, for example, in legal regimes for protection of semiconductor chips, which are essentially based on a model of copyright protection. The U.S. Semiconductor Protection Act (SCPA) and the European Semiconductor Protection Directive[1114] provide legal protection for the layout of semiconductor chips based on a requirement of originality similar to that in copyright law.[1115] Similar to copyright protection of (the source and object code of) computer programs, these semiconductor protection laws protect subject matter that is highly functional and not directed at communication with humans. Unlike copyright law, however, the SCPA, as well as, for example, the Dutch implementation of the directive,[1116] contain a registration requirement as a prerequisite to semiconductor protection.[1117] Some commentators have suggested protecting computer programs under a similar model.[1118] Such a model would thus offer protection in return for registration of the computer program's source code.

Recall however, that copyright's restrictions on reverse engineering of computer programs are aimed precisely at *limiting* access to the source code.[1119] Section 3.1.2 already observed that copyright's role in protecting computer programs lies, *inter alia*, in preventing access to their source code because copyright can offer only 'thin' protection for the valuable know-how embedded in this source code. Copyright protection for computer programs is essentially a reinforced trade secret regime, which clearly conflicts with a requirement of source code disclosure.[1120]

Compared to registration of a computer program's source code, however, a more limited registration requirement for the program's interface specifications would be less intrusive from the rightsholder's perspective. An interface registration requirement does not primarily relate to the work itself (the source code of the computer program) but rather to its technical delimitation (its interface specifications). As this study is limited to interoperability and interface specifications, it cannot serve as a basis for broader disclosure requirements.

1113. See also section 6.5.
1114. Directive 87/54/EEC.
1115. Gielen 2007, p. 103; Hugenholtz & Spoor 1987, p. 68; Samuelson 1985, p. 497.
1116. Topografiewet. Note that the EU Directive does not prescribe a registration requirement.
1117. Gielen 2007, p. 103.
1118. Guibault 1997. See also Samuelson 1985, p. 514.
1119. See section 3.1.2a.
1120. In addition, the *absence* of formal requirements for copyright protection was one of the rationales behind the protection of computer programs by copyright law: it lowered the costs of protection. See section 3.1.1a.

The primary rationale for an interface registration requirement would thus be to balance the incentive function of copyright protection, by maintaining effective protection of a computer program's source code, with competitors' need to interoperate with that program through registration of its interface specifications. This rationale could arguably be regarded as a combination of the known rationales of *quid-pro-quo*, limiting transaction costs and safeguarding the public domain (see *supra*). Although interface registration does not teach others how the computer program functions (*quid-pro-quo*) because the source code is not disclosed, it does teach them how to interoperate with it. Transaction costs are limited because disclosure of interface specifications obviates the need for third parties to invest substantially in acquiring the information they need to interoperate with the relevant computer program. Finally, disclosure of interfaces safeguards the public domain by effectively limiting copyright protection to the relevant computer program itself, rather than to the domain of interoperable programs as well.[1121]

A disclosure requirement limited to interface specifications could, however, introduce difficulties of its own. For instance, it must be established how an incomplete disclosure of interface specifications is to be discovered, given the fact that the source code is normally kept secret.[1122] Moreover, one must determine how an incomplete registration should be sanctioned and, particularly, whether loss of copyright protection is an appropriate remedy for *any* omittance of interface specifications in the registration. This is all the more relevant because of the 'accordion-like nature of the term interface'.[1123] A third party could point at an 'interface' that the rightsholder had not intended as such, which would result in loss of copyright protection. This introduces legal uncertainty. Patent law offers more instruments to deal with issues of (insufficient) disclosure of a technical nature, suggesting that a patent approach to interfaces might be preferable to the introduction of an interface registration requirement in copyright law (see also section 6.5).

One possibility to stimulate a more comprehensive disclosure of relevant interface specifications might be to relate the scope of copyright protection of a (complex) computer program to the degree of disclosure of its individual modules' interface specifications. Complex computer programs that consist of multiple modules could, for purposes of the scope of protection, be treated as a single work if few of its interface specifications were disclosed, or as multiple works if more interface specifications were disclosed. Registration of interface specifications of a complex computer program's individual modules could, for instance, serve as prima facie evidence that the modules constituted (individually) copyrightable works. Conversely, individual modules whose interface specifications were not individually disclosed would not be treated as separate, copyrightable works. For the rightsholder, copyright protection

1121. See also section 3.1.1a.
1122. See section 2.1.
1123. Lake et al. 1989, p. 432. See also section 2.1.2.

for each individual module is arguably more attractive than protection of the entire, complex computer program because there are better opportunities to exploit each module separately. However, in order to obtain such a broad scope of protection, the rightsholder would be required to disclose the interface specifications of or those between the individual modules. Nonetheless, the question remains whether these incentives would indeed be greater than those caused by competitors' abilities to decompile the computer program.

For the reasons mentioned, *supra*, mandatory disclosure of interface specifications is not recommended. Instead, a regulatory authority could significantly loosen restrictions on reverse engineering, which should provide an incentive for a rightsholder to disclose the interface specifications 'voluntarily'.[1124] If reverse engineering proves no viable option, other intellectual property regimes, such as patent and trade secret law, contain more established and tested disclosure requirements that could obviate problems of access to interface specifications. Note that, moreover, mandatory disclosure may still be achieved as a remedy for abuse of a dominant position under competition law, in particular where the prohibitive difficulty of reverse engineering was not anticipated in the *ex-ante* copyright regime (see section 4.2 and section 6.4).

6.4. INSTRUMENTS WITHIN COMPETITION LAW

Chapter 4 examined the role of competition law in providing access to a computer program's interface specifications. On the instrumental side, the first part of that chapter questioned the application of competition law as a structural tool to address interoperability, indicating a preference for a more substantial *ex-ante* approach instead. The current *ex-ante* approach to interoperability in the Software Directive was critically examined in Chapter 3, while the contours of an alternative approach were further explored in section 6.3. On the substantive side, the second part of Chapter 4 questioned the rigidity of the analytical framework used by the competition courts to examine unilateral refusals to supply. It also noted that the current analytical framework may not be suitable for the specific situation in which the unilateral refusal to supply concerns interface information. In sum, Chapter 4 identified some room for improvements. To that end, this section suggests substantive changes – namely, a need for more flexibility and for explicit consideration of the indirect effects of control over interface specifications on competition and innovation – and instrumental changes, namely, more substantial deference to an *ex-ante* approach to interoperability in software copyright law.

It is beyond the scope of this study – and perhaps any study – to provide a comprehensive analytical framework for competition law to assess cases involving refusals to supply interface information. Indeed, section 4.2 already

1124. See section 6.3.2b.

criticized the 'checklist approach' currently employed by the courts. A detailed framework appears to be difficult to reconcile with the case-by-case function of competition law. The European Commission has expressed this particularly well in its *Microsoft* decision, observing, '[t]here is no persuasiveness [to] an exhaustive checklist of exceptional circumstances'.[1125] Its value, instead, lies in a flexible, case-by-case assessment of exceptional, abusive behavior. The risks of scrutinizing a dominant firm's behavior too rigidly have already been demonstrated in section 4.2: application of the existing framework on refusals to deal to refusals to supply interoperability information has led to an arguably erroneous analysis.

Notwithstanding these arguments in favor of more flexibility, however, a number of more general remarks can be made with respect to instrumental and substantive aspects of the application of competition law. On the substantive side, Chapter 2 demonstrated that, to the extent that control over interoperability information is welfare enhancing, this is primarily due to the incentives for firms to achieve substantial market power by competing for, rather than in, the market. The prospect of achieving significant market power based on a proprietary network can significantly stimulate firms to innovate. In such cases, dominance may not be as much of a concern as long as it is temporary. Competition law as applied by the European courts is, however, somewhat biased towards models of competition in the market, in which dominance is largely established without consideration of pressure from subsequent competitors.[1126] A more rigorous analysis of entry barriers and possible pressure from subsequent competitors, therefore, may be useful.

Similarly, if a duty to license an intellectual property right in interface specifications reduces incentives to innovate, it is not in the creation of these interface specifications themselves that incentives are reduced, as presumed under Article 102 TFEU and particularly under the new-product test,[1127] but rather in the inability to continue to control proprietary network effects. The new-product test does not appear to serve as an adequate proxy for these effects and does not, therefore, fulfill a useful function in cases involving control over standards and interface specifications in particular.[1128] The application of this test in cases involving standards, lastly by the General Court in its *Microsoft* judgment, may thus deserve reconsideration.[1129] Courts may be well advised to abandon the automatic application of the new-product test in favor of more rigor in analyzing the effects of control over interface specifications and a lack of interoperability on entry barriers and future dominance. In general, for full scrutiny of any positive effects of a refusal to

1125. *Microsoft Decision* (European Commission 2004), §555.
1126. See section 4.2.2a.
1127. See section 4.2.2b.
1128. *Id.*
1129. See section 4.2.1b.

supply interoperability information, it appears worthwhile considering any incentives arising from the ability to temporarily exploit a closed network.

Instrumentally, competition law should be applied with careful consideration of the complementary relationship between intellectual property rights and competition law. This theory of complementarity demands compromises from both intellectual property rights and competition law: the former should be sufficiently curtailed to enable competition in foreseeable circumstances, whereas the latter should give deference to these *ex-ante* balancing acts save exceptional circumstances. This study has suggested several instruments to improve the *ex-ante* treatment of interoperability. These instruments should enable a generally adequate *ex-ante* balancing act between openness and control of interoperability information. If such an approach is indeed adopted, there is less reason for competition law to structurally review the scope of these intellectual property rights in detail. In other words, it would be appropriate for competition law to provide some deference to the balance already struck in intellectual property rights. The role of the new-product test in this respect was critically examined in section 4.2.2b. A different approach to granting deference to *ex-ante* intellectual property rights, therefore, may be needed.

There are two main areas where the presence of the *ex-ante* approach to interoperability could be taken into account, such that the scope of the *ex-post* approach is limited: first, in the analysis of dominance, and, second, in the analysis of abusive behavior. It was already observed that competition law could only be used to force access to interface specifications on the part of a dominant firm. Whether a firm is dominant depends on the market definition and the market power of the subject firm on that market, which, in turn, depends, *inter alia*, on entry barriers, or whether competitors can easily join the market. In a network market, the ability of competitors to join the market depends significantly on their access to interface specifications of the allegedly dominant firm. Because the Software Directive's reverse engineering provisions are essentially designed to reduce entry barriers caused by controlled interface specifications, the possibility of reverse engineering appears relevant as part of the analysis.[1130] In *Microsoft*, the Commission, indeed, examined whether the possibility of reverse engineering reduced entry barriers.[1131]

In addition to dominance, the Software Directive could also play a role in the analysis of abusive behavior. As noted, one of the primary requirements of application of the essential facilities doctrine is that the facility, in this case the interface specifications, sought access to be indispensable to competition. Because the Software Directive already provides for a mechanism to access these specifications, active disclosure of interface specifications through

1130. See sections 3.1.2 and 3.2.2. See also Katz & Shelanski 2005, pp. 9, 11; Sucker 1993, p. 16.

1131. *Microsoft Decision* (European Commission 2004), §5.2.1.3, §454, §455.

competition law may not be indispensable. In order to properly align the roles of *ex-ante* copyright law (the reverse engineering instrument in the Software Directive) and *ex-post* competition law, the *ex-ante* instrument of reverse engineering should thus arguably be exhausted before mandatory access could be considered as indispensable. The proper inquiry, therefore, would not be merely whether interoperability is indispensable to compete, but, in addition, whether active supply of this information is indispensable considering the possibility to reverse engineer the information.[1132] In the light of the Software Directive's reverse engineering provisions, it would appear worthwhile to examine the indispensability of the active supply of interface specifications.[1133] An inquiry into the state of the art in reverse engineering technology would be desirable to assess whether reverse engineering is a viable option.[1134] If a more flexible limitation permitting reverse engineering is, indeed, implemented to address access to interoperability information *ex-ante*, as section 6.3.2b suggested, the informed opinion of the regulatory authority suggested in that section might enable the competition authority to consider whether the *ex-ante* instrument for access to interface specifications was sufficient, or whether intervention through competition law is appropriate, for example, because reverse engineering proves prohibitively difficult.

In *Microsoft*, the Commission had found, and the GC confirmed,[1135] that reverse engineering constituted no viable alternative for the active supply of the interoperability information because 'reverse-engineering of the interfaces of a program as voluminous as Windows requires considerable efforts with uncertain chances of success' and because Microsoft could easily change its interfaces in order to frustrate any fruitful reverse engineering attempts.[1136] However, the Commission did not consider the possibility of reverse engineering against the stringent indispensability test of the *Bronner* judgment.[1137] It instead appears to have applied a lower indispensability threshold by observing that reverse engineering proved prohibitively difficult for the relatively small Samba group.[1138]

Naturally, not all abuses of a dominant position in the software industry are caused by exercise of intellectual property rights in interfaces and their specifications. An abuse may also comprise, for example, tying or predatory pricing. Such abuses are not generally anticipated by intellectual property rights and continue to warrant full scrutiny by the competition authority.

1132. See also Bay 1993, p. 186.
1133. See, generally, van Rooijen 2007b, p. 134.
1134. See section 3.2.2c.
1135. *Microsoft Decision* (European Commission 2004), §5.3.1.2.3.3; *Microsoft* (GC 2007), §362, §435.
1136. *Microsoft Decision* (European Commission 2004), §685, §686. See also section 3.2.2d.
1137. See sections 3.2 and 4.2.1b.
1138. *Microsoft Decision* (European Commission 2004), §685. See also van Rooijen 2007b, p. 134.

In sum, changes in the *ex-ante* approach to interoperability should ultimately enable competition law to return to the role it was arguably designed for, namely, the scrutiny of exceptional circumstances and abusive behavior. In this role, competition law should preferably be applied with more flexibility and more consideration of the indirect effects of control over interface specifications and other standards than is currently the case.

6.5. OUTLOOK

In closing, some observations are offered regarding future developments in software interoperability.

For one, it appears high time to consider the effects that intellectual property rights, corrected in some instances by competition rules, can have on standardization, and, thereby, on innovation and competition in certain industries. Currently, intellectual property control over standards is often dealt with similarly to any other intellectual property right. This is true both within intellectual property rights and for their treatment in the competition case law. Yet, this undifferentiated control over standards can impede competition and innovation in industries that substantially rely on standardization because network effects can amplify the market power of the firm controlling the standard. This study has demonstrated that several courts have found a way out to the problem of too much control over standards, in particular within copyright law. However, because standardization considerations are not yet substantially incorporated in the intellectual property laws and competition case law, the courts have necessarily done so without expressly basing their judgments on the effects of standardization. The outcome of these cases is, therefore, of little help to a sustainable standards policy. The suggested reconsideration of control over standards is a matter of competition policy, and competition authorities, therefore, may play an important role in this process.

As to the copyright protection of computer programs, one might also reconsider the relevance and effects of protecting computer programs as literary works under the Berne Convention. The rationale for this form of protection appears to have been the strong need that was felt to establish an international framework for providing incentives to develop computer programs. This was most straightforward to conceive by treating computer programs as 'yet another' literary work within the meaning of the Berne Convention. However, it was already observed that copyright protection of computer programs has very little to do with protecting traditional literary works. It is effectively a form of *sui generis* protection that focuses on preventing access to know-how (source code) of the computer program. Moreover, the literary works rhetoric can have negative consequences for a problem that was perhaps not yet recognized at the time, namely, interoperability and protection of interface specifications. After all, these specifications constitute source or object code similar to the rest of the program and, therefore, might be considered copyrightable subject matter.

Based in part on the TRIPS agreement, the WCT and the European Software Directive, the majority of states have come to protect computer programs in this way (i.e., as literary works under the Berne Convention), even if the obligation to protect computer programs as literary works arguably does not arise from the Berne Convention itself. Now that the original objective of creating an international level playing field for software protection has thus been achieved, and now that the problem of interoperability arguably manifests itself as one of similar importance to protection of computer programs as such, it may be an appropriate time to reconsider this specific form of protection under copyright law, giving more weight to the problem of interoperability and protection of interface specifications.

Taking this thought one step further, the question arises whether copyright law should indeed be the primary *ex-ante* instrument to address the interoperability problem in computer programs. Menell has argued that network features of computer programs (interfaces) should be protected, if at all, by patent law, because of its focus on innovation (rather than originality) and its shorter term of protection.[1139] Interestingly, a patent approach to protection of interfaces might also obviate the problem of access to interface specifications because patent law contains a strong disclosure requirement.[1140]

Some of the ways in which standardization issues could be addressed might be borrowed from trademark law. Unlike copyright law, trademark law expressly deals with *ex-post* standardization issues. In particular through its 'genericide' doctrine, trademark law recognizes that a mark can lose protection if it becomes a *de-facto* standard.[1141] An interesting and important characteristic of trademark law, which also applies to the protection of interface specifications, is its goodwill function: the protection of signs under trademark law encourages firms to establish goodwill associated with their mark and thus, indirectly, to innovate. The incentives provided by trademark law are thus directed at the goodwill behind the mark, not primarily at the creation of the mark itself. This resembles the important indirect function of providing for control over interface specifications: control over interface specifications should not primarily lead to advances in interface technology but should, to a limited extent, enable

---

1139. Menell 1998. See also Kroes 2008, p. 3.

1140. In some instances, a failure to disclose interface specifications for an interface or related patent might violate patent law's enabling disclosure requirement. See, for example, *Decision on patent application number EP84100264: Communications switching system* (EPO Board of Appeals 1990) ('It is noted that Claim 1 only specifies that interface means and processing and scheduling means are provided for carrying out these necessary functions. No further details as to the format of the commands and responses or to the design of the processor and interface means are given.'). However-owever, it may well be possible to patent an interface at a higher level of abstraction, such that the particular interface specification actually used by the rightsholder not be part of the patented invention, and is, therefore, not necessarily disclosed. Samuelson 2008a, p. 28.

1141. See also Koelman 2006, p. 832.

the rightsholder to exploit a closed network. As noted in Chapters 3 and 4, respectively, neither current copyright law nor competition law adequately recognize this important indirect function of control over interface specifications, which can lead to inadequate analyzes.

In this outlook, a final question is how the problem of interoperability in proprietary software will be affected by the ongoing evolution in software development, use and distribution. For one, the increasing use of open source software purposely reduces the developers' control over source code, including interface specifications, thus significantly facilitating interoperability. Another development is the increasing use of hosted applications or *software as a service*, which do not run on the end-user's computer but rather on a remote server, which the end-user is provided access to via a network connection. Although this type of computing could be traced back to the early days of mainframes, more modern and feature-rich applications had not proven suitable for such hosted use until the recent emergence of more bandwidth and enabling technologies, such as virtualization.[1142] As a result of these technologies, software applications are now increasingly being offered as a hosted service, run on a remote server rather than on the end-user's computer.[1143] In such models, the rightsholder can maintain complete control over his or her computer program,[1144] making decompilation for interoperability purposes difficult. Consequently, the reproduction right in copyright law, which plays a central role in regulating decompilation of locally run computer programs, will have little bearing on this form of software use.[1145] The role of contract law and the law of misappropriation, however, may become more significant for regulating these relationships.

1142. Carr 2008, pp. 58, 75.
1143. *Id.*, p. 63.
1144. See also Zittrain 2008, p. 123.
1145. See, for example, *Pendula* (Voorzieningenrechter Rechtbank Leeuwarden 2005) (with case comment by Koelman). In this case, software was not run locally but rather on the defendant's remote server. The plaintiff, who sought to migrate to a new vendor and convert the data stored on the server, relied on the Software Directive's decompilation provision, arguing that the defendant had a duty to cooperate in the conversion process. The District Court of Leeuwarden (Netherlands) agreed, but, as commentator Koelman has observed, erroneously so: the software was not run on the plaintiff's local computer, and the actions required for the conversion of data did not involve decompilation or any other reproductions of the software on the local computer. The decompilation provision was simply not applicable.

Appendix

Following are several examples of API interface *specifications* (note that no implementations are disclosed here). Each of these specifications is written in the C programming language. Other languages use comparable syntaxes. In the C language, the specification typically consists of three parts: an interface name, a return value and a parameter list. The middle part, printed following in bold text, is the name of the interface. The name is typically short and descriptive; it informs the programmer about what the interface does (**`ldap_add, GetFileSize, gotoNextSentence`**). The left part, printed following in italics, is the return type of the interface. This informs the programmer of the type of data the interface returns on completion of its task (*`int, DWORD, boolean`*). Although not all interfaces return a value, most do. A frequently used return type is *`bool`* or *`boolean`*: this type of variable can only be true or false, usually indicating whether the call to the interface was successful. The right part of the specification is the list of arguments the interface requires. If the interface is called on without the proper parameters in the appropriate order, it will not function. This part of the specification lists the type of parameters, their number and their arrangement. The parameters are separated by commas. Each request for a parameter consists of two parts: the left part indicates the type of the variable, such as a number or text value (`int` and `char*`, respectively), whereas the right part is the name of the variable. Like the name of the function itself, the name of a variable typically indicates to the interoperable developer what the variable is used for within the context of the purpose of the interface (`attrs` for 'attributes', `hFile`, `Expand`). The interface specification, thus comprising the name, return type and parameters, should normally suffice for quick reference. That is, an interoperable developer must normally be able to understand from the specifications which interface he or she requires for a specific task, what to expect when the interface has completed its task, and what information to provide the interface with – all without knowledge of the interface implementation.

LDAP Directory service interfaces for searching, modification and addition of directory information in workgroup networks:[1146]

```
int ldap_add( LDAP *ld, char *dn, LDAPMod *attrs[] );
int ldap_search( LDAP *ld, char *base, int scope, char *filter, char
*attrs[], int attrsonly );
int ldap_modify( LDAP *ld, char *dn, LDAPMod *mods[] );
```

Microsoft Win32 API interfaces for requesting a file's size and for changing the system's time zone information:[1147]

```
DWORD GetFileSize( HANDLE hFile, LPDWORD lpFileSizeHigh );
BOOL SetTimeZoneInformation( const TIME_ZONE_INFORMATION* lpTimeZoneIn-
formation );
```

OpenOffice.org API interfaces for positioning the cursor in the word processor:[1148]

```
boolean gotoNextSentence( [in] boolean Expand );
boolean gotoPreviousSentence( [in] boolean Expand );
boolean gotoStartOfSentence( [in] boolean Expand );
boolean gotoEndOfSentence( [in] boolean Expand );
```

The interfaces are called on by the interoperable developer through the reference to the interface's name and the appropriate parameters in their specified order. For example, the first interface of each of the example API sets, *supra*, would be invoked through the following three respective commands:

```
iResult = ldap_add( &ldap, strDomain, attributes );
dwSizeOfMyFile = GetFileSize( hMyFile, &dwFileSizeHigh );
bResult = gotoNextSentence( true );
```

If one would attempt to call on an interface using a different format – such as a different order or number of parameters, the result would be either a compiler or a runtime error.[1149] For instance, the following calls would likely generate errors:

```
iResult = ldap_add( strDomain, attributes, &ldap );
dwSizeOfMyFile = GetFileSize( &dwFileSizeHigh );
bResult = gotoNextSentence( );
```

1146. Howes & Smith, The LDAP Application Programming Interface, available at <http://tools.ietf.org/html/rfc1823> (last visited July 26, 2006).

1147. Microsoft, MSDN, available at <http://msdn.microsoft.com/> (last visited December 22, 2008).

1148. Sun Microsystems, OpenOffice.org 2.0 Developer's Guide, available at <http://api.openoffice.org/docs/DevelopersGuide/DevelopersGuide.xhtml> (last visited July 26, 2006).

1149. The compiler detects a compiler error before completing the conversion of the source code into object code. A runtime error may not be detected by the compiler in advance but is likely to have unintended consequences when the program is executed.

Bibliography

PRIMARY SOURCES

Access Directive
Directive 2002/19/EC of the European Parliament and of the Council of 7 March 2002 on access to, and interconnection of, electronic communications networks and associated facilities, *Official Journal L108, 24/04/2002* 7 (2002).

Berne Convention
Berne Convention for the Protection of Literary and Artistic Works (1971).

COM(1993) 342 Final
Proposal for a European Parliament and Council Regulation on the Community Design (1993).

Community Design Regulation
Council Regulation (EC) No. 6/2002 of 12 December 2001 on community designs, *Official Journal L3, 5/1/2002* 1–24 (2001).

Database Directive
Directive 96/9/EC of the European Parliament and of the Council of 11 March 1996 on the legal protection of databases, *Official Journal L077, 27/03/1996* 20–28 (1996).

Directive 87/54/EEC
Council Directive 87/54/EEC of 16 December 1986 on the legal protection of topographies of semiconductor products, *Official Journal L024, 27/01/1987* 36–40 (1986).

Directive 98/71/EC
Directive 98/71/EC of the European Parliament and of the Council of 13 October 1998 on the legal protection of designs, *Official Journal L289*, 28–33 (1998).

Framework Directive
Directive 2002/21/EC of the European Parliament and of the Council of 7 March 2002 on a common regulatory framework for electronic communications networks and services, *Official Journal L108, 24/4/2002* 33–50 (2002).

InfoSoc Directive
Directive 2001/29/EC of the European Parliament and of the Council of 22 May 2001 on the harmonisation of certain aspects of copyright and related rights in the information society, *Official Journal L167, 22/06/2001* 10–19 (2001).

Proposal amending Directive 98/71/EC
Proposal for a Directive of the European Parliament and of the Council amending Directive 98/71/EC on the legal protection of designs, 2004 0582 (European Commission 2004).

Regulation 1/2003
Council Regulation (EC) No. 1/2003 of 16 December 2002 on the implementation of the rules on competition laid down in Articles 81 and 82 of the Treaty, *Official Journal L1, 4/1/2003* 1–25 (2002).

Software Directive
Directive 2009/24/EC of the European Parliament and of the Council of 23 April 2009 on the legal protection of computer programs (Codified version), *Official Journal L111, 5/5/2009* 16–22 (2009).

Software Directive, Amended Proposal
Amended Proposal for a Council Directive on the legal protection of computer programs (European Commission 1990).

Software Directive, Proposal
Proposal for a Council Directive on the legal protection of computer programs (European Commission 1989).

Term Directive
Council Directive 93/98/EEC of 29 October 1993 harmonizing the term of protection of copyright and certain related rights, *Official Journal L290, 24/11/1993* 9–13 (1993).

Topografiewet
Wet van 28 oktober 1987, houdende regelen inzake de bescherming van oorspronkelijke topografieën van halfgeleiderprodukten, *Staatsblad 1987* 484.

TRIPS
Agreement on Trade-Related Aspects of Intellectual Property Rights (1994).

Vorschlag für eine Richtlinie des Rates über den Rechtsschutz von Computerprogrammen' 1989
'Vorschlag für eine Richtlinie des Rates über den Rechtsschutz von Computerprogrammen', *GRUR Int.* 564 (1989).

WCT
WIPO Copyright Treaty (1996).

SECONDARY SOURCES

Akzo
Akzo Chemie B.V. v. Commission of the European Communities, 1991 ECR I-03359 (ECJ 1991).

Apple v. Franklin
Apple Computer, Inc. v. Franklin Computer Corporation, 714 F.2d 1240 (US Court of Appeals, Third Circuit 1983).

Apple v. Microsoft
Apple Computer, Inc. v. Microsoft Corporation, 759 F.Supp 1444 (US Court of Appeals, Ninth Circuit 1994).

Aspen Skiing
Aspen Skiing Company v. Aspen Highlands Skiing Corporation, 472 U.S. 585 (US Supreme Court 1985).

Atari v. Nintendo
Atari Games Corp. v. Nintendo of America Inc., 975 F.2d 832 (US Court of Appeals, Federal Circuit 1992).

Baker v. Selden
Baker v. Selden, 101 U.S. 99 (US Supreme Court 1879).

Betriebssystem
Betriebssystem, 1991 CR 80 (Bundesgerichtshof 1990).

Bigott v. Doucal
C.A. Cigarrera Bigott Sucs. v. British American Tobacco Co., 1999 NJ 697 (Hoge Raad 1999).

British Airways
British Airways plc v. Commission of the European Communities, 2007 ECR I-2331 (ECJ 2007).

British Telecom
Italian Republic v. Commission of the European Communities, 1985 ECR 873 (ECJ 1985).

Bronner
Oscar Bronner GmbH & Co. KG v. Mediaprint Zeitungs- und Zeitschriftenverlag GmbH & Co. KG, Mediaprint Zeitungsvertriebsgesellschaft mbH & Co. KG and Mediaprint Anzeigengesellschaft mbH & Co. KG, 1998 ECR I-07791 (ECJ 1998).

Commercial Solvents
Istituto Chemioterapico Italiano S.p.A. and Commercial Solvents Corporation v. Commission of the European Communities, 1974 ECR 223 (ECJ 1974).

Computer Associates Int'l
Computer Associates International v. Faster and Altai, 166 RIDA 324 (Tribunal de Commerce de Bobigny 1995).

Computer Associates v. Altai
Computer Associates International, Inc. v. Altai, Inc., 982 F.2d 693 (US Court of Appeals, Second Circuit 1992).

Consten and Grundig v. European Commission
Établissements Consten S.à.R.L. and Grundig-Verkaufs-GmbH v. Commission of the European Economic Community, ECR 299 (ECJ 1966).

Consumers Union v. General Signal Corp.
Consumers Union of United States, Inc. v. General Signal Corp. and Grey Advertising, Inc., 724 F.2d 1044 (US Court of Appeals, Second Circuit 1983).

Continental Can
Europemballage Corporation and Continental Can Company Inc. v. Commission of the European Communities, 1973 ECR 215 (ECJ 1973).

Creative v. Aztech
Creative Technology Ltd v. Aztech Systems Pte Ltd, 1997 F.S.R. 491 (Singapore Court of Appeal 1996).

Data General
Data General Corporation v. Grumman Systems Support Corporation, 36 F.3d 1147 (US Court of Appeals, First Circuit 1994).

Decision on patent application number EP84100264: Communications switching system
Decision on patent application number EP84100264: Communications switching system (EPO Board of Appeals 1990).

Deutsche Grammophon
Deutsche Grammophon Gesellschaft mbH v. Metro-SB-Großmärkte GmbH & Co. KG, 1971 ECR 487 (ECJ 1971).

Dior v. Evora
Parfums Christian Dior SA v. Evora BV, 1996 NJ 682 (Hoge Raad 1995).

Elwood
Benetton v. G-Star, 2006 BIE (Hoge Raad 2006).

ERT
Elliniki Radiophonia Tiléorassi AE and Panellinia Omospondia Syllogon Prossopikou v. Dimotiki Etairia Pliroforissis and Sotirios Kouvelas and Nicolaos Avdellas and others, 1991 ECR I-02925 (ECJ 1991).

Hoffmann-La Roche
Hoffmann-La Roche & Co. AG v. Commission of the European Communities, 1979 Jur. 461 (ECJ 1979).

Höfner
Klaus Höfner and Fritz Elser v. Macrotron GmbH, 1991 ECR I-01979 (ECJ 1991).

IBM Undertaking
IBM Undertaking, 1984 EC Bulletin 95 (European Commission 1984).

Illinois Tool Works v. Independent Ink
Illinois Tool Works Inc. v. Independent Ink, Inc., 126 S.Ct. 1281 (US Supreme Court 2006).

IMS Health
IMS Health GmbH & Co. OHG v. NDC Health GmbH & Co. KG, 2004 ECR I-05039 (ECJ 2004).

In re ISO Antitrust Litigation
In re Independent Service Organizations Antitrust Litigation, 203 F.3d 1322 (US Court of Appeals, Federal Circuit 2000).

Inkassoprogramm
Sudwestdeutsche Inkasso KG v. Bappert and Burker Computer GmbH, 94 BGHZ 279 (Bundesgerichtshof 1985).

Inno v. Atab
SA G.B.-INNO-B.M. v. Association des détaillants en tabac (ATAB), 1977 ECR 02115 (ECJ 1977).

Kodak
Eastman Kodak Company v. Image Technical Services, Inc., 504 U.S. 451 (US Supreme Court 1992).

Case T-270/06 (Lego)
Lego Juris A/S v. Office for Harmonisation in the Internal Market (Trade Marks and Designs), ECR (GC 2008).

Lotus v. Borland
Lotus Development Corporation v. Borland International Inc., 49 F.3d 807 (US Court of Appeals, First Circuit 1995).

Lotus v. Borland
Lotus Development Corporation v. Borland International, Inc., 799 F.Supp 203 (US District Court Massachusetts 1992).

Lotus v. Paperback
Lotus Development Corporation v. Paperback Software International, 740 F.Supp 37 (US District Court, Massachusetts 1990).

Magill
Radio Telefis Eireann (RTE) and Independent Television Publications Ltd v. Commission of the European Communities, 1995 ECR 492 (ECJ 1995).

MAI v. Peak
MAI Systems Corp. v. Peak Computer, Inc., 991 F.2d 511 (US Court of Appeals, Ninth Circuit 1993).

MCI v. AT&T
MCI Communications Corporation v. American Telephone and Telegraph Company, 708 F.2d 1081 (US Court of Appeals, Seventh Circuit 1983).

Merci
Merci convenzionali porto di Genova SpA v. Siderurgica Gabrielli SpA, 1991 ECR I-05889 (ECJ 1991).

Microsoft
Microsoft Corporation v. Commission of the European Communities (Case T-201/04), (GC 2007).

Microsoft Decision
Commission Decision of 24.03.2004 relating to a proceeding under Article 82 of the EC Treaty (European Commission 2004).

Morrisey v. Proctor & Gamble
Morrisey v. Proctor & Gamble, 379 F.2d 675 (US Court of Appeals, First Circuit 1967).

Navitaire v. EasyJet
Navitaire Inc. v. EasyJet Airline Co., Bulletproof Technologies Inc., 2005 E.C.D.R. 160 (UK High Court of Justice, Chancery Division 2004).

Nichols v. Universal Pictures Corporation
Nichols v. Universal Pictures Corporation, 45 F.2d 119 (US Court of Appeals, Second Circuit 1930).

Nomaï
Nomaï v. Iomega, 1992 Droit de l'Informatique & des Télécoms 2/65 (Paris Court of Appeals 1997).

NYMEX
New York Mercantile Exchange, Inc. v. Intercontinental Exchange, Inc., 323 F.Supp.2d 559 (US District Court, S.D. New York 2004).

Pendula
Openbaar Onderwijs Zwolle en Regio v. Pendula B.V., 29 AMI 143 (Voorzieningenrechter Rechtbank Leeuwarden 2005).

Peregrine v. Exa
Peregrine Systems v. Exa Communications, 2003 BIE 24 (District Court The Hague 2002).

Philips v. Vomar
Philips Domestic Appliances and Personal Care BV v. Coöperatieve Inkoopvereniging Integro BA and Vomar Voordeelmarkt BV, 2002 IER 323 (Voorzieningenrechter Rechtbank Haarlem 2002).

Philips v. Remington
Philips Electronics v. Remington Consumer Products, 2003 BIE 89 (ECJ 2002).

Renault
Consorzio italiano della componentistica di ricambio per autoveicoli and Maxicar v. Régie nationale des usines Renault, 1988 ECR 6039 (ECJ 1988).

Sega v. Accolade
Sega Enterprises Ltd v. Accolade, Inc., 977 F.2d 1510 (US Court of Appeals, Ninth Circuit 1992).

Sirena
Sirena S.r.l. v. Eda S.r.l. and Others, 1971 ECR 69 (ECJ 1971).

Softimage
X and Y v. Softimage Co, 2006 Légipresse 229-12 (Supreme Court 2005).

Taylor Instrument
Taylor Instrument Co. v. Fawley-Brost, 1943.

Technip
Technip Benelux B.V. v. Goossens, 2007 NJ 37 (Hoge Raad 2006).

Terminal Railroad
United States of America v. Terminal Railroad Association of St. Louis et al., 224 U.S. 383 (US Supreme Court 1912).

TIPS v. Daman
Total Information Processing Systems Limited v. Daman Limited, 1992 F.S.R. 171 (UK High Court of Justice, Chancery Division 1991).

Trinko
Verizon Communications Inc. v. Law Offices of Curtis V. Trinko, LLP, 540 U.S. 398 (US Supreme Court 2004).

United Brands
United Brands Company and United Brands Continentaal BV v. Commission of the European Communities, 1978 ECR 207 (ECJ 1987).

United States v. Microsoft
United States v. Microsoft Corporation, 34 F.3d 34 (US Court of Appeals, DC Circuit 2001).

Volvo
AB Volvo v. Erik Veng (UK) Ltd, 1988 ECR 6211 (ECJ 1988).

Whelan v. Jaslow
Whelan Associates, Inc. v. Jaslow Dental Laboratory, Inc., 797 F.2d 1222 (US Court of Appeals, Third Circuit 1986).

TERTIARY SOURCES

Ahlborn et al. 2005
Christian Ahlborn et al., 'The Logic and Limits of the "Exceptional Circumstances Test" in *Magill* and *IMS Health*', 28 *Fordham International Law Journal* 1109–1156 (2005).

Ahn 1999
Hyo-Jil Ahn, *Der urheberrechtliche Schutz von Computerprogrammen im Recht der Bundesrepublik Deutschland und der Republik Korea*, Baden-Baden: Nomos 1999.

Airbus
Airbus, *Specifications Airbus A330-200*, available at <http://www.airbus.com/en/aircraftfamilies/a330a340/a330-200/specifications/> (last visited December 31, 2009).

Angel 2001
John Angel, 'The Telecommunications Regime in the United Kingdom', in: Ian Walden & John Angel, *Telecommunications Law*, London: Blackstone Press 2001, pp. 53–73.

Appeldoorn 2005
Jochen Appeldoorn, 'He Who Spareth His Rod, Hateth His Son? Microsoft, Super-Dominance and Article 82 EC', 26 *European Competition Law Review* 653–658 (2005).

Areeda 1990
Phillip Areeda, 'Essential Facilities: An Epithet in Need of Limiting Principles', 58 *ABA Antitrust Law Journal* 841 (1990).

Areeda & Hovenkamp 1994
Phillip Areeda & Herbert Hovenkamp, *Antitrust Law: An Analysis of Antitrust Principles and Their Application*, New York: Aspen 1994.

Bainbridge 2006
David I. Bainbridge, *Intellectual Property*, Harlow: Pearson Education 2006.

Bakels & Hugenholtz 2002
Reinier Bakels & P. Bernt Hugenholtz, *The Patentability of Computer Programs: Discussion of European-Level Legislation in the Field of Patents for Software*, European Parliament, 2002.

Baldwin & Cave 1999
Robert Baldwin & Martin Cave, *Understanding Regulation: Theory, Strategy and Practice*, Oxford: Oxford University Press 1999.

Band & Durney 1995
Jonathan Band & Edward Durney, 'Protection of Computer Programs under Japanese Copyright Law', in: *Tricks of the Trade: Intellectual Property in the United States and Japan*, Austin: IC2 Institute 1995.

Band & Katoh 1995
Jonathan Band & Masanobu Katoh, *Interfaces on Trial: Intellectual Property and Interoperability in the Global Software Industry*, Boulder: Westview Press 1995.

Band et al. 1992
Jonathan Band et al., 'The US Decision in *Computer Associates v. Altai* Compared to the EC Software Directive: Transatlantic Convergence of Copyright Standards Favoring Software Interoperability', 8 *Computer Law & Practice* 137–143 (1992).

Bartmann 2005
Jeannine Bartmann, *Grenzen der Monopolisierung durch Urheberrechte am Beispiel von Datenbanken und Computerprogrammen: Eine rechtsvergleichende Studie des europäischen, deutschen und US-amerikanischen Rechts*, Cologne/Berlin/Munich: Carl Heymanns Verlag 2005.

Barton 1997
John H. Barton, 'The Balance between Intellectual Property Rights and Competition: Paradigms in the Information Sector', 18 *European Competition Law Review* 440–445 (1997).

Bath 2002
Ulrika Bath, 'Access to Information vs. Intellectual Property Rights', 24 *European Intellectual Property Review* 138–146 (2002).

Bay 1993
Matteo Bay, 'EC Competition Law and Software IPRs', 9 *Computer Law & Practice* 176–193 (1993).

Bechtold 2007
Stefan Bechtold, *Die Kontrolle von Sekundärmärkten: eine juristische und ökonomische Untersuchung im Kartell- und Immaterialgüterrecht*, Baden-Baden: Nomos 2007.

Beier 1994
Friedrich-Karl Beier, 'Protection for Spare Parts in the Proposals for a European Design Law', 25 *IIC* 840–879 (1994).

Belloir 1998
Philippe Belloir, 'La décompilation d'une disquette, est-elle illicite?', *Expertises des systèmes d'information* 190 (1998).

Benjamin et al. 2006
Stuart Minor Benjamin et al., *Telecommunications Law and Policy*, Durham: Carolina Academic Press 2006.

Bently 2006
Lionel Bently, 'Computer Programs Directive', in: Thomas Dreier & P. Bernt Hugenholtz, *Concise European Copyright Law*, Alphen aan den Rijn: Kluwer Law International 2006, pp. 211–238.

Bently & Sherman 2004
Lionel Bently & Brad Sherman, *Intellectual Property Law*, Oxford: Oxford University Press 2004.

Besen & Farrell 1994
Stanley M. Besen & Joseph Farrell, 'Choosing How to Compete: Strategies and Tactics in Standardization', 8 *The Journal of Economic Perspectives* 117–131 (1994).

Bitan 2006
Hubert Bitan, *Protection et contrefaçon des logiciels et des bases de données*, Paris: Lamy 2006.

Boomerang
Boomerang, available at <http://boomerang.sourceforge.net/> (last visited January 12, 2009).

Borenstein et al. 1995
Severin Borenstein et al., 'Antitrust Policy in Aftermarkets', 63 *Antitrust Law Journal* 455 (1995).

Bork 1978
Robert Bork, *The Antitrust Paradox: A Policy at War with Itself*, New York: Free Press 1978.

Bouwman et al. 2004
Harry Bouwman et al., *Interconnectie: het vaste telefoonnet, het mobiele net en internet*, The Hague: SDU 2004.

Breuer & Bowen 1994
Peter T. Breuer & Jonathan P. Bowen, 'Decompilation: The Enumeration of Types and Grammars', 16 *ACM Transactions on Programming Languages and Systems* 1613–1647 (1994).

Buendia Sierra 1999
José Louis Buendia Sierra, *Exclusive Rights and State Monopolies under EC Law: Article 86 (Formerly Article 90) of the EC Treaty*, Oxford: Oxford University Press 1999.

Calliess & Blanke 2002
Christian Calliess & Hermann-Josef Blanke, *Kommentar des Vertrages über die Europäische Union und des Vertrages zur Gründung der Europäischen Gemeinschaft*, Neuwied: Luchterhand 2002.

Carr 2008
Nicholas Carr, *The Big Switch: Rewiring the World, from Edison to Google*, New York/London: Norton 2008.

Chikofsky & Cross II 1990
Elliot J. Chikofsky & James H. Cross II, 'Reverse Engineering and Design Recovery: A Taxonomy', 7 *IEEE* 13–17 (1990).

Cifuentes 1999
Cristina Cifuentes, 'The Impact of Copyright on the Development of Cutting Edge Binary Reverse Engineering Technology', in: *Sixth Working Conference on Reverse Engineering*, Washington, DC: IEEE-CS Press, 1999, pp. 66–76.

Cifuentes 2001
Cristina Cifuentes, 'Reverse Engineering and the Computing Profession', 34 *Computer* 166–168 (2001).

Cifuentes & Fitzgerald 1998
Cristina Cifuentes & Anne Fitzgerald, 'Interoperability and Computer Software Protection in Australia', 4 *Computer and Telecommunications Law Review* 271–276 (1998).

Cifuentes et al. 1998
Cristina Cifuentes et al., 'Assembly to High-Level Language Translation', in: *14th IEEE International Conference on Software Maintenance*, Washington, DC 1998, p. 228.

Clapes et al. 1987
Anthony L. Clapes et al., 'Silicon Epics and Binary Bards: Determining the Proper Scope of Copyright Protection for Computer Programs', 34 *UCLA Law Review* 1493 (1987).

Cohen-Jehoram 1994
H. Cohen-Jehoram, 'The EC Copyright Directives, Economics and Author's Rights', 25 *IIC* 821–839 (1994).

Cohen-Jehoram 2007
H. Cohen-Jehoram, 'De Hoge Raad erkent verwatering van auteursrecht door merkenrechtelijke verwording van een werk tot onbeschermde stijl. Een uniek

monstrum en een nieuw obstakel voor het Europese vrij verkeer van goederen', 2007 *Bijblad bij de Industriële Eigendom* 12–16 (2007).

Cooter & Ulen 2007
Robert Cooter & Thomas S. Ulen, *Law and Economics*, Pearson 2007.

Cornish 1989
William R. Cornish, 'Inter-Operable Systems and Copyright', 11 *European Intellectual Property Review* 391–393 (1989).

Cornish 1993
William R. Cornish, 'Computer Program Copyright and the Berne Convention', in: Michael Lehmann & Colin Tapper, *A Handbook of European Software Law*, Oxford: Oxford University Press 1993, pp. 183–201.

Cornish & Llewellyn 2003
William R. Cornish & David Llewellyn, *Intellectual Property: Patents, Copyright, Trade Marks and Allied Rights*, London: Sweet & Maxwell 2003.

Cornish & Llewellyn 2007
William R. Cornish & David Llewellyn, *Intellectual Property: Patents, Copyright, Trade Marks and Allied Rights*, London: Sweet & Maxwell 2007.

Correa 2001
Lisa Correa, 'The Economics of Telecommunications Regulation', in: Ian Walden & John Angel, *Telecommunications Law*, London: Blackstone Press 2001, pp. 16–52.

Cotter 1999
Thomas F. Cotter, 'Intellectual Property and the Essential Facilities Doctrine', 44 *Antitrust Bulletin* 211 (1999).

Craig & de Búrca 2003
Paul Craig & Gráinne de Búrca, *EU Law: Text, Cases, and Materials*, Oxford: Oxford University Press 2003.

Cringeley 1996
Robert X. Cringeley, *Accidental Empires: How the Boys of Silicon Valley Make Their Millions, Battle Foreign Competition, and Still Can't Get a Date*, Collins Business 1996.

Czarnota & Hart 1991
Bridget Czarnota & Robert J. Hart, *Legal Protection of Computer Programs in Europe: A Guide to the EC Directive*, London: Butterworths 1991.

Dam 1995
Kenneth W. Dam, 'Some Economic Considerations in the Intellectual Property Protection of Software', 24 *Journal of Legal Studies* 321 (1995).

David 1985
Paul A. David, 'Clio and the Economics of QWERTY', 75 *The American Economic Review* 332–337 (1985).

David & Bunn 1988
Paul A. David & Julie Ann Bunn, 'The Economics of Gateway Technologies and Network Evolution: Lessons from Electricity Supply History', 3 *Information Economic and Policy* 165–202 (1988).

De Cock Buning 2007
Madeleine De Cock Buning, 'The History of Copyright Protection of Computer Software: The Emancipation of a Work of Technology toward a Work of Authorship', in: Karl De Leeuw & Jan Bergstra, *The History of Information Security: A Comprehensive Handbook*, Amsterdam: Elsevier 2007, pp. 121–140.

Deene 2007
Joris Deene, 'Originality in Software Law: Belgian Doctrine and Jurisprudence Remain Divided', 2 *Journal of Intellectual Property Law & Practice* 692–698 (2007).

Van den Bergh 1998
Roger Van den Bergh, 'The Role and Social Justification of Copyright: A "Law and Economics" Approach', 1998 *Intellectual Property Quarterly* 17–34 (1998).

Derclaye 2000
Estelle Derclaye, 'Software Protection: Can Europe Learn from American Case Law? Part 1', 22 *European Intellectual Property Review* 7–16 (2000).

Derclaye 2003
Estelle Derclaye, 'Abuse of Dominant Position and Intellectual Property Rights: A Suggestion to Reconcile the Community Courts Case Law', 26 *World Competition* 685 (2003).

DeSanti & Cohen 2001
Susan DeSanti & William Cohen, 'Competition to Innovate: Strategies for Proper Antitrust Assessments', in: Rochelle Cooper Dreyfuss et al., *Expanding the Boundaries of Intellectual Property: Innovation Policy for the Knowledge Society*, Oxford: Oxford University Press 2001, pp. 317–341.

Doherty 2001
Barry Doherty, 'Just What Are Essential Facilities?', 38 *Common Market Law Review* 397–436 (2001).

Dolmans et al. 2007
Maurits Dolmans et al., 'Article 82 EC and Intellectual Property: The State of the Law Pending the Judgment in *Microsoft v. Commission*', 3 *Competition Policy International* 106 (2007).

Dommering 1992
Egbert J. Dommering, 'De software richtlijn uit Brussel en de Nederlandse Auteurswet', 16 *AMI* 83–89 (1992).

Dommering 1994
Egbert J. Dommering, 'Het auteursrecht spoelt weg door het elektronisch vergiet: enige gedachten over de naderende crisis van het auteursrecht', 1994 *Computerrecht* 109 (1994).

Dommering et al. 1999
Egbert J. Dommering et al., *Handboek Telecommunicatierecht: Inleiding tot het recht en de techniek van de telecommunicatie*, The Hague: SDU 1999.

Dommering et al. 2001a
Egbert J. Dommering et al., 'Toezicht en regulering in de telecommunicatiemarkt', 2001 *Mediaforum* 186–190 (2001).

Dommering et al. 2001b
Egbert J. Dommering et al., *Toezicht en regulering in de telecommunicatiemarkt*, Amsterdam: Instituut voor Informatierecht 2001.

Dreier 1991a
Thomas Dreier, 'Rechtsschutz von Computerprogrammen: Die Richtlinie des Rates der EG vom 14. Mai 1991', 7 *Computer und Recht* 577–584 (1991).

Dreier 1991b
Thomas Dreier, 'The Council Directive of 14 May 1991 on the Legal Protection of Computer Programs', 13 *European Intellectual Property Review* 319–330 (1991).

Dreier 1993
Thomas Dreier, 'Die internationale Entwicklung des Rechtsschutzes von Computerprogrammen', in: Michael Lehmann, *Rechtsschutz und Verwertung von Computerprogrammen*, Cologne: Verlag Dr. Otto Schmidt 1993, pp. 31–68.

Dreier 2001
Thomas Dreier, 'Balancing Proprietary and Public Domain Interests: Inside or Outside of Proprietary Rights?', in: Rochelle Cooper Dreyfuss et al., *Expanding the Boundaries of Intellectual Property: Innovation Policy for the Knowledge Society*, Oxford: Oxford University Press 2001, pp. 295–316.

Dreier & Hugenholtz 2006
Thomas Dreier & P. Bernt Hugenholtz (eds.), *Concise European Copyright Law*, Alphen aan den Rijn: Kluwer Law International 2006.

Dreier & Schulze 2004
Thomas Dreier & Gernot Schulze, *UrhG: Urheberrechtsgezetz, Urheberrechtswahrnehmungsgesetz, Kunsturhebergesetz*, Munich: C.H. Beck 2004.

Drexl 1994
Josef Drexl, *What Is Protected in a Computer Program?*, Weinheim: VCH 1994.

Drexl 2004
Josef Drexl, 'Intellectual Property and Antitrust Law – *IMS Health* and *Trinko* – Antitrust Placebo for Consumers Instead of Sound Economics in Refusal-to-Deal Cases', 2004 *IIC* 788 (2004).

Drexl 2006
Josef Drexl, 'Abuse of Dominance in Licensing and Refusals to License – A "More Economic Approach" to Competition by Imitation and to Competition by Substitution', in: Claus Dieter Ehlermann & Isabela Atanasiu, *European Competition Law Annual 2005: The Interaction between Competition Law and IP Law*, Oxford: Hart Publishing 2006, pp. 647–664.

Drexl 2008
Josef Drexl, 'The Relationship between Legal Exclusivity and Economic Market Power: Links and Limits', in: Inge Govaere & Hanns Ullrich, *Intellectual Property, Market Power and the Public Interest*, Brussels: PIE-Peter Lang 2008.

Drexl et al. 2005
Josef Drexl et al., 'Design Protection for Spare Parts and the Commission's Proposal for a Repairs Clause', 36 *IIC* 448–457 (2005).

Drexl et al. 2006
Josef Drexl et al., 'Comments of the Max Planck Institute for Intellectual Property, Competition and Tax Law (Munich) on the DG Competition Discussion Paper of December 2005 on the Application of Article 82 of the EC Treaty to Exclusionary Abuses', 2006 *IIC* 558 (2006).

Ehlermann 1993
Claus Dieter Ehlermann, 'Managing Monopolies: The Role of the State in Controlling Market Dominance in the European Community', 14 *European Competition Law Review* 61–69 (1993).

European Commission 1985
European Commission, *Completing the Internal Market: White Paper from the Commission to the European Council*, 1985.

European Commission 1987
European Commission, *Towards a Dynamic European Economy: Green Paper on the Development of the Common Market for Telecommunications Services and Equipment*, 1987.

European Commission 1988
European Commission, *Green Paper on Copyright and the Challenge of New Technology – Copyright Issues Requiring Immediate Action*, 1988.

European Commission 1991
European Commission, *Green Paper on the Legal Protection of Industrial Design*, 1991.

European Commission 1998
European Commission, *Notice on the Application of the Competition Rules to Access Agreements in the Telecommunications Sector*, 1998.

European Commission 1999
European Commission, *Towards a New Framework for Electronic Communications Infrastructure and Associated Services: The 1999 Communications Review*, 1999.

European Commission 2000
European Commission, *Report from the Commission to the Council, the European Parliament and the Economic and Social Committee on the implementation and effects of Directive 91/250/EEC on the legal protection of computer programs*, 2000.

European Commission 2002
European Commission, *Commission Guidelines on Market Analysis and the Assessment of Significant Market Power under the Community Regulatory Framework for Electronic Communications Networks and Services*, 2002.

European Commission 2004a
European Commission, *Commission Notice Guidelines on the Application of Article 81 of the EC Treaty to Technology Transfer Agreements*, 2004a.

European Commission 2004b
European Commission, *Commission Staff Working Paper on the Review of the EC Legal Framework in the Field of Copyright and Related Rights*, 2004b.

European Commission 2004c
European Commission, *Proposal for a Directive of the European Parliament and of the Council amending Directive 98/71/EC on the Legal Protection of Designs: Extended Impact Assessment*, 2004c.

European Commission 2005
European Commission, *Article 82 Discussion Paper*, 2005.

European Commission 2007
European Commission, *Commission Staff Working Document: Report to the Council, the European Parliament and the Economic and Social Committee on the Application of Directive 2001/29/EC on the Harmonisation of Certain Aspects of Copyright and Related Rights in the Information Society*, 2007.

European Commission 2009
European Commission, *Guidance on the Commission's Enforcement Priorities in Applying Article 82 of the EC Treaty to Abusive Exclusionary Conduct by Dominant Undertakings*, 2009.

European Parliament 2007
European Parliament, *Report on the Proposal for a Directive of the European Parliament and of the Council Amending Directive 98/71/EC on the Legal Protection of Designs*, Committee on Legal Affairs 2007.

Evans et al. 2002
David S. Evans et al., 'Tying in Platform Software: Reasons for a Rule-of-Reason Standard in European Competition Law', 25 *World Competition* 509–514 (2002).

Evans & Schmalensee 1996
David S. Evans & Richard Schmalensee, 'A Guide to the Antitrust Economics of Networks', *Antitrust* 36 (1996).

ExeToC
ExeToC, *ExeToC*, available at <http://sourceforge.net/projects/exetoc> (last visited January 12, 2009).

Farrell 1989
Joseph Farrell, 'Standardization and Intellectual Property', 30 *Jurimetrics Journal* 35–50 (1989).

Farrell 1995
Joseph Farrell, 'Arguments for Weaker Intellectual Property Protection in Network Industries', 3 *StandardView* 46–49 (1995).

Farrell & Katz 1998
Joseph Farrell & Michael L. Katz, 'The Effects of Antitrust and Intellectual Property Law on Compatibility and Innovation', 43 *Antitrust Bulletin* 609 (1998).

Farrell & Klemperer 2004
Joseph Farrell & Paul Klemperer, 'Coordination and Lock-In: Competition with Switching Costs and Network Effects', in: *Handbook of Industrial Organization*, Elsevier 2004, pp. 1967–2056.

Farrell & Saloner 1985
Joseph Farrell & Garth Saloner, 'Standardization, Compatibility, and Innovation', 16 *The RAND Journal of Economics* 70–83 (1985).

Farrell & Saloner 1986
Joseph Farrell & Garth Saloner, 'Installed Base and Compatibility: Innovation, Product Preannouncements, and Predation', 76 *The American Economic Review* 940–955 (1986).

Farrell & Saloner 1992
Joseph Farrell & Garth Saloner, 'Converters, Compatibility, and the Control of Interfaces', XL *The Journal of Industrial Economics* 9–35 (1992).

Faull & Nikpay 1999
Jonathan Faull & Ali Nikpay (eds.), *The EC Law of Competition*, Oxford: Oxford University Press 1999.

Faull & Nikpay 2007
Jonathan Faull & Ali Nikpay (eds.), *The EC Law of Competition*, Oxford: Oxford University Press 2007.

Federal Trade Commission 2003
Federal Trade Commission, *To Promote Innovation: The Proper Balance of Competition and Patent Law and Policy*, Federal Trade Commission, 2003.

Ficsor 2002
Mihály Ficsor, *The Law of Copyright and the Internet: The 1996 WIPO Treaties, Their Interpretation and Implementation*, Oxford: Oxford University Press 2002.

Forrester 2005
Ian S. Forrester, 'Article 82: Remedies in Search of Theories?', 28 *Fordham International Law Journal* 919 (2005).

Fowler 2002
Martin Fowler, 'Public versus Published Interfaces', 19 *IEEE Software* 18–19 (2002).

Frischmann & Weber-Waller 2008
Brett Frischmann & Spencer Weber-Waller, 'Revitalizing Essential Facilities', 75 *Antitrust Law Journal* 1 (2008).

Furse 1995
Mark Furse, 'The Essential Facilities Doctrine in Community Law', 16 *European Competition Law Review* 469–472 (1995).

Geiger 2008
Christophe Geiger, 'Die Schranken des Urheberrechts als Instrumente der Innovationsförderung – Freire Gedanken zur Ausschließlichkeit im Urheberrecht', *GRUR Int.* 459–468 (2008).

Geradin 2004
Damien Geradin, 'Limiting the Scope of Article 82 of the EC Treaty: What Can the EU Learn from the US Supreme Court's Judgment in *Trinko* in the wake of *Microsoft, IMS,* and *Deutsche Telekom*', 41 *Common Market Law Review* 1519–1553 (2004).

Geradin & Kerf 2003
Damien Geradin & Michel Kerf, *Controlling Market Power in Telecommunications: Antitrust vs Sector-specific Regulation*, Oxford: Oxford University Press 2003.

Gervais 2003
Daniel Gervais, *The TRIPS Agreement: Drafting History and Analysis*, London: Sweet & Maxwell 2003.

Ghezzi et al. 1991
Carlo Ghezzi et al., *Fundamentals of Software Engineering*, Englewood Cliffs, NJ: Prentice Hall 1991.

Gibson 2005
James Gibson, 'Once and Future Copyright', 81 *Notre Dame Law Review* 167–243 (2005).

Gielen 2007
Charles Gielen (ed.), *Kort begrip van het intellectuele eigendomsrecht*, Deventer: Kluwer 2007.

Gijrath 2006
Serge J.H. Gijrath, *Interconnection Regulation and Contract Law*, Amsterdam: deLex 2006.

Gilbert & Shapiro 1996
Richard J. Gilbert & Carl Shapiro, 'An Economic Analysis of Unilateral Refusals to License Intellectual Property', 93 *PNAS* 12749–12755 (1996).

Gilbert-Macmillan 1993
Kathleen Gilbert-Macmillan, 'Intellectual Property Law for Reverse Engineering Computer Programs in the European Community', 9 *Santa Clara Computer and High Technology Law Journal* 247 (1993).

Ginsburg 1994
Jane C. Ginsburg, 'Four Reasons and a Paradox: The Manifest Superiority of Copyright over *Sui Generis* Protection of Computer Software', 94 *Columbia Law Review* 2559 (1994).

Glazer & Lipsky Jr. 1995
Kenneth L. Glazer & Abbott B. Lipsky Jr., 'Unilateral Refusals to Deal under Section 2 of the Sherman Act', 63 *Antitrust Law Journal* 749–800 (1995).

Goldberg 2005
Matthew A. Goldberg, 'Message in a Bottleneck: The Need for FCC-Mandated Interoperability among Instant Messaging Providers', 9 *Marquette Intellectual Property Law Review* 133 (2005).

Goldstein 1986
Paul Goldstein, 'Infringement of Copyright in Computer Programs', 47 *University of Pittsburgh Law Review* 1119 (1986).

Goldstein 1993
Paul Goldstein, 'The EC Software Directive: A View from the United States of America', in: Michael Lehmann & Colin Tapper, *A Handbook on European Software Law*, Oxford: Oxford University Press 1993, pp. 203–216.

Goldstein 2001
Paul Goldstein, *International Copyright: Principles, Law and Practice*, Oxford: Oxford University Press 2001.

Van Gompel 2009
Stef J. Van Gompel, 'Les formalités sont mortes, vive les formalités! Copyright Formalities and the Reasons for Their Decline in Nineteenth Century Europe', in: Ronan Deazley et al., *Privilege and Property: Essays on the History of Copyright*, Cambridge: Open Book 2009, p. forthcoming.

Gordon 1998
Sean E. Gordon, 'The Very Idea! Why Copyright Law Is an Inappropriate Way to Protect Computer Programs', 20 *European Intellectual Property Review* 10–13 (1998).

Goth 2005
Greg Goth, 'Open Source Business Models: Ready for Prime Time', 22 *IEEE Software* 98–100 (2005).

Govaere 1996
Inge Govaere, *The Use and Abuse of Intellectual Property Rights in E.C. Law*, London: Sweet & Maxwell 1996.

Gowers 2006
Andrew Gowers, *Gowers Review of Intellectual Property*, London: Bristows 2006.

Grosheide 1986
F.W. Grosheide, *Auteursrecht op maat*, Deventer: Kluwer 1986.

Gual et al. 2005
Jordi Gual et al., *An Economic Approach to Article 82*, EAGCP 2005.

Guibault 1997
Lucie M.C.R. Guibault, 'Les programmes d'ordinateur et le droit d'innovation technologique', 9 *Cahiers de Propriété Intellectuelle* 171–202 (1997).

Guibault 2002
Lucie M.C.R. Guibault, *Copyright Limitations and Contracts: An Analysis of the Contractual Overridability of Limitations on Copyright*, Amsterdam: University of Amsterdam 2002.

Guibault & Van Daalen 2006
Lucie M.C.R. Guibault & Ot Van Daalen, *Unravelling the Myth around Open Source Licenses*, The Hague: TMC Asser Press 2006.

Guibault et al. 2007
Lucie M.C.R. Guibault et al., *Study on the Implementation and Effect in Member States' Laws of Directive 2001/29/EC on the Harmonisation of*

Certain Aspects of Copyright and Related Rights in the Information Society, Institute for Information Law 2007.

Haberstumpf 1993
Helmut Haberstumpf, 'Der urheberrechtliche Schutz von Computerprogrammen', in: Michael Lehmann, *Rechtsschutz und Verwertung von Computerprogrammen*, Cologne: Verlag Dr. Otto Schmidt 1993, pp. 69–167.

Haeck 1998
J.F. Haeck, *Idee en programmaformule in het auteursrecht*, Amsterdam: University of Amsterdam 1998.

Haratsch et al. 2006
Andreas Haratsch et al., *Europarecht*, Tübingen: Mohr Siebeck 2006.

Helberger 2005
Natali Helberger, *Controlling Access to Content*, Amsterdam: University of Amsterdam 2005.

Helberger 2008
Natali Helberger, 'Access Directive', in: Oliver Castendyk et al., *European Media Law*, Austin/Boston/Chicago/New York/The Netherlands: Wolters Kluwer 2008, p. 1127.

Herndon 2002
Jill Boylston Herndon, 'Intellectual Property, Antitrust, and the Economics of Aftermarkets', 47 *Antitrust Bulletin* 309 (2002).

Holmes & Torok 2006
Josh Holmes & Gabriel Torok, 'Reduce Your Code Vulnerability', 16(4) *Visual Studio Magazine* 30 (2006).

Horton 1994
Audrey Horton, 'European Design Law and the Spare Parts Dilemma: The Proposed Regulation and Directive', 16 *European Intellectual Property Review* 51–57 (1994).

Hovenkamp 2007
Herbert Hovenkamp, 'Standards Ownership and Competition Policy', 48 *Boston College Law Review* 87–109 (2007).

Hovenkamp et al. 2002–2007
Herbert Hovenkamp et al., *IP and Antitrust: An Analysis of Antitrust Principles Applied to Intellectual Property Law*, New York: Aspen Law & Business 2002–2007.

Hovenkamp et al. 2005
Herbert Hovenkamp et al., 'Unilateral Refusals to License in the US', in: François Lévêque & Howard A. Shelanski, *Antitrust, Patents and Copyright: EU and US Perspectives*, Cheltenham/Northampton: Edward Elgar 2005, pp. 12–55.

Howes & Smith 1995
T. Howes & M. Smith, *The LDAP Application Programming Interface*, available at <http://tools.ietf.org/html/rfc1823> (last visited July 26, 2006).

Hugenholtz 1991
P. Bernt Hugenholtz, 'Protection of Compilation of Facts in Germany and The Netherlands', in: Egbert J. Dommering & P. Bernt Hugenholtz, *Protecting Works of Fact: Copyright, Freedom of Expression and Information Law*, Deventer/Boston: Kluwer Law and Taxation 1991, pp. 59–65.

Hugenholtz 1998
P. Bernt Hugenholtz, 'Het Internet: het auteursrecht voorbij?: Preadvies voor de Nederlandse Juristenvereniging 1998', 128 *Recht en Internet – Handelingen Nederlandse Juristen-Vereniging* 197–260 (1998).

Hugenholtz 2008
P. Bernt Hugenholtz, 'Open Letter Concerning European Commission's "Intellectual Property Package"', 30 *European Intellectual Property Review* 497–499 (2008).

Hugenholtz et al. 2006
P. Bernt Hugenholtz et al., *The Recasting of Copyright and Related Rights for the Knowledge Economy: Final Report*, Amsterdam: Institute for Information Law 2006.

Hugenholtz & Okediji 2008
P. Bernt Hugenholtz & Ruth L. Okediji, *Conceiving an International Instrument on Limitations and Exceptions to Copyright*, Institute for Information Law/University of Minnesota Law School 2008. Report by Open Society Institute.

Hugenholtz 1989
P. Brent Hugenholtz, *Auteursrecht op informatie: auteursrechtelijke bescherming van feitelijke gegevens en gegevensverzamelingen in Nederland, de Verenigde Staten en West-Duitsland: Een rechtsvergelijkend onderzoek*, Amsterdam: Universiteit van Amsterdam 1989.

Hugenholtz & Spoor 1987
P. Brent Hugenholtz & Jaap H. Spoor, *Auteursrecht op software*, Amsterdam: Otto Cramwinckel 1987.

Johnson-Laird 1994
Andrew Johnson-Laird, 'Software Reverse Engineering in the Real World', 19 *University of Dayton Law Review* 843–902 (1994).

Jones & Sufrin 2001
Alison Jones & Brenda Sufrin, *EC Competition Law: Text, Cases, and Materials*, Oxford: Oxford University Press 2001.

Jones II & Turner 1997
Bryce J. Jones II & James R. Turner, 'Can an Operating System Vendor Have a Duty to Aid Its Competitors?', 37 *Jurimetrics Journal* 355–394 (1997).

Karjala 1999
Dennis S. Karjala, 'Copyright Protection of Operating Software, Copyright Misuse, and Antitrust', 9 *Cornell Journal of Law and Public Policy* 161 (1999).

Katz 2002
Michael L. Katz, 'Intellectual Property Rights and Antitrust Policy: Four Principles for a Complex World', 1 *Journal on Telecommunications & High Technology Law* 325 (2002).

Katz & Shapiro 1985
Michael L. Katz & Carl Shapiro, 'Network Externalities, Competition, and Compatibility', 75 *The American Economic Review* 424–441 (1985).

Katz & Shapiro 1994
Michael L. Katz & Carl Shapiro, 'Systems Competition and Network Effects', 8 *Journal of Economic Perspectives* 93–115 (1994).

Katz & Shapiro 1999
Michael L. Katz & Carl Shapiro, 'Antitrust in Software Markets', in: Jeffrey A. Eisenach & Thomas M. Lenard, *Competition, Convergence and the Microsoft Monopoly*, Boston/Dordrecht/London: Kluwer 1999, pp. 29–81.

Katz & Shelanski 2005
Michael L. Katz & Howard A. Shelanski, '"Schumpeterian" Competition and Antitrust Policy in High-Tech Markets', 14 *Competition* 47 (2005).

Katz & Shelanski 2007
Michael L. Katz & Howard A. Shelanski, 'Mergers and Innovation', 74 *Antitrust Law Journal* (2007).

Kaufmann 1982
P.J. Kaufmann, 'De lof der nabootsing: Een kritische herbezinning op de leer der "slaafse navolging"', 25 *TVVS* 216 (1982).

Keuchenius et al. 1990
Petra Keuchenius et al., *Computerprogramma's en Auteursrecht in de Europese Gemeenschap: Enige opmerkingen over het 'voorstel voor een Richtlijn van de Raad betreffende de rechtsbescherming van computerprogramma's'*, Amsterdam: Universiteit van Amsterdam 1990.

Klemperer 1987
Paul Klemperer, 'Markets with Consumer Switching Costs', 102 *The Quarterly Journal of Economics* 375–394 (1987).

Koelman 2006
Kamiel J. Koelman, 'An Exceptio Standardis: Do We Need an IP Exemption for Standards?', 2006 *IIC* 823–843 (2006).

Koenig & Loetz 2002
Christian Koenig & Sascha Loetz, 'Framework for Network Access and Interconnection', in: Christian Koenig et al., *EC Competition and Telecommunications Law*, The Hague/London/New York: Kluwer Law International 2002, pp. 359–439.

Korah 2006
Valentine Korah, *Intellectual Property Rights and the EC Competition Rules*, Oxford: Hart Publishing 2006.

Koschtial 2005
Ulrike Koschtial, 'Design Law: Individual Character, Visibility and Functionality', 36 *IIC* 297–313 (2005).

Kovacic & Reindl 2005
William E. Kovacic & Andreas P. Reindl, 'An Interdisciplinary Approach to Improving Competition Policy and Intellectual Property Policy', 28 *Fordham International Law Journal* 1062 (2005).

Kroes 2008
Neelie Kroes, 'Being Open about Standards', in: *OpenForum Europe – Breakfast Seminar* 2008.

Kuhn & Van Reenen 2007
Kai-Uwe Kuhn & John Van Reenen, 'Interoperability and Foreclosure in the European Microsoft Case', 2007 *SSRN* 1013929 (2007).

Kur 1999
Annette Kur, '"Freeze Plus" Melts the Ice – Observations on the European Design Directive', 30 *IIC* 620–632 (1999).

Lai 2000
Stanley Lai, *The Copyright Protection of Computer Software in the United Kingdom*, Oxford/Portland: Hart Publishing 2000.

Lake et al. 1989
William T. Lake et al., 'Seeking Compatibility or Avoiding Development Costs? A Reply on Software Copyright in the EC', 11 *European Intellectual Property Review* 431–434 (1989).

Landes & Posner 2003
William M. Landes & Richard A. Posner, 'Indefinitely Renewable Copyright', 70 *University of Chicago Law Review* 471–518 (2003).

Larouche 2000
Pierre Larouche, *The Basis of EC Telecommunications Law after Liberalization*, Maastricht: Universiteit Maastricht 2000.

Larouche 2007a
Pierre Larouche, 'Contrasting Legal Solutions and the Comparability of US and EU Experiences', in: François Lévêque & Howard A. Shelanski, *Antitrust and Regulation in the EU and US: Legal and Economic Perspectives*, Cheltenham: Edward Elgar 2007.

Larouche 2007b
Pierre Larouche, 'Europe and Investments in Infrastructure with Emphasis on Electronic Communications', *SSRN* 1020899 (2007).

Larouche 2008
Pierre Larouche, 'The European Microsoft Case at the Crossroads of Competition Policy and Innovation', *SSRN* 1140165 (2008).

Lea & Hall 2004
Gary Lea & Peter Hall, 'Standards and Intellectual Property Rights: An Economic and Legal Perspective', 16 *Information Economics and Policy* 67–89 (2004).

Legal Advisory Board 1995
Legal Advisory Board, *Reply to the Green Paper on Copyright and Related Rights in the Information Society*, 1995.

Lehmann 1989
Michael Lehmann, 'Freie Schittstellen ("Interfaces") und freier Zugang zu den Ideen ("Reverse Engineering"): Schranken des Urheberrechtsschutzes von Software', 5 *Computer und Recht* 1057–1063 (1989).

Lehmann 1991
Michael Lehmann, 'Die Europäische Richtlinie über den Schutz von Computerprogrammen', 1991 *GRUR Int.* 327–336 (1991).

Lehmann 1992
Michael Lehmann, 'Standardization and the EC Directive of 14 May 1991 on the Legal Protection of Computer Programs', in: Willem F. Korthals Altes et al., *Information Law Towards the 21st Century*, Deventer/Boston: Kluwer Law and Taxation 1992, pp. 363–368.

Lehmann 1993
Michael Lehmann, 'Die Europäische Richtlinie über den Schutz von Computerprogrammen', in: Michael Lehmann, *Rechtsschutz und Verwertung von Computerprogrammen*, Cologne: Verlag Dr. Otto Schmidt 1993, pp. 1–29.

Lemley 2002
Mark A. Lemley, 'Intellectual Property Rights and Standard Setting Organizations', 90 *California Law Review* 1889 (2002).

Lemley & McGowan 1998
Mark A. Lemley & David McGowan, 'Legal Implications of Network Economic Effects', 86 *California Law Review* 479 (1998).

Lemley et al. 2000
Mark A. Lemley et al., *Software and Internet Law*, Gaithersburg: Aspen Law & Business 2000.

Lemley & Shapiro 2005
Mark A. Lemley & Carl Shapiro, 'Probabilistic Patents', 19 *Journal of Economic Perspectives* 75 (2005).

Lévêque 2005
François Lévêque, 'Innovation, Leveraging and Essential Facilities: Interoperability Licensing in the EU Microsoft Case', 28 *World Competition* 71–91 (2005).

Lévêque & Méniere 2004
François Lévêque & Yann Méniere, *The Economics of Patents and Copyright*, Berkeley: Berkeley Electronic Press 2004.

Levin & Richman 2003
Katrine A. Levin & Monica B. Richman, 'A Survey of Design Protection in the European Union and the United States', 25 *European Intellectual Property Review* 111–124 (2003).

Lewinski 2008
Silke von Lewinski, *International Copyright Law and Policy*, Oxford: Oxford University Press 2008.

Liebowitz & Margolis 1990
Stan J. Liebowitz & Stephen E. Margolis, 'The Fable of the Keys, 30 *Journal of Law and Economics* 1–26 (1990).

Lipsky Jr. & Sidak 1999
Abbott B. Lipsky Jr. & J. Gregory Sidak, 'Essential Facilities', 51 *Stanford Law Review* 1187 (1999).

Lloyd & Mellor 2003
Ian Lloyd & David Mellor, *Telecommunications Law*, London: LexisNexis 2003.

Loewenthal 2005
Paul John Loewenthal, 'The Defence of "Objective Justification" in the Application of Article 82 EC', 28 *World Competition* 455–477 (2005).

Van Loon 2008
Sophie C. Van Loon, *Licentieweigering als misbruik van machtspositie: Intellectuele eigendom, artikel 82 EG en de belemmering van innovatie*, Amstelveen: deLex 2008.

Madou et al. 2005
Matias Madou et al., 'Hybrid Static-Dynamic Attacks against Software Protection Mechanisms', in: *5th ACM Workshop on Digital Rights Management*, New York: ACM Press, 2005, pp. 75–82.

Marquardt & Leddy 2003
Paul D. Marquardt & Mark Leddy, 'The Essential Facilities Doctrine and Intellectual Property Rights: A Response to Pitofsky, Patterson, and Hooks', 70 *Antitrust Law Journal* 847 (2003).

Maxwell 2002
Winston Maxwell (ed.), *Electronic Communications: The New EU Framework*, New York: Oceana Publications 2002.

May & Levine 2005
Randolph J. May & Richard O. Levine, *Interconnection without Regulation: Lessons for Telecommunications Reform from Four Network Industries*, Washington DC: Progress and Freedom Foundation 2005.

Mayrhauser & Vans 1994
A. von Mayrhauser & A.M. Vans, *Program Understanding – A Survey*, Colorado State University, Department of Computer Science 1994.

McGowan 1996
David McGowan, 'Regulating Competition in the Information Age: Computer Software as an Essential Facility under the Sherman Act', 18 *Hastings Communications and Entertainment Law Journal* 771 (1996).

McKean 2005
Erin McKean, *The New Oxford American Dictionary*, New York: Oxford University Press 2005.

Menell 1987
Peter S. Menell, 'Tailoring Legal Protection for Computer Software', 39 *Stanford Law Review* 1329 (1987).

Menell 1989
Peter S. Menell, 'Analysis of the Scope of Copyright Protection for Application Programs', 41 *Stanford Law Review* 1045 (1989).

Menell 1998
Peter S. Menell, 'An Epitaph for Traditional Copyright Protection of Network Features of Computer Software', 43 *Antitrust Bulletin* 651 (1998).

Merges 1999
Robert P. Merges, *Who Owns the Charles River Bridge? Intellectual Property and Competition in the Software Industry*, 1999 *SSRN* 208089 (1999).

Merges 2007
Robert P. Merges, 'Software and Patent Scope: A Report from the Middle Innings', 85 *Texas Law Review* 1626–1676 (2007).

Merges et al. 2003
Robert P. Merges et al., *Intellectual Property in the New Technological Age*, New York: Aspen 2003.

Meyer & Colombe 1990a
Caroline Meyer & Michel Colombe, 'Interoperability Still Threatened by EC Software Directive: A Status Report', 12 *European Intellectual Property Review* 325–329 (1990).

Meyer & Colombe 1990b
Caroline Meyer & Michel Colombe, 'Seeking Interoperability: An Industry Response', 12 *European Intellectual Property Review* 79–83 (1990).

Microsoft
Microsoft, *MSDN*, available at <http://msdn.microsoft.com/> (last visited December 22, 2008).

Mueller 1993
Milton Mueller, 'Universal Service in Telephone History: A Reconstruction', 17 *Telecommunications Policy* 352–369 (1993).

National Commission on New Technological Uses of Copyrighted Works 1978
National Commission on New Technological Uses of Copyrighted Works, *Final Report of the National Commission on New Technological Uses of Copyrighted Works*, 1978.

Neumann 2002
Andreas Neumann, 'The European Regulatory Framework for Standardisation in the Telecommunications Sector', in: Christian Koenig et al., *EC Competition and Telecommunications Law*, The Hague/London/New York: Kluwer Law International 2002, pp. 617–690.

Newman 1999
Jon O. Newman, 'New Lyrics for an Old Melody: The Idea/Expression Dichotomy in the Computer Age', 17 *Cardozo Arts and Entertainment Law Journal* 691 (1999).

Nihoul & Rodford 2004
Paul Nihoul & Peter Rodford, *EU Electronic Communications Law*, Oxford: Oxford University Press 2004.

Nimmer & Nimmer looseleaf
Melville B. Nimmer & David Nimmer, *Nimmer on Copyright: A Treatise on the Law of Literary, Musical and Artistic Property, and the Protection of Ideas*, New York: Matthew Bender looseleaf.

O'Donoghue & Padilla 2006
Robert O'Donoghue & A. Jorge Padilla, *The Law and Economics of Article 82 EC*, Oxford: Hart Publishing 2006.

Ofcom 2006
Ofcom, *End-to-End Connectivity*, London: Ofcom 2006.

Open Source Alliance 2007
Open Source Alliance, *Inter-Open Customer Forum Series: Summary Report*, OSA 2007.

Ortiz Blanco 2006
Luis Ortiz Blanco (ed.), *European Community Competition Procedure*, Oxford: Oxford University Press 2006.

Ottow 2006
A.T. Ottow, *Telecommunicatietoezicht: de invloed van het Europese en Nederlandse bestuurs(proces)recht*, The Hague: SDU Uitgevers 2006.

Page & Lopatka 2007
William H. Page & John E. Lopatka, *The Microsoft Case: Antitrust, High Technology, and Consumer Welfare*, Chicago/London: The University of Chicago Press 2007.

Palmer & Vinje 1992
Alan K. Palmer & Thomas C. Vinje, 'The EC Directive on the Legal Protection of Computer Software: New Law Governing Software Development', 2 *Duke Journal of Comparative and International Law* 65 (1992).

Parnas 1972
D.L. Parnas, 'A Technique for Software Module Specification with Examples', 15 *Communications of the ACM* 330–336 (1972).

Pilny 1990
Karl H. Pilny, 'Schnittstellen in Computerprogrammen: Zum Rechtsschutz in Deutschland, den USA und Japan', *GRUR Int.* 431–442 (1990).

Pilny 1992
Karl H. Pilny, 'Legal Aspects of Interfaces and Reverse Engineering – Protection in Germany, the United States and Japan', *IIC* 196–218 (1992).

Pinckaers 2007
J.C.S. Pinckaers, 'De techniekrestrictie in het modellenrecht en de relevantie van alternatieven', in: D.J.G. Visser & D.W.F. Verkade, *Spoorbundel: Een eigen, oorspronkelijk karakter: Opstellen aangeboden aan prof.mr. Jaap H. Spoor*, Amstelveen: deLex 2007, pp. 257–273.

Pitofsky 2001
Robert Pitofsky, 'Antitrust and Intellectual Property: Unresolved Issues at the Heart of the New Economy', 16 *Berkeley Technology Law Journal* 535 (2001).

Pitofsky et al. 2002
Robert Pitofsky et al., 'The Essential Facilities Doctrine under U.S. Antitrust Law', 70 *Antitrust Law Journal* 443–462 (2002).

Plana 2007
Sandrine Plana, 'La recherche de la nature juridique du logiciel: La quête du Graal', *Revue Internationale du Droit d'Auteur* 87–137 (2007).

Posner 1995
Bernhard Posner, 'The Proposal of an EU Design', 11 *IER* 121–128 (1995).

Posner 2001
Richard A. Posner, 'Antitrust in the New Economy', 68 *Antitrust Law Journal* 925 (2001).

Quaedvlieg 1987
A.A. Quaedvlieg, *Auteursrecht op techniek: De auteursrechtelijke bescherming van het technisch aspecten van industriële vormgeving en computerprogrammatuur*, Zwolle: W.E.J. Tjeenk Willink 1987.

Quaedvlieg 1992
A.A. Quaedvlieg, *Auteur en aantasting, werk en waardigheid*, Zwolle: W.E.J. Tjeenk Willink 1992.

Quaedvlieg 2006
A.A. Quaedvlieg, 'Case Comment: *Technip Benelux B.V. v. Goossens*', 2006 *AMI* 155 (2006).

Raikow 2007
David Raikow, *iPhone Hacker Slams Apple Security*, available at <http://www.crn.com/security/201202993> (last visited February 19, 2009).

Ramamoorthy & Tsai 1996
C.V. Ramamoorthy & Wei-tek Tsai, 'Advances in Software Engineering', 29 *Computer* 47–58 (1996).

Ramsey 1927
Frank P. Ramsey, 'A Contribution to the Theory of Taxation', 37 *Economic Journal* 47–61 (1927).

Raubenheimer 1996
Andreas Raubenheimer, 'Implementation of the EC Software Directive in Germany – Special Provisions for Protection of Computer Programs', 27 *IIC* 609–648 (1996).

Reichman 1994
Jerome H. Reichman, 'Legal Hybrids between the Patent and Copyright Paradigms', 94 *Columbia Law Review* 2432 (1994).

Reinbothe & Von Lewinski 2002
Jörg Reinbothe & Silke Von Lewinski, *The WIPO Treaties 1996: The WIPO Copyright Treaty and The WIPO Performances and Phonograms Treaty: Commentary and Legal Analysis*, London: Butterworths 2002.

Ricketson 1987
Sam Ricketson, *The Berne Convention*, London/The Hague: Query Mary College/Kluwer 1987.

Ricketson & Ginsburg 2006
Sam Ricketson & Jane C. Ginsburg, *International Copyright and Neighbouring Rights: The Berne Convention and Beyond*, Oxford: Oxford University Press 2006.

Ritter 2005
C. Ritter, 'Refusal to Deal and "Essential Facilities": Does Intellectual Property Require Special Defence Compared to Tangible Property?', 28 *World Competition* 281–298 (2005).

Robinson & Cargill 1996
Gary S. Robinson & Carl Cargill, 'History and Impact of Computer Standards', 29 *Computer* 79–85 (1996).

van Rooijen 2006
Ashwin van Rooijen, 'Liever misbruikt dan misplaatst auteursrecht: het doelcriterium ingezet tegen oneigenlijk auteursrechtgebruik', 2006 *AMI* 45–51 (2006).

van Rooijen 2007a
Ashwin van Rooijen, 'Case Comment', *AMI* 192–194 (2007).

van Rooijen 2007b
Ashwin van Rooijen, 'Essential Interfaces: Exploring the Software Directives Equilibrium between Intellectual Property Rights and Competition Law', 8 *Computer Law Review International* 129–137 (2007).

van Rooijen 2008
Ashwin van Rooijen, 'The Role of Investments in Refusals to Deal', 31 *World Competition* 63–88 (2008).

Sammet 1972
Jean E. Sammet, 'Programming Languages: History and Future', 15 *Communications of the ACM* 601–610 (1972).

Samuelson 1985
Pamela Samuelson, 'Creating a New Kind of Intellectual Property: Applying the Lessons of the Chip Law to Computer Programs', 70 *Minnesota Law Review* 471 (1985).

Samuelson 1994
Pamela Samuelson, 'Comparing U.S. and E.C. Copyright Protection for Computer Programs: Are They More Different Than They Seem?', 13 *Journal of Law and Commerce* 279–300 (1994).

Samuelson 2001
Pamela Samuelson, 'Economic and Constitutional Influences on Copyright Law in the United States', 23 *European Intellectual Property Review* 409–422 (2001).

Samuelson 2007a
Pamela Samuelson, 'Preliminary Thoughts on Copyright Reform', 2007 *Utah Law Review* 551–571 (2007).

Samuelson 2007b
Pamela Samuelson, 'Questioning Copyright in Standards', 48 *Boston College Law Review* 193–224 (2007).

Samuelson 2007c
Pamela Samuelson, 'Why Copyright Law Excludes Systems and Processes from the Scope of Its Protection', 85 *Texas Law Review* 1921 (2007).

Samuelson 2008a
Pamela Samuelson, 'Are Patents on Interfaces Impeding Interoperability?', *Berkeley Center for Law and Technology. Law and Technology Scholarship (Selected by the Berkeley Center for Law and Technology)* (2008).

Samuelson 2008b
Pamela Samuelson, *The Strange Odyssey of Software Interfaces in Intellectual Property Law*, 1998 *SSRN* 1323818 (2008).

Samuelson et al. 1994
Pamela Samuelson et al., 'A Manifesto Concerning the Legal Protection of Computer Programs', 94 *Columbia Law Review* 2308–2430 (1994).

Samuelson & Scotchmer 2002
Pamela Samuelson & Suzanne Scotchmer, 'The Law and Economics of Reverse Engineering', 111 *Yale Law Journal* 1575 (2002).

Schaerr 1985
Gene C. Schaerr, 'The Cellophane Fallacy and the Justice Department's Guidelines for Horizontal Mergers', 94 *Yale Law Journal* 670–693 (1985).

Schelven & Struik 1995
P.C. van Schelven & H. Struik, *Softwarerecht. Bescherming en gebruik van programmatuur sedert de Richtlijn Softwarebescherming*, Deventer: Kluwer 1995.

Schmidtchen & Koboldt 1993
Dieter Schmidtchen & Christian Koboldt, 'A Pacemaker That Stops Halfway: The Decompilation Rule in the EEC Directive on the Legal Protection of Computer Programs', 13 *International Review of Law and Economics* 413–429 (1993).

Schneider 1990
Jörg Schneider, 'Vervielfältigungsvorgänge beim Einsatz von Computerprogrammen: Vorrang urheberrechtlicher Grundwertungen gegenüber technischen Zufälligkeiten', 6 *Computer und Recht* 503–508 (1990).

Schotter 2003
Andrew Schotter, *Microeconomics: A Modern Approach*, Upper Saddle River: Prentice Hall International 2003.

Schovsbo 1998
Jens Schovsbo, 'As If Made for Each Other – Intellectual Property Rights and Protection of Compatible Products', 29 *IIC* 510–534 (1998).

Schricker 1999
Gerhard Schricker, *Urheberrecht*, Munich: C.H. Beck 1999.

Schulte 1992
Dieter Schulte, 'Der Referentenentwurf eines Zweiten Gesetzes zur Änderung des Urheberrechtsgesetzes', 8 *Computer und Recht* 648 (1992).

Schumpeter 1942
Joseph A. Schumpeter, *Capitalism, Socialism and Democracy*, New York: Harper & Row 1942.

Scotchmer 2004
Suzanne Scotchmer, *Innovation and Incentives*, Cambridge/London: The MIT Press 2004.

Severance 1999
Charles Severance, 'Posix: A Model for Future Computing', 32 *Computer* 131–132 (1999).

Shapiro 1995
Carl Shapiro, 'Aftermarkets and Consumer Welfare: Making Sense of Kodak', 63 *Antitrust Law Journal* 483 (1995).

Shapiro 1999a
Carl Shapiro, 'Competition Policy in the Information Economy, 1999', in: Einar Hope, *Competition Policy Analysis*, London/New York: Routledge 2000, pp. 109–132.

Shapiro 1999b
Carl Shapiro, 'Exclusivity in Network Industries', 7 *George Mason Law Review* 673 (1999).

Shapiro 2000
Carl Shapiro, 'Setting Compatibility Standards: Cooperation or Collusion?', in: Rochelle Dreyfuss et al., *Expanding the Boundaries of Intellectual Property: Innovation Policy for the Knowledge Society*, Oxford: Oxford University Press 2000, pp. 81–122.

Shapiro & Teece 1994
Carl Shapiro & David J. Teece, 'Systems Competition and Aftermarkets: An Economic Analysis of Kodak', 39 *Antitrust Bulletin* 135 (1994).

Shapiro & Varian 1999
Carl Shapiro & Hal R. Varian, *Information Rules: A Strategic Guide to the Network Economy*, Boston: Harvard Business School Press 1999.

Shelanski 2002
Howard A. Shelanski, 'From Sector-Specific Regulation to Antitrust Law for U.S. Telecommunications: The Prospects for Transition', 2002 *SSRN* 300600.

Shelanski 2007
Howard A. Shelanski, 'Adjusting Regulation to Competition: Toward a New Model for U.S. Telecommunications Policy', 24 *Yale Journal on Regulation* 55–105 (2007).

Shelanski & Sidak 2001
Howard A. Shelanski & J. Gregory Sidak, 'Antitrust Divestiture in Network Industries', 68 *University of Chicago Law Review* 1 (2001).

Sheremata 1997
Willow A. Sheremata, 'Barriers to Innovation: A Monopoly, Network Externalities, and the Speed of Innovation', 42 *Antitrust Bulletin* 937 (1997).

Simonyi 1999
Charles Simonyi, *Hungarian Notation*, available at <http://msdn.microsoft.com/library/default.asp?url=/library/en-us/dnvs600/html/hunganotat.asp> (last visited July 25, 2006).

Souza et al. 2004
Cleidson R.B. de Souza et al., 'Sometimes You Need to See Through Walls – A Field Study of Application Programming Interfaces', in: *Computer Supported Cooperative Work*, New York: ACM Press, 2004, pp. 63–71.

Souza et al. 2005
Sergio Cozzetti B. de Souza et al., 'A Study of the Documentation Essential to Software Maintenance', in: *23rd Annual International Conference on Design of Communication: Documenting & Designing for Pervasive Information*, New York: ACM Press, 2005, pp. 68–75.

Sparta 2005
Sparta, *State-of-the-Art in Decompilation and Disassembly*, Columbia: Sparta 2005.

Spoor 1994
Jaap H. Spoor, 'Copyright Protection and Reverse Engineering of Software: Implementation and Effects of the EC Directive', 19 *University of Dayton Law Review* 1063 (1994).

Spoor et al. 2005
Jaap H. Spoor et al., *Auteursrecht: auteursrecht, naburige rechten en databankenrecht*, Deventer: Kluwer 2005.

Sprigman 2004
Christopher Sprigman, 'Reform[aliz]ing Copyright', 57 *Stanford Law Review* 485 (2004).

Staffelbach 2003
Oliver Staffelbach, *Die Dekompilierung von Computerprogrammen gemäss Art. 21 URG*, Bern: Stämpfli 2003.

Stern 1986
Richard H. Stern, 'The Bundle of Rights Suited to New Technology', 47 *University of Pittsburgh Law Review* 1229 (1986).

Straus 2005
Joseph Straus, 'Design Protection for Spare Parts Gone in Europe? Proposed Changes to the EC Directive: The Commission's Mandate and Its Doubtful Execution', 27 *European Intellectual Property Review* 391–404 (2005).

Stuurman 1995
Cees Stuurman, *Technische normen en het recht: Beschouwingen over de interactie tussen het recht en technische normalistie op het terrein van informatietechnologie en telecommunicatie*, Deventer: Kluwer 1995.

Sucker 1993
Michael Sucker, 'The Software Directive – Between the Combat against Piracy and the Preservation of Undistorted Competition, in: Michael Lehmann & Colin Tapper, *A Handbook on European Software Law*, Oxford: Oxford University Press 1993, pp. 11–24.

Sun Microsystems 2006
Sun Microsystems, *OpenOffice.org 2.0 Developer's Guide*, available at <http://api.openoffice.org/docs/DevelopersGuide/DevelopersGuide.xhtml> (last visited July 26, 2006).

Swanson & Baurnol 2005
Daniel G. Swanson & William J. Baurnol, 'Reasonable and Nondiscriminatory (RAND) Royalties, Standards Selection, and Control of Market Power', 73 *Antitrust Law Journal* 1 (2005).

Teasley 1994
Barbee E. Teasley, 'The Effects of Naming Style and Expertise on Program Comprehension', 40 *International Journal of Human-Computer Studies* 757–770 (1994).

Temple Lang 1994
John Temple Lang, 'Defining Legitimate Competition: Companies' Duties to Supply Competitors, and Access to Essential Facilities', 18 *Fordham International Law Journal* 437–524 (1994).

Temple Lang 1997
John Temple Lang, 'European Community Antitrust Law – Innovation Markets and High Technology Industries', 20 *Fordham International Law Journal* 717–818 (1997).

Temple Lang 2005
John Temple Lang, 'The Application of the Essential Facility Doctrine to Intellectual Property Rights under European Competition Law', in: François Lévêque & Howard A. Shelanski, *Antitrust, Patents and Copyright: EU and US Perspectives*, Cheltenham/Northampton: Edward Elgar 2005, pp. 56–84.

Tiemann 2006
Michael Tiemann, 'An Objective Definition of Open Standards', 28 *Computer Standards & Interfaces* 495–507 (2006).

Tridgell 2003
Andrew Tridgell, *How Samba Was Written*, available at <http://samba.org/ftp/tridge/misc/french_cafe.txt> (last visited April 11, 2006).

Turney 2005
James Turney, 'Defining the Limits of the EU Essential Facilities Doctrine on Intellectual Property Rights: The Primacy of Securing Optimal Innovation', 3 *Northwestern Journal of Technology and Intellectual Property* 179 (2005).

Ullrich 2001
Hanns Ullrich, 'Intellectual Property, Access to Information, and Antitrust: Harmony, Disharmony, and International Harmonization', in: Rochelle Cooper Dreyfuss et al., *Expanding the Boundaries of Intellectual Property: Innovation Policy for the Knowledge Society*, Oxford: Oxford University Press 2001, pp. 365–402.

US Department of Justice & Federal Trade Commission 1992
US Department of Justice & Federal Trade Commission, *Horizontal Merger Guidelines*, 1992.

US Department of Justice & Federal Trade Commission 2007
US Department of Justice & Federal Trade Commission, *Antitrust Enforcement and Intellectual Property Rights: Promoting Innovation and Competition*, 2007.

Valkonen & White 2007
Sami J. Valkonen & Lawrence J. White, 'An Economic Model for the Incentive/Access Paradigm of Copyright Propertization: An Argument in Support of the Orphan Works Act', 29 *Hastings Communications and Entertainment Law Journal* 359–400 (2007).

Vandenberghe 1984
Guy Vandenberghe, *Bescherming van computersoftware*, Antwerpen: Kluwer 1984.

Vandenberghe 1989
Guy Vandenberghe, 'Copyright Protection of Computer Programs: An Unsatisfactory Proposal for a Directive', 11 *European Intellectual Property Review* 409–414 (1989).

Vaver 1986
David Vaver, 'The National Treatment Requirements of the Berne and Universal Copyright Conventions, Part One', 1986 *IIC* 577 (1986).

Verstrynge 1993
Jean-François Verstrynge, 'Protecting Intellectual Property Rights within the New Pan-European Framework: Computer Software', in: Michael Lehmann & Colin Tapper, *A Handbook on European Software Law*, Oxford: Oxford University Press 1993, pp. 39–84.

Vinje 1991
Thomas C. Vinje, 'The Development of Interoperable Products under the EC Software Directive', 8 *The Computer Lawyer* 1–12 (1991).

Vinje 1992
Thomas C. Vinje, 'Magill: Its Impact on the Information Technology Industry', 14 *European Intellectual Property Review* 397–402 (1992).

Vinje 1993
Thomas C. Vinje, 'The Legislative History of the EC Software Directive', in: Michael Lehmann & Colin Tapper, *A Handbook on European Software Law*, Oxford: Oxford University Press 1993, pp. 39–84.

Visser 1997
D.J.G. Visser, *Auteursrecht op toegang: De exploitatierechten van de auteur in het tijdperk van digitale informatie en netwerkcommunicatie*, Leiden: Rijksuniversiteit Leiden 1997.

Visser 2007
D.J.G. Visser, 'Verwatering, "verknoeling" en verandering van wezenlijke waarde: reactie op het artikel van prof. mr. H. Cohen Jehoram', 2007 *Bijblad bij de Industriële Eigendom* 16–21 (2007).

Vivant 2007
Michel Vivant (ed.), *Lamy Droit de l'informatique et des reseaux*, Rueil-Malmaison: Lamy 2007.

Walter et al. 2001
M.M. Walter et al. (eds.), *Europäisches Urheberrecht: Kommentar: insbesondere Software-, Vermiet- und Verleih-, Satelliten- und Kabel-, Schutzdauer-, Datenbank-, Folgerecht-, Informationsgesellschaft-Richtlinie, Produktpiraterie-Verordnung*, Vienna: Springer 2001.

Webber 2003
Adam Brooks Webber, *Modern Programming Languages: A Practical Introduction*, Wilsonville: Franklin, Beedle & Associates 2003.

Weber 2005
Steven Weber, *The Success of Open Source*, Cambridge: Harvard University Press 2005.

Weber Waller 2008
Spencer Weber Waller, 'Areeda, Epithets, and Essential Facilities', 2008 - *Wisconsin Law Review* 359 (2008).

Weinreb 1998
Lloyd L. Weinreb, 'Copyright for Functional Expression', 111 *Harvard Law Review* 1149 (1998).

Weiser 2003
Philip J. Weiser, 'The Internet, Innovation, and Intellectual Property Policy', 103 *Columbia Law Review* 534 (2003).

Werden 1987
Gregory Werden, 'The Law and Economics of the Essential Facilities Doctrine', 32 *St. Louis University Law Journal* 433 (1987).

Whinston 1990
Michael D. Whinston, 'Tying, Foreclosure and Exclusion', 80 *American Economic Review* 837–859 (1990).

Whish 2003
Richard Whish, *Competition Law*, London: LexisNexis UK 2003.

World Intellectual Property Organization 1978
World Intellectual Property Organization, 'Model Provisions on the Protection of Computer Software', 14 *Copyright* 6 (1978).

Zittrain 2008
Jonathan Zittrain, *The Future of the Internet – And How to Stop It*, New Haven/London: Yale University Press 2008.

Index

D

E

INFORMATION LAW SERIES

1. Egbert J. Dommering, *Protecting Works of Fact: Copyright, Freedom of Expression and Info*, 1991 (ISBN/ISSN 90-654-4567-6).
2. W.F. Korthals Altes, *Information Law Towards the 21st Century*, 1992 (ISBN/ISSN 90-654-4627-3).
3. Jacqueline Seignette, *Challenges to Creator Doctrine, Authorship, Copyright Ownership*, 1994 (ISBN/ISSN 90-654-4876-4).
4. P. Bernt Hugenholtz, *The Future of Copyright in a Digital Environment*, 1996 (ISBN/ISSN 90-411-0267-1).
5. Julius C.S. Pinckaers, *From Privacy Toward a New Intellectual Prop Right In Persona*, 1996 (ISBN/ISSN 90-411-0355-4).
6. Jan J.C. Kabel & Gerard J.H.M. Mom, *Intellectual Property and Information Law, Essays in Honour of Herman Cohen Jehoram*, 1998 (ISBN/ISSN 90-411-9702-8).
7. Ysolde Gendreau, Axel Nordemann and Rainer Oesch, *Copyright and Photographs, An International Survey*, 1999 (ISBN/ISSN 90-411-9722-2).
8. P. Bernt Hugenholtz, *Copyright and Electronic Commerce: Legal Aspects of Electronic Copyright Management*, 2000 (ISBN/ISSN 90-411-9785-0).
9. Lucie M.C.R. Guibault, *Copyright Limitations and Contracts, an Analysis of the Contractual Overridability of Limitations on Copyright*, 2002 (ISBN/ISSN 90-411-9867-9).
10. Lee A. Bygrave, *Data Protection Law, Approaching its Rationale, Logic and Limits*, 2002 (ISBN/ISSN 90-411-9870-9).
11. Niva Elkin-Koren & Neil Weinstock Netanel, *The Commodification of Information*, 2002 (ISBN/ISSN 90-411-9876-8).
12. Mireille M.M. van Eechoud, *Choice of Law in Copyright and Related Rights: Alternatives to the Lex Protectionis*, 2003 (ISBN/ISSN 90-411-2071-8).
13. Martin Senftleben, *Copyright, Limitations and the Three-Step Test*, 2004 (ISBN/ISSN 90-411-2267-2).
14. Paul L.C. Torremans, *Copyright and Human Rights*, 2004 (ISBN/ISSN 90-411-2278-8).
15. Natali Helberger, *Controlling Access to Content: Regulating Conditional Access in Digital Broadcasting*, 2005 (ISBN/ISSN 90-411-2345-8).
16. Lucie M.C.R. Guibault & P. Bernt Hugenholtz, *The Future of Public Domain: Identifying the Commons in Information Law*, 2006 (ISBN 978-90-411-2435-7).
17. Irini Katsirea, *Public Broadcasting and European Law: A Comparative Examination of Public Service Obligations in Six Member States*, 2008 (ISBN 978-90-411-2500-2).
18. Paul L.C. Torremans, *Intellectual Property and Human Rights: Enhanced Edition of Copyright and Human Rights*, 2008 (ISBN 978-90-411-2653-5).

INFORMATION LAW SERIES

19. Mireille van Eechoud, P. Bernt Hugenholtz, Stef van Gompel, Lucie Guilbault and Natali Heiberger, *Harmonizing European Copyright Law: The Challenges of Better Lawmaking*, 2009 (ISBN 978-90-411-3130-0).
20. Ashwin van Rooijen, *The Software Interface between Copyright and Competition Law: A Legal Analysis of Interoperability in Computer Programs*, 2010 (ISBN 978-90-411-3193-5).